Criminal Evidence
in Context

Criminal Evidence
in Context

Jonathan Doak and Claire McGourlay

LawMatters
PUBLISHING

To our parents

Published by Law Matters Publishing

Law Matters Ltd
33 Southernhay East
Exeter EX1 1NX
Tel: 01392 215560
info@lawmatters.co.uk
www.lawmatterspublishing.co.uk

British Library Cataloguing-in-Publication Data

A catalogue record for this book is available from the British Library.

ISBN 1 84641 004 5

Typeset by Pantek Arts Ltd, Maidstone, Kent

Printed by Ashford Colour Press Ltd, Gosport, Hampshire

Contents

Preface

This is an intriguing, if a somewhat challenging time, to author a text on the law of criminal evidence. The task is intriguing since the law has undergone a radical overhaul in recent years, and the appellate courts have been awash with cases concerning the impact and scope of such reforms. However, the project has also been demanding, because the law continues to evolve in a rapid and unpredictable fashion. Three major pieces of legislation have come into force within the past five years. The Human Rights Act 1998 took effect in October 2000, and imported a fresh canon of interpretation into the English courts. It was followed in 2002 by the implementation of (most of) the measures contained in Part II of the Youth Justice and Criminal Evidence Act, which introduced major new procedural and evidential safeguards for vulnerable witnesses testifying in court. Most recently, the Criminal Justice Act 2003 has introduced and provided for wide-ranging reforms of rules relating to the admissibility of character evidence and hearsay.

Against this backdrop of changes, we have found that students of Criminal Evidence often find it difficult to find coherency within the subject. The rule themselves have been developed, reformed and implemented in something of a disordered and haphazard manner. In writing this book, we have sought to produce a clear and accessible text, through presenting the relevant law in a comprehensive, yet systematic, way. As such, it is hoped that the book will be of interest not only to Law students, including those taking the Legal Practice Course or Bar Vocational Course, but also to non-lawyers who would like to gain some understanding of the evidential rules that underpin the criminal trial. It is also anticipated that the text should provide some useful insights into recent changes in the law for criminal practitioners.

Each chapter begins with a brief overview of the particular subject matter in question. The text is then broken down using various levels of subheadings. We have included, were relevant, references to major scholarly works and other sources of interest, that may help to reinforce the reader's understanding of individual topics. We have also attempted to present the law in a slightly wider, social context than other texts in the field. In addition to offering our description and analysis of the recent changes in the law, we have attempted to give some explanation as to why such changes came about, and what the reform process may have in store for the future. It was also our intention to highlight the practical significance of the law of evidence. Throughout the text, we have included various examples and case scenarios to assist students in developing that oft-elusive skill of applying the law to a factual scenario in a clear and logical fashion.

We would like to offer our sincere thanks to those who have helped and advised us in the preparation of this text. In particular, Ken Lidstone provided us with some excellent teaching materials that he had used in his Criminal Evidence course at the University of Sheffield over many years, and was glad to offer his advice and expertise to us throughout the drafting process. Thanks also to Jeremy Stein from Law Matters, and to David Stott for his helpful suggestions. Our sincere gratitude is also extended to Bill Antrobus, for his assistance in the production process. We would also like to thank our families, friends and colleagues at the School of Law, University of Sheffield for their support and advice.

Jonathan Doak
Claire McGourlay
Sheffield
September 2005

Table of Cases

Table of Statutes

Table of Statutory Instruments

1 Introduction to Criminal Evidence

All material which is produced at court is subject to regulation by the laws of evidence. Decisions on the application of these rules of evidence are taken by the trial judge, and will often be concerned with whether or not the evidence should be admitted. The law of evidence is adjectival rather than substantive law. The substantive law is the criminal law – murder, manslaughter, theft, burglary, rape, violence to the person and other crimes – that defines the conduct and mental element that is required for the particular crime. The law of criminal evidence is the law that governs how these criminal offences are to be proved.

The subjects are not totally separate. For example, in a murder case the jury have to decide whether the defendant intended to kill or to cause really serious bodily harm. In directing a jury that there has to be a 'virtual certainty of death' and that the defendant(s) had to have an 'appreciation that such was the case', the trial judge is stating a rule of evidence not one of substantive law (see *R v Mathews and R v Alleyne* [2004] QB 69). Knowledge of the law of criminal evidence is essential to a full understanding of the criminal legal process. No matter how well versed you are in the criminal law, you cannot properly advise a client, or decide whether to prosecute a case, without knowledge of the law of evidence. For advocates dealing with the criminal law, a sound knowledge the law of evidence is even more essential.

From the outset, it must be clearly understood that in the prosecution of most serious crimes the burden is on the prosecution to prove beyond reasonable doubt that the defendant did the prohibited act with the required mental element. This is not always possible. Take the following case: Baby X is found dead. The autopsy shows that a blow to the head killed him, probably by coming into contact with a wall or similar hard, flat surface. Marks on the legs suggest that the baby was swung against the flat surface while held by the legs. The baby was seen alive the day before he was found dead. Only the mother and her boyfriend had contact with the baby during this period. An open and shut case? By no means, if the mother and the boyfriend maintain their right to refuse to answer questions and refuse to offer any explanation for the child's death. Without evidence that one or the other, or both, did the act which killed the child, neither can be charged with murder or manslaughter. It is not possible to say that it must have been one of them so charge both and let the jury decide which one did it. If one or both were charged, each could refuse to give evidence and would not be exposed to cross-examination, which might reveal the truth. Since the Criminal Justice and Public Order Act 1994, the jury may draw proper inferences from the failure to answer police questions or to give evidence, but these provisions do not replace the requirement for evidence that the defendant intentionally, recklessly or negligently did an act, or failed to do an act, which caused the death of the child.

If there was a prosecution in this case the lack of evidence would result in an acquittal, and until recently the law was that one cannot thereafter be tried for the same offence. However, Pt 10 of the Criminal Justice Act 2003 provides for the retrial of a person who has been acquitted of a qualifying offence where there is new and compelling evidence that the person was guilty of that offence. The principle had already been breached by ss 54 to 57 of the Criminal Procedure and Investigation Act 1996, which permit prosecution of a defendant acquitted as the result of jury tampering or witness intimidation, and, as we shall see, the House of Lords has recently held that the previous acquittals of an accused can, in certain circumstances, be used to prove the guilt of the accused when charged with an offence committed in a similar way to those of which he was acquitted.

The trial

The function of the judge and jury

The criminal trial almost always involves questions of law and fact. In jury trials the general rule is that questions of law are to be decided by the trial judge, while questions of fact are to be decided by the jury. Matters such as the competence of witnesses, the admissibility of evidence and matters relating to the substantive law are matters of law for the judge. Matters such as the credibility of a witness who has been declared competent, the weight to be attached to any evidence and the existence, or non-existence, of the facts in issue are questions of fact for the jury. In the case of trial by lay justice or by stipendiary magistrates there is no jury, and the magistrate(s) must decide questions of law and questions of fact. Lay magistrates will rely heavily on the legally qualified clerk in deciding questions of law.

Although questions of fact are normally to be decided by the jury, there are times when the judge must investigate the preliminary facts in order to decide, for example, whether evidence is admissible, or to determine whether there is sufficient evidence on a particular issue to go before a jury and to evaluate the evidence in order to comment on it when summing up the evidence for the jury.

As one might expect, there are a number of special cases where questions of fact may be treated as questions of law, or where what many would argue should be questions of law are treated as questions of fact. For example, while the construction of a statute is a matter of law, the construction of ordinary words used in the statute may be a question of fact. The phrase 'insulting behaviour' in s 5 of the Public Order Act 1936 (now replaced by the Public Order Act 1986) was thought to be a matter of law, but in *Cozens v Brutes* [1973] AC 854 the House of Lords held that where a word in a statute is used in its ordinary sense, it is a question of fact for the jury or magistrates to determine whether the proved conduct amounted to insulting behaviour. Applying this dictum, the word 'dishonestly' as used in the Theft Act 1968 was held to be an ordinary word in common use and therefore a question of fact for the jury. Similarly, the question whether an act is 'more than merely preparatory to the commission of an offence' for the purposes of s 1 of the Criminal Attempts Act 1981 is one of fact (*DPP v Stonehouse* [1978] AC 854 and see now s 4(3) of the 1981 Act). Of more relevance to this account is the decision of the Court of Appeal in *R v Fulling* [1987] QB 426, where the word 'oppression' in s 76(2)(a) of the Police and Criminal Evidence Act 1984 (which governs the admissibility of confessions) was given its ordinary dictionary meaning despite a partial definition in s 76(8).

There is, however, no consistency of approach. *Cozens v Brutus* is often ignored. Even the House of Lords disregarded it in *MPC v Caldwell* [1978] AC 55, where the word 'recklessly', as used in the Criminal Damage Act 1971, was said to be used in its ordinary sense and yet was given a legal definition which differed from that given in the case of *R v Cunningham* [1957] QB 396. In *R v G* [2003] 4 All ER 765, the House of Lords reconsidered their decision in *Caldwell* and departed from it, holding that it was just to do so (recklessness is now subjective as in *Cunningham*, as opposed to objective as in *Caldwell*). There are, however, countless other examples of ordinary words being legally defined simply because without such definition juries (and judges) are likely to produce different interpretations.

Trial procedure

A brief look at the way in which a typical trial on indictment proceeds (assuming the jury have been selected and the opening address to the jury by prosecution and defence counsel has taken place) may assist in understanding the above. There are broadly four phases in the criminal trial (see **Figure 1.1**).

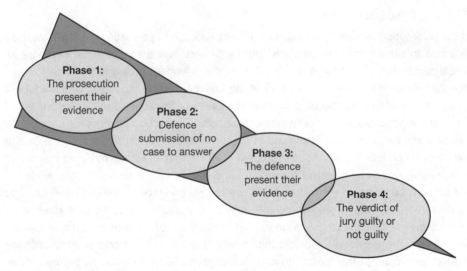

Figure 1.1 The English adversarial trial

Phase 1: the prosecution case

The first task of the prosecution (Phase 1) is to adduce sufficient evidence to persuade the judge that there is a case to answer. The prosecution will call their witnesses, who will be led through their evidence by prosecuting counsel (examination-in-chief). The defence will cross-examine those witnesses in an attempt to undermine the evidence given, or, as is too often the case, to discredit the witnesses. After cross-examination, prosecuting counsel will re-examine in order to emphasise the evidence given and to restore the credibility of the witness if damaged in cross-examination. Once the prosecution have presented sufficient evidence to persuade the trial judge that there is a case to answer, that is the end of Phase 1. It is not permissible for the prosecutor to introduce further evidence after the close of its case (*R v Rice* [1963] 1 QB 857). The prosecution case may, however, be strengthened by cross-examination of the defendant and/or any witnesses for the defence. Equally, cross-examination of the victim and any prosecution witnesses, together with evidence from the defendant and/or defence witnesses, may weaken the prosecution case.

Phase 2: a case to answer?

At the end of the prosecution case the defence may submit that there is 'no case to answer', if there appears to be insufficient evidence to persuade a reasonable jury of the defendant's guilt (Phase 2). If the judge agrees, the prosecution will have failed to discharge the evidential burden and the judge will withdraw the case from the jury and direct an acquittal (*Practice Direction (Submission of No Case)* [1962] 1 WLR 227). In most cases which go to trial the prosecution succeed in discharging the evidential burden, which means that the case proceeds and the defence present their case (see Phase 3, below). But this does not mean that the prosecution have discharged the persuasive burden; the jury must be persuaded of the defendant's guilt beyond reasonable doubt (see **Chapter 3**). In a case tried on indictment, whether the prosecution have done so or not will not be known until the jury reach their verdict.

Phase 3: the defence case

If the prosecution succeed in producing sufficient evidence to persuade the judge that there is a case to answer, the case proceeds and the defence may then give evidence (Phase 3). The defence must at this stage decide whether the defendant is to give evidence. Counsel for the defence will be aware that s 35 of the Criminal Justice and Public Order Act 1994 provides that inferences may be draw from the failure of the accused to give evidence or if he, without good cause, refuses to answer questions. The section provides for a procedure under which the court must at the end of the prosecution case satisfy itself (in the case of proceedings on indictment) that the accused is aware that the stage has been reached at which evidence can be given for the defence and that he can, if he wishes, give evidence. He will also be told of the effect of his failure to give evidence or without good cause to answer questions (that a proper inference may be drawn). This puts the defendant under some degree of coercion to give evidence, but the strength of the prosecution case will also exert a certain pressure. If the prosecution have presented a strong case which calls for an answer, the failure of the accused to answer it suggests to the jury that he has no answer. The jury may then accept the evidence presented by the prosecution and conclude that he is guilty as charged. If the defendant does give evidence, he may succeed in casting sufficient doubt on the prosecution case to justify an acquittal. However, it is also possible that the defence evidence actually strengthens the prosecution case. For example, a defence witness may admit under cross-examination that he lied to help the defendant, or the defendant himself may under cross-examination make damaging admissions. Where a defendant gives evidence it is evidence for all purposes, and may be evidence for him also but against his co-accused. Thus, where there are a number of defendants and each seeks to blame the others, their evidence supports the prosecution case against the others. However, if a defendant has made a confession then that confession becomes part of the prosecution case, but only against the person who made it, and assists them in discharging the evidential burden and the legal or persuasive burden.

At this point in the trial the defence may have an evidential burden to adduce sufficient evidence of a defence they are relying on, for example self-defence or provocation on a charge of murder. If the defence do not adduce sufficient evidence of a particular defence to make it an issue, and there is no other evidence of that defence, the trial judge will not put that defence to the jury and the prosecution are not required to adduce evidence rebutting that defence. It follows that if the defence are relying on a particular defence, the accused or defence witnesses will usually have to give evidence of that defence. There may be occasions when prosecution witnesses suggest a defence in their evidence, eg the witness says he saw the victim punch the accused who then punched him back – suggesting self-defence. Defence witnesses may also give such evidence, but few juries will accept such a defence if the accused does not himself give evidence and is not subjected to cross-examination. If there is sufficient evidence to make the particular defence an issue – and this will be for the trial judge to determine – the prosecution must then disprove that defence by persuading the jury beyond reasonable doubt that the particular defence does not apply.

Like prosecuting counsel, defence counsel will lead the witness through his or her evidence and will re-examine defence witnesses after cross-examination. Sometimes the defence will bear the legal or persuasive burden of proving certain defences, eg insanity or diminished responsibility, or that defendants have an excuse or justification for their action. Reversing the legal or persuasive burden means that the defence must persuade the jury (on the balance of probabilities) that, at the time he did the act, the defendant was insane or suffering from diminished responsibility, or has the excuse or justification pleaded (see **Chapter 3**).

Summing Up

After the conclusion of all the evidence and closing speeches by counsel in a trial on indictment, the trial judge must sum up the case for the jury. He must direct them on the relevant substantive law, remind them of the evidence that has been given and direct them on a number of evidential matters. He begins with a direction on which side bears the burden of proof and the standard of proof required before they can be satisfied that the matters have been proved. He will normally take the jury through the prosecution evidence and, importantly, point out any defence which that evidence discloses, even if the defence have not relied on that particular defence (eg, on a charge of murder the defendant pleads self-defence but the evidence also raises the defence of provocation; the jury will be directed to consider self-defence but, if that fails, to go on to consider provocation). What evidential directions are given will depend on the nature of the particular case. Thus where the case depends wholly or substantially on identification evidence, a direction on the special need for caution will be required (see *R v Turnbull* [1977] QB 224). If there are a number of defendants, but if only one of them has confessed, the jury must be directed that the confession is evidence only against that particular defendant (see **Chapter 7**).

The judge may also comment on the plausibility and credibility of witnesses, and on the weight which might be attached to particular evidence (see the judge's comments on the evidence of witness Bromley in the *Damilola Taylor* case *Daily Telegraph*, 22 February 2002). He may express his opinion quite strongly, but he must tell the jury that they are in no way bound by any view he expresses. He should not give an express indication of his belief or disbelief. He should not, for example, say 'it is obvious to everyone, in this court, is it not, that the accused is lying'; though he may say 'you may think that the defendant's explanation is not worthy of belief, but that ladies and gentlemen of the jury, is a matter for you'.

Many believe that the summing up often unduly influences the jury and could be dispensed with – see Lord Bingham's criticism of the summing up of one of his predecessors in title, Lord Goddard, in the case of Derek Bentley, which was heavily biased in favour of a conviction (*The Times*, 31 July 1998). Indeed, there are numerous cases where a conviction has been quashed on appeal because of improper comment by the trial judge, but these cases represent the extreme. A majority of judges are more circumspect and their influence over the jury cannot be ascertained without proper research. Since the law does not permit such research, we may never know the true impact of the summing up on the verdict of the jury.

Phase 4: the verdict

At the end of the trial, the jury will deliver the verdict (Phase 4). One should note that it is commonly supposed that a verdict of 'not guilty' equates with innocence. This is not so. It simply means that the prosecution have failed to satisfy the jury of the defendant's guilt beyond reasonable doubt. The failure to satisfy the jury is often due to a lack of evidence, or to an inability to adduce relevant evidence because it is excluded or inadmissible. Thus the defendant's confession may be excluded because of some improprieties in the obtaining of that confession, which under s 76 of the Police and Criminal Evidence Act 1984 is to be excluded, even if true, if the prosecution cannot prove beyond reasonable doubt that it was not obtained in breach of s 76 or in some other way which justifies its exclusion under s 78 of that Act (see **Chapter 7**). The defendant may be acquitted of rape (or any other crime) despite the fact that he has several convictions for rape (or other crimes), those previous convictions being inadmissible prior to the Criminal Justice Act 2003, unless the manner in which they were committed is such as to make them relevant to prove that the defendant raped the complainant in the instant case (the 2003 Act changes the law and in future the previous convictions of the accused, when relevant, may be admissible to prove his guilt – see **Chapter 5**).

The Law Commission recognised that an acquittal does not necessarily mean innocent in its report *Double Jeopardy and Prosecution Appeals* (Law Com No 267, 2001). It recommended that the rule against double jeopardy, which prevents a further prosecution for the same offence following an acquittal, should be subject to an exception in certain cases where new evidence is discovered after an acquittal, but only where the offence of which the defendant was acquitted was murder, genocide consisting of the killing of any person, or (if and when the Law Commission's recommendations on involuntary manslaughter are implemented) reckless killing. The Criminal Justice Act 2003 has now enacted this recommendation.

In a similar vein, one may also note that the fact that an appellate court quashes a conviction does not mean that the convicted person was in fact innocent. Occasionally an appeal court will declare that the convicted person is innocent of the crime, but more often the conviction is quashed because it is seen as unsafe. This may be because of a fault in the trial, such as the judge's failure to give a direction to the jury or his having given the wrong direction. In *R (Mullen) v Secretary of State for the Home Department* [2004] UKHL 18, the Home Secretary appealed against a decision of the Court of Appeal where it was held that Mullen, whose conviction for conspiracy to cause explosions was quashed as unsafe, because he had been unlawfully removed from Zimbabwe and brought to the United Kingdom for trial, was entitled to ex gratia compensation. It was accepted that Mullen, who had served 10 years of a 30-year sentence, had been properly convicted, there being no doubt that he was a quartermaster for the IRA and was in possession of bombs and bomb-making equipment, but the manner of his removal from Zimbabwe to UK was seen as blatantly unlawful and therefore an abuse of executive power which justified the quashing of his conviction. The Divisional Court held that the Home Secretary was right to refuse to pay Mullen ex gratia compensation, such payments being intended for persons who were wrongly convicted and shown, by virtue of some new or newly discovered fact, to have been innocent. The Court of Appeal took the opposite view, holding that if Parliament had intended that compensation be paid only to those proved to be innocent it would have said so. The Court did not therefore consider proof of innocence to be a prerequisite of entitlement to compensation. The House of Lords quashed the decision of the Court of Appeal and restored the decision of the Divisional Court.

Media communication frequently represents both acquittals at first instance and successful appeals as authoritative statements of innocence and full acceptance of the defence cases, thereby both reinforcing and responding to the general public expectation that a miscarriage of justice equates to innocence of an alleged crime. Precise legal meanings are thereby often lost in the reportage of criminal cases (see further R Nobles and D Schiff, *Understanding Miscarriages of Justice* (2000)).

The function of the criminal court

The English criminal trial is not a search for truth but an attempt to do justice within the constraints placed upon it by the law of evidence and the procedural requirements. In contrast, the inquisitorial mode of trial, used in many continental criminal justice systems, is much more concerned with the truth, or what passes for truth in a legal inquiry. Inquisitorial systems embark on a long and detailed inquiry led by an investigating magistrate (see, for example, the inquiry into the death of Diana, Princess of Wales, and the more recent trial of Francisco Arce Montes for the murder of Caroline Dickinson, extensively reported in the newspapers from 8 June 2004). In contrast, common law adversarial systems prefer to do justice within a much shorter time frame.

The most obvious evidential constraint in the common law system is that the court itself cannot undertake a search for relevant evidence; it must rely almost entirely on the prosecution and defence. The prosecution have at their disposal the huge resources of the police and forensic services. The defence have little in the way of investigative resources and have to rely on private detectives for any real investigation. The imbalance has led to the creation of many rules of evidence and procedure that are favourable to the defence. The law has long been that the prosecution must disclose their entire case to the defence before trial, while the defence were only obliged to disclose an alibi and any reliance on expert evidence. In recent times the law has required the prosecution disclosure of all unused material. The failure to disclose relevant material led to a number of well-publicised acquittals (see, eg, *R v Ward (Judith)* [1993] 2 All ER 577). The pendulum is now swinging the other way, toward a more balanced position according to government and prosecution, though many civil libertarians see it differently.

The Criminal Procedure and Investigations Act 1996 requires disclosure by the prosecution of previously undisclosed material. This is to be followed by the defence disclosing to the prosecution certain information about the defence case. On receipt of that, the prosecution will be required to disclose any material relevant to the defence case as disclosed (Pt 5 of the Criminal Justice Act 2003 amends this procedure to increase the amount of defence disclosure). Stemming from the recommendations of the *Auld Review of the Criminal Courts* (see p 23 below), the central purpose of the legislation was said to be administrative efficiency, so that issues that remain in contention can effectively be identified.

The Criminal Justice and Public Order Act 1994 requires disclosure of facts at the stage when the suspect is cautioned and questioned about the offence. Provided that a solicitor is present when the defendant is interviewed, proper inferences may be drawn from the defendant's failure to mention facts when questioned under caution which are later relied upon at trial, or from the failure to explain the presence of objects or marks on the person or clothing, or one's presence at or near the scene of a crime. Inferences can also be drawn from the failure of the accused to give evidence, or from his refusal, without good cause, to answer questions while giving evidence (see further **Chapter 2**).

The concept of relevance

The general rule governing the admissibility of evidence is that all relevant evidence is admissible. The legal definition of relevance was set out by Lord Simon in *R v Kilbourne* [1973] AC 729. Evidence was considered to be 'relevant' if 'if it is logically probative or disprobative of some matter which requires proof' (at 756).

This definition is not a decisive indicator as to what evidence should be excluded and what should be included. It does not amount to a legal test for relevance. As Professor Dennis observes, it is frequently referred to as a legal 'concept' as it has no statutory or common law definition or test (I Dennis, *The Law of Evidence* (2002), 50).

The legal concept of relevance is thus somewhat elusive and open to subjective interpretation. As such, it has also been subject to considerable criticism, particularly from feminist commentators, who have attacked the way in which the concept of relevance has been applied in rape and sexual assault cases. Until the Youth Justice and Criminal Evidence Act 1999 clamped down on the use of previous sexual history evidence, it was commonplace for complainants in rape cases to be cross-examined in detail about their sexual history because trial judges frequently deemed it relevant to the issue of consent. Jennifer Temkin has argued that judges' beliefs and assumptions about sexual relationships fail to take account of the way in which the role of sex in society has undergone a radical transformation over the past 40 years. She contends that multiple sexual partners over a period of time are relatively commonplace in contemporary society, and that the use of such evidence 'can shed no light on whether she [the complainant] consented to this particular defendant on the occasion in question' (J Temkin, *Rape and the Legal Process* (2002), 199).

The House of Lords took relevance to what may be described as its logical extreme in *R v Blastland* [1985] 2 All ER 1095. The accused was charged with the murder of a young boy. He claimed that the murderer was another man, M, who had been in the vicinity while the accused was with the boy. M was investigated by the police but was not charged. M had made a number of statements to the police in which he admitted the crime, but he later withdrew them. These were inadmissible at Blastland's trial because they were hearsay. However, the defence wished to call a number of witnesses who would say that M had told them of the boy's death at a time when the only way he could have known of it was if he himself had killed him. The House of Lords upheld the trial judge's decision to exclude the evidence of these witnesses on the ground that it was not relevant. The issue at the trial was whether Blastland had committed the crime, and what was relevant to that issue was not the fact of M's knowledge but how he came by it. Since he might have come by it in a number of different ways, there was no rational basis on which the jury could be invited to draw an inference as to how M came by that knowledge or that M, rather than the accused, was the killer.

There are thus various degrees of relevance: a fact may be only slightly relevant; or highly relevant; or somewhere between these two extremes. Until recently, the common law test for the admissibility of evidence of previous convictions or bad character required a high degree of relevance in order to outweigh the prejudicial effect of admitting such evidence. However, in general the degree of relevance does not affect the admissibility of the evidence, though the less relevant the evidence is, the less likely it is that one will rely upon it. This pertains to what is known as the 'weight' to be given to the evidence: whether or not a particular piece of evidence is deemed to be relevant will often depend upon the weight, or importance, that ought to be attached to it. Thus in evidence of identification, if a witness caught only a fleeting glimpse of the alleged offender as he ran from the scene, that evidence might be relevant and admissible but carries little weight. On the other hand, the fact that a witness recognises a robber as a man with whom he went to school and who lives only a few streets away from the witness, is highly relevant, and doubtless the jury will give much greater weight to that evidence. The weight of the evidence will also be affected by the way in which it is given, the character of the witness, and whether or not that witness is discredited in cross-examination. Thus a witness may give what appears to be highly relevant evidence but is then discredited in cross-examination. For example, the eyewitness who claims to recognise the defendant as a person he went to school with and whom he knows well, is shown to have a grudge against the defendant, which he has nurtured since his schooldays. He may therefore not be entirely truthful in his evidence implicating the accused.

The trial of Rosemary West in the Autumn of 1995 revealed a number of witnesses who had been paid by newspapers, or who had entered into contracts with newspapers to publish their story after conviction (*The Times*, 4 November 1995). Their evidence, though highly relevant, carried less weight if the jury accepted the suggestion that they embellished their evidence to ensure a conviction because they had been promised more money if West was convicted. In the 1970s the former Liberal Party leader, Jeremy Thorpe, was acquitted of various offences, in part because a central prosecution witness had been promised more money for his story if Thorpe was convicted. Witness Bromley, a 15-year-old girl who gave evidence in the trial of the boys accused of murdering Damiola Taylor, had been promised a reward of £50,000 in return for evidence leading to the conviction of those responsible for the killing. The discussion of the reward with the interviewing police officer, which suggested more interest in the reward than in giving honest evidence, was a factor in the judge's decision to instruct the jury that her evidence was not credible. There have been suggestions since that case that legislation should make payments to witnesses unlawful; these have not been acted upon, but the Code of Practice governing newspapers states that payments should not be made to witnesses before trial.

Judicial discretion to exclude evidence

Many forms of evidence have traditionally been held back from the British jury on the basis that the jury cannot be trusted. For example, it is feared that jurors may give too much weight to previous convictions and not enough to other evidence. The law against hearsay evidence is similarly based on a lack of faith in the jury to consider evidence fairly. Fear of concoction and manufacturing of evidence led to the creation of other rules excluding previous statements made by a witness which are consistent with what he says in court. In addition to certain forms of evidence which are automatically inadmissible by virtue of common law or statute, there is also an important general judicial discretion to exclude any other evidence that may otherwise be admissible.

The common law discretion

The discretion to exclude admissible evidence is confined to evidence produced by the prosecution (see *Lobban v The Queen* [1995] 2 All ER 602, PC, where the Privy Council confirmed that there is no discretion to exclude, at the request of one co-accused, evidence tendered by another co-accused). In *R v Sang* [1980] AC 492, the House of Lords stated the common law discretion in the following terms:

> *(1) The trial judge at a criminal trial has always a discretion to refuse to admit evidence if in his opinion its prejudicial effect outweighs its probative value.*

> *(2) Save with regard to admissions and confessions and generally with regard to evidence obtained from the accused after the commission of the offence, he has no discretion to refuse to admit relevant admissible evidence on the ground that it was obtained by improper or unfair means. The court is not concerned with how it was obtained but how it is used at trial.*

Sang was concerned with the argument that the offence was instigated by an agent provocateur. The trial judge, on the assumption that the offence was so instigated, ruled that he had no discretion to exclude the evidence. The House of Lords agreed that the fact that the evidence was obtained by the use of an agent provocateur, or by the police or an informant inciting the offence, was not a ground on which the trial judge could exclude evidence. It was emphasised that there was no defence of entrapment in English law. Their Lordships went on to consider the discretion more generally, defining the discretion in the terms stated above (it will be noted that admissions and confessions are excluded from the above statement: they were subject to a different regime at common law and are now subject to s 76 of the Police and Criminal Evidence Act 1984).

The law before *Sang* was replete with statements of a broader discretion to exclude real evidence, but in no case was the suggested discretion actually exercised. Thus evidence obtained after an illegal search was admissible in *Jeffrey v Black* [1978] QB 490); and drugs seized following an unlawful entry onto premises were also admitted into evidence in *R v Adams* [1980] QB 575. In more recent times, the Court of Appeal refused to exclude the evidence of involvement in the illegal importation of drugs obtained by a trespassory bugging of a dwelling house (*R v Khan* [1994] 4 All ER 426). The House of Lords (*R v Khan* [1996] 3 WLR 162) confirmed this decision while doing little to clarify an area of law which has been confused by the addition of a statutory discretion to exclude evidence under s 78 of the Police and Criminal Evidence Act 1984 (see pp 268–88 below). Their Lordships found it unnecessary to consider whether and, if so, to what extent English law provided a right to privacy, holding that even if there were such a right and the evidence was obtained unlawfully, it remained admissible, subject to the judge's power to exclude it at his discretion. Their Lordships also found it unnecessary to consider the common law discretion apart from s 78 of the Police and Criminal Evidence Act 1984.

It was argued that in exercising its discretion the court ought to take account of the European Convention on Human Rights, in particular Article 8, which provided for a limited right to respect for private life. However, their Lordships held that whether the evidence was obtained in breach of English law or European law made no difference, and that on the facts of the instant case the circumstances in which the evidence was obtained, even if in breach of Article 8, entitled the trial judge to hold that the facts were not such as to require the exclusion of the evidence (note that this case was heard before the Human Rights Act 1998 took effect).

The statutory discretion

Section 78 of the Police and Criminal Evidence Act 1984 provides:

> *In any proceedings the court may refuse to allow evidence on which the prosecution proposes to rely to be given if it appears to the court that, having regard to all the circumstances, including the circumstances in which the evidence was obtained, the admission of the evidence would have such an adverse effect on the fairness of the proceedings that the court ought not to admit it.*

In *Khan* [1996] 3 WLR 162, s 78 was argued alongside the common law discretion, but the evidence of conversations, which showed that Khan was involved in the illegal importation of drugs, was admitted. Unfortunately the appeal centred on whether a trial judge, in exercising his discretion at common law or under the statute, was obliged to take account of the European Convention on Human Rights and in particular Article 8. There is no doubt that in the light of the decision of the European Court in *Malone v United Kingdom* (1984)

7 EHRR 14, the *Guidelines on Aural Surveillance*, under which the police operated in *Khan*, were in breach of Article 8 because they were not law and were not readily available (the Government has since accepted that the Guidelines are in breach of the Convention and has put them into statutory form). That, however, missed the point that the courts have never been overly concerned with how the evidence was obtained. Their primary concern is with how the evidence is used at trial and whether that use affects the fairness of the trial. The common law has often applied the dictum of Crompton J in *R v Leatham* (1861) 8 Cox CC 498, 501, that 'it matters not how you get it if you steal it even, it would be admissible in evidence'. It seems clear that s 78 is not going to change that approach, but the way in which the defence put their case on appeal meant that the opportunity to clarify the law and provide some indication of how s 78 should be interpreted was lost. Section 78 has been far more widely, and arguably often incorrectly, relied upon to exclude confession evidence (see **Chapter 7**).

A further statutory discretion, worded almost exactly as that in s 78, is provided by s 101(3) of the Criminal Justice Act 2003. This replaces the common law discretion to exclude bad character evidence when its probative force is outweighed by its prejudicial effect. That discretion was based on a mistrust of the jury, while s 78 is based on an overall view of the effect of the evidence on the fairness of the trial. However, the *Explanatory Notes* accompanying the 2003 Act state that the discretion will be exercised when the probative value of the evidence is outweighed by its prejudicial effect, suggesting that there will be little change in practice.

Glossary of terms

Repeated reference will be made in forthcoming chapters to terms such as 'facts in issue', 'collateral facts', 'real evidence', 'circumstantial evidence' and so on. These, and other terms, are explained below.

Facts in issue

These are the facts that the prosecution must prove in order to succeed. It is noted in **Chapter 3** that the burden of proving the facts that in a criminal case amount to the defined offence, is always on the prosecution, who must prove those facts beyond reasonable doubt. If the defendant pleads not guilty, all the facts are in issue; that is the prosecution must prove the actus reus of the offence and any mental element required.

For example, in a case of theft the prosecution must prove that the article alleged to have been stolen was property belonging to another and that the defendant appropriated that property dishonestly with the intention of permanently depriving the owner, or person in possession or control, of that property. If the accused's plea of guilty is based on a lack of dishonesty he may admit the actus reus, so that the only fact in issue is whether on not he was dishonest when he appropriated the property belonging to another. In many rape cases, the fact that intercourse took place is often admitted, but the defendant claims it was consensual. In such a case there is no need to prove that the accused had intercourse with the complainant; the only fact in issue is whether she consented (or the defendant held a reasonable belief that she was consenting) to the admitted act of intercourse. In other cases, the sole issue may be the identity of the defendant as the rapist.

Collateral facts

These are facts that are not directly relevant to the facts in issue. In the main collateral facts are facts that go to the credit of the witness (including the victim). As we shall see, largely in order to cut down on extraneous examination or cross-examination, the law limits such examination in relation to collateral facts by obliging the cross-examining party to accept the answer given and denying him the opportunity to bring rebutting evidence unless the line of questioning falls into recognised categories. In relation to the crime of rape, and some related offences, there is a statutory limitation on cross-examination of the complainant. Cross-examination as to credit is designed to undermine the credibility of the witness in the eyes of the jury and persuade them to give less weight to the evidence of the particular witness. The fact that the witness has a contract with a newspaper for his story is a collateral fact, but because it shows a likely bias on the part of the witness the cross-examining party is permitted to prove that there is such a contract if the witness were to deny it. Previous convictions were regularly put to a witness (other than the defendant) in cross-examination on the basis that a person with previous convictions is a less credible witness, though there is no scientific basis for the belief.

It is often suggested that witnesses are mistaken or, even worse, liars, and many who have given evidence at a criminal trial will say that it felt as if they were on trial and they would think twice before volunteering to give evidence in future. Section 100 of the Criminal Justice Act 2003 restricts the admissibility of the bad character of a witness with the intention of preventing some of the abuses of cross-examination of witnesses. Until recently, the accused was permitted to cross-examine his alleged victim in person. Children and adult victims of rape and other offences were particularly intimidated by this practice. In one case the victim of rape was faced by her alleged attacker who cross-examined her while wearing the same clothes he was alleged to have worn while raping her (*The Times*, 5 April 2000). The Youth Justice and Criminal Evidence Act 1999 has now changed the law to prevent cross-examination by the defendant in person of children or victims of sexual offences, and judges have discretion to prevent such cross-examination in other appropriate cases. In addition, the Act seeks to control the use of evidence of the sexual behaviour of the complainant in a case of rape and other sexual offences. As noted above, in the past the previous sexual behaviour of the complainant had been used by the defence to suggest that the complainant was of loose moral character and probably consented to the intercourse which took place. This was a factor in the extremely low conviction rate for rape, particularly the form known as acquaintance rape, where the defendant and complainant were known to each other and might well have been intimate in the past.

This 'legal intimidation' of witnesses is certainly distressing, but many witnesses also have to face illegal intimidation from defendants, their families and/or their associates. Such intimidation is an offence, but that fact rarely deters the intimidators, and it is a threat to the criminal justice system that depends on the evidence of witnesses. Witness protection programmes are available to protect against intimidation, and at the extreme witnesses can be relocated and have their names changed, but that is a high price to pay for doing one's duty as a citizen. Most witnesses faced with such a choice will choose not to give evidence. As we shall see, there are now provisions to allow witnesses to give evidence anonymously, via a live link or by video, which helps to overcome the low-level fear of giving evidence. Where the fear is greater and the witness has made a statement to the police, there is a provision that allows the statement to be read without the need for oral evidence from the witness.

Forms of evidence

Direct oral testimony

This is the oral statement of a witness made on oath in open court and tendered as evidence of the truth of the facts asserted. 'Direct' means that the witness himself perceived the facts asserted with one of his five senses – usually he saw or heard the facts to which he testifies. An eyewitness, one who actually saw the events described, would give direct oral testimony. Such testimony, which is always admissible if it is relevant and the witness is competent, is usually contrasted with hearsay evidence (see below), which is usually not admissible unless subject to an exception. If evidence is given through a live link or by pre-recorded video, the authorising statutes state that such evidence is to be treated as direct oral evidence.

Hearsay evidence

Hearsay evidence is any statement other than one made by the witness in the course of giving his evidence in the proceedings in question, which is tendered as evidence of the truth of the facts asserted. Such evidence is inadmissible unless subject to a common law or statutory exception. Thus while the statement by a witness P that 'I saw the defendant strike the victim' is direct testimony, a statement by another witness that 'P told me that he had seen the defendant striking the victim' is hearsay if tendered to prove that the defendant struck the victim. One must emphasise that a statement is hearsay only if tendered to prove the truth of the facts asserted. Thus if the defendant is claiming that he acted under threats from X, the statement 'X said he would kill me if I did not do what he said' is not hearsay, because the purpose of the statement is not to prove that X intended to kill the defendant but to prove that the statement was made and that it amounted to duress.

There are numerous exceptions to the rule against hearsay. The unreliability of hearsay evidence is the main reason why it is excluded, though there are a number of examples of reliable hearsay evidence being excluded. The Criminal Justice Act 2003 reforms the law and in doing so preserves some of these exceptions. The Act and the preserved exceptions are considered in **Chapter 6**.

Documentary evidence

As the name implies, documentary evidence consists of documents produced in evidence before a court. 'Document' now means not only the written or typed form but includes maps, plans, graphs, drawings, photographs, tapes (audio and visual), films, negatives and disks, CDs or DVDs – in short, every means of communicating information other than the direct spoken word. The purpose in producing a document varies according to the document and the particular case. Maps may be produced simply to provide the court with a visual picture of the scene of an accident or a crime. In the Rosemary West trial, detailed plans of the house in which a number of bodies were found were produced to provide a visual picture of the location of the various bodies. The formal evidence of the finding of the bodies came from the police and forensic pathologists.

Our main concern is with documentary evidence that replaces the oral evidence of witnesses. Most witnesses in criminal cases make a written statement to the police (or defence solicitors if a defence witness). These written statements may be used by the witness to refresh his memory before or while giving evidence if made fairly soon after the events described. Under the provisions of the Criminal Justice Act 2003, statements in a document, whether made by a witness to the crime or a business document made for the purposes of the business, are admissible in evidence subject to certain conditions and judicial discretion. These provisions contradict the tradition of orality that is, or was, a cornerstone of the adversarial system, and are considered in **Chapter 6**.

Real evidence

This is usually taken to mean some material object that is produced to the court for inspection, so that the court may draw its own inference from observation of the particular object. Though often an important element in the prosecution case (sometimes also the defence case), it is often of little evidential value without some accompanying testimony. Thus in a case of murder by stabbing, a knife produced to the court is real evidence, but unless other evidence is available to show that it was the murder weapon and that it is linked to the accused, eg it was found in his car and has the victim's blood on it, it proves nothing. Real evidence may also be an original document, a visit to the scene of the murder(s) by the judge and jury, a tape-recording of the kidnapper's voice which the jury are asked to compare with the voice of the defendant or, increasingly, footage from a surveillance camera which purports to catch the defendant(s) in the act of committing the crime. In *R v Luttrell, Dawson and Hamberger* [2004] 2 Cr App R 520, lip-reading evidence given by an expert who had studied silent video-tape of the defendants in conversation was accepted as a species of real evidence subject to the qualifications of the lip reader and the particular circumstances, and subject to a warning to the jury as to the limitations of such evidence and the risk of error.

Real evidence is a term also used to distinguish between hearsay evidence, which has traditionally been inadmissible unless subject to a statutory or common law exception, and real evidence which is admissible if relevant. Thus in a recent case involving the distribution of indecent pictures of children by use of a computer, it was held that a document obtained from the company running the child pornography website, containing a breakdown of the defendant's successful and unsuccessful attempts to enter the website, and charges made to his credit card, was real evidence rather than hearsay.

Circumstantial evidence

Circumstantial evidence is evidence of relevant facts from which the existence, or non-existence, of the facts in issue may be inferred. Such evidence may include any of the above forms of evidence except, of course, direct testimony relating to the facts in issue. It is with direct oral testimony that circumstantial evidence is contrasted. One often hears circumstantial evidence being referred to in rather derogatory terms such as 'the case against the accused is only circumstantial', but circumstantial evidence has convicted far more than direct oral testimony, if only because it is in the nature of most crimes that they are not committed in the presence of eyewitnesses and therefore circumstantial evidence is the only available evidence. Cross and Tapper cite Pollock CB in *R v Exall* (1866) F & F 922, who likened such evidence to a multi-stranded rope:

> *One strand of the cord might be insufficient to sustain the weight, but three stranded together might be of sufficient strength. Thus … there may be a combination of circumstances, not one of which would raise a reasonable conviction or more than mere suspicion: but the three taken together may create a conclusion of guilt with as much certainty as human affairs can require.* (Cross and Tapper on Evidence *(10th edn), 929)*

Take the following example: D is charged with the murder of V by stabbing him in an alleyway behind a club they both frequented. On the night of V's death, D and V were playing cards in the club. V accused D of cheating and D was thrown out of the club at around 9.30 pm. D, who was a chef in a nearby restaurant, though off duty, was seen in the restaurant bar shortly after 10.00 pm, where he consumed several small whiskies. As he left at 11.30 pm he was heard to say, 'I'll get the bastard. He can't do this to me and get away with it.' V left the club at 11.45 pm, using the rear door into the alley. At about 11.50 pm a man fitting D's description was seen running from the alleyway in which V was found dying, a few minutes after witnesses heard loud voices followed by a scream. D's jacket was stained with lime wash, which was identical to that used on a wall in the alley where V was found, and a button from the jacket was found at the scene of the murder. The murder weapon, a carving knife, was similar to one used in the restaurant where D works. It was a well-known make, and a knife of that make, which had been in use shortly before D returned to the restaurant, was missing afterwards.

While there is no direct evidence of D's involvement, when the various strand of evidence are tied together there is a very strong case against D.

Motive

Those familiar with substantive criminal law will be aware of the distinction between motive and mental element (or mens rea). The fact that the defendant hates the victim, or that the defendant stood to benefit from the death of a particular person, is not part of the substantive law and contributes nothing to the question whether the defendant intended to kill the victim when he struck him. However, it is a useful piece of evidence, because it is more probable that a man with a motive to kill actually did so. By itself, it is not sufficient to convict the defendant, but when added to the other pieces of evidence it strengthens the prosecution case. Equally, the absence of a motive might weaken the prosecution case. In the above example the accused had a strong motive to kill the victim.

Corroboration

Corroboration is evidence that supports the truth of facts asserted by another witness. At its simplest it could mean no more than another independent witness giving the same evidence so that each supports the other, but it may be more complex and comprise much confirmatory detail. Forensic evidence often provides corroboration, although DNA evidence is now seen as direct, and often conclusive, evidence. In appropriate cases where it is alleged that the defendant committed the same offence against a number of victims, such as a multiple rape, the jury may take the evidence of other victims into account when considering the count against a particular victim, so that each victim supports the evidence of the other victims, thus providing mutual corroboration.

Corroboration was not generally required as a matter of law, though in practice the lack of any corroboration meant that the case was too weak to prosecute or, if prosecuted, to persuade the jury of the defendant's guilt. However, the common law created mandatory requirements that the jury be warned of the danger of convicting on the uncorroborated evidence of certain categories of witnesses. There were three such categories:

(a) accomplices giving evidence for the prosecution;

(b) complainants in sexual cases; and

(c) children giving sworn evidence.

In addition, s 38 of the Children and Young Persons Act 1933 required that children giving unsworn evidence be corroborated by other evidence, and other statutes provided that a conviction for certain offences (eg, speeding, perjury or treason) was not possible on the evidence of only one witness (these requirements, other than s 38 of the 1933 Act, remain in force).

The growth of the corroboration requirements illustrates how many of our evidential rules developed as a form of protection for the accused based on what may have been a mistaken belief that such rules were essential to a fair trial. The mistrust of evidence given by an accomplice was understandable, but the mistrust of victims of sexual offences and children was less so. It can be traced back to the writings of Hale in the seventeenth century, where he warned of the danger of false accusation in rape cases, observing that the charge was 'an accusation easy to be made and hard to be proved, and harder to be defended by the party accused, tho' never so innocent' (Sir Matthew Hale, *The History of the Pleas of the Crown* (1736), 635–6). Hale went on to state that if the complainant was of good fame (character) and reported the crime promptly, the greater her credibility; though if of bad fame and slow to complain, the less credible she was. Hale's observations became the stock-in-trade of defence lawyers, and some judges included them in their summing up.

The Criminal Law Amendment Act 1885 created several new sexual offences, including one intended to stop what became known as the 'white slave trade', abducting young girls for sexual purposes, and, in line with Hale's strictures, included a requirement of corroboration. However, rape remained a common law offence, and it was not until 1910 that the Court of Appeal laid down a requirement that the judge should warn the jury that it is dangerous to act on the unsupported evidence of the complainant in sexual cases (*R v Graham* (1910) 4 CAR 218). The requirement soon became mandatory and developed a life of its own.

The mandatory warning, as it became known, developed over the years into an excessively technical requirement that contributed greatly to the difficulties experienced in prosecuting alleged rapists and child molesters. The 'full' warning comprised four requirements:

(a) the warning to the jury that it was dangerous to convict on the uncorroborated evidence of the particular witness, though they might convict despite the absence of any corroboration;

(b) an explanation of corroboration, which had developed a technical meaning;

(c) a direction as to what evidence was, or was not, capable of amounting to corroboration; and

(d) a direction that it was for them (the jury) to decide whether that evidence did in fact constitute corroboration.

Sometimes the warning was accompanied by a justification for it. In respect of accomplices, this was usually that the witness might have a purpose of his own to serve in giving evidence for the prosecution; he might exaggerate the role of others, while minimising his role in the hope of a lighter sentence. In respect of victims of sexual offences, the justification was usually based on the likelihood of false accusation based on sexual neurosis, spite or shame at having consented to intercourse, which the victim now regretted. So far as children were concerned, it was assumed, without any supporting evidence, that a child's evidence was less trustworthy than that of an adult. The failure to give the warning led to a quashing of the conviction, and there were numerous unjustified acquittals resulting from this or from a failure correctly to identify the evidence that was capable of being corroboration. Precisely what the effect of this warning was on the jury can, however, only be a matter of speculation.

The corroboration requirement in respect of children was the first to be abolished. Section 34 of the Criminal Justice Act 1988 abrogated the requirement of a warning in respect of children giving sworn evidence and the requirement of actual corroboration in respect of children giving unsworn evidence. These requirements were helpful to the defence, and an attempt to require judges to give a cautionary warning, and in effect continue the old law, was rejected by the Court of Appeal in *R v Pryce* [1991] Crim LR 379.

The other two requirements (in respect of sexual complainants and accomplices) were abolished by s 32 of the Criminal Justice and Public Order Act 1994. Inevitably, that was not the end of the matter. Whilst the statute abolished the need for 'obligatory' warnings, it remained possible for a judge to warn a jury in a particular case that it might be dangerous to convict on the uncorroborated evidence of a particular witness where there was a particular reason to do so. In *R v Makanjuola* [1995] 3 All ER 730, counsel for the defendant tried unsuccessfully to re-impose the common law rule when he argued on appeal that where a judge does exercise his discretion to warn the jury, he had to give the full warning ((a) to (d) above). Lord Taylor CJ, speaking for the Court of Appeal, rejected this submission and summarised the relevant principles as follows:

(a) Section 32(1) abrogates the requirement to give a corroborative direction in respect of an alleged accomplice or a complainant of a sexual offence simply because the witness falls into one of those categories.

(b) It is a matter for the judge's discretion what, if any, warning he considers appropriate. Whether he chooses to give a warning and in what terms will depend on the circumstances of the case, the issues raised and the content and quality of the witness's evidence.

(c) In some cases, it may be appropriate for the judge to warn the jury to exercise caution before acting on the unsupported evidence of a witness. This will not be so simply because the witness is a complainant of a sexual offence or an accomplice. There will need to be an evidential basis for suggesting that the evidence of the witness may be unreliable. An evidential basis does not include mere suggestions by cross-examining counsel.

(d) If any question arises as to whether the judge should give a special warning in respect of a witness, it is desirable that the question be resolved by a discussion with counsel in the absence of the jury before final speeches.

(e) Where the judge does decide to give some warning in respect of a witness, it will be appropriate to do so as part of the judge's review of the evidence and his comments as to how the jury should evaluate it rather than a set-piece legal direction.

(f) Where some warning is required, it will be for the judge to decide the strength and terms of the warning. It does not have to be invested with the whole florid regime of the old corroboration rules.

(g) It follows that we emphatically disagree with the tentative submission that if the judge does give a warning, he should give a full warning. Attempts to re-impose the straitjacket of the old corroboration rules are strongly to be deprecated.

(h) Finally, this court will be disinclined to interfere with a judge's exercise of his discretion save in a case where the exercise is unreasonable in the Wednesbury *sense.*

It is now clear that the common law rules have finally been laid to rest. The judge retains a discretion to warn the jury in terms appropriate to the facts of a particular case. Where a witness has been shown to be unreliable, the judge may consider it necessary to urge caution. In a more extreme case, if the witness is shown to have lied, to have made previous false complaints or to bear the defendant a grudge, a stronger warning may be appropriate and the judge may suggest that it would be wise to look for supporting material before acting on the impugned witness's evidence. For a reaffirmation of the principles set out in *Makanjuola*, see *R v Muncaster* [1999] Crim LR 409 and *R v Causeley* [1999] Crim LR 572.

Identification

Eighteenth- and nineteenth-century lawyers were well aware of the fallibility of identification evidence, but the fact that such evidence was a frequent source of false convictions failed to lead to any formal safeguards. However, many judges, perhaps personally aware of the risk of false conviction, took to warning the jury of the possible dangers of convicting on identification evidence alone, or even went so far as to direct an acquittal where they thought the identification was too poor to sustain a conviction. It was the false conviction of one Adolf Beck, who had been mistakenly identified by a number of victims of theft and fraud, which led to the creation of the Court of Appeal in 1907. Despite that, it was not until 1977 that the Court of Appeal laid down guidelines relating to possible mistaken identification.

The Court of Appeal was responding to the Devlin Report (*The Report of the Committee on Evidence of Identification in Criminal Cases* (Cmnd 338, 1976)). That Report recommended that there should be no conviction in a case in which the prosecution relied wholly or mainly on the evidence of visual identification by one or more witnesses. The guidelines laid down by the Court of Appeal in *R v Turnbull* [1977] QB 224 did not go so far:

> *First, whenever the case against an accused depends wholly or substantially on the correctness of one or more of the identifications of the accused, which the defence alleges to be mistaken, the judge should warn the jury of the special need for caution before convicting the accused in reliance on the correctness of the identification(s). In addition he should instruct them as to the reason for the need for such a warning and should make some reference to the possibility that a mistaken witness can be a convincing one and that a number of witnesses can be mistaken.*
>
> *Secondly, the judge should direct the jury to examine closely the circumstances in which the identification by each witness came to be made. How long did the witness have the accused under observation? At what distance? In what light? Was the observation impeded in any way, as for example by passing traffic or a press of people? Had the witness ever seen the accused before? How often? If only occasionally, had he any special reason for remembering the accused? How long elapsed between the original observation and the subsequent identification to the police? Was there any material discrepancy between the description of the accused given to the police by the witness when first seen by them and his actual appearance?*
>
> *Recognition may be more reliable than identification of a stranger; but even when the witness is purporting to recognise someone whom he knows, the jury should be reminded that mistakes in recognition of close relatives and friends are sometimes made.*
>
> *All these matters go to the quality of the identification evidence. If the quality is good and remains good at the close of the accused's case, the danger of a mistaken identification is lessened; but the poorer the quality, the greater the danger.*
>
> *In our judgement when the quality is good, as for example when the identification is made after a long period of observation, or in satisfactory conditions by a relative, a neighbour, a close friend, a workmate and the like, a jury can safely be left to assess the value of the identifying evidence even though there is no other evidence to support it: provided always, however, that an adequate warning has been given about the special need for caution ...*
>
> *When in the judgement of the trial judge, the quality of the identification evidence depends solely on a fleeting glance or on a longer observation made in difficult circumstances the situation is very different. The judge should then withdraw the case from the jury and direct an acquittal unless there is other evidence, which goes to support the correctness of the identification. ...*
>
> *A failure to follow these guidelines is likely to result in a conviction being quashed and will do so if in the judgement of this court on all the evidence the verdict is either unsatisfactory or unsafe.*

The Court of Appeal has had numerous opportunities to emphasise the importance of following these guidelines, which apply not only to what may be described as 'pure identification cases' but equally to cases in which the witness claims to recognise the accused and a warning must be given even if the defence do not claim mistaken identity.

Supportive evidence of identification may consist of lies other than a false alibi. Such lies may also be indicative of guilt, but before the jury use them in this way they must be satisfied:

(a) that the lie was deliberate and relates to a material issue;

(b) that there was no innocent purpose for the lie (the jury must be reminded that people lie for a variety of motives, eg to bolster a just cause, or because they are ashamed or wish to hide disgraceful conduct;

(c) the lie must be established by evidence other than that of a witness whose evidence needs to be corroborated (*R v Goodway* [1993] 4 All ER 894).

The voir dire or 'trial within a trial'

There are a number of occasions when the admissibility of certain evidence is in dispute. If the issue were to be determined in the presence of the jury, they might be prejudiced by hearing evidence which is then ruled inadmissible. The most common example is where the prosecution propose to rely on a confession made by the accused which the defence argue is inadmissible because it was obtained in breach of s 76 of the Police and Criminal Evidence Act 1984, or in some other way which renders it liable to exclusion under s 78 of that Act. In the Crown Court the issue of admissibility and/or exclusion is determined in the absence of the jury on a voir dire, or trial within a trial. Counsel for the defence will have informed the prosecution that they intend to object to the admissibility of the confession (or other evidence). At the point when the prosecution would have adduced the confession (or other evidence) counsel for the prosecution will intimate to the judge that a point of law has arisen which falls to be determined in the absence of the jury. The jury will then be asked to retire and the issue of the admissibility of the confession (or other evidence) will be determined by calling the prosecution witnesses to whom the confession was made, usually the police, who give evidence on oath about how the confession (or other evidence) was obtained.

It will often be necessary for the defendant to give evidence, particularly if he is alleging some malpractice or illegality in the obtaining of the evidence. If the judge decides the evidence is not admissible, the jury are recalled and the trial continues, but the jury hear nothing of the excluded evidence. If he decides that the evidence is admissible, the jury are recalled and the evidence is presented in the normal way. In the context of confession evidence, how it was obtained will be put to the jury in the hope that they will give little or no weight to it after hearing such evidence.

In magistrates' courts, where the magistrates are judges of both law and fact, there are obvious difficulties in deciding issues such as the admissibility of a confession. There can be no question of a trial within a trial as in the Crown Court, but if the defence represent that a confession was or may have been obtained in breach of s 76 of the Police and Criminal Evidence Act 1984, the magistrates must hold a trial within a trial, that is the trial proper is stopped and the issue of the admissibility of the confession is then determined as a separate issue by the magistrates, who will hear evidence as to how it was obtained. Having done so, if they rule in favour of admissibility, it is not necessary for them to hear evidence about the confession repeated at the trial proper. If they rule against admissibility they must then put the evidence of the confession out of their minds and resume the trial. The defence are entitled to a ruling on the admissibility of any evidence before or at the end of the prosecution case. If a confession is inadmissible, it may be that the prosecution cannot persuade the magistrates that there is a case to answer in the absence of a confession. The defendant is then entitled to an acquittal.

Abuse of process

At common law the criminal courts have an inherent jurisdiction to control their own proceedings in the interests of justice and to secure a fair trial. The judicial and statutory discretions mentioned above allow judges to ensure the fairness of a trial by excluding evidence which would have an adverse effect on that fairness. A judicial stay of proceedings for abuse of process allows judges to prevent a prosecution where something has been done prior to the trial which compromises the integrity of the trial. Arguably this properly belongs to the remit of criminal procedure, but it is related to the exclusion of evidence which sometimes has the effect of stopping a trial.

The first application of the principle to the criminal trial came in the landmark decision of the House of Lords in *Connelly v DPP* [1964] AC 1254, where the question was whether the accused could be prosecuted and convicted of robbery when he had already been convicted of murder arising from the same incident, an armed robbery in which a person had been killed. In *R v Horseferry Road Magistrates' Court, ex p Bennett* [1994] 1 AC 42, the British and South African police colluded (apparently with the tacit agreement of the CPS) to have Bennett deported from South Africa via London Heathrow Airport, where he could be arrested and brought to trial, effectively an illegal kidnapping rather than a legal extradition. Lord Griffiths noted (at 62) that the courts could not 'contemplate for a moment the transference to the executive of the responsibility for seeing that the process of law is not abused. The judiciary should accept a responsibility for the maintenance of the rule of law that embraces a willingness to oversee executive action and to refuse to countenance behaviour that threatens either basic human rights or the rule of law.'

In *R v Latif* [1996] 1 WLR 104, the House of Lords confirmed that the principle applies to cases of entrapment, though entrapment is not a substantive defence. Exclusion of evidence may have the same effect in such a case, but a stay for abuse of process is to be preferred (*R v Looseley; AG's Reference (No 3 of 2000)* [2001] 1 WLR 2060).

The future: reforming the adversarial system

A number of well-publicised acquittals (such as the Birmingham Six, Judith Ward and the Guildford Four) many years after conviction were instrumental in bringing about a crisis of confidence in the criminal justice system during the 1990s. In response to fears that justice was being denied to accused persons and those already convicted of offences, the Government established a Royal Commission on Criminal Justice (Cmnd 2263, 1993). In time, very specific components of the adversarial system came under scrutiny. These included the treatment of victims and witnesses in court (Home Office, *Speaking Up for Justice* (1998)); adjournments and delays (Audit Commission, *The Route to Justice* (June

2002)); and the role of the Crown Prosecution Service (Glidewell, *Review of the Crown Prosecution Service* (Cmnd 3960, 1998)).

Sir Robin Auld's *Review of the Criminal Courts in England and Wales* (Cmnd 9376, 2001) contained a number of radical proposals designed to streamline criminal procedure and radically overhaul the law of evidence. The Review recommended the adoption of a number of inquisitorial-style features into the English system. For example, it was conceded that adversarial combat in the pre-trial phase was inappropriate and a more co-operative regime of disclosure was recommended. Other features were somewhat reminiscent of practices in continental jurisdictions and were aimed at tempering the very partisan nature of the adversarial justice system. These included the recommendation to codify the criminal law and law of evidence; a greater managerial role for trial judges; and further pre-trial co-operation between the parties. Sir Robin's observation that the adversarial system should 'move away from technical rules of inadmissibility to trusting judicial and lay fact finders to give relevant evidence the weight it deserves' (Ch 2, para 17) also reflects the approach followed in most inquisitorial trials. As such, judges would play a much more pro-active role in the trial, and have a much broader discretion in relation to the admissibility of evidence. It is also worth noting that Lord Justice Auld acknowledged of some of the drawbacks of oral evidence, including the effects of stress and delay upon witnesses.

Auld appears to have used this observation as a springboard for a number of his recommendations, which included the relaxation of the rules on admissibility of previous witness statements, the relaxation of the hearsay rule, and the extension of the use of televised evidence. He seemed to accept that indirect testimony can, in certain circumstances, be as reliable and cogent as direct oral evidence. The Criminal Justice Act 2003 gives legislative effect to most of these reforms and thus forms a central plank of many of the subsequent chapters in this book.

Technology is also set to change the ways in which evidence is given. Already evidence can be given via satellite link, so that a witness in America can give evidence without crossing the Atlantic. Instead of pouring over mountains of documents, some juries can now call up the evidence on a computer screen, now commonplace in large fraud cases involving many documents (note, however, that once Pt 7 of the Criminal Justice Act 2003 takes effect, prosecutors will be able to apply to have such cases heard without a jury). The Youth Justice and Criminal Evidence Act 1999 provides that children and other vulnerable witnesses can give their evidence-in-chief by means of a pre-recorded video, and also may be cross-examined and re-examined on video so that they need never be present in court (although this particular provision now seems unlikely to be implemented). Part 8 of the Criminal Justice Act 2003 extends the use of live links in criminal proceedings, enabling witnesses other than vulnerable witnesses who are in the United Kingdom but unable to come to court to give evidence via a live link without appearing in court. Doubtless the rules of evidence will continue to be amended and modified for the new age. The Crime (International Co-operation) Act 2003 allows evidence requested by foreign countries to be taken by telephone. It is not improbable that in the future we will be able to give evidence via a mobile phone with a video picture being transmitted.

Some commentators have argued that tinkering with evidential and procedural rules and introducing new technology are unlikely to tackle many of the system's current problems in an effective manner (see, eg, L Ellison, *The Adversarial Process and the Vulnerable Witness* (2001); W Pizzi, *Trials Without Truth* (1999)). Whilst a number of law reform and working groups throughout the common law world have mooted the idea of replacing our adversarial system with a more continental style of process, they have proceeded to defend staunchly the retention of the adversarial system with what has been described by Van Kessel as 'self-righteous adoration' ('Adversary Excesses in the American Criminal Trial' 67 Notre Dame LR 403, 409 (1992)). While many of these groups do recognise certain inherent weaknesses in the system, none has gone so far so as to recommend its outright abolition, and most display a strong aversion to any prospect of transplanting inquisitorial procedures.

In England, the reports of various reform bodies have failed to address the idea of introducing an inquisitorial system in any real depth. The notion was considered summarily before being promptly dismissed in the Philips Royal Commission of 1981 and the Runciman Royal Commission of 1993. The latter Commission suggested that it would be content to see the system move in a more inquisitorial direction, while the more recent *Auld Review of the Criminal Courts* was happy to recommend the 'grafting' of certain elements of inquisitorial procedure onto the adversarial framework. However, not all commentators are agreed that such an approach can work effectively: Edwards comments that cherry-picking and transplanting individual components of inquisitorial systems risks diffusing 'the worst tendencies of combativeness in the Anglo-American system, while retaining some of the salutary features of the continental inquisitorial system' (H Edwards, 'Comments on Mirjan Damaska's "Of Evidentiary Transplants"' 45 American J of Comp Law 853, 855; see also D Corker, 'The Worst of Both Worlds' (2002) 152 (1997) NLJ 1741).

The prospect of transplanting an inquisitorial model into the legal system of England and Wales has few supporters within the legal profession, law reform bodies or political parties. It thus remains highly unlikely that such radical reform would occur in the short to medium term, although it does appear that criminal justice policy is currently in a process of transformation, with policy-makers seemingly more ready to acknowledge the shortcomings of the adversarial trial system and look for solutions outside the adversarial framework. There appears to be an increasing tendency to borrow the facets of other systems which are believed to work effectively. Pizzi notes that among the judiciary, legislature and legal profession there is 'less attachment to failed doctrinal structures of the past and a willingness to look for what will work' (*Trials Without Truth* (1999), 231). A need to temper adversarial processes has been broadly acknowledged, and both the Auld Review and the latest Criminal Justice Act have laid down a pathway for a more radical rethink of the perceived merits of the adversarial model of justice. The restriction of the right to trial by jury, the dismantling of a number of exclusionary rules of evidence, and permitting more witnesses to give evidence by way of a televised link or video recording are all recent developments in modern criminal justice policy which sit uneasily alongside traditional perceptions of the adversarial paradigm.

New international criminal trial systems, such as the International Criminal Court and the International Criminal Tribunal for the Former Yugoslavia, have been instrumental in developing something approaching an international consensus on best trial practice, and the emphasis placed on victims' rights within these institutions probably acted as a catalyst in the improved protections now available to vulnerable witnesses and the erosion of exclusionary rules of evidence. As international harmonisation continues, it can legitimately be speculated that such international norms will serve to inform the reform process within discrete domestic jurisdictions. In time, international convergence is likely to become a powerful catalyst in effecting more widespread reform to the adversarial system.

2 Giving Evidence

The oath

The modern criminal trial relies heavily on the oral testimony of witnesses as the major source of proof. The general rule is that a witness must attend court to give live evidence in person under oath or solemn affirmation. At one time the common law required all witnesses to testify on oath on the Bible. This served to exclude all non-Christians and atheists, who were for that reason incompetent. This rule was modified in the eighteenth century and has been further modified subsequently. The modern law is to be found in the Oaths Act 1978. Section 1 provides for the manner of the administration of the oath to Christians and those of the Jewish faith. The oath is administered routinely unless the witness objects. In the case of witnesses of a religion other than Christian or Jewish, the Act (s 1(3)) provides that the oath shall be administered in any lawful manner. Such witnesses will usually take the oath upon whichever holy book is appropriate to their religion. In *R v Kemble* [1990] 1 WLR 1111, it was decided that whether an oath was lawful depended not on the intricacies of the particular religion, but on whether the oath appears to the court to be binding on the conscience of the witness and, if so, whether the witness himself considers the oath to be binding on his conscience.

If the witness objects to the taking of an oath, he or she may make a solemn affirmation (Oaths Act 1978, s 5). Such affirmation may replace the oath if the court is not equipped to administer the oath in accordance with the religion of the witness (s 5(2)). To avoid the possibility that a non-religious witness might claim that his evidence given on oath is invalid, s 4(2) provides that the fact that a person had at the time of taking the oath no religious belief 'shall not for any purpose affect the validity of the oath'. Wilfully making a material statement on oath or affirmation that is known to be false, or which the witness does not believe to be true, is the offence of perjury.

There have been a number of proposals to abolish the religious oath on the basis that perhaps a majority of witnesses have no particular religion. Nothing has come of these proposals, though there are now categories of witnesses who may give evidence unsworn. The most important of these are children under 14 who are, by virtue of s 55(2) of the Youth Justice and Criminal Evidence Act 1999, not permitted to be sworn for the purposes of giving evidence in court, it being assumed that they do not have sufficient appreciation of the solemnity of the occasion and the particular responsibility to tell the truth which is involved in taking the oath. Adult witnesses who are able to give intelligible testimony are presumed to have such an appreciation. However, s 56 of the 1999 Act also provides a power to receive the unsworn evidence of a person who is over 14, provided they are competent but for some reason do not have sufficient appreciation of the solemnity of the occasion and the particular responsibility to tell the truth which is involved in taking the oath. Thus for the first time in the history of the English criminal justice system, certain adult witnesses will be able to give evidence unsworn.

Competency and compellability

Competent and compellable witnesses

Section 53 of the Youth Justice and Criminal Evidence Act 1999 provides that all witnesses are competent, and, as a general rule, all competent witnesses are compellable. In other words, all witnesses are under a legal obligation to give evidence if called upon to do so and may be subject to a legal penalty for failure to carry out that duty. A competent witness may be compelled to give evidence by the threat of being held in contempt (punishable by imprisonment) for failing to do so (see *R v Renshaw* [1989] Crim LR 811; *R v Holt and Bird* (1996) *The Times*, 31 October).

Although it is usually the case that competence will automatically give rise to compellability, there are three major exceptions to this rule. First, the spouse of an accused is now a competent witness by virtue of s 53(1) of the Youth Justice and Criminal Evidence Act 1999. However, he or she is only compellable for the prosecution against the accused spouse, or a co-accused, in the limited circumstances provided for in s 80(3) of the Police and Criminal Evidence Act 1984 (as amended by the Youth Justice and Criminal Evidence Act 1999; see further pp 37–42 below). Secondly, the accused was made a competent witness in his own defence by the Criminal Evidence Act 1898 (see further pp 30–31 below), but is not a competent witness for the prosecution in any proceedings so long as he remains charged with an offence in the proceedings. Lastly, diplomats, foreign heads of state and the sovereign are competent but not compellable witnesses.

All witnesses who are compellable have a privilege against self-incrimination that permits them to refuse to answer questions if the answer would incriminate them (sometimes referred to as the right to silence). Lawyers may refuse to answer questions about advice given to clients on the grounds of legal professional privilege, and government and quasi-government bodies may be able to rely on public interest immunity to refuse to answer certain questions. Otherwise a witness can be punished for contempt of court if he or she refuses to answer questions. This includes priests, doctors and others in a confidential relationship, who have no legal right to refuse to answer questions, though most prosecutors would be reluctant to put such a person in the position of having to breach the moral duty of confidentiality unless absolutely necessary. Journalists can not normally be required to disclose their source of information, but there is a procedure under s 10 of the Contempt of Court Act 1981 under which they can be required to do so.

An accused person is not compellable, but if he chooses to give evidence he has no privilege against self-incrimination in respect of the offences with which he is charged (see s 1(2) of the Criminal Evidence Act 1898).

Problematic witnesses

Children

All witnesses of whatever age were at one time treated the same. All children who were deemed capable of distinguishing between good and evil were expected to take the oath and give evidence orally from the witness box in open court (*R v Brasier* (1779) 1 Leach 199). This situation was widely considered to be unsatisfactory and led to s 38 of the Children and Young Persons Act 1933 (now repealed), which permitted a child of tender years (under 14) to give evidence unsworn if the child understood the duty to speak the truth, and the child was of sufficient intelligence to justify the reception of his evidence.

R v Hayes [1977] 2 All ER 288 produced a more secular approach. Thereafter the question for the trial judge, who had to decide whether a child was competent to give sworn evidence, was 'whether the child has a sufficient appreciation of the solemnity of the occasion and the added responsibility to tell the truth which is involved in taking an oath, over and above the duty to tell the truth which is an ordinary duty of normal social contact'. In practice, there was little difference between this test for giving sworn evidence and that in s 38 of the Children and Young Persons Act 1933 for unsworn evidence. However, mistrust of children's evidence continued in the common law requirement that children giving sworn evidence had to be the subject of a warning to the jury of the danger of acting on their uncorroborated evidence, though they could act on it even if uncorroborated. Additionally, a child giving unsworn evidence under s 38 of the Children and Young Persons Act 1933 required actual corroboration in the form of other independent evidence supporting his evidence, otherwise there could be no conviction.

These corroboration requirements, together with the reluctance to treat young children as competent witnesses, created difficulties for prosecutors and were a major reason why (before 1990) so few prosecutions of child abusers were commenced. They provided a potent source of unjustified acquittal of those who were prosecuted, because of a failure to give the warning in respect of sworn child witnesses and the incorrect identification or absence of actual corroboration.

Both requirements were removed by s 34 of the Criminal Justice Act 1988 (corroboration warnings in respect of accomplices and victims of sexual offences were abolished by s 32 of the Criminal Justice and Public Order Act 1994; see pp 16–19 above). With the removal of the corroboration requirements there were two issues for the trial judge to consider in determining the competence of a child to give evidence:

(a) whether the child was capable of giving evidence at all; and

(b) if so, whether that evidence should be sworn or unsworn.

The first raised issues beyond the obvious question whether the child was capable of giving coherent and intelligible evidence. There is the trauma involved in attending court and giving evidence in public in open court, and being faced by the alleged assailant. The common law made no concession to children of whatever age. If they gave evidence they did so as if they were adults, apart from giving their evidence unsworn. However, historically judges had adopted a protective approach which ignored the question of whether the child was capable of giving evidence. This involved treating the very young child witness as incompetent, even though the child might have been able to understand questions and give intelligible answers.

Sections 53 to 57 of the Youth Justice and Criminal Evidence Act 1999 now provide for a much more straightforward approach, in that there is a presumption that all witnesses are competent regardless of age, unless they are unable to understand the questions and give answers that can be understood (s 53(3)). It is of course conceivable that this could exclude a very young child; if doubts are raised as to the competence of a witness, it is for the party calling the witness to prove that he is able to communicate intelligibly on the balance of probabilities (s 54(2)). The Act also provides that no witness under the age of 14 is to be sworn, and that witnesses over 14 are eligible to be sworn only if they understand the solemnity of a criminal trial and that taking an oath places a particular responsibility on them to tell the truth (s 55(2)(a)). Such witnesses may, however, give evidence unsworn (s 56).

In *R v Day* [1997] 1 Cr App R 181, it was held that where a child aged under 14 when the video was made but over 14 when the video is presented as evidence is cross-examined in court or via a TV link, the child should be sworn. This is likely to be the position under the 1999 Act. It follows that fewer children will appear in court; but if the situation in *Day* is repeated and the child witness is then over 14 years of age when the video is tendered in evidence then, consistent with s 55(2) of the 1999 Act, he can only give sworn evidence. It is the practice when video-taping an interview with a child close to 14, who might well be over that age when appearing in court, for the child to affirm at the beginning of the interview.

As John Spencer has observed, the new rules governing the competency of child witnesses are of symbolic, as well as practical, importance. He notes that the rules 'mark the final transition from a system where the courts refused to hear all sorts of persons for fear they might not tell the truth, to one where the courts listen to everybody, and try to decide whether they are truthful or not on the basis of what they have said' (J Spencer, 'The Youth Justice and Criminal Evidence Act 1999: The Evidence Provisions', *Archbold News*, January 2000, 5–8). Combined with a new range of special measures that has been made available to assist such witnesses (see pp 53–59 below), it is hoped that the rights of children coming to court will be respected and protected in a much more comprehensive fashion than has traditionally been the case in criminal trials in England and Wales.

Witnesses with physical and learning disabilities

Those witnesses who suffer from disabilities, physical or mental, that affect their ability to communicate, have traditionally presented problems to the courts. There are many different forms of physical disability that affect the ability to speak without necessarily affecting the mind and the ability to understand. People with learning disabilities face particular problems as witnesses. They have problems recalling information, and often have difficulty in understanding questions and responding to them. They may understand the question but may recall the incident in pictures rather than words, and may find it difficult to put their recollection into words. Some learning-disabled witnesses have particular traits that may influence their experience of the criminal justice system. People with Down's Syndrome, for example, can be particularly sensitive to negative emotion. They tend to be suggestible and respond to what they perceive as aggression (such as 'tough' questioning) by trying to appease the questioner. Questioners who fail to appreciate this can undermine the reliability of such witnesses' information.

At common law, 'persons of unsound mind' who were not capable of understanding the nature of the oath and of giving rational evidence were not competent witnesses. The test was whether the witness understood the nature of the oath and the divine sanction. Thus in *R v Hill* (1851) 2 Den 254, the witness was an inmate of a lunatic asylum who suffered from the delusion that he had numerous spirits who talked to him. Medical evidence was given that the witness was capable of giving an account of any transaction that he witnessed. The judge ruled that he was competent and the Court of Appeal upheld his ruling, holding that where it is contended that a witness is of too weak an intellect to give evidence, it is for the trial judge to examine him and determine whether he understands the nature of the oath. In *R v Bellamy* (1985) 82 Cr App R 222, the complainant in a rape case was aged 33 but had a mental age of 10. It was made clear that there was then no provision for adult witnesses to give unsworn evidence. After examining her and taking evidence from a social worker, the judge ruled that the complainant was not incompetent but she did not have a sufficient belief in God to take the oath. He ruled that she should affirm. The Court of Appeal dismissed the appeal against conviction, but held that if a witness is competent and does not object to being sworn he or she must be sworn. The Court went on to state that it is no longer necessary that the witness have an awareness of the divine sanction of the oath in order to be sworn. The more secular approach of *Hayes* in relation to children applied to adults. As noted above, s 56 of the Youth Justice and Criminal Evidence Act 1999 now enables such adults to give unsworn evidence if they are competent, that is they can understand questions put to them and give answers which can be understood, even if they do not, because of their affliction, have sufficient appreciation of the solemnity of the occasion.

In appropriate cases when the witness was competent but unable to communicate, the provisions of s 23 of the Criminal Justice Act 1988 (now replaced by s 116 of the Criminal Justice Act 2003), which allowed the statement of the witness to be admitted in evidence without the need for the witness to give oral evidence, could be of assistance if certain conditions were satisfied. A condition laid down by s 23(2)(a) (now s 116(2)(b) of the 2003 Act) is that the person who made the statement is by reason of his bodily or mental condition unfit to give evidence. For example, in *R v Duffy* [1999] QB 919, the accused was convicted of the manslaughter of V. The deceased's son witnessed the killing. He was physically handicapped with very poor power of speech, and the only person capable of understanding him was a social worker. The social worker attended a police interview with the deceased's son which was video recorded. He asked the questions and confirmed the answers for the benefit of the camera. He subsequently compiled a transcript of the interview. The trial judge accepted that the video amounted to a document for the purposes of s 23 of the Criminal Justice Act 1988, but refused to admit the video under that provision on the grounds that the video was of poor quality and the fact that it needed translation by the interviewer meant that it was effectively the evidence of the interviewer, not that of the deceased's son. The Court of Appeal held that the video was a document within s 23 and was therefore admissible as first hand hearsay; and although most of the evidence given by the deceased's son was incomprehensible to all but the social worker, he was in a position akin to a translator who could give admissible evidence of his interpretation of what the witness was saying in the interview.

Taken in isolation, the transcript of the interview made by the social worker was not admissible, as it was not a document coming within s 23 of the Criminal Justice Act 1988, as the deceased's son had neither signed it nor approved it as a correct record of his evidence. However, the transcript was akin to the notes of a witness made at the time of an event and referred to later. The judge should have considered the video and the transcript together, which left no doubt as to the evidence of the deceased's son and should therefore have been admitted, subject to the judge's discretion under s 26 of the 1988 Act (now s 116(4) of the Criminal Justice Act 2003). This decision made it possible for some witnesses in this category to give evidence. In Scotland the provisions applying to children – video-recorded testimony and live televised link – had been extended to include adult witnesses who fell into this category.

Such witnesses, along with other 'vulnerable' and 'intimidated' witnesses such as children, were the subject of a major study by a working group set up by the Home Office. Their report, *Speaking Up for Justice, the Report of the Interdepartmental Working Group on the Treatment of Vulnerable or Intimidated Witnesses in the Criminal Justice System* (1998), made a number of recommendations that paved the way for a radical overhaul of the law by P II of the Youth Justice and Criminal Evidence Act 1999. In addition to the amendments to the rules on competency, the Act also provided for a range of special measures which could be used in court to ease the strain traditionally brought about through giving live testimony in open court. These are considered in more detail at pp 53–59 below.

The accused

Section 1 of the Criminal Evidence Act 1898 (as amended by the Youth Justice and Criminal Evidence Act 1999) made the accused person competent in his own defence, but it did not make him a compellable witness. The accused may choose to go into the witness box and give evidence in his defence, but he cannot be compelled to do so. Since the right to make an unsworn statement from the dock was abolished by s 72 of the Criminal Justice Act 1982, the accused must, if he decides to give evidence, do so on oath from the witness box and be exposed to cross-examination. When he does give evidence, that evidence is evidence for all purposes, including evidence against his co-accused (where co-defendants seek to put the blame on another co-defendant it is known as a 'cut throat' defence for obvious reasons).

When the accused gives evidence he may be cross-examined:

(a) as to the offence charged (s 1(2) of the Criminal Evidence Act 1898 makes it clear that the accused has no privilege against self-incrimination in respect of the offence charged);

(b) in order to incriminate a co-accused; and

(c) on behalf of a co-accused, whether he has given evidence against that co-accused or not.

However, the accused may not be cross-examined about his bad character or previous convictions, except in the circumstances provided for in the Criminal Justice Act 2003, considered in **Chapter 5**.

The accused is not a competent witness for the prosecution so long as he is a person charged in the proceedings, that is named in the indictment, whether alone or with others (Youth Justice and Criminal Evidence Act 1999, s 53(4)). There are, nonetheless, four ways in which an accused can be removed from the indictment, thus making him a competent and compellable witness for the prosecution:

(a) he is acquitted, the prosecution offering no evidence;

(b) he pleads guilty and is removed from the indictment (if those who were his co-accused plead not guilty, they go to trial);

(c) the Attorney-General enters a *nolle prosequi* – a writ that stays the prosecution against the person named on it. Thus if the accused is the subject of such a writ, he cannot be prosecuted in respect of the offence(s) with which he is charged and is removed from the indictment. The trial proceeds against the others charged in the indictment;

(d) the accused is removed from the indictment and is tried separately.

In each case the accused is then a competent and a compellable witness for the prosecution against his co-accused.

If the defendant gives evidence against those with whom he was involved in committing the crime he will be seen as an accomplice, and until 1994 his evidence had to be the subject of a mandatory warning to the jury of the danger of convicting on his uncorroborated evidence. As noted at p 18 above, this requirement was abolished by s 32(1) of the Criminal Justice and Public Order Act 1994, and any similar requirement in respect of summary trials was abolished by s 32(3). The abolition of the mandatory requirement of a warning in respect of accomplices also does away with the overly technical rules defining an accomplice. Judges are not now required to, and will no longer, warn the jury automatically about the danger of relying on the uncorroborated evidence of an accomplice, or a witness who might be an accomplice or who might have a purpose of his own to serve in giving evidence for the prosecution. Such a warning may be given if there is some evidence of bias or partiality of a particular witness, the strength of the warning depending on the particular witness and the particular case (*R v Makanjuola* [1995] 3 All ER 730). It will, of course be made clear to the jury by the defence that a particular witness was a participant in the crime with which the defendants are charged, and they will doubtless suggest that his evidence is suspect for that reason.

The privilege against self-incrimination

Section 1(b) of the Criminal Evidence Act 1898 originally forbade comment by the prosecution on the failure of the defendant to give evidence. The ability of the trial judge to comment on the failure of the accused to give evidence has been the subject of numerous appeal cases over the years. The latest in a long line of such cases is *R v Martinez-Tobon* [1994] 1 WLR 388. There, the defendant, charged with drug smuggling, claimed that he thought he was carrying emeralds through customs rather than prohibited drugs, but he did not himself give evidence of this. Commenting on the trial judge's direction to the jury, the Court of Appeal held that the following principles applied:

(a) The judge should give a direction along the lines of the Judicial Studies Board specimen direction based on *R v Bathurst* [1968] 2 QB 99. That is:

> *The defendant does not have to give evidence. He is entitled to sit in the dock and require the prosecution to prove its case. You must not assume that he is guilty because he has not given evidence. The fact that he has not given evidence proves nothing one way or the other. It does not establish his guilt. On the other hand, it means that there is no evidence from the defendant to undermine, contradict or explain the evidence put before you by the prosecution.*

(b) The essentials of that direction are that the defendant is under no obligation to testify, and the jury should not assume he is guilty because he has not given evidence.

(c) Provided those essentials are complied with, the judge may think it appropriate to make a stronger comment where the defence case involves alleged facts which are at variance with the prosecution evidence, or additional to it and exculpatory, and must, if true, be within the knowledge of the defendant.

(d) The nature and strength of such comment must be a matter for the discretion of the judge and will depend on the circumstances of the individual case. However, it must not be such as to contradict or nullify the essentials of the conventional direction.

A number of changes have been made by the Criminal Justice and Public Order Act 1994 and the Criminal Procedure and Investigations Act 1996, which, while not denying the accused his right not to answer questions, disclose his defence or to decline to give evidence, may penalise the exercise of these rights. The Criminal Procedure and Investigations Act 1996, which has been added to and amended by Pt 5 of the Criminal Justice Act 2003, provides for primary disclosure of prosecution material to the defence that is to be followed by disclosure by the defence of a statement containing the outline of their defence, including any alibi, the matters about which it takes issue with the prosecution and the reasons. This will be followed by secondary disclosure by the prosecution of any material that is relevant in the light of the defence disclosed or issues raised. Section 11 provides that where the defence are required to disclose their defence under s 5 and the accused:

(a) fails to give the prosecutor a defence statement under s 5;

(b) gives the prosecutor a defence statement but does so only after the expiry of the specified period;

(c) sets out inconsistent defences in the defence statement given under s 5;

(d) puts forward a defence which is different from that disclosed in the defence statement;

(e) at his trial adduces evidence in support of an alibi without having given particulars of the alibi in the defence statement; or

(f) at his trial calls a witness to give evidence in support of an alibi without having provided the prosecution with the name of that witness and any information necessary to trace him;

the court or any other party (with the leave of the court) may make such comment as appears appropriate, and the court or jury may draw such inferences as appear proper in deciding whether the accused is guilty of the offence concerned.

This will, of course, be added to the existing provisions of the Criminal Justice and Public Order Act 1994 which effected radical changes in this area, and allows for 'such inferences as appear proper' to be drawn by the factfinder in four situations:

(a) where an accused fails to mention any facts when being questioned under caution before charge that he later relies upon in his defence at trial (s 34);

(b) where he fails to give evidence at his trial (s 35).

(c) where he fails to account for the presence of any object, substance or mark on his person, clothing or footwear, or otherwise in his possession or at any place in which he is at the time of arrest (s 36); or

(d) where he fails to account for his presence at a place at or about the time of the commission of an offence (s 37).

In changing the law to allow inferences to be drawn from the accused's silence, the Government had rejected the majority recommendation of the Royal Commission on Criminal Justice that the status quo be retained and went back to the recommendations of the Criminal Law Revision Committee (11th Report, *Evidence (General)* (1972, Cmnd 4991)). The Committee's proposals were put into effect in Northern Ireland by the Criminal Evidence (Northern Ireland) Order 1988 (SI 1988/1987). The difficulty in convicting terrorist suspects in Northern Ireland at the time was said to justify this move, but studies have suggested that the provisions have had little impact upon conviction rates (see J Jackson, K Quinn and M Wolfe, *Legislating Against Silence: The Northern Ireland Experience* (1995)). Despite widespread scepticism about the wisdom of abrogating a such a longstanding component of the common law trial, the Government was persuaded that the 1994 Act's provisions were necessary to restore the balance following the introduction of the Police and Criminal Evidence 1984 and its many safeguards for the accused.

It is arguable that the only significant change to the position at common law is that the prosecution are now able to comment on the failure of the accused to give evidence. It is questionable whether s 35 has any real effect on the common law as set out in *R v Martinez-Tobon*. The Government clearly intended to change the law, but whether it has succeeded in doing so remains to be seen. Two points deserve to be emphasised. First, the silence of the accused is not of itself evidence, and his silence adds nothing to the prosecution case. If he is to be convicted, the conviction must be based on all the evidence presented to the jury. It is suggested that is wrong to speak of 'inferences from silence'; instead it should perhaps be 'inferences from the prosecution evidence and lack of rebutting or contradictory evidence from the accused'. Inferences are drawn from the evidence and the silence of the accused serves only to leave the prosecution evidence unchallenged. If it is unchallenged the jury may then infer that it is true and, if they are satisfied beyond reasonable doubt, they may convict. At the heart of the principles laid down in *Martinez-Tobon* is the principle that the silence of the accused adds nothing to the prosecution case, nor does it take anything away. Secondly, s 38(3) makes it clear that, inter alia, no conviction can be made solely on the on inferences drawn under s 35. The inferences, if any, will be drawn from the evidence. It may be that in the appropriate case the only proper inference is that the accused is guilty, but that conclusion stems from the fact that the prosecution have presented a strong case that persuades the jury that the accused is guilty beyond any reasonable doubt.

The House of Lords in *Murray v DPP* [1994] 1 WLR 1 (a decision based on the Northern Ireland legislation) appear to have rejected any suggestion that the Northern Ireland Order, (and thus by implication the similarly-worded 1994 Act) is merely declaratory of the common law. The trial judge told the jury that it was remarkable that the accused, in the light of the cumulative strength of circumstantial and forensic evidence against him, had not given evidence, and that it was only common sense to infer 'that he was not prepared to assert his innocence on oath because that was not the case'. The House of Lords upheld the conviction for murder and said that in appropriate circumstances the inference that the person was guilty of the offence with which he was charged is permissible. Put in such stark terms, the decision can be seen as suggesting that the silence of the accused can be used as direct evidence of guilt. However, silence is never direct evidence of anything; rather, it is negative evidence in the sense suggested by *Martinez-Tobon* – it leaves the prosecution evidence unchallenged but neither adds to nor detracts from it. If, therefore, the prosecution have produced an overwhelming case against the accused who does not give evidence, it may well be common sense to infer that he is guilty as charged but – and it is an important *but* – the inference is drawn from the fact that the prosecution case is unchallenged and uncontradicted. The jury then convict on the prosecution evidence, not on the silence of the accused.

Prosecuting counsel are now permitted to comment on the failure of the accused to give evidence, and will doubtless emphasise that the prosecution case is unchallenged and uncontradicted. The trial judge may direct the jury that they may draw proper inferences and indicate what those proper inferences are in the particular case, drawing attention to the fact that the prosecution case has not been challenged or contradicted. He may also in an appropriate case point out that if the accused had been able to contradict, undermine or explain the prosecution evidence, they may conclude that the reason why he has not chosen to do so is that he is unable to do so (following *Murray*, above). It will be a perverse jury who find a doubt in the failure of the accused to provide an answer when the evidence calls for one. If they then convict, it will be the evidence that has not been challenged.

The European Court of Human Rights has also considered the *Murray* case (*Murray v United Kingdom* (1996) 22 EHRR 29). Murray alleged that the failure to allow him access to a lawyer (under the Prevention of Terrorism (Temporary Provisions) Act 1989 access to a solicitor may be delayed for up to 48 hours) was a breach of Article 6 of the European Convention on Human Rights, as was the drawing of inferences under the Northern Ireland Order of 1988, which contains provisions that are the equivalent of ss 34 to 38 of the 1994 Act. Significantly, the Court found the UK Government to be in breach of Article 6 in denying the accused access to a solicitor, but not in breach of that Article in permitting inferences to be drawn from the failure of the accused to explain his presence at the scene of the crime, or his failure to give evidence at his trial. Whilst the right to remain silent under police questioning and the privilege against self-incrimination are at the heart of the notion of a fair trial, the Court held that the right of silence was not absolute, and inferences could be drawn where a defendant had failed to provide an explanation in circumstances where the facts called for such an explanation. Nonetheless, the Court stated that certain safeguards ought to be in place before such inferences were drawn, and these included the weight of the evidence against the accused; the discretion exercised by the trial judge as to whether to draw inferences or not; and the availability of reasons for drawing them.

Section 58 of the Youth Justice and Criminal Evidence Act 1999 has now amended each of ss 34, 36 and 37 in the light of the decision in *Murray* (see also *Condron v UK* (2001) 31 EHRR 1), so that no inferences can be drawn if the accused was in police detention and did not have access to a solicitor (see further the apparently contradictory decisions of the Court of Appeal on this point in *R v Betts and Hall* [2001] 2 Cr App R 257 and *R v Howell* [2005] 1 Cr App R 1).

In *R v Cowan, R v Gayle and R v Ricciardi* [1996] QB 373, the Court of Appeal allowed two out of three appeals following directions to the jury on the application of s 35. The judges in the trials of Cowan and Gale had to direct the jury without the benefit of guidance from the Judicial Studies Board, whereas the judge in the third case had the benefit of that guidance. The issues before the Court were whether the discretion to draw inferences from silence under s 35(3) should be open in the generality of cases, or only exceptionally; and if it were to apply in a jury trial, then in what form should the trial judge issue such a direction.

It was argued by defence counsel that s 35 was so at variance with established principle that its operation should be reduced and marginalised as far as possible. Therefore, defending counsel ought to be allowed to present reasons or excuses for not drawing inferences from the failure of the accused to give evidence without the need for evidence. One suggested reason for not drawing inferences was said to be that the fact that the accused had a criminal record and, having attacked the character of prosecution witnesses, he could not be cross-examined on his record if he did not give evidence. If he did give evidence, his past record would be put before the jury (see discussion of the Criminal Evidence Act 1898 in **Chapter 5**). The Court rejected this argument, pointing out that this would lead to the bizarre result that a defendant with previous convictions would be in a more privileged position than one with a clean record. The Court accepted that, apart from the mandatory provisions of s 35, it would be open to a court to decline to draw an adverse inference from silence at trial and for a judge to direct or advise a jury against drawing such inference if the circumstances of the case justified such a course. However, there would need to be some evidential basis for doing so, or some exceptional factors in the case making that a fair course to take. It had to be stressed that the inferences permitted by s 35 were only such 'as appear proper'. Use of that phrase was doubtless intended to leave a broad discretion to a trial judge to decide in all the circumstances whether any proper inferences were capable of being drawn by the jury. If not, he should tell them so, otherwise it was for the jury to decide whether in fact an inference should properly be drawn. By way of guidance the Judicial Studies Board has suggested a specimen direction in the following terms:

The defendant has not given evidence. That is his right. He is entitled to remain silent and to require the prosecution to make you sure of his guilt. You must not assume he is guilty because he has not given evidence. But two matters arise from his silence.

In the first place, you try this case according to the evidence, and you will appreciate that the defendant has not given evidence at this trial to undermine, contradict or explain the evidence put before you by the prosecution.

In the second place, his silence at this trial may count against him. This is because you may draw the conclusion that he has not given evidence because he has no answer to the prosecution's case, or none that would bear examination. If you do draw that conclusion, you must not convict him wholly or mainly on the strength of it, but you may treat it as some additional support for the prosecution's case.

However, you may draw such a conclusion against him only if you think it is a fair and proper conclusion, and you are satisfied about two things: first, that the prosecution's case is so strong that it clearly calls for an answer by him; and second, that the only sensible explanation for his silence is that he has no answer, or none that would bear examination.

It is, of course, impossible to anticipate all the circumstances in which a judge might think it right to direct or advise a jury against drawing adverse inferences, and the Board has recommended that it would not be wise even to give examples as each case had to turn on its own facts (citing *R v McLernon* (1990) 10 NIJB 91, 102). In taking into account the opinion of the European Court of Human Rights in *Murray*, it was stressed that while decisions of the Court were not binding on domestic courts, they were of assistance to resolve any ambiguity in domestic law, but here no ambiguity was found in s 35. It was added that the Court of Appeal would not lightly interfere with a judge's exercise of discretion to direct or advise the jury as to the drawing of inferences from silence and as to the nature, extent and degree of such inferences. It was also made clear that the rule against advocates giving evidence dressed up as a submission applied in the present context. It could not be proper for a defence advocate to give to the jury reasons for his client's silence at trial in the absence of evidence to support such reasons.

This leading case on s 35 makes it clear that, as suggested above, where inferences are to be drawn, the proper inference can only be that the prosecution have proved their case which, because the accused has not offered any explanation or answered the case made out, stands unanswered. If the jury believe the prosecution witnesses and accept that there is a case to answer, the failure to answer that case entitles them to draw the proper inference that the case is proved. If they are then sure that the accused is guilty they will convict, but they convict on the evidence not on the silence of the accused.

One may therefore conclude that s 35 merely serves to underline and emphasise a commonsense process which juries have applied for decades. It does not affect the burden of proof, nor does it detract from the accused's right to remain silent and to refuse to give evidence. It does, however, add another layer of bureaucracy to an already overly bureaucratic system.

The spouse of the accused

The common law rules relating to the competence and compellability of the accused's spouse were complex and confused. The wife or husband of a person charged in the proceedings was generally incompetent, but was thought to be competent and compellable in a small number of cases. The House of Lords' decision in *Hoskyn v Metropolitan Police Commissioner* [1979] AC 474 changed this view, holding that a wife was not a competent witness on a charge of violence toward her. Thereafter the common law rule was that the wife or husband of a defendant could not give evidence for the prosecution no matter what the charge or how serious the charge.

The Criminal Law Revision Committee (1972, Cmnd 4991) accepted that a wife ought not to be compelled to testify against her husband. The Committee felt that compulsion could unnecessarily disrupt marital harmony and place the wife in the invidious position of having to incriminate her spouse. It concluded, however, that she should be compellable to testify for certain offences against the person of the wife or children (aged under 16) of the same household as the accused; otherwise these offences might go undetected – or, if detected, unpunished – given that there are rarely any other witnesses to domestic crimes of this nature. It was further felt that in relation to crimes against children of the household, the wife might be guilty of some complicity and for that reason reluctant to testify without the compulsion of law. These two factors, combined with the serious nature of the offences, justified compellability. However, the Committee emphasised that seriousness of the offence was not in itself sufficient to justify compelling a spouse to testify against the other spouse (paras 143–157).

Nevertheless, some 12 years later, when the Police and Criminal Evidence Bill was going through Parliament, concern about increased levels of child abuse persuaded the Government, in enacting the Committee's proposals, to extend compellability to include sexual offences against, or assaults upon, any child under 16, not simply those in the same household as the spouse. Section 80 of the 1984 Act, as amended by the Youth Justice and Criminal Evidence Act 1999, forms the basis of the current legal framework.

Section 80(2A) makes a wife compellable for the prosecution or a co-defendant (unless she is jointly charged with her husband) if, and only if, the offence constitutes a 'specified offence'. Under s 80(3), an offence is defined as a specified offence for the purposes of s 80(2A) if:

(a) it involves an assault on, or injury or threat of injury to, the wife or husband or a person who was at the material time under the age of 16;

(b) it is a sexual offence alleged to have been committed in respect of a person who was at the material time under that age; or

(c) it consists of attempting or conspiring to commit, or of aiding, abetting, counselling, procuring or inciting the commission of, an offence falling within para (a) or (b) above.

A wife or husband is now competent in all cases (unless also charged in the proceedings) and can give evidence in any case, but can only be compelled to do so in the limited circumstances provided for in s 80(3)(a), (b) and (c) (a specified offence). The section creates anomalies. For example, a wife cannot be compelled to give evidence against her husband charged with the rape and murder of a girl aged 16 years and 1 month, but can be compelled to give evidence against her husband if he is charged with indecent assault on a 15-year-old girl by pinching her bottom. This is consistent with the Criminal Law Revision Committee's refusal to be swayed simply by the seriousness of the offence. Take the case of Frederick West. He and his wife were jointly charged with more than 10 murders of young girls. If the wife had not been charged with West, she would have been compellable for the prosecution on charges of rape and murder of girls aged under 16, but not in respect of the same charges where the victims were 16 or over.

That case also demonstrates another anomaly. For example, where the husband is charged with rape of a 15-year-old (a specified offence under s 80(3)(b)) and the rape of a woman over 16 at the time of the offence, the wife is a compellable witness in respect of the 15-year-old but not in respect of the woman aged over 16 (see s 80(2A)(b)). In such a case the evidence may be intermingled, so that it may be difficult to separate the evidence in respect of the specified offence from that in respect of the unspecified offence. Nevertheless, the wife is entitled to refuse to give evidence in respect of the latter offence, creating problems for the prosecution and court, who must determine what evidence is relevant to which offence and what evidence the wife can be compelled to give and what evidence she can refuse to give. It would have been more sensible to state that where the accused is charged with a specified offence in respect of which his spouse is compellable, and with other offences in respect of which she is not compellable, she should be compellable in respect of all offences charged.

In effect the spouse has been given a privilege against being compelled to give evidence against the other spouse unless the offence falls within s 80(3). He or she can waive the privilege and give evidence if he or she wishes to do so in those cases to which s 80(3) does not apply, but why, particularly in serious cases, should it be left to the spouse to decide whether or not to give evidence? Where such testimony is crucial, the spouse effectively has a veto on conviction. Any waiver of the privilege must be made in full knowledge of his or her right not to give evidence. Thus, where a spouse who is not compellable chooses to give evidence, the trial judge must ensure that the decision to give evidence is made in the knowledge that he or she is not compelled to do so (*R v Pitt* [1983] QB 25).

It is questionable as to whether the scope of s 80(3)(a) includes a sexual offence against the spouse. Could it be the case, for example, that the wife of the accused could be compellable to give evidence against her husband accused of raping her? The question was not considered by the Criminal Law Revision Committee in 1972, nor by the framers of the Police and Criminal Evidence Act 1984, because in those days there was no offence of marital rape. When the husband's immunity at common law for marital rape was abolished by the decision of the House of Lords in *R v R* [1992] 1 AC 599, the issue arose of whether the wife was a compellable witness for the prosecution. Given that rape usually involves an assault or threat of an assault, the answer would appear to be 'yes'. However, in their report *Rape Within Marriage* (Law Com No 205, 1990), the Law Commission drew attention to the presumably intended contrast between s 80(3)(a), which refers to assault, and s 80(3)(b), which refers to 'sexual' offences committed against persons under 16. If rape is considered to be a sexual offence, it follows that a wife is not compellable on a charge against her husband of raping her. The argument that she is not compellable gains further support from the redefinition of 'rape' in s 1 of the Sexual Offences Act 2003, which, while including lack of consent, speaks of 'intentional penetration' of the vagina, anus or mouth. It is likely that the courts will interpret rape as including an assault for the purposes of s 80(3)(a), given that any touching without consent is an assault. Such an interpretation is supported by s 2 of the 2003 Act, which creates the offence of assault by penetration by parts of the body or anything else other than the penis. Apart from the use of the penis in s 1, the offences are identically worded. It would thus appear that rape of a spouse would now fall within the ambit of s 80(3)(a) of the 1984 Act.

It was also thought that s 80(3) would assist in the prosecution of husbands who battered their wives, but it in practice it has not been of much assistance. It is often the case that a wife withdraws her complaint before a file is passed to the Crown Prosecution Service (CPS), resulting in no charge being preferred. Where a file is submitted, the CPS tends to discontinue a prosecution for sexual or physical abuse of the wife when the wife is a reluctant witness, on the basis that there is little prospect of conviction in such cases (see further Her Majesty's Chief Inspector of Constabulary and Her Majesty's Chief Inspector of the Crown Prosecution Service, *Violence at Home*, 2004).

In cases where the wife withdraws her charge the prosecution can use s 80(3) and threaten the wife with punishment for contempt if she refuses to testify; but if she continues to refuse we end up with the paradoxical situation in which the victim is imprisoned and the alleged offender goes free. There is also some evidence from other jurisdictions that a policy of pursuing prosecutions regardless of the witness's reluctance can result in less reporting of domestic violence (see generally E Buzawa and C Buzawa, *Domestic Violence: The Criminal Justice Response* (2002)). If the victim is in fear because of threats of intimidation, she qualifies for the measures discussed at pp 53–59 below, which will assist her to give evidence. There is also the possibility that her statement of evidence can be admitted in documentary form under s 116(2)(e) of the Criminal Justice Act 2003 (replacing s 23 of the Criminal Justice Act 1988). These measures can overcome the fear of testifying but not reliance on the privilege provided by s 80(3), or the refusal to testify based on the emotional tie between victim and offender.

The reluctant wife, if she is compellable, or if she decides to waive her privilege and is called to testify, but refuses to give the expected testimony, can be treated as a hostile witness under s 3 of the Criminal Procedure Act 1865. Under this provision, previous statements made to the police that are inconsistent with what the witness says in the witness box can be put to the witness and, if accepted as correct, be put in evidence (and now, under s 120 of the Criminal Justice Act 2003, as evidence of the truth of the facts asserted). However, the weight given to such evidence is much reduced by the process, and the jury may not give much credence to a witness who has said one thing to the police and another in court.

It seems to follow that laws alone do not have much impact on the prevention or prosecution of domestic violence. Would the removal of the privilege in respect of other serious crimes result in spouses giving evidence against the accused spouse? Few cases fail simply because the wife refuses to testify against her husband. Crime fiction sometimes has the murderer marrying the eyewitness to the crime on the basis that, as his wife, she cannot testify against him. She can if she wishes to, but, assuming the victim was not under 16, she cannot be compelled to do so. In real life few women would marry a murderer so that they can take advantage of the privilege afforded by s 80(3) (but see *R (CPS) v Registrar-General for Births, Deaths and Marriages* [2003] 1 QB 1222, discussed at p 41 below). In any event, there is usually other evidence sufficient to convict.

It should be noted that it is only the wife or husband who has the right to refuse to give evidence in cases not covered by s 80(3). Partners, no matter how long they have lived together, are competent and compellable in all cases; so are children of the marriage and other close relatives. This is somewhat anomalous given the increasing tendency to put partners in the same position as spouses (note the recent passage of the Civil Partnership Act 2004) and the fact that the blood relationship can be as strong as, if not stronger than, the marital bond. Compelling a partner, son or daughter to give evidence against the other partner or parent, or compelling the partner or parent to give evidence against their children, is likely to have as great an impact on the family as compelling the legal spouse is likely to have on the marriage. However, the law is not concerned with what compelling a spouse to give evidence does to the family, only with what it might do to the marriage. In *R v Pearce* [2002] 1 Cr App R 551, the Court of Appeal confirmed that partners and children were not within s 80(3). In that case, it was argued on behalf of the appellant that compelling partners and children of the marriage to give evidence constituted a breach of Article 8(1) of the European Convention on Human Rights. However, the Court of Appeal rejected the argument, holding that such compulsion was necessary in a democratic society to prevent crime.

The institution of marriage has, of course, undergone radical transformation in the decades since s 80 came into force. Originally the wife was not a competent witness because of the unity principle that the common law recognised. However, one in four marriages now ends in divorce, and with marriage on the decline and cohabitation now the vogue, it might be asked whether a more modern approach should be enacted which would place on the spouse the same social responsibility to give evidence as non-spouses? This would involve repealing s 80 and putting spouses under the same moral and legal obligation as any other witness who can choose not to testify, but on pain of punishment. Thus a priest has no legal privilege and cannot lawfully refuse to disclose matters confided to him, even under the seal of the confessional. Journalists have gone to prison rather than testify as to the source of information obtained. Why should a spouse be in a more privileged position?

Alternatively, it may be argued that the emphasis should be on preserving family relationships, so that the privilege should be extended to include partners, children and close relatives. However, given the increase in abuse within families, the exceptions contained in s 80(3) must remain if the family members are to be protected from criminal abuse.

A number of Australian states, including Victoria, New South Wales and South Australia, have adopted a discretionary approach in various forms, whereby the spouse is compellable in all cases, but the trial judge has a discretion to exempt the spouse from giving evidence where the public interest in obtaining the spouse's evidence is outweighed by private interests, such as the likely damage to the marital relationship or the harshness of compelling the spouse to testify. Factors to be considered in exercising that discretion include the nature of the offence charged, the likely significance of the spouse's evidence in the case, the state of the relationship between the spouses and the likely effect upon it of compelling the spouse to testify. Under such a discretionary system a wife is unlikely to be compelled to testify against her husband who is charged with a minor offence, but is likely to be compelled when she has evidence of some significance and the offence is a serious one.

In 1972, the Criminal Law Revision Committee refused to recommend reform based on the seriousness of the crime, stating that 'the law has never ... made the seriousness of an offence by itself a ground for compellability, and we do not do so now' (Cmnd 4991, at para 152). Instead the Committee sought a balance between 'the desirability that all available evidence which might conduce to the right verdict should be before the court, against (i) the objection on social grounds to disturbing marital harmony more than is absolutely necessary, and (ii) what many regard as the harshness of compelling a wife to give evidence against her husband'.

Suppose a man is charged with the abduction, rape and murder of several teenage girls, all over 16. All the crimes were allegedly committed in the family home, but the bodies of the victims were found in various locations some distance from the home. There is forensic evidence of the presence of some of the victims in the home, but no witnesses other than the wife. A psychologist states that the wife is under the influence of the husband, but if compelled to give evidence she might overcome that influence. Where should the balance lie in such a case?

It is worth noting that the failure of the wife or husband of the accused to give evidence shall not be made the subject of any comment by the prosecution. A similar constraint applied under s 1 of the Criminal Evidence Act 1898 regarding the failure of the accused to give evidence until it was abolished by s 168 of and Sch 11 to the Criminal Justice and Public Order Act 1994 (see pp 31–36 above). The judge may comment on the failure of the spouse to testify, but there is little that can be said about the wife whose loyalty to her husband causes her to decline to give evidence against him.

Former spouses, future spouses and polygamous 'spouses'

Under s 80(5) of the Police and Criminal Evidence Act 1984, former spouses shall be competent and compellable to give evidence as if that person and the accused had never been married. Only those who have had the divorce decree made absolute are compellable (*R v Cruttenden* [1991] Crim LR 537).

The position regarding future spouses was considered in *R (Crown Prosecution Service) v Registrar-General of Births, Deaths and Marriages* [2003] 1 QB 1222, where the accused, charged with murder and held on remand, sought permission to marry his long-term partner. Since she was a witness for the prosecution, and would by virtue of s 80 of the 1984 Act cease to be a compellable witness at his trial, the CPS attempted to persuade the Registrar-General and the director of the prison not to allow the marriage to take place until after the trial. When both declined to do so, their decision was challenged by way of judicial review. The Court of Appeal held that there was no power to prevent, on the grounds of public policy, the marriage between a prisoner on remand and his long-term partner, despite the fact that the marriage would make her a non-compellable witness at his forthcoming trial for murder. It was accepted that the duty of the Registrar-General under s 31 of the Marriage Act 1949 was absolute. There were, however, circumstances in which that absolute duty would be subject to implied limitations on public policy grounds. Authorities were cited to show that no person should profit from his own serious crime, and that statutes should be interpreted to prevent a grave crime being committed or the course of justice perverted. However, entering into a lawful marriage, despite the consequences that followed from the provisions of s 80 of the 1984 Act, did not amount to perverting the course of justice.

The application of s 80 to a polygamous marriage was considered by the Court of Appeal in *R v Khan* (1987) 84 Cr App R 44. Khan, who was already married under English law, underwent a Muslim marriage taking a second 'wife'. The marriage was not recognised in England, and it was thus held that his second 'wife' was competent and compellable for the prosecution on the charges against Khan. Although this case was decided before s 80 came into force, the decision would be the same under s 80 either because the woman is not married to a person charged in the proceedings and must therefore be treated as any other witness, or because s 80(5) operates to treat her as not married.

Vulnerable witnesses

Research suggests that giving evidence in open court is a highly distressing affair for many victims. In particular, there is a great deal of evidence to suggest that vulnerable witnesses, such as children and complainants in sexual offence cases, find the demands of the adversarial trial system particularly onerous.

Child witnesses

There is a considerable body of literature that highlights the stress that can be caused to children when they are called on to testify at court. Many children find the experience extremely daunting and confusing. A survey of child witnesses in Australia identified 13 different linguistic devices which were used regularly by advocates to confuse them (M Brennan and R Brennan, *Strange Language: Child Victims under Cross-Examination* (1988)). The use of complex sentence structures and advanced vocabulary serves to exacerbate the unfamiliar situation which children already experience, and the researchers found that questions were frequently highly stylised (eg, 'I put it to you …'; 'I suggest to you') or employed complex grammatical structures involving negatives (eg, 'Now you did have a bruise, did you not, near one of your breasts?'; 'Now this happened on a Friday, did it not?'). Cordon et al cite a number of other studies which arrived at similar findings. They note that advocates will frequently try to lure child witnesses into a false sense of security, by asking non-substantive questions about the child's background and interests, before subtly moving on to elicit substantive information which contradicts the child's original testimony. They also present evidence which suggests that cross-examiners typically capitalise on children's tendencies to be suggestible and to fantasise. The goal in many cross-examinations, they argue, is to 'keep the child off balance to increase the chance of inconsistencies' (I Cordon et al, 'Children in Court' in P J Van Koppen and S D Penrod (eds), *Adversarial versus Inquisitorial Justice* (2003), 175–7).

During the late 1980s, a moral panic had emerged over the perceived problems surrounding child abuse, in light of the widespread media coverage of several high profile cases. In response to this public concern, in 1986 the then Home Secretary, Douglas Hurd, outlined his plans for a new Criminal Justice Bill that would contain procedures to enable children under the age of 14 to give evidence in child abuse cases out of the view of the alleged attacker. On introducing the Bill into Parliament, the Home Office issued a discussion document on the way in which all forms of video technology might be used in the courtroom, as well as commissioning an evaluation by the Home Office Research and Planning Unit into the reliability of children's evidence.

Section 32 of the Criminal Justice Act 1988 provided for witnesses aged under 14 to give their evidence via a live link (closed circuit TV) if the offence charged involved violence or sexual misconduct (this was extended by the subsequent Criminal Justice Act 1991 to include children under 17, where the offence was a sexual offence as defined by s 32(2)(c) of that Act). There were, however, a number of limitations. Principally, the link was to be available only for trials on indictment (Crown Court), or on an appeal from such a trial; and the procedure could not be used in magistrates' courts, where reliance had to be placed on screens. Screens remained an option for the Crown Court when the technology was not available or was out of action. Where the live link was used the child was to be in a room outside the courtroom, which would be linked to the courtroom by closed circuit television. Each courtroom that was equipped with the technology had three workstations with which receive and transmit sound and pictures by means of a screen with a built-in camera and microphone. The judge had one, as did prosecution and defence counsel. The jury had a large television monitor enabling them to see and hear the child witness, and there was one or more monitors positioned so that the defendant and others in the court could see and hear the child's evidence. Thus all those in the court could see and hear the child. They could also see any person accompanying the child, usually an usher, or a social worker or both. The child sat in another room facing another workstation, but saw and heard only the person speaking. Commonly the judge and counsel removed their wigs so as to appear less intimidating on screen. The child did not see the defendant, though the defendant could see the child. The child's evidence-in-chief was given via the TV link and cross-examination or re-examination took place via the link, so that the child never appeared in person in the courtroom.

The TV link procedure first became available on 1 January 1989, and in the first two years of operation it was used 544 times. The link was not automatically available to child witnesses even if they satisfied the requirements of the statute; it was a matter for the discretion of the trial judge. The advantages of the live link, apart from the obvious reduction in stress produced by the fact that the child does not have to be physically present in court and face the accused, include:

(a) enabling younger children to give evidence;

(b) allowing better contact with the child witness, who is not overawed or distracted by seeing others in the court;

(c) the fact that jurors appear to pay more attention to the child's evidence and then realise that the child is capable of giving accurate evidence.

One disadvantage suggested by research by Davies and Noon (*An Evaluation of the Live Link for Child Witnesses* (1991) Home Office), is that the TV image distances the child from the jury, leading to a reduction in sympathy. The fact that the child is on screen and not there in person also appears to lead to more vigorous cross-examination. Training of judges and barristers in the use of the TV link is likely to lead to improvements in cross-examination techniques, including more use of child-friendly language and greater control over cross-examination, when it takes place, by the trial judge.

Given the extensive debates that had taken place in Parliament on the scope of the legislation, the Government established an advisory group in 1989, chaired by Judge Thomas Pigot QC, to consider its full implications. The terms of reference of the advisory group were to examine the 'growing body of support for a change in the law, so that video recordings of interviews with victims could be readily used as evidence in trials for child abuse'. However, the Home Secretary also made clear that the Government could not contemplate the effacement of the defendant's right to cross-examination, thus effectively rejecting the possibility of pre-recorded cross-examination before the group had even commenced its enquiry. The group based its work around two 'rudimentary principles':

(a) that child witnesses' involvement in criminal proceedings should be concluded as rapidly as possible without compromising the interests of justice; and

(b) that children should give evidence in surroundings and circumstances which do not intimidate or overawe them, and the number of people present should be kept to a minimum.

The Pigot Committee recognised that the TV link was only a partial solution and recommended that:

(a) no child under 14 (17 in sexual offences) should have to give evidence in open court where the offence involved is one of violence or of a sexual nature, or cruelty or neglect;

(b) children's evidence-in-chief should be replaced by a video-taped interview;

(c) cross-examination of the child should take place at an out-of-court preliminary hearing when the judge and counsel would be present, the videoed evidence and cross-examination being shown to the jury at the appropriate point in the trial when the child would have given evidence.

These proposals would have meant that, without being unjust to the accused, a physically or sexually abused child (and some other vulnerable witnesses) need never appear in court and, importantly, the child's evidence-in-chief, the cross-examination and re-examination could (in theory) be taken fairly soon after the offence had been committed without the need for the child to give evidence in court. The Pigot proposals would have meant that in all but the most exceptional cases, the child's entire evidence could be taken shortly after the offence and the child could start the healing process very soon after the commission of the crime.

The Pigot Report envisaged a procedure in which a judge, counsel for the prosecution and counsel for the defence took the child's evidence-in-chief and cross-examined him in an informal atmosphere as soon as possible after the alleged crime but before trial. The whole process would be recorded on video and would then be replayed to the jury at the trial. The child's evidence would have been tested by cross-examination in the informal pre-trial process. The Pigot Committee recommended that their proposals for video-taped testimony and the use of live TV links to lessen the trauma for children of giving evidence, should also apply to other vulnerable witnesses. They offered no definition, but would have included victims of rape and elderly victims of crime.

The Criminal Justice Act 1991 (amending the Criminal Justice Act 1988) stopped well short of implementing the Pigot recommendations. The legislation gave effect to the proposals to allow the evidence-in-chief of the child witness to be videoed and that video be admitted as the child's evidence-in-chief. However, the child witness still had to attend court to be cross-examined on that evidence, though such cross-examination was to be done through a TV link. Only children under 15 (physical abuse) or under 17 (sexual abuse) could take advantage of the provision. Nonetheless, the reform was given a broad welcome. For the first time, the Government had accepted that courts had duties to safeguard the interests of certain witnesses, and acknowledged their status as victims, as opposed to mere servants of the criminal justice system. However, the legislation still fell well short of offering a fully comprehensive set of procedural protections for vulnerable witnesses, and was severely limited in a number of respects.

First, the legislation applied only to a limited class of persons for a limited range of specified offences in criminal cases only. The reforms failed to deal with other vulnerable witnesses, such as adult complainants in sexual cases, or the physically disabled and mentally ill. Their position had not improved. The provisions may be contrasted with art 81 of the Police and Criminal Evidence (Northern Ireland) Order 1989 (SI 1989/1341 (NI 12)), which provided for use of the link system in Northern Ireland in any case where 'the witness will not give evidence through fear'. In England and Wales, only child victims of sexual assault or violence could make use of the measures in the Act. This somewhat artificial distinction between child witnesses who had allegedly been victims of violence and sexual crimes as opposed to those who were alleged victims of other sorts of crimes, was based on flawed assumptions about the effects of various criminal acts upon children.

Secondly, even where child witnesses were deemed eligible to make use of such measures, the range of measures open to them remained very limited. For example, only the child's evidence-in-chief was to be pre-recorded. The key recommendation of the Pigot Committee, that children should not be forced into giving any evidence in court against their will, was ignored: s 54 of the 1991 Act required as a condition of the admissibility of the video evidence that the child be available for cross-examination. The fact that such cross-examination would be conducted using the live link softened the blow, but the fact that the child had to be available for cross-examination at the time of trial took the edge off what was a radical change in the law. The child victim-witness still had to live with the trauma of the crime and the prospect of having to attend court to be cross-examined, and that, even with accelerated arrangements for trial, could often mean a wait in excess of nine months. During this time they were often not given the therapy they needed, for fear that the therapy might taint the evidence they were yet to give. Video evidence was not therefore the major advance on the TV link that it could have been. It might also have been a disadvantage to the child, who might have seen the video recording of his evidence-in-chief only at trial. The gap in time might result in the child not fully remembering what he said on the video, and under cross-examination the child could be portrayed as a less credible witness than ought to be the case.

Thirdly, the nature of legislation created an overly complex and piecemeal framework of rules on children's evidence, contained in three separate statutes: the Children and Young Persons Act 1933; the Criminal Justice Act 1988; and the Criminal Justice Act 1991. The Government failed to seize the opportunity to consolidate the law in the 1991 Act, and its scope thus remained uncertain and confusing. The provisions of the Act were overly complex, poorly drafted, and they also gave rise to numerous legal lacunae. For example, whereas the live link and the use of video-recorded evidence were limited to trial on indictment and in youth courts, no provision was made for children who had to testify in magistrates' courts. Another major omission was the lack of any comprehensive guidance or criteria, other than the rather ambiguous 'interests of justice' test (Criminal Justice Act 1988, s 32A(3)(c)). Likewise, no mechanisms were in place for ascertaining the child witness's expectations or desires; there was no guidance as to whether the views of the child should be taken into account, or indeed how such views were to be ascertained. Such omissions and complexities resulted in an uncertain regime where judicial discretion had a key role to play. In the absence of comprehensive guidelines, the prevailing climate of uncertainty and inconsistent practice was bound to be perpetuated.

The failure of the Government to introduce a more comprehensive system of protecting child witnesses can be attributed to its fear of opposition from the legal profession, and possibly from within some quarters of the Government itself. The legislation was nonetheless significant in so far as it did constitute a willingness to start addressing the problems facing complainants in court. Pressure continued for implementation of the 'full Pigot', which would enable the child to close an unpleasant chapter in his life as soon as possible rather than have it drag on until trial. Much more radical protections for child witnesses were eventually made available by Pt II of the Youth Justice and Criminal Evidence Act 1999 (see pp 53–59 below).

Complainants in sexual cases

Trials for sexual offences differ from other criminal hearings in a number of respects. Often, the fact that intercourse actually took place is not a contested issue. Most rape cases usually turn upon the issue of consent, which can give rise to a number of evidential difficulties, particularly where the complainant and the accused have previously engaged in a consensual sexual relationship. Since the complainant and the accused will usually be the only witnesses to the incident in question, rape trials frequently boil down to a battle of credibility between the accused and the alleged victim. One of the main methods used by defence counsel to attack the character of the rape complainant is to suggest that she is sexually disreputable, alluding to loose moral values and a decadent lifestyle. In assessing this, the jury are invited to take into account a wide range of deeply personal and embarrassing details touching upon such issues as underwear, make-up, social lifestyle, menstrual cycle and drug addiction (see, eg, S Less, *Rape on Trial* (1996); Department of Women for New South Wales, *Heroines of Fortitude – The Experiences of Women in Court as Victims of Sexual Assault,* (1996); I Bacik et al, *The Legal Process and Victims of Rape* (1998)).

Section 2 of the Sexual Offences (Amendment) Act 1992 provides that the identity of the complainant in a case of rape cannot be made public, but the accused and his defence team will know the complainant's name and other details, the prohibition being directed mainly at the media. That prohibition was extended to other sexual offences by the Criminal Justice and Public Order Act 1994, Sch 9, para 52. Restrictions on the reporting of alleged offences involving persons under 18, and similar restrictions on the reporting of alleged offences involving certain adult witnesses, are contained in ss 40 to 49 of the Youth Justice and Criminal Evidence Act 1999, which are considered in **Chapter 4**.

Witnesses in fear of intimidation

Fear of giving evidence in open court may be based simply on the fear of appearing in public, a fear akin to stage fright. This is probably best overcome by some of the measures to be described later that can shield witnesses from public gaze. However, it may stem from fear for one's personal safety, or the safety of those close to the witness. Witness intimidation is an increasing problem, particularly if the alleged offenders are part of the community in which the witness lives, or where the community is hostile to the police. *The Times* (5 April 1997) reported the trial of four men for causing grievous bodily harm to a witness to a murder. The witness was sitting in a crowded pub when he was set upon by four masked men, one of whom hacked off his hand with a butcher's knife. Section 51 of the Criminal Justice and Public Order Act 1994 sought to deal with the problem by creating a new offence of witness intimidation; however, this has done little to reduce the amount or the effect of intimidation.

Witness protection programmes, which are widely used in the United States, are becoming increasingly common in this country. The Metropolitan Police and Greater Manchester Police have had such a programme for some years. *In extremis*, what is known as 'first tier protection' can involve moving the witness and his family from the area and changing identities. More often a lesser degree of protection is required, which might involve supplying the witness with a 'panic button', a device that alerts the police to the need for assistance in the event of a threat.

Before Pt II of the Youth Justice and Criminal Evidence 1999 extended the range of measures to assist frightened or intimidated witnesses, judges were able to use their common law powers to permit such witnesses to give evidence behind screens so that they would be hidden from the defendant and the public (*R v X, Y and Z* (1989) 91 Cr App R 36). The use of screens was not limited to any particular category of witness, but it was made clear in *R v Schaub and Cooper* [1994] Crim LR 531 that they should be used in respect of adult witnesses only in very exceptional circumstances because, even if the trial judge warns the jury not to make any adverse assumptions against the accused, their use may be potentially prejudicial to the accused. In this particular instance, the Court of Appeal found that the case was exceptional (it involved the multiple rape of a 21-year-old woman) and upheld the judge's decision to allow the witness to be screened (although the appeal was allowed on another point).

As an alternative to the erection of a physical screen, certain witnesses were able to give their evidence anonymously with the leave of the court. This was always potentially more contentious than the use of screens, since it is widely accepted that defendants have a fundamental right at common law to know the identity of their accusers, including witnesses for the prosecution. This right can be denied only in rare and exceptional circumstances, and whether such circumstances exist is a matter for the trial judge to determine in the exercise of his discretion. The witness can be protected from undue publicity where to publicise his name and other details might endanger his safety, or where it is necessary to the fair and proper administration of justice. Thus he may be permitted to write down his name and other details rather than identify himself in open court, but his name, etc, is known to the parties to the trial (*R v Socialist Worker, ex p Attorney-General* [1975] 1All ER 142). Victims of blackmail are often permitted to give evidence incognito, a practice confirmed by the House of Lords in *Attorney-General v Leveller Magazine* [1979] AC 440. Section 11 of the Contempt of Court Act 1981 permits the court to prohibit the publication of the name of a witness or other matters in connection with proceedings. This is justified only where publication would frustrate or render impracticable the administration of justice (see *R v Malvern JJ, ex p Evans; R v Evesham JJ, ex p McDonagh* [1988] QB 540). Child witnesses are protected against publicity by s 39 of the Children and Young Persons Act 1933, and see also s 25 of the Youth Justice and Criminal Evidence Act 1999 (discussed at p 55 below). Occasionally this means that the defendant cannot be identified where, for example, he is the child's father and to identify him would be to identify the child. Section 4 of the Sexual Offences (Amendment) Act 1992 prevents the publication of the name or other identification of the complainant in a rape case.

In *R v Watford Magistrates' Court, ex p Lenman* [1993] Crim LR 388, the Divisional Court applied the principles set out by Lord Lane CJ in *R v DJX* (1988) 91 Cr App R 36 as a suitable guide to be used in determining whether to withhold the identity of a witness or take other precautions. In *R v DJX*, the court emphasised the overriding duty of the trial judge to see that justice is done by ensuring that the system operates fairly to all those concerned: prosecution, defence and witnesses. If a magistrates' court is satisfied that there is a real risk to the administration of justice, because witnesses for the prosecution have reasonable grounds for fearing for their safety if their identities are disclosed, the court has the power to take reasonable steps to protect the witnesses. However, if the rights of the accused to prepare and conduct his defence would be prejudiced thereby, then justice requires that the court balance the prejudice to him and the interests of justice. The appellate courts should not interfere with such a decision unless it is shown to be so unreasonable that no magistrate properly considering it and properly directing himself could have reached such a conclusion. In the instant case the witnesses gave evidence on charges of violent disorder involving a number of youths who rampaged through the town, violently attacking a number of witnesses, one of whom was seriously stabbed. The identities of the witnesses were withheld because of fears for their own safety. In their statements to the police they were permitted to use pseudonyms; and the prosecution applied for them to be allowed to give evidence from behind screens, using voice-distortion equipment to disguise their voices. The magistrates granted the application subject to arrangements being made for defence solicitors to see the witnesses. The Divisional Court refused an application for judicial review of the magistrates' decision.

The decision in *ex p Lenman* was followed in *R v Taylor (Gary)* (1994) *The Times*, 17 August. There, the prosecution sought leave to allow Miss A, whose evidence was the only relevant corroboration, to testify from behind a screen where counsel and the jury could still see her, and also that she be allowed to remain anonymous. The defendants, who were charged with disposing of the body of a murdered man by dismembering, could not see her directly but only through a TV monitor. The trial judge granted the application. The question raised on appeal was whether he was correct in doing so. In holding that he was, the Court of Appeal confirmed that the decision to grant witnesses protection by these means was pre-eminently one for the discretion of the trial judge. The Court further recognised that the possible grounds for anonymity might include the witness's fear for his family or other persons. The Court offered the following guidelines to which a trial judge should have regard in exercising his discretion:

(a) There must be real grounds for fear of the consequences if evidence was given. In practical terms it might be sufficient to draw a parallel with s 23(3)(b) of the Criminal Justice Act 1988 (now s 117 Criminal Justice Act 2003), which is concerned with the admissibility of statements where the witness does not give oral evidence through fear (see pp 209–214 below), but in principle it might not be necessary for the witness to be concerned for himself alone, the concern could be for other persons or for his family.

(b) The evidence must be sufficiently relevant and important to make it unfair to make the Crown proceed without it.

(c) The Crown must satisfy the court that the creditworthiness of the witness had been fully investigated and disclosed.

(d) The court must be satisfied that there is no undue prejudice to the accused, although some prejudice is inevitable, even if it is only the qualification placed on the right of the accused to confront a witness. There might also be factors pointing the other way, for example where the defendant could see the witness on a TV screen.

(e) The court could balance the need for protection of the witness, including the extent of that protection, against the unfairness or the appearance of unfairness.

(f) There is no reason in principle why the same considerations should not apply to defence witnesses.

In *R v Lord Saville of Newdigate and others, ex p A and others* [1999] 4 All ER 860, the Divisional Court allowed an application for judicial review of a decision by a tribunal appointed under the Tribunal of Inquiry (Evidence) Act 1921 to inquire into the events of Bloody Sunday on 30 January 1972, which led to the loss of life in Londonderry, Northern Ireland, not to permit the soldiers involved to remain anonymous. The court's decision was based largely on the fact that because the tribunal was inquisitorial in nature, its ability to discover the truth would not be impeded by granting anonymity, and it could not reasonably have concluded that the additional degree of openness gained by disclosure of names was so compelling a public interest as to warrant subjecting the soldiers to a significant danger to their lives. For that reason, in a later application, soldiers required to give evidence were permitted to do so by means of a video link rather than travelling to Northern Ireland and giving evidence in person.

Admission of a written statement

A third means of helping a frightened witness was provided by s 23 of the Criminal Justice Act 1988 (now s 116(2)(e) and (4) of the Criminal Justice Act 2003). In certain circumstances (see **Chapter 6**), the statement of the frightened witness may be read out in court, thus avoiding the need for the witness to give oral evidence. There is no opportunity for cross-examination (a factor taken into account in determining whether to admit the statement), although there is a means by which the credibility of the witness can be impugned in his absence. In objecting to alternative means of giving evidence, such as anonymity or screens (or by a TV link, or by video), defence counsel should bear in mind that even if the witness does give evidence by one of these alternative means, he can still be cross-examined, and the creditworthiness of the witness will have been investigated and disclosed by the prosecution. If the witness is in fear and these methods are not permitted, the alternative might be that the statement is admitted under s 116(2)(e) of the 2003 Act (formerly s 23(3)(b) of the 1988 Act) and there will be no opportunity for cross-examination.

Special measures

As with other classes of vulnerable witnesses, the range of protections available to witnesses in fear of intimidation has been substantially extended by the provisions of Pt II of the Youth Justice and Criminal Evidence Act 1999 (hereafter 'the 1999 Act').

Following the election of the Labour Government in May 1997, the new Home Secretary, Jack Straw, announced the setting up of a Home Office Interdepartmental Working Group, to examine and make recommendations on the treatment of vulnerable and intimidated witnesses within the criminal justice system. Its terms of reference included the identification of measures at all stages of the criminal justice process which would improve the treatment of vulnerable witnesses, and further measures that might encourage witnesses to give evidence in court. Members of the Group were drawn from a range of government departments, and included representatives of Victim Support and the Association of Chief Police Officers. Special conferences were held to facilitate discussion with the judiciary and legal profession, and in drawing up their recommendations the Group drew heavily on the findings of a number of academic studies. The Group published its report, *Speaking Up for Justice*, in June 1998.

The Report made a total of 78 recommendations, 26 of which required legislation. It highlighted the need for training for all those involved in the criminal justice system to assist them in responding to the needs of vulnerable witnesses, including children. A plethora of recommendations dealt with a variety of victims' issues, including measures to combat witness intimidation and a wide range of measures to protect vulnerable and intimidated witnesses within the trial itself. The Group identified two categories of witness who should receive assistance at the discretion of the court. First, the Report concluded that those witnesses whose vulnerability related to the effects of age, disability or illness (category 'a' witnesses) would automatically be entitled to some form of special protection. However, in the case of witnesses who may be vulnerable or intimidated for reasons relating to their particular situation or the circumstances of the case (category 'b' witnesses), it was recommended that the trial judge retain discretion in determining whether or not the granting of such measures would be appropriate. In contrast to the half-hearted attempt to implement the Pigot Report in 1991 (see pp 44–45 above), most of the *Speaking Up for Justice* recommendations were implemented in P II of the 1999 Act.

Eligibility for special measures

Like the 1988/1991 regime (see pp 43–46 above), the provisions concerning eligibility for special assistance are something of a statutory minefield. Applications for special measures directions can be made before the trial begins, usually during the Plea and Case Management Hearing. In determining whether or not to issue a special measures direction, the court has to concern itself with three issues:

(a) the eligibility of the witness;

(b) the availability of the range of special measures; and

(c) the desirability of making a special measures direction in the circumstances of the case.

In keeping with the recommendations of the Working Group, the eligibility of a witness for a special measures direction will depend upon the characteristics of an individual witness, rather than hinging on whether or not the witness falls within a list of closed categories

Child witnesses

Under s 16(1)(a) of the 1999 Act, a child witness is eligible for special measures if he is less than 17 years old at the time of the hearing. However, once it has been established that a child is eligible, the court must then consider which special measure(s) should be made available. Where an application is made on behalf of a young witness, the court must apply a series of presumptions contained in s 21 of the Act before issuing the special measures direction. Section 21(2)–(5) dictates that child witnesses under the age of 17 should normally give their main evidence by means of a video-recorded interview, and any further evidence and cross-examination should take place via live link. To a large extent, this reflects the position under the 1988/1991 regime. However, s 21(6) identifies a separate category for 'child witnesses in special need of special protection'; where they are the alleged victims of a sexual offence as defined under s 35(3)(a), then the special measures direction that the witness's evidence be video-recorded, as provided for in s 27, must also provide that the cross-examination also take place on video as provided by s 28. Section 21(8) provides that where a witness has turned 17 before he begins to give evidence and is not eligible for special measures for any other reason, the direction will be revoked. However, if the witness turns 17 after he has begun to give evidence, the special measures direction will continue to apply. This subsection is made subject to s 21(9), which provides that where the witness is eligible only because he is under 17 and the special measures direction provides for the examination-in-chief and cross-examination to be conducted by video recording under ss 27 and 28, then the direction may still apply if the witness is over 17 by the time the trial proper commences, provided he was under 17 when the video recording was made.

The intention is to reduce confusion for the witness and the court by providing clear rules, but it does put undue emphasis on a particular date. If a witness who is 16 years and 6 months old is a witness to a heinous crime, the need for special measures may be just as necessary six months later when he turns 17. In practice other sections may assist. For example, a child who is eligible under s 16(1)(a) may also be eligible under s 17 if he is in fear or distress; and if the witness is a victim of a sexual offence, s 17(4) creates a presumption that the witness is eligible for special measures. If the child witness is eligible under both sections then it matters not that he turns 17 before or during the trial s 21(8) applies to a child witness eligible for special measures only under s 16(1)(a).

Child witnesses in need of special protection who get the benefit of special measures under ss 27 and 28 will get the benefit of these special measures after they are 17 so long as they were under 17 when the cross-examination by video was recorded. It follows that s 21(8) will only apply to a witness to a non-sexual offence who obtains the special measures simply on age and for no other reason. Such witnesses may well be able to cope without them.

Section 22 of the Act purports to deal with the rather unusual situation in which a person under 17 is a witness to or victim of a crime, and who was under that age when a video recording of his evidence-in-chief was made but over 17 when the court had to determine whether any special measures should apply. He will then be deemed a 'qualifying witness' as defined by s 22(1). If he was a witness to or victim of a sexual offence, or an offence of assault or kidnapping, he is a qualifying witness 'in need of special protection'. Section 21(2)–(7) apply to such witnesses, so that they too are to be treated as child witnesses under s 21. They must therefore be allowed to give their evidence-in-chief by means of a video recording and, if victims of or witnesses to sexual offences, be cross-examined on video as well. Other special measures that might improve the quality of their evidence can also be made available, as they can to child witnesses within s 21.

Adult witnesses

Section 16(2) of the 1999 Act implements the recommendations of the Working Group that, like children, those suffering from mental or physical disability should automatically be entitled to special measures. Such witnesses are basically those affected by mental disorder or impairment of intelligence and social functioning, and those affected by a physical disability or disorder. The court should consult witnesses prior to trial in relation to their wishes (s 16(4)), although it remains to be seen what weight, if any, might be attached to the evidence of expert witnesses or carers. The appropriateness of any special measure will effectively depend on the nature of the disability.

Section 17 provides that a witness is eligible for special measures if the quality of his evidence 'is likely to be diminished by reason of fear or distress'. Nevertheless, unless the witness is a complainant in a sexual case (s 17(4) see – below), the fact that a witness produces evidence that he suffers from fear or distress about the prospect of testifying does not give rise to automatic eligibility. Section 17(2) requires the court to consider a range of factors in arriving at its determination. These are:

(a) the nature and alleged circumstances of the offence to which the proceedings relate;

(b) the age of the witness;

(c) such of the following matters as appear to the court to be relevant, namely –

    (i) the social and cultural background and ethnic origins of the witness,

    (ii) the domestic and employment circumstances of the witness, and

    (iii) any religious beliefs or political opinions of the witness;

(d) any behaviour towards the witness on the part of –

    (i) the accused,

    (ii) members of the family or associates of the accused, or

    (iii) any other person who is likely to be an accused or a witness in the proceedings.

In addition, s 17(3) provides that the court must also consider any views expressed by the witness.

Once the court determines that the adult witness is eligible for a special measures direction, it must decide which measure(s) would be likely to optimise the quality of that witness's evidence under s 19. In doing so, it should have regard to all the circumstances of the case, including in particular any views expressed by the witness and whether the measure or measures might tend to inhibit such evidence being effectively tested by a party to the proceedings (s 19(2)–(3)). In summing up, the trial judge should give the jury such warning as he considers necessary to ensure that the fact that the direction was given does not prejudice the accused (s 32).

Under s 17(4), the court must presume that a sexual complainant is an 'eligible witness', unless the witness expresses the wish not to be treated as one, although the defence may attempt to rebut the presumption. Nevertheless, this provision is particularly welcome, in that police can now guarantee sexual complainants that, if they have to go to court, they should normally be eligible at least for one or more of the special measures.

The defendant

It will be noted that the provisions of the 1999 Act do not apply to a witness who is the accused. It is possible this could constitute a potential breach of the principle of equality of arms under the European Convention. This concept states that when the prosecution and defence are in court, there must be a level playing field between them. In *Delcourt v Belgium* (1970) 1 EHRR 355, it was held that the accused should not be placed in a position where he is at a substantial disadvantage in presenting his case compared to the prosecution. In the joined cases of *T v United Kingdom; V v United Kingdom* (2000) 30 EHRR 121, the European Court of Human Rights found no breach of Article 6 in relation to the well-publicised trial of two 10-year-olds convicted for the murder of toddler Jamie Bulger. However, the Court went on to stress the need for special provisions to be made available for child defendants in order that they could fully participate in the proceedings against them.

In light of the judgment, the Attorney-General issued guidance to the Crown Courts dealing with young defendants tried on indictment that applies some of the measures considered above to such juveniles (*Practice Direction (Crown Court: Trial of Children and Young Persons)* [2000] 1 WLR 659). Although the Practice Direction set out a number of measures which courts should adopt when trying juveniles, such as the right of the accused to sit with family or friends and the removal of wigs and gowns by counsel, it did not alter the fact that juvenile defendants are still excluded from applying for special measures under the 1999 Act; and it also failed to address the key concern of the European Court as to whether it is ever appropriate to try children in a forum designed for the trial and sentencing of adults. Since one of the most commonly cited reasons for introducing the legislation was to enable children to give the best evidence in court, it seems odd that child defendants should not be allowed to rely on this mechanism.

Types of special measures

Screens

The use of screens is the first of the special measures to be outlined in the 1999 Act. It is provided for under s 23 of the legislation. This measure is perhaps the least contentious of the shielding measures, in so far as the witness is still seated in the actual courtroom. He will then sit behind an erected screen while giving evidence. As noted at p 47 above, screens have been used in court at common law, and although they act to obscure the witness from the view of the accused, their use has been relatively non-contentious. They are also easy to use and require few resources. Both the defendant and the victim will remain in the actual courtroom, so the disruptive effect on proceedings will be minimal.

Live link

Section 24 of the 1999 Act provides for witnesses to give evidence by live link. The Criminal Justice Act 1988 made provision for witnesses outside the United Kingdom to give evidence through a live television link (s 32(1)(a), which continues in force; see further below) and for child witnesses to do so where the offence was an offence of violence or a sexual offence. Section 32(1)(b) is repealed and replaced with s 24 of the 1999 Act, where the procedure is described as a 'live link'. This will usually mean a closed circuit television link, but the section is drafted sufficiently widely to include any technology with the same effect. Section 24(2) and (3) are intended to create a presumption that a witness who gives evidence by live link for part of the proceedings will continue to give evidence via this means throughout the proceedings.

Section 24(5) and (6) make it clear that the live link procedure applies to magistrates' courts, whereas under the 1988 Act provisions it applied only to Crown Courts. Where a particular magistrates' court does not have the facilities, temporary facilities may be made available, and the court can sit in another area, if necessary, in order to make use of such facilities. The magistrates may also move to a nearby Crown Court if facilities are available there. The usual procedure will involve the witness giving evidence from a room within the court precincts, but it can be used more widely. For example, in what may have been the first case under this provision, in August 2002 a paralysed patient gave evidence from her bed in a nursing home via a live link, and told Lewes Crown Court how the defendant, a male nurse, had indecently assaulted her.

Section 32(1)(a) of the Criminal Justice Act 1988 provides that a person, other than the accused, may give evidence through a live television link if the witness is outside the United Kingdom. This provision, recently used to take the evidence of a witness in the United States in a major fraud trial, is built upon by ss 29 to 31, which permit the courts, following a request from a recognised 'external authority', to take evidence from persons outside the United Kingdom through a live television link, and from witnesses in the United Kingdom by telephone. These provisions to not apply to the ordinary criminal trial and will not be considered further. They do, however, demonstrate the extent to which our system has moved away from the traditional common law view that the only way to give evidence was to attend court in person and give oral evidence directly to the court.

The Criminal Justice Act 2003 and the Crime (International Co-operation) Act 2003 extend the use of the live link procedure. The Government considered the recommendation of Sir Robin Auld in his *Review of the Criminal Courts* (2001) that expert witnesses be permitted to give evidence by live link, but the Acts go further by extending the live link provision to any witness, other than the defendant, where it is in the interests of efficiency or effectiveness. These provisions are in addition to the provisions of the 1999 Act (see pp 53–59 above) and are not conditional on the vulnerability of the witness. The criterion is that the use of the live link is in the interests of the efficient and effective administration of justice. It is, in effect, an extension of s 32 of the Criminal Justice Act 1988 (above), under which the court can take evidence via a television link if the witness is outside the United Kingdom. Section 51 of the Criminal Justice Act 2003 applies to witnesses inside the United Kingdom who, for good reason, are unable to travel to the court, or where such travel would be very inconvenient or commercially damaging – for example, a one-man company who is required to travel some distance to give evidence, whose business would suffer unduly if he did so. If there are suitable facilities nearby, the court may sanction the giving of evidence via a live link. In some cases the equipment may be taken to the witness, or the witness may use his own equipment as he would in what is known as a video-conference. The day may not be too far away when the court will be able to accept testimony via a mobile camera phone which is within the broad definition of live link. Section 56(5) makes it clear that the provisions in s 51 do not affect the inherent discretion of the court to authorise evidence to be heard by live link in circumstances not covered by s 51, or to make any other directions or orders in relation to witnesses including the defendant. The Crime (International Co-operation) Act 2003 makes provision for evidence in criminal cases requested by other countries to be taken by British courts using a live link.

Evidence given in private

Section 25 of the 1999 Act empowers the judge to order the courtroom to be cleared of people who do not need to be present while a witness gives evidence. The direction will apply to individuals or groups of people, rather than areas of the court, and will mostly affect those in the public gallery. The court must allow at least one member of the press to remain if one has been nominated by the press. The measure will only be available in a case involving a sexual offence, or when the court is persuaded that someone has tried to intimidate, or is likely to try to intimidate, the witness. These are relatively narrow grounds, which mean that many child witnesses and those with learning difficulties will not be able to benefit from such a direction.

Removal of wigs and gowns

Section 26 of the 1999 Act stipulates that a special measures direction may provide for the wearing of wigs or gowns to be dispensed with during the giving of the witness's evidence. As with the power to clear the public gallery (above), such a procedure has always remained within the power of the court at common law. The measure was introduced to reduce the intimidating formality of the proceedings. It would particularly aid young witnesses, who may feel over-awed by the austere atmosphere of the trial setting. Unlike some of the other special measures, this has not proved to be particularly contentious. It has, however, been mooted that some witnesses may feel that they prefer the judge and counsel to wear their wigs and gowns, so that the trial is a formal rather than a casual procedure and gives them a sense that the process is being taken seriously (*Guardian*, 17 January 2003). Louise Ellison has also suggested that some witnesses may expect wigs to be worn from their knowledge of the legal system, and may thus be 'thrown' by their absence (L Ellison, *The Adversarial Process and the Vulnerable Witness* (2001), (34). Obviously if the child has indicated that he does not want this sort of 'special treatment', no such application would normally be made, and he would be free to give evidence in the normal setting.

Video-recorded evidence-in-chief

As a matter of course, video-recorded interviews are conducted by the police in accordance with a Home Office Memorandum that takes account of the rules of evidence. Despite this, video-recorded interviews often contain inadmissible statements, and occasionally the interviewer will allow his prejudices to show and render the video interview inadmissible because it assumed the defendant's guilt. Section 27 of the Youth Justice and Criminal Evidence Act 1999 provides for a video-recorded interview with an eligible witness to be substituted for that witness's examination-in-chief. However, certain protections are in place for the accused: such a direction may not be given if the court considers that it would be against the interests of justice to do so (s 27(2)). Furthermore, the court must balance any prejudice to the accused with the desirability of showing the whole of the recorded interview (s 27(3)); and the court may direct that the recording should not be admitted if it appears that the witness will not be available for cross-examination, or that rules of disclosure have not been followed (s 27(4)). A witness giving evidence in this way must be called by the party tendering it in evidence (s 27(5)(a)) and may not give evidence-in-chief through means other than the recording without the permission of the court.

It is intended that when a video recording is made of an interview with a witness aged 14 or over then, in anticipation of an application being made for a direction under this section, the witness should be asked to make an affirmation at the beginning of the interview unless an affirmation would be wholly inappropriate. Where an affirmation is not made, the evidence admitted will be evidence given unsworn (see *R v Duffy*) [1999] QB 919.

As with evidence given by live link (see pp 54–55 above), the Criminal Justice Act 2003 adopted the recommendation of Lord Justice Auld in his *Review of the Criminal Courts* by extending the use of video-recorded evidence beyond the rather narrow confines of the 1999 Act. Section 137 of the 2003 Act gives a judge the power to issue a direction that a video recording of the evidence-in-chief of a witness should be admitted in trials of offences triable on indictment and prescribed offences triable either way, if it enables the witness to give better evidence and it is in the interest of justice to do so. The criteria for admitting a video recording of the witness's evidence are:

(a) that the person claims to be a witness to the offence (or part of it) or to events closely connected to the offence;

(b) that the video recording was made at a time when the events were fresh in the witness's memory; and

(c) that the alleged offence is triable only on indictment in the Crown Court, or is an either way offence prescribed by an order of the Secretary of State.

The central purpose is to ensure that the quality and accuracy of the evidence is the highest possible. Thus only if the recorded account is likely to be significantly better than the witness's oral account in court will the video recording be admitted. It seems to be common sense that a video-recorded account given soon after the offence is likely to be better than an oral account given many months after the offence was committed, and the section reflects this approach. The section also ties in with demands from reformers that witness statements be video-recorded to ensure that the witness gives an account of what he saw or heard rather than what the interviewing officer would like the witness to have seen or heard. It is easy to influence an uncertain witness into a state of certainty by prompting him. This may be done consciously or unconsciously by a police officer who has a version of the facts of the offence and is seeking confirmation from the witness.

Unlike s 27 of the 1999 legislation, it is not a condition of admissibility that the witness be available for cross-examination, and there is no provision for extending the provision in s 28 of the 1999 Act to permit cross-examination by means of a video recording (see below). However, given that the central reason for admitting the video recording of the evidence-in-chief is that the recorded evidence would be significantly better than the oral evidence, suggesting a choice between oral and recorded evidence, it seems that the witness must be available for cross-examination. As with s 27 of the 1999 Act, provision is made in s 138 that the witness (other than the defendant – s 137(3)) may not give evidence-in-chief otherwise than by means of the recording, unless the court is of the opinion that the matter has not been dealt with adequately in the recording. In considering whether any part of the recording should not be admitted, the court must consider whether admitting that part would carry a risk of prejudice to the defendant and, if so, whether the interests of justice nevertheless require it to be admitted in view of the desirability of showing the whole, or substantially the whole, of the recorded interview.

Video-recorded cross-examination and re-examination

Section 28 of the 1999 Act constitutes a radical departure from tradition that was recommended by the Pigot Committee in 1991 (referred to as the 'full Pigot'; see pp 44–45 above). It provides that where the court has already allowed a video recording to be admitted as the witness's main evidence, the cross-examination and re-examination of that witness may also be pre-recorded in advance of the trial. The video-recorded cross-examination may, but need not, take place in the physical presence of the judge or magistrates and the defence and legal representatives. However, a judge or magistrate will have to be able to control the proceedings. It is intended that the judge or magistrate in charge of this procedure will normally be the trial judge. All the people mentioned in this paragraph will have to be able to see and hear the witness being cross-examined and communicate with anyone who is in the room with the witness, such as an intermediary acting under s 29 below (see pp 58–59).

The provision was aimed at preventing the sort of disparaging cross-examination directed at the 15-year-old witness known as 'Bromley' in the Damilola Taylor murder trial. That case showed the need for proper testing of the evidence of a witness by cross-examination, but can also be seen as an example of the abuse of cross-examination, the 15-year-old being exposed to 15 hours of cross-examination by four experienced counsel. The police and prosecution say that the witness – a young, under-achieving girl – was cross-examined into confusion by four Oxbridge graduates. The defence claim that she was an ill-prepared witness who, by sensitive but probing techniques of skilled criminal advocacy, was shown to be inconsistent and unreliable. The s 28 procedure would still allow for proper cross-examination and testing of the witness's evidence, but under more controlled conditions. It is possible that in a case where there are a number of defendants, one or two counsel might cross-examine for all rather than four. Alternatively the procedure under s 29 – cross-examination by an intermediary, discussed below – could be used to reduce the stress of being cross-examined by a number of counsel.

Receiving the entire testimony of a child outside the formal courtroom environment clearly holds the potential significantly to reduce fear and apprehension and allow the child to achieve some sense of closure within a relatively short timeframe after the offence. However, the Government declined to implement this provision when most of the other special measures came into force in July 2002, and announced in December 2004 that it would not take effect at all because of perceived difficulties with the rules on disclosure. It was basically envisaged that pre-recorded cross-examination would have been rendered ineffective unless the defence had full disclosure of the prosecution case. Even if the case had been fast-tracked to get it to court in the shortest possible time, there would have been a delay of some weeks or months before the defence would have been in a position to cross-examine the witness on video. As part of a wide-ranging review set up by the Government to assess the needs of child witnesses, views are now being sought as to how this provision might be reformulated in order to sidestep such difficulties.

Examination of a witness through an intermediary

One of the most radical provisions of the 1999 Act was contained in s 29, which allows an intermediary not only to communicate questions and answers to and from a witness, but also to explain the questions and answers to enable them to be understood. The intermediary should be specially qualified and trained by the court, and must declare that he or she will perform the role faithfully. The judge, jury and legal representatives must be able to see and hear the proceedings, and to communicate with the intermediary (s 29(3)). The procedure cannot be used in relation to a recorded interview with a witness, unless the court issues a further special measures direction (s 29(6)).

The idea of an intermediary was first proposed by the Pigot Committee in 1989. It was the only proposal of the Committee that was not unanimous. The rationale for the introduction of the mechanism would appear to have been that it would reduce the stress levels for child witnesses, and as such would enhance the quality of their evidence. Whilst the use of screens, television links and pre-recorded evidence-in-chief have now been in place for some years with relatively few opponents, the use of intermediaries is particularly contentious as it is viewed as being so alien to the nature of the adversarial process. A major perceived risk is that the traditional role of counsel would be significantly undermined, since questions would be put to the child by the intermediary, who would be free to use very different voice tones and interrogative techniques than those which defence counsel might believe to be in the interests of his client. As Hoyano points out, there is obviously the potential for a particular meaning or emphasis to be lost, which in turn could lead to disputes between the questioner and the intermediary on which the trial judge would have to adjudicate (L Hoyano, 'Variations on a Theme by Pigot: Special Measures Directions for Child Witnesses' [2000] Crim LR 250, 272).

It is easy to imagine situations in which it might be necessary to call upon the services of an intermediary at an early stage in an investigation or proceedings involving a witness who has a particular problem in communicating. Where intermediaries are used at an early stage of the investigation or proceedings, and subsequently an application is made for a video recording of an interview in which they were involved to be admitted as evidence, that direction can be given despite the judge, magistrate or legal representative not having been present. However, the intermediary who was involved must still gain the court's approval retrospectively before the recording can be admitted. Intermediaries will have to declare that they will perform their functions faithfully. They will have the same obligation as foreign language interpreters not to make a wilfully false or misleading statement to the witness or the court. If they do make such statements they will commit an offence under the Perjury Act 1911.

Some indication of the full effect of this measure will be evident when the outcomes of pilots are published, but it could be said that it holds significant potential to spare young child witnesses the trauma of cross-examination.

Aids to communication

Under s 30 of the 1999 Act, a special measures direction may provide for the witness, while giving evidence (whether by testimony in court or otherwise), to be provided with such aids as the court considers appropriate, with a view to enabling questions or answers to be communicated to or by the witness despite any disability or disorder the witness has or suffers from. Such devices might include sign boards, communications aids for the disabled, and other aids that may allow deaf or dumb witnesses to communicate more effectively. It is not intended to include devices for disguising speech, sometimes used to preserve anonymity.

A new era for vulnerable witnesses?

Research carried out for the Home Office, *Are special measures working? Evidence from surveys of vulnerable and intimidated witnesses*, Research Report No 283 (2004), shows that:

(a) 9 out of 10 witnesses using the live link found this helpful;

(b) a similar proportion found using video-recorded evidence helpful;

(c) around half of witnesses who had the opportunity to give evidence with the aid of special measures said they would have found special measures helpful;

(d) witnesses who used special measures were significantly more confident that the criminal justice system was effective in meeting the needs of victims;

(e) 44% of victims of sexual offences said they would not have given evidence without special measures;

(f) one-third of all witnesses using special measures said they would not have been willing and able to give evidence without them;

(g) the satisfaction of witnesses who fear intimidation increased from 66% to 80%.

It would thus appear, prima facie, that the special measures provided for by Pt II of the Youth Justice and Criminal Evidence Act 1999 mark a positive step forward for vulnerable witnesses. Many witnesses will no longer have to give live oral evidence and undergo detailed questioning about their private lives in open court, and so the legislation can be said to strike a better balance between the interests of the various parties involved in the criminal action. It is also indicative that certain key principles of the adversarial trial, such as orality, confrontation and live cross-examination, may no longer be viewed as principles so sacrosanct that they ought to operate to prevent radical reform of the criminal trial.

While the Youth Justice and Criminal Evidence Act 1999 marked a great leap forward for vulnerable witnesses, the legislation was by no means perfectly formulated. In addition to some of the concerns outlined in the previous section, it has also been argued that the legislation does not go far enough in addressing secondary victimisation. The Act will only come to the aid of witnesses who are legally eligible for assistance under the statute. The vast majority of witnesses, including victims of crime, will continue to give live, oral evidence. Even for those witnesses who do fall under the ambit of the legislation, the excesses of the adversarial trial are only partially reduced, rather than removed. Even if witnesses give evidence via a television link, for example, they will still be then subjected to the same techniques and devices commonly used to disorientate or intimidate witnesses during cross-examination (see generally L Ellison, 'The Mosaic Art: Cross-examination and the Vulnerable Witness' (2001) 21(3) LS 353). Indeed, Louise Ellison has argued that that as long as orality and cross-examination are regarded as sacrosanct features of the English criminal trial, complainants in court are unlikely to be relieved of secondary victimisation. She maintained that effective solutions to the problems facing vulnerable witnesses can be found only by looking *beyond* the adversarial system, since there is an inherent 'basic conflict between the needs and interests of vulnerable witnesses and the resultant evidentiary safeguards of the adversarial trial process'. In spite of the changes introduced by the Act, Ellison believes that a radical overhaul of the adversarial system remains 'an indeterminate prospect', given that many practitioners would seem to be concerned with the loss of effect of evidence upon the jury, and view televised testimony as being 'artificial, remote and less compelling' (L Ellison, *The Adversarial Process and the Vulnerable Witness* (2001), 60).

Other concerns with special measures stem from the idea that the accused has a 'right of confrontation', that is, that he has a right to be physically present to view the opposing witnesses when they are giving evidence against him. While this is a constitutional right in the United States of America, such a right does not have any grounding either in English common law, or under the European Convention on Human Rights. Instead, both parties to the trial are said to have the right to put forward and challenge effectively the evidence adduced by the opposition. While the common law has traditionally recognised the right of the accused to be present during his trial (*R v Lee Kun* [1916] 1 KB 337), there is no authority to suggest that this right should entail physical confrontation (J Doak, 'Shielding Vulnerable Witnesses from Adversarial Showdown: A Bridge Too Far?' (2000) 16(3) *Journal of Civil Liberties* 216).

Similarly, the right of confrontation does not appear to form part of the fair trial requirements of the European Convention. While Article 6(3)(d) gives the accused the right 'to examine or have examined witnesses against him and to obtain the attendance and examination of witnesses on his behalf under the same conditions as witnesses against him', the wording of the Convention itself gives little guidance as to whether physical confrontation is an element of Article 6(3)(d). While the case law would appear to place an emphasis on the need for witnesses at least to attend the trial proper and be available to have their evidence challenged, it does not bear out the argument that confrontation is an essential ingredient to meaningful cross-examination. It is clear from the Convention case law that special measures to shield vulnerable witnesses from the accused will not contravene the Convention, provided they are strictly necessary (*Kostovski v Netherlands*

(1989) 12 EHRR 434; *Doorson v Netherlands* (1996) 22 EHRR 330; *Van Mechelen v Netherlands* (1998) 25 EHRR 657).

Indeed, the compatibility of special measures with the Convention was recently considered by the House of Lords in the case of *R (D) v Camberwell Green Youth Court* [2005] UKHL 4. Here, the applicants challenged the requirement for the court, under s 21(5) of the Youth Justice and Criminal Evidence Act 1999, to give a special measures direction in favour of video-recording their evidence-in-chief where child witnesses were 'in need of special assistance' (ie, where they were victims of sexual abuse). It was alleged that this requirement deprived the court of any power to consider whether the restriction on the rights of the defence was necessary or in the interests of justice. The House of Lords rejected the appeal, holding that just because some of the evidence was produced by contemporaneous television transmission, the fair trial rights of the accused were not compromised since he could see and hear the evidence, and had every opportunity to challenge and question the witnesses against him at the trial itself.

The potential of special measures to alleviate the plight of vulnerable witnesses in court will become evident in the fullness of time, but it could be said in the meantime that they do provide evidence of a gradual shift away from the principle of orality which traditionally has been perceived as a fundamental component of the adversarial trial. Coupled with other radical reforms to the law of evidence discussed throughout this work, such as the erosion of the hearsay rule, the relaxation of the rules of admissibility of previous witness statements and the extension of the use of televised evidence, it may be the case that indirect testimony is increasingly becoming perceived as evidence that can be every bit as reliable and cogent as direct oral evidence.

Further reading

Birch, D, 'A Better Deal for Vulnerable Witnesses?' [2000] Crim LR 223.

Cooper, D, 'Pigot unfulfilled: video-recorded cross-examination under section 28 of the Youth Justice and Criminal Evidence Act 1999' [2005] Crim LR 456.

Ellison, L, *The Adversarial Process and the Vulnerable Witness* (2001).

Ellison, L, 'Cross-examination and the intermediary: bridging the language divide?' [2002] Crim LR 114.

McEwan, J, 'In Defence of Vulnerable Witnesses: The Youth Justice and Criminal Evidence Act 1999' (2000) 4(1) E & P 1.

3 The Burden of Proof

The 'golden thread'

In modern times every jury must be directed on the burden of proof. Nothing should be said which detracts from the principle that the burden of proof is on the prosecution. A failure to give a direction, or to suggest that the defendant has the onus of proof when he does not, will be a misdirection and, unless corrected, will render the verdict unsafe.

A central feature of the adversarial system of criminal justice is that the prosecution have the burden of proving the guilt of the accused person beyond reasonable doubt. In *Woolmington v DPP* [1935] AC 462, the House of Lords held that it was for the prosecution to prove all the elements of the crime, including, in the case of murder, malice (or as we would say in modern times, the intention to kill or to cause really serious bodily harm). In *Woolmington,* the accused was charged with murdering his estranged wife. He admitted shooting her, but claimed that he had threatened to shoot himself unless she returned to him and had shot her by accident. The trial judge directed the jury that once it was established that the victim had died as a result of the defendant's act, he had the burden of proving that it was an accident rather than an intentional killing. The House of Lords held this to be a misdirection and Viscount Sankey stated the law thus:

> While the prosecution must prove the guilt of the prisoner, there is no ... burden laid
> on the prisoner to prove his innocence and it is sufficient for him to raise a doubt as to
> his guilt. Throughout the web of English criminal law one golden thread is always to be
> seen, that it is the duty of the prosecution to prove the prisoner's guilt subject to the
> defence of insanity and subject also to any statutory exception ... No matter what the
> charge or where the trial, the principle that the prosecution must prove the guilt of the
> prisoner is part of the common law of England (and Wales) and no attempt to whittle it
> down can be entertained.

It was this decision in 1935 which first clearly established the 'golden thread' of English criminal law: the principle that it is for the prosecution to prove the defendant's guilt subject only to the common law exception of insanity and any statutory exception created by Parliament. The importance of this principle can be seen from the language used by their Lordships and from the fact that the European Convention on Human Rights adopts this principle in Article 6(2), which states that 'Everyone charged with a criminal offence shall be presumed innocent until proved guilty according to law.'

Legal and evidential burdens

Whilst the expression 'burden of proof' is properly used to describe the 'legal' or 'persuasive' burden (ie, the legal obligation on the prosecution to prove all the facts necessary to establish the defendant's guilt), it is also (incorrectly) used to describe the 'evidential' burden (ie, the obligation upon either the prosecution or the defence to produce sufficient evidence to establish the facts, more correctly referred to as the 'burden of adducing evidence').

It is vitally important to distinguish the two burdens (see Lord Hope of Craighead's comments in *R v DPP, ex p Kebilene* [2000] 2 AC 326). So far as the prosecution are concerned, the persuasive and evidential burdens are two sides of the same coin – without adducing sufficient evidence of the facts of the offence they could not discharge their persuasive burden. If the prosecution adduce sufficient evidence to make a prima facie case, the defence may then respond by calling the defendant and/or witnesses for the defence. The defence do not have to disprove the prosecution case, though they will if they can. It is sufficient for them to raise a reasonable doubt in the minds of the magistrate or district judge in cases tried summarily, or in the minds of the jury if the case is tried on indictment. The defence may take the chance that the prosecution case will not satisfy the jury beyond reasonable doubt and decide not to call any evidence, or may call some evidence but not put the accused on the witness stand. However, in the majority of cases the defence cannot take that risk and will challenge the evidence of the prosecution by calling their own witnesses and the defendant to give evidence.

Where the defence rely on a particular defence, the passing of the evidential burden to the defence means that they must adduce sufficient evidence of the defence relied upon to make it an issue which the prosecution must rebut. For example, if the accused relies on self-defence on a charge of murder (see further below), the defence must adduce evidence of that defence if it is to be put before the jury. This will often mean that the defendant must give evidence himself and/or call witnesses to substantiate any defence. Thus, in the vast majority of cases the jury will hear evidence from the prosecution and the defence. Since the Criminal Evidence Act 1898 made the accused a competent witness in his own defence, the accused can give evidence but cannot be compelled to do so. The vast majority of defendants do give evidence, as to decide not to is usually risky; and when the defendant has a defence, he usually has to call evidence and give evidence himself. The defendant's failure to call or give evidence means that the prosecution case is uncontested. If the prosecution have presented a strong prima facie case to answer and there is no good reason why the accused should not give evidence, the jury will probably draw a commonsense inference that he has no answer. As noted in **Chapter 2**, under s 35 of the Criminal Justice and Public Order Act 1994, the trial judge may direct the jury that they may draw proper inferences from the failure of the accused to give evidence. The jury are then likely to convict in the absence of evidence from the defence.

If the defence to a charge of wounding or murder is self-defence, the defendant has the evidential burden of raising the defence, which, put simply, means he or his witnesses must give evidence of the need to use reasonable force in defence of himself or another. The prosecution, who have the legal burden of proof on the issue once it is raised, must then rebut that defence beyond reasonable doubt. The rule as to evidential burdens was stated in *R v Gill* (1963) 47 Cr App R 166, 172 (in the context of duress) as follows:

The accused, either by cross-examination of the prosecution witnesses or by evidence called on his behalf, or by a combination of the two, must place before the court such material as makes duress a live issue fit and proper to be left to the jury. But, once he has succeeded in doing this, it is then for the Crown to destroy that defence in such a manner as to leave in the jury's minds no reasonable doubt that the accused cannot be absolved on the grounds of alleged compulsion.

The prosecution are not required to rebut every possible defence to a charge; some evidence of the defence must be adduced to the court before they can be required to do so. As indicated above, it is usually for the defence, to adduce evidence of a defence, but this may sometimes come from the prosecution evidence. For example, a prosecution witness speaks of the victim attacking the defendant and the defendant retaliating. However, if there is no evidence of self-defence in the prosecution case, it is for the defence to raise the issue – they have the evidential burden. Once they have done so, it is for the prosecution to prove (beyond reasonable doubt) that the defendant did not act in self-defence but did the act with the necessary mental element.

The defence of provocation under s 3 of the Homicide Act 1957 imposes an evidential burden on the accused to provide sufficient evidence of provocation in order for the issue to go before the jury. If he does so, the prosecution then have the legal or persuasive burden of proving that the defendant killed the victim intentionally and without provocation, or that no reasonable person would have reacted as he did to the alleged provocation. This is also true of the defence of duress (*per minas*, or of circumstances). It is not sufficient simply to say 'I was forced into doing it'. There must be sufficient evidence of the defence to oblige the judge to leave the issue to the jury; and he must put the defence to the jury if, properly directed, a reasonable jury might acquit as a result. The prosecution must, if, and only if, there is sufficient evidence of the defence, rebut it by proving beyond reasonable doubt that the defendant did not act because of the pressure of the threat.

It should be noted that there are circumstances in which the defence may run a particular defence which is inconsistent with another defence which may be raised by the evidence (from the prosecution or the defence) but is not relied upon by the defence. For example, If the defendant is charged with the murder of the victim who the defendant says verbally abused and physically attacked him, the best defence may be self-defence, which, if it succeeds, will result in an acquittal. In such circumstances, to plead provocation, which is in effect a plea of guilty to manslaughter, is contradictory. If, however, there is sufficient evidence of provocation, the judge is under a duty to put that defence to the jury.

The defence must now also disclose their defence(s) to the prosecution before trial. The prosecution will therefore be aware of the possibility of an alternative defence being put to the jury, and will seek to rebut it by direct evidence, or in cross-examination of the witnesses or defendant if he gives evidence. The trial judge will direct the jury on the alternative defence even if the defence have not themselves raised it (see S Doran, 'Alternative defences: the "invisible burden" on the trial judge' [1991] Crim LR 878 and *R v Watson* [1992] Crim LR 434). It may be noted that in relation to many defences, the defence often bear an evidential burden simply because the evidence of that defence is within the knowledge of the defence. It is then seen as reasonable that the defendant should bear the evidential burden of raising that defence as an issue. However, a practical consequence of an evidential burden, and more so of the reverse legal burden, and perhaps the purpose behind them, is that the defendant is compelled to go into the witness box and give evidence of the defence. He will then be exposed to cross-examination by the prosecution (see the comments of the Criminal Law Revision Committee, 11th Report (Cmnd 4991) (1972), para 140).

As we shall see later in this chapter, there is also one common law provision (insanity) and many statutory provisions which place the legal or persuasive burden of proof of a defence on the defence. As indicated, a consequence of those provisions is that the defendant has to give evidence of the defence (and face cross-examination), and he may be convicted if he adduces sufficient evidence to raise a doubt about his guilt but fails to convince the jury on the balance of probabilities. Previously, when faced with a statutory provision which placed a reverse legal burden on the accused, the courts had to accept that this was the will of Parliament and apply the law no matter how unfair it might have seemed. However, the position has changed since the Human Rights Act 1998 came into force in 2000. The Act incorporates the European Convention on Human Rights into our domestic law and provides a procedure under which a court can declare a statutory provision incompatible with the European Convention or, relying on s 3, interpret the statutory provision so as to avoid any incompatibility. In the context of reverse burdens of proof this provision has been relied upon to 'read down' a provision which imposes a reverse legal burden of proof on the defendant when it is seen as incompatible with Article 6(2) of the European Convention, so that it reads as an evidential burden which is not incompatible. Thus the word 'prove' is interpreted as requiring the defendant to adduce sufficient evidence to make it an issue which the prosecution must disprove, rather than as imposing a requirement on the defendant to prove the issue on the balance of probabilities. So far as serious offences are concerned, the courts and Parliament have gone some way toward accepting the recommendation of the Criminal Law Revision Committee by, in the case of the courts, 'reading down' provisions imposing legal burdens on the defence and making them evidential burdens. In the case of Parliament, there is an acceptance that reverse legal burdens are not always necessary; see, for example, s 118 of the Terrorism Act 2000, which converts a number of reverse legal burdens contained in various sections of the Act to evidential burdens.

The standard of proof

'Standard of proof' means the level or degree of proof which must be established. There are only two standards: the criminal standard of proof, which is 'proof beyond reasonable doubt'; and the civil standard, which is proof 'on the balance of probabilities'.

Proof beyond reasonable doubt

In criminal trials where the prosecution bear the legal or persuasive burden, they must establish the defendant's guilt beyond reasonable doubt. This standard applies in all criminal trials, whether before magistrates or on indictment before a jury. If there is a reasonable doubt created by the evidence given either by the prosecution or by the defence, the prosecution have not made out their case and the defendant must be acquitted (*Woolmington v DPP* [1935] AC 462). Many judicial attempts have been made to define what is, or is not, a reasonable doubt. Most create more problems than they solve. It is clear that the standard is high; but certainty is not required, still less scientific proof. Perhaps the best definition is that given by Lord Denning in *Miller v Minister of Pensions* [1947] 2 All ER 372, at 373,

> *That degree is well settled. It need not reach certainty, but it must carry a high degree of probability. Proof beyond reasonable doubt does not mean proof beyond a shadow of a doubt. The law would fail to protect the community if it admitted of fanciful possibilities to deflect the course of justice. If the evidence is so strong against a man as to leave only a remote possibility in his favour which can be dismissed with the sentence, 'of course it is possible but not in the least probable,' the case is proved beyond reasonable doubt but nothing short of that will suffice.*

Even this definition has been criticised, and there have been numerous attempts by judges to define reasonable doubt in terms which a jury might better understand. Thus, in *Walters v R* [1969] 2 AC 26, the Privy Council approved the definition as 'that quality of doubt which when you are dealing with matters of importance in your own affairs, you allow to influence you one way or another'. This was disapproved of in *R v Gray* (1973) 58 Cr App R 177 because it pitched the standard too low. The reference to 'important affairs' was more acceptable, because decisions on such important matters make one more reflective and likely to apply a higher standard. In *R v Ching* (1976) 63 Cr App R 7, the use of the analogy between buying a house and taking out a mortgage was approved; the jury would have to be as sure as they would be in taking out a residential mortgage before they had proof beyond reasonable doubt. But these definitions merely highlight the fact that the jury are taking an important decision and do little to indicate what degree of doubt justifies an acquittal. They are also highly subjective and relative to individual jurors' experiences. The Court of Appeal in *Ching* said that judges would be well advised not to attempt any gloss on what is meant by 'sure' or 'reasonable doubt'; and in *R v Adey*, unreported (97/5306/W2), the Court of Appeal cautioned against any attempt at a more elaborate definition of 'being sure' or 'beyond reasonable doubt'. Also, in *R v Stephens* (2002) *The Times*, 27 June, the Court of Appeal said that it was unhelpful to seek to distinguish between being 'sure' and 'certain'. This advice is also backed by the Judicial Studies Board in their Specimen Directions, first published in 1991.

The higher standard of proof in criminal cases may explain why a defendant in a criminal case who is found not guilty can nevertheless be found liable in damages in a civil claim. There the standard of proof is lower – on the balance of probabilities (see below) – so that while a jury in a criminal trial say 'not guilty', a civil court can say 'guilty' on exactly the same evidence. However, it may be that the absence of the jury in civil cases, with the exception of libel, is as good an explanation. When someone is sued in a claim which suggests dishonesty or serious criminality, the civil standard, of proof is in reality little different from the criminal standard, the consequences of finding against the defendant being so serious as to require something close to the criminal standard. The real difference may be that the trial judge considers the evidence, unaffected by irrelevant issues which may have affected the lay jury.

Proof on the balance of probabilities

On those relatively rare occasions where the defence bear the legal burden on an issue, they must prove it on the balance of probabilities. Again, Lord Denning in *Miller v Minister of Pensions* [1947] 2 All ER 372 produced the best definition when he said that this standard is not as high as that required in criminal cases. 'If the evidence is such that the tribunal may say "we think it is more probable than not" the burden is discharged, but if the probabilities are equal it is not.' The Judicial Studies Board suggests the following direction to the jury:

> If the prosecution has not made you sure that the defendant has (set out what the prosecution must prove), that is an end of the matter and you must find the defendant 'Not Guilty'. However, if and only if, you are sure of those matters, you must consider whether the defendant [eg, had a reasonable excuse etc for doing what he did]. The law is that that is a matter for him to prove on all the evidence; but whenever the law requires a defendant to prove something, he does not have to make you sure of it. He has to show that it is probable, which means it is more likely than not, that [eg, he had reasonable excuse etc for doing it]. If you decide that probably he did [eg, have a reasonable excuse etc for doing it], you must find him 'Not Guilty'. If you decide that he did not, then providing that the prosecution has made you sure of what it has to prove, you must find him 'Guilty'.

The Judicial Studies Board also recommends that this direction is appropriate where the defence bear the 'legal' or 'persuasive' burden of proof, but not where the defence bear only an 'evidential' burden. For an example of the former, see *Lynch v DPP* [2002] 1 Crim App R 420. For examples of the latter, see *R v Lambert* [2002] AC 545 and *R v Carass* [2002] 2 Cr App R 77.

Tarnishing the 'golden thread' – exceptions to *Woolmington*

Despite the injunction of their Lordships in *Woolmington v DPP* [1935] AC 462, that no whittling down of the principle should be entertained, there has been a significant tarnishing of the golden thread. This has been brought about by an increasing number of express statutory provisions reversing the burden of proof or creating presumptions against the defence, a process which their Lordships accepted but could not have anticipated in such numbers. While one must accept that Parliament can reverse the burden of proof, it has not always expressed itself clearly, leaving it to the courts to determine what Parliament's intention is in relation to a particular statute or a section within a statute. The courts could have upheld the fundamental nature of the principle in *Woolmington* by refusing to accept any displacement of that principle without a clearly expressed statutory provision. However, the House of Lords in *R v Hunt* [1987] AC 352 accepted that the fundamental principle can be displaced by implication, as well as by an express statutory provision. The reversing of the burden of proof by statute, expressly or by implication, which inevitably leads to a tarnishing of the golden thread, will be considered below. First, though, the common law exceptions to the principle that the burden of proof is on the prosecution will be addressed.

Common law exceptions

During the eighteenth and nineteeth centuries, in trials on indictment (so called because each trial was preceded by the drawing up of an indictment containing a list of the offences charged and their details) in what are now Crown Courts, it was generally accepted that it was for the prosecution to prove guilt beyond reasonable doubt, but juries were often directed in different forms. For example Chitty's *Criminal Law*, published in 1816, stated that the direction ought to be that the jury should convict if guilt was proved (or clearly proved) to their (complete) satisfaction, or if they believed the prosecution witnesses. Despite this fairly clear statement that the burden of proof was on the prosecution, there was a growing body of opinion that the burden on the prosecution did not include a duty to disprove defences raised by the accused at trial. Text writers and judges often wrote and talked as if the burden of proving defences was on the accused. One defence upon which the accused undoubtedly did bear the persuasive burden of proof was insanity. The common law presumed a man to be sane, and if an accused relied upon insanity as a defence it was for him to produce evidence rebutting that presumption. This had been clear law since *Arnold's Case* (1724) 16 St Tr 694, at 764, and was confirmed by the decision in *M'Naghten's Case* (1840) 10 Cl & Fin 200, which remains the law on insanity in English criminal law. Numerous cases placed the persuasive burden of disproving defences on the accused in relation to defences such as duress or self-defence. In cases of murder, it was accepted that once the prosecution had proved that the accused killed the victim, the burden was then on him to prove that the case was not one of murder by proving that the killing was an accident or was in self-defence, or was manslaughter due to provocation or lack of an intent to kill. It follows that throughout the eighteenth and nineteenth centuries the rule that the prosecution bore the burden of proof referred only to the prosecution's duty to prove that the act alleged to be criminal had been committed by the accused – what today we would describe as the actus reus. The law on the mental element required to be proved in major crimes such as murder had yet to be clarified (in murder cases the law presumed malice from the fact of killing), but it is clear from the requirement that the accused prove that the killing was not murder, that the prosecution were not required to prove an intention to kill, rather it was for the accused to prove a lack of such an intention.

The defence of insanity nonetheless remains a common law exception to the principle that the prosecution have the legal burden of proof. There is a presumption of law that every person is sane until the contrary is proved, and it is for the defence to prove that the defendant is insane. The defence have the legal burden of proving, on the balance of probabilities, that the defendant is insane.

Express statutory reversal

With the exception of insanity (above), the 'golden thread' established in *Woolmington* remains intact at common law. However, constitutionally the courts must accept the will of Parliament; and in this context, if Parliament states a clear intention to place the burden of proof on the defence, the court must accept that and cannot overrule a statute. There is a variety of ways in which a statute may reverse the burden of proof. In most cases, the legislation will stipulate quite clearly that the defence must prove certain circumstances to be in existence in order to make use of an available defence. For example, s 139(4) of the

Criminal Justice Act 1988 provides a defence for an accused charged with possession of a bladed weapon in a public place, if he can establish some 'lawful authority or reasonable excuse' for being in possession of the offensive article.

There is generally less concern about the placing of burdens on the defendant when the offence is triable only summarily, where the offence is considered to be minor and punishable by a fine and no more than 12 months' imprisonment. It follows that Parliament is more ready to reverse the burden of proof in such cases (see 1 of the Prevention of Crime Act 1953; ss 139 and 141 of the Criminal Justice Act 1988; s 69 of the Criminal Justice and Public Order Act 1994; s 40 of the Health and Safety at Work Act 1974; and s 206(1) of the Insolvency Act 1986). Such offences are often regulatory offences dealing with matters of great importance to society, and the courts have had little difficulty in determining the reverse legal burden to be necessary, justifiable and proportionate in the circumstances (see, eg, *L v DPP* [2002] Crim LR 320; *R v Matthews*; *R v Alleyne* [2004] QB 69).

Another common device used by draftsmen who seek to place the burden of proof on the defence is to include a presumption of fact or law which the court must accept as proved unless the defence rebut that presumption. For example, where a person is driving a motor vehicle having consumed alcohol, the proportion of alcohol in his blood will depend on a number of factors, most importantly when he last consumed the alcohol. The body absorbs and destroys alcohol, and if a driver has recently consumed alcohol the amount in his blood will be rising as the body absorbs it. This can work in the driver's favour given that a sample taken immediately after consumption before the body has absorbed the alcohol may not show excess alcohol, though a later sample may do so. If he stops drinking, there will come a point when the body ceases to absorb the alcohol and starts to destroy it. Some drivers, when they fail a breath test and are required to provide a specimen of blood or urine seek until take advantage of this process by delaying the taking of a sample until a time when they believe their body is destroying the alcohol, hoping that by then the sample will show a legal amount of alcohol in the blood. Alternatively, the driver may claim that the sample taken an hour or more after he had ceased to drive, which shows an illegal amount of alcohol, did not reflect the lower, and legal, amount when he was driving. In order to counter these possibilities (and suggestions of post-offence consumption of alcohol), the statute provides for back-calculation to show the blood alcohol level at the time of the offence, rather than that shown some hours later when the sample was taken. Section 15(2) of the Road Traffic Offenders Act 1988, as amended by the Road Traffic Act 1991, provides:

> *Evidence of the proportion of alcohol or any drug in a specimen of breath, blood, or urine provided by the accused shall, in all cases ... be taken into account and ... it shall be assumed that the proportion of alcohol in the accused's breath, blood or urine at the time of the alleged offence was not less than the specimen.*

This section goes further than simply placing the legal burden of proof on the defendant. It is in effect an irrebuttable presumption (or assumption) that the proportion of alcohol in the defendant's blood at the time of the offence was not less than that shown in the specimen. The assumption will not be made if the accused's proves that he consumed alcohol before he provided the specimen and after he ceased to drive attempted to drive or was in charge of the vehicle (s 15(3)), but there is no opportunity to rebut the presumption by proving that the proportion of alcohol in the blood was less than that shown by the analysis.

The absence of such an opportunity to prove that the blood alcohol level at the time of the offence was in fact less than shown by the specimen was the subject of challenge under the Human Rights Act 1998 in *Parker v DPP* [2001] RTR 240. The defendant failed a roadside breath test and about one hour later provided a specimen of blood that exceeded the prescribed proportion of alcohol. He was convicted of driving with excess alcohol. He appealed against his conviction based on the assumption under s 15(2), arguing that the section was incompatible with Article 6(2) of the European Convention unless words were read into the section to the effect that the assumption would not be made 'unless proved to the contrary'. Dismissing the appeal, Lord Justice Waller stated that since it was consumption before driving at which the offence was aimed, it was not to rebut the presumption of innocence to assume that the quantity of alcohol shown in the breath test or blood specimen test carried out at the police station was the quantity which the motorist had in his blood at the time that he would be driving. Even if that were taking it too far, having regard to the importance of what is at stake, the assumption was a reasonable one and well within limits. The language of the section provided for an irrebuttable presumption. In his Lordship's view, there was no infringement of Convention rights by providing for such an irrebuttable presumption in the context of the legislation as a whole.

Similar facts were present in *Sheldrake v DPP* [2005] AC 246. Here, the defendant was found over the limit in his car in a public place, and later claimed he had been trying to get a lift from a friend. Section 5(2) of the 1988 Act affords a potential defence if it can proved that, at the time of the alleged offence, the circumstances were such that there was no likelihood of the motorist driving the vehicle while he remained above the prescribed limit. It was held that this placed the legal or persuasive burden of proof on the defendant. In this case, having failed to persuade the court on the balance of probabilities that there was no likelihood of him driving while over the limit, the defendant was convicted. The Divisional Court allowed the appellant's appeal by a majority of 2:1. Lord Justice Clarke argued that the prosecution had failed to show that it was necessary to impose a legal burden on the accused to show that there was no likelihood of his driving while over the limit. To do so would be disproportionate. Thus, s 5(2) of the 1988 Act should be read down under s 3 of the Human Rights Act 1998 so that it imposed only an evidential burden. The House of Lords, by a majority of 3:2, took a different view to that of the majority of the Divisional Court. Assuming that the section infringed the presumption of innocence and that it was directed to a legitimate object – the prevention of death, injury and damage caused by unfit drivers – Lord Bingham asked whether the provision met the test of acceptability identified in the Strasbourg jurisprudence (discussed at p 86 below). Accepting that it plainly did, he went on to say that he did 'not regard the burden placed on the defendant as beyond reasonable limits or in any way arbitrary'. He also concluded that it was not 'objectionable to criminalise a defendant's conduct in the circumstances without requiring a prosecutor to prove a criminal intent', on the basis that 'the defendant has a full opportunity to show that there was no likelihood of his driving, a matter so closely conditioned by his own knowledge and state of mind at the material time as to make it more appropriate for him to prove on the balance of probabilities that he would not have been likely to drive than for the prosecutor to prove, beyond reasonable doubt, that he would'. In their Lordships' opinion, the imposition of a legal burden did not go beyond what was necessary and it was not unfair to the defendant, given the legitimate object of the legislation of protecting society from the very real dangers of driving, or being likely to drive, with excess alcohol in the blood.

In *R v Drummond* [2002] RTR 21, it was held that s 15(3) of the Road Traffic Offenders Act 1988, which prevents the presumption in s 15(2) (considered above in *Parker*) from operating if the accused proves that he consumed alcohol before he gave the specimen and after he had ceased to drive, attempt to drive or was in charge of a motor vehicle, imposed a legal burden of proof on the accused. The court took the view that the legislative interference with the presumption of innocence was justified and was no greater than necessary to minimise the social evil of driving while over the legal limit.

Unfortunately, not all statutes are clearly expressed, and it may be unclear as to where the burden should fall. Some statutes contain provisions in which the burden of proof is clearly placed on the defendant, while other sections or subsections are silent as to which party bears the burden of proof. For example, *Polychronakis v Richards and Jerrom Ltd* [1998] Env LR 346, highlighted an apparent ambiguity in s 80(1) of the Environmental Protection Act 1990. The legislation contained two subsections which clearly imposed the legal burden of proving a specified defence on the accused; but a third subsection provided for a defence of reasonable excuse but did not specify whether the prosecution should the absence or the defence the presence of that excuse. In such circumstances, the court must interpret the statute or section and try to determine whether Parliament intended to place the legal burden of proof on the prosecution or the defendant.

Such interpretation will, since the Human Rights Act 1998, involve a consideration of whether the imposition of a reverse legal burden is justifiable and proportionate to the particular mischief with which the statute seeks to deal (see discussion at pp 77–83 below).

Implied statutory exceptions

One would expect that the displacement in a statute of the fundamental principle that it is for the prosecution to prove all aspects of the offence would be the subject of an express provision in any legislation. However, such displacement, together with the question whether the statutory defence required a mental element, was often not mentioned expressly, and it was left to the courts to interpret the intention of Parliament.

Summary offences

As Parliament grew in strength during the eighteenth and nineteenth centuries, it started creating statutory offences, many of which were comparatively minor and were triable by magistrates' courts. These became known as summary offences, being tried summarily without the need to draw up an indictment. In the middle of the nineteenth century Parliament sought to bring the trial of summary offences into line with the trial of indictable offences by passing the Summary Jurisdiction Act 1848. This Act required that where the defendant relied in his defence upon any exemption, proviso, excuse or qualification, then it was for him to prove that he came within the exception, etc. The 1848 Act has been re-enacted over the years and is now contained in s 101 of the Magistrates' Courts Act 1980 (see below). After the 1848 Act the common law and statute law proceeded on a parallel course, both modes of trial placing the burden on the defendant to prove any defence relied upon in the nature of an excuse, such as accident or self-defence in indictable offences, or that the defendant fell within any exception, exemption, etc, in relation to summary offences.

Section 101 of the Magistrates' Courts Act 1980 states:

> Where the defendant to an information or complaint relies for his defence on an exception, exemption, proviso, excuse or qualification whether or not it accompanies the description of the offence or matter of complaint in the enactment creating the offence or on which the complaint is founded, the burden of proving the exception, exemption, proviso, excuse or qualification shall be on him and this notwithstanding that the information or complaint contains an allegation negativing the exception, etc.

Section 101 applies only to magistrates' courts, that is to summary offences or either way offences which are tried summarily. There are numerous examples of statutes expressly worded so as to make an act an offence unless done by someone licensed or qualified to do the act, or if done without lawful authority or excuse. For example, driving a motor vehicle without being the holder of a licence to drive; keeping a vehicle without an excise licence; selling intoxicating liquor without a licence; possessing a firearm without a licence; possessing certain drugs without a doctor's certificate; delivering a child while not being a qualified midwife; practising medicine being unqualified, obstructing the highway without lawful authority or excuse; possessing forged currency without lawful authority or excuse, and many, many more. In *Gatland v Metropolitan Police Commissioner* [1968] 2 QB 279 and *Nimmo v Alexander Cowan Ltd* [1968] AC 107, it was held that the defendant in cases to which s 101 applies bears the legal or persuasive burden of proving that he comes within the exception, proviso, excuse or qualification upon which he relies, and not simply the burden of adducing evidence that he does so. Thus it is not sufficient to produce some evidence of a defence and, as in a defence like self-defence, leave it to the prosecution to rebut it; the defence must prove that they come within the exception, proviso, etc, though only on the balance of probabilities.

The court must analyse the statute to determine whether s 101 applies – the defence will frequently deny that it does and claim that the prosecution bear the entire legal burden. Section 101 distinguishes between 'the description of the offence' and 'any exception', etc. Any matter which is part of the description of the offence must be proved by the prosecution; it is only as to exceptions, proviso, excuse or qualification that the onus of proof is on the defendant. In *Woolmington v DPP* [1935] AC 462 the House of Lords expressed the fundamental principle as applying 'No matter what the charge or where the trial'. However, Parliament is supreme and so the fundamental principle must give way to an express statutory provision. Section 101 is such a provision and, as indicated above, there are numerous express statutory provisions which place the burden of proving a defence to a summary offence on the defence.

While there is no doubt that these provisions are also a significant whittling down of the fundamental principle, it is unlikely that they will be found to be in breach of Article 6(2) of the European Convention on Human Rights. In *Salabiaku v France* (1991) 13 EHRR

379 (see p 76 below), the European Court of Human Rights accepted that all the Convention States make use of reverse burdens and presumptions, but required States to confine them within reasonable limits which take into account the importance of what is at stake and maintain the rights of the defence. Given that a summary offence is punishable by a fine or a sentence of imprisonment not exceeding 12 months, it is not seen as serious. In addition, many are regulatory offences passed for the protection of society, which makes it easier to justify the reverse burden (see the case of *Parker* and the breath test assumption, at p 71 above).

Indictable offences

Section 101 of the Magistrates' Courts Act 1980 applies only to summary proceedings, but in *R v Edwards* [1975] QB 27 the Court of Appeal enunciated an almost identical principle which applies to trial on indictment. *Edwards* interpreted the forerunner to s 101 as an expression of common law rule. This was deduced from the fact that the origins of the provision are to be found in s 14 of the Summary Jurisdiction Act 1848, which stated that 'it shall not be necessary for the Prosecutor or Complainant in that behalf to prove a Negative, but the Defendant may prove the Affirmative thereof in his Defence, if he would have Advantage of the Same'. In passing this legislation Parliament was doing no more than putting into statutory form the common law rule which then applied and which, as we have seen, was applied by the court of trial and the Court of Appeal in *Woolmington v DPP* (though later overruled by the House of Lords). Since a majority of offences, even in 1974, when *Edwards* was decided, were statutory, the Court of Appeal saw no reason why the statutory rule in what is now s 101 of the Magistrates' Court Act 1980, which expresses the common law rule (at least before the decision of the House of Lords in *Woolmington*), should not be applied by the common law so that statutory offences tried on indictment would be dealt with exactly as statutory offences tried summarily. After all, there was no reason why an either way offence should be tried according to different rules depending on whether it was tried summarily or on indictment.

In *Edwards*, the defendant was convicted under s 160 of the Licensing Act 1964 of selling alcohol without a justices' licence (now a summary offence but then triable on indictment). The prosecution called no evidence that the appellant did not hold a justices' licence, leaving him to show, if he could, that he did possess one. The conviction was upheld by the Divisional Court and by the Court of Appeal. Giving judgment in the Court of Appeal, Lawton LJ said: 'It is limited to offences arising under enactments which prohibit the doing of an act save in specified circumstances or by persons of specified classes or with specified qualifications or with the licence or permission of specified authorities.' In this case it would have been just as easy for the defendant to produce evidence of the possession of a licence, if he had one, as for the prosecution to prove he did not have one. Such records are kept by clerks to the justices and are easily available to either party. However, the decision in *Edwards* is not limited to cases when the defendant has peculiar knowledge, or where one party can more easily prove the particular defence. Instead it is based on the linguistic structure of the statute, so that whenever the statute is expressed to prohibit certain acts subject to provisos, exemptions and the like, the defendant bears the legal burden of proving that proviso, exemption, etc. It follows from this that the Court of Appeal confined the decision of the House of Lords in *Woolmington* to common law offences, such as murder, and statutory offences which are not framed to prohibit the doing of acts subject to a proviso or exemption, etc. Those statutory offences which are framed to prohibit the doing of acts subject to a proviso or exemption are placed outside the fundamental principle expressed in that case.

The decision in *R v Edwards* received qualified approval by the House of Lords in *R v Hunt* [1987] AC 352. As we have seen, the decision in *Edwards* was limited to certain issues. The House of Lords in *R v Hunt* said that Lawson LJ's statement was better regarded as a guide to construction of the statute than as an exception to the rule that the prosecution bear the burden of proof. Their Lordships stated that the question whether the defendant bears a legal burden of proof is not always to be determined by the wording of the particular statute. The words 'any statutory exception' in *Woolmington* (see p 63 above) were not confined to statutory exceptions in which the burden of proof was expressly placed on the defendant. A statute can do so expressly or impliedly, that is on its true construction. Therefore, when the statute was not clear it was a matter of construction in which a number of considerations applied. Hunt was charged with possession of a controlled drug, morphine, contrary to s 5(2) of the Misuse of Drugs Act 1971. A search of his house revealed a fold of paper containing morphine, a controlled drug, mixed with caffeine and atropine which are not controlled drugs. The prosecution called no evidence as to the proportion of morphine in the mixture. The defence submitted that there was no case to answer because Sch 1 to the Misuse of Drugs Regulations 1973 (SI 1973/797), as amended by the Misuse of Drugs (Amendment) Regulations 1983 (SI 1983/788), provided that a preparation containing not more than 0.2% morphine which was not readily recoverable was not within s 5. Since the prosecution had failed to prove that the amount of morphine in the mixture exceeded 0.2%, there was no evidence that the mixture was a controlled drug within s 5. The trial judge rejected the submission, and the Court of Appeal upheld this ruling on the ground that the defendant bore the burden of proving that the mixture fell within the exception provided by Sch 1 to the 1973 Regulations. The House of Lords overturned this decision, holding that the prosecution bore the burden of proving that the mixture did not come within the exception. Properly analysed the offence consisted not of being in possession of morphine, but of being in possession of morphine other than a preparation as specified in Sch 1 to the 1973 Regulations. The percentage of morphine was part of the description of the offence, not an exception to it. It followed that the prosecution had to prove that the morphine was in the prohibited form, ie more than 0.2%.

It is arguable that the courts applying the common law significantly failed to protect their own fundamental principle by allowing its displacement by implication, rather than insisting on an express provision as the House of Lords did in *Hunt*. Insisting on an express provision would have had the effect of placing the responsibility for undermining such a fundamental right of its citizens squarely on Parliament, which would then have to give reasons for imposing a reverse burden of proof in particular statutes. Instead the courts conspired, wittingly or unwittingly, in the undermining of fundamental rights, using the smoke screen of an unspoken intention of Parliament to justify it. This led to a loss of respect in the legislature for the fundamental principle, and meant that a potential buffer between the practical power of the state and the comparative weakness of the individual was considerably diminished.

Today the decisions themselves are of less practical importance for three major reasons:

(a) As was emphasised by Lord Griffiths in *Hunt*, 'the principle is limited .... I have little doubt that the occasions on which the statute will be construed as imposing a burden of proof on a defendant which do not fit within this formulation are likely to be exceedingly rare'.

(b) Over the years such offences as described which are triable on indictment have become rarer, if not extinct. Almost all statutory offences which are comparatively minor offences and contain an exception, exemption, proviso or qualification, are now triable only in magistrates' courts to which s 101 of the Magistrates' Courts Act 1980 applies. See, for example, *Edwards*, a liquor licensing case, which today is exclusively in the jurisdiction of magistrates.

(c) The attitude of the courts has also changed since the coming into force of the Human Rights Act 1998, which is discussed in some depth below. If there is a serious indictable offence which prohibits the doing of an act in specified circumstances, or except by persons of specified classes or without specified qualifications, or without the licence or permission of specified authorities, which does not expressly state which party has the legal burden of proving that the defendant fits within the circumstances or is of the specified class, etc, it is highly unlikely that a court would imply a reverse legal burden on the accused in the light of Article 6(2) of the European Convention on Human Rights, the Terrorism Act 2000 (see p 78 below), *Lambert* (see p 80 below) and the other decisions discussed above. It is far more likely that the courts will interpret the relevant provision as imposing the burden of proof on the prosecution, or only an evidential burden on the accused.

It follows that the above cases should be seen as being of historical interest only.

The European Court of Human Rights and the presumption of innocence

Article 6(2) of the Convention

As indicated at p 63 above, Article 6(2) of the European Convention on Human Rights protects the right to be presumed innocent until proven guilty, and in doing so enshrines the fundamental principle of criminal law enunciated in *Woolmington v DPP*. To date there have been few cases in which the European Court or Commission has considered the principle, but one such is *X v United Kingdom*, Application No 5124/71 (1972). There the Commission upheld the presumption contained in s 30(2) of the Sexual Offences Act 1956, under which a man who lives habitually with a prostitute, or who exercises control or influence over her movements in a way which shows he is aiding and abetting or compelling her prostitution, shall be presumed to be knowingly living on the earnings of prostitution, unless he proves to the contrary. The Commission held that such a presumption does not violate Article 6(2) provided it is rebuttable and reasonable. But if such a provision was widely or unreasonably worded, it could have the same effect as a presumption of guilt and would violate Article 6(2). Alternatively, the presumption related to matters which were peculiarly within the knowledge of the defendant.

In *Salabiaku v France* (1991) 13 EHRR 379, the European Court of Human Rights upheld a provision of the French Criminal Code which placed the burden of proof squarely on the defendant. The Court said (at para 28) that:

> *Presumptions of fact or law operate in every legal system. Clearly the Convention does not prohibit such presumptions in principle. It does, however, require the Contracting State to remain within certain limits in this respect as regards criminal law .... Article 6(2) does not, therefore, regard presumptions of law or fact with indifference. It requires States to confine them within the reasonable limits which take into account the importance of what is at stake and maintains the rights of the defence.*

The guidance in *Salabiaku* was applied by the Commission in *H v United Kingdom*, Application No 15023/89, 4 April 1990, in rejecting the complaint that the burden on the accused in criminal proceedings to prove insanity on the balance of probabilities was contrary to the presumption of innocence and in violation of Article 6. (See also *Bates v United Kingdom*, Application No 26280/95, 16 January 1996.)

The impact of the Human Rights Act 1998

The Prevention of Terrorism (Temporary Provisions) Act 1989

The Human Rights Act 1998 already had an impact in the area under discussion even before it came into force in October 2000. Sections 16A and 16B of the Prevention of Terrorism (Temporary Provisions) Act 1989 had created the offence of possession of articles for the purposes of terrorism and the offence of collecting or recording information for such a purpose. These provisions clearly and unequivocally placed the burden of proof on the defendant. Section 16A stipulated that the accused would have to prove that the possession of the articles was not for the purposes of terrorism, or else that that he was not in possession of those articles; and similarly, in relation to the offence under s 16B, the defendant had to prove that he had a reasonable excuse for collecting or recording the information.

In *R v DPP, ex p Kebilene and others* [2000] AC 326, three Algerians were prosecuted for offences under ss 16A and 16B of the 1989 Act. At the close of the prosecution case the defence obtained a ruling that the sections were incompatible with Article 6(2) of the European Convention on Human Rights. The Director of Public Prosecutions, whose consent was required before a prosecution could be undertaken, appeared before the trial judge to argue that the judge's ruling was wrong. The trial judge maintained his position and the case went to the Divisional Court, which agreed with the trial judge. At the time the Human Rights Act 1998 was not in force, having been delayed until October 2000, but the Divisional Court, having decided that the sections undermined the presumption of innocence protected by Article 6(2) in a blatant and obvious way, pointed out that the prosecution would be a waste of time and money since the defendants would, if convicted, appeal; and if by the time of the appeal the 1998 Act was in force, they would rely on ss 7(1)(b) and 22(4) and their appeal would be allowed. If the 1998 Act was not in force at the time of appeal, the case would be taken to the European Court of Human Rights in Strasbourg with the same result, at much cost to the public purse. The Divisional Court held that the Director of Public Prosecutions had acted unlawfully and granted a declaration to this effect.

The Director of Public Prosecutions appealed to the House of Lords and their Lordships held that the courts had no power to review a decision of the Director of Public Prosecutions. That was sufficient to dispose of the appeal and a majority expressed no concluded views on the compatibility of the sections with Article 6(2), though some considered the issue arguable. Lord Hobhouse pointed out that presumptions and reverse burdens were not uncommon, nor were they confined to the United Kingdom, and were not necessarily incompatible with the Convention. Lord Hope adopted the suggestion of Counsel for the Director of Public Prosecutions that three questions should be considered in determining whether a reverse burden strikes a balance between the rights of the individual and those of the State (as will be seen, these questions have been applied in later cases):

(a) What does the prosecution have to prove in order to transfer the onus to the defence?

(b) What is the burden of the accused – does it relate to something which is likely to be difficult for him to prove, or does it relate to something which is likely to be within his knowledge or to which he readily has access?

(c) What is the nature of the threat faced by society which the provision is designed to combat?

Lord Hope believed that no concluded view as to whether the provisions in ss 16A and 16B were compatible with Article 6(2) was possible until the trial had been concluded, but in suggesting that the matter was open to argument he appeared to disagree with the Divisional Court's view that they were incompatible. However, a majority suggested that once the 1998 Act was in force, reverse legal burdens might have to be interpreted as imposing merely an evidential burden on the accused. The prosecution proceeded, but was abandoned after a witness, said to be an agent working for MI5, refused to give evidence because he feared for his life. Unfortunately the sections therefore remained untested.

The Terrorism Act 2000

In 2000, Parliament decided to repeal the Prevention of Terrorism (Temporary Provisions) Act 1989, which required annual renewal by Parliament, and to replace it with a permanent statute. Parliament responded to the comments in *Kebilene* (above) by re-enacting ss 16A and 16B of the 1989 Act as ss 57 and 58 of the Terrorism Act 2000, but added s 118, which converts what were reverse legal burdens into evidential burdens. Section 58 makes it an offence, punishable to the same extent as s 57, to collect or make a record of information likely to be useful to a person committing or preparing an act of terrorism, or to possess a document or record containing information of that kind. Section 58(3) also provides that it is a defence for a person charged with an offence under this section to prove that he had a reasonable excuse for his action or possession. Sections 12(4), 39(5)(a), 54, 77 and 103 also contain provisions making it a defence for the accused to prove certain facts or for presumptions to be made. For example, the court may assume that the accused possessed the article, unless he proves that he did not know of its presence on the premises or that he had no control over it. At first sight it appeared that the Government was ignoring the opinion of the various judges in *Kebilene*. However, s 118 contains provisions which make it clear that the Government has listened to the court and other critics of the earlier provisions.

In the absence of s 118, the accused charged with an offence under this Act would bear the legal or persuasive burden. That would mean that the matter in question must be taken as proved against the accused unless he satisfies the court or jury, on the balance of probabilities, to the contrary. However, the provisions make it clear that the defendant charged with offences under the relevant sections bears only an evidential burden. This means that the matter must be taken as proved against the accused unless the accused adduces sufficient evidence to raise an issue on the matter; but that if sufficient evidence to raise the issue is adduced by the accused, then the prosecution have the burden of satisfying the court or jury as to the matter beyond reasonable doubt (see the rule as to evidential burdens stated in *R v Gill* (1963) 47 Cr App R 166, 172, set out at p 64 above). In addition, the phrase 'a live issue' or, as in s 118(2) and (4), 'an issue' means that it is not enough merely to allege the fact in question; the accused must raise sufficient evidence to make it an issue which can be put to the court or jury. In jury trials it is for the judge to determine whether the accused has adduced sufficient evidence of the matter to make it an issue which the jury must determine. If he decides the accused has done so, he will direct the jury to determine whether, in the light of that evidence, the prosecution have disproved that evidence beyond reasonable doubt. If he decides there is insufficient evidence to raise the issue, he will direct the jury to consider the matter proved in accordance with the provisions of the particular section.

There may also be other opportunities for challenge to the above provisions. A close look at, for example, s 57, shows that the legal or persuasive burden on the prosecution has been made lighter by the fact that there need only be reasonable suspicion that the article is possessed for the purposes of terrorism. 'Reasonable suspicion' is normally sufficient to ground an arrest, but not proof that an offence has been committed. The need to prove possession arises only if the accused adduces evidence that the article, though in his possession, was not possessed for the purposes of terrorism. Only then need the prosecution prove beyond reasonable doubt that it was possessed for that purpose. Similarly, where the article is on the premises occupied or habitually used by the accused, otherwise than as a member of the public, possession is assumed unless the accused adduces evidence that he did not know of its presence, or, if he did, that he had no control over it. Only if such evidence is adduced are the prosecution required to prove that he did know of it, or had control over it. It follows that if the accused decides not to give evidence, he might be convicted by virtue of presumptions against him and on reasonable suspicion falling short of proof, one of the reasons why the Divisional Court in *Kebilene* believed the predecessor of s 57 was in breach of the European Convention on Human Rights. The Criminal Law Revision Committee, Eleventh Report, *Evidence (General)* (Cmnd 4991, 1971), recommended that whenever statute placed a burden on the accused, it should be treated as an evidential rather than a persuasive burden. Section 118 of the Terrorism Act 2000 does this and is to be welcomed. Almost certainly the relevant sections of the Terrorism Act 2000 which reverse the burden of proof, or provide for assumptions against the accused, would have been challenged under the Human Rights Act 1998 and would, given the seriousness of the offences, probably have been found to be in breach of Article 6(2) of the European Convention on Human Rights. By providing for evidential burdens only, s 118 precludes any such challenge.

It should not, however, be assumed that a serious offence cannot be the subject of a reverse legal burden and therefore compatible with Article 6(2). For example, not all reverse legal burdens in the Terrorism Act 2000 are covered by s 118. This suggests that in relation to those sections which imposed a reverse burden of proof on the defendant and which are not mentioned in s 118, Parliament had considered the matter and intended to place a reverse burden on the defendant. Traditionally that would have meant that the courts were bound by such an intention (*Attorney-General's Reference (No 4 of 2002)* [2003] 3 WLR 1153). However, in *Attorney-General's Reference (No 4 of 2002); Sheldrake v DPP (Conjoined Appeals)* [2005] 1 AC 264, the House of Lords held that s 11(2) of the Terrorism Act 2000 did not impose a reverse burden of proof on the defence and did not infringe the presumption of innocence so as to breach Article 6(2) of the Convention:

> The task of the court is never to decide whether a reverse burden should be imposed on a defendant, but always to assess whether a burden enacted by Parliament unjustifiably infringes the presumption of innocence. It may nonetheless be questioned whether … 'the assumption should be that Parliament would not have made an exception without good reason'. Such an approach may lead the court to give too much weight to the enactment under review and too little to the presumption of innocence and the obligation imposed on it by s 3 [of the Human Rights Act 1999].
> (*per* Lord Bingham, at para 31)

This statement underlines the impact of the Human Rights Act 1998 in altering the orthodox role of the courts in statutory interpretation: the express intention of Parliament to impose a reverse burden is no longer conclusive; it must be shown that a reverse onus is both necessary and proportionate in relation to the particular statute.

The Misuse of Drugs Act 1971/the Homicide Act 1957

In *R v Lambert, Ali and Jordan* [2001] 1 All ER 1014, the first appellant, Lambert, had been convicted of possession of a class A drug with intent to supply contrary to s 5 of the Misuse of Drugs Act 1971. The section makes it clear that is for the accused to prove, inter alia, that he neither knew nor suspected the existence of some fact alleged by the prosecution if he is to be acquitted of the offence charged. Ali and Jordan had both been convicted of murder, but had pleaded the defence of diminished responsibility under s 2 of the Homicide Act 1957.

Both these defences were subject to an appeal based on the argument that both sections were in breach of Article 6 of the European Convention on Human Rights. The appeals anticipated that the Human Rights Act 1998 was in force, but in each case the Court of Appeal dismissed the appeal holding that neither section breached Article 6.

So far as the defence of diminished responsibility was concerned, the Court had no difficulty in finding no breach of Article 6. The fact that there was no power to examine a defendant, and that an uncooperative defendant could make it very difficult for the prosecution to prove a negative, was important, as was the fact that the prosecution were required to prove all the ingredients of the offence. Section 2 of the Homicide Act 1957 was of benefit to defendants who were in a position to take advantage of it. It did not matter whether it was treated as creating a defence to a charge of murder or an exception, or as dealing with the capacity to commit the act of murder – s 2 did not contravene Article 6.

Lambert, who was found in possession of a controlled drug, argued that he did not know the bag he carried contained such drugs. However, s 28(3) of the Misuse of Drugs Act 1971 provides that the accused:

(a) shall not be acquitted of the offence charged by reason only of proving that he neither knew or suspected nor had reason to suspect that the substance or product in question was the particular controlled drug alleged; but

(b) shall be acquitted … if he proves that he neither believed nor suspected nor had reason to suspect that the substance or product in question was a controlled drug…

In relation to s 28, the Court emphasised the fact that for the defendant to be guilty of possession of drugs, the prosecution must prove an identifiable actus reus and mens rea. However, it was not necessary to prove that the defendant knew that the box contained drugs, only that he knew it contained something which proved to be drugs. This was a deliberate policy of Parliament. The Court regarded the substance of the offence as being reflected in the language of the sections. Sections 5(4) and 28 did not impose additional ingredients which had to be proved to complete the offence, but provided a way of avoiding liability for what would otherwise be an offence. It was commonplace for the defendant to seek to avoid his guilt by saying he thought he had pornography or gold and not drugs in the box, and such a defence was difficult to rebut. What the offence did was to make the defendant responsible for making sure he did not take into his possession containers which in fact contained drugs. In addition, the Court held that there was a clear social objective in discouraging trading in drugs and that the level of sentence would reflect the extent to which the defendant was responsible for the drugs in his possession. It did not consider that the chosen course of the legislator contravened Article 6. In the opinion of the Court, there was an objective justification for the choice in the case of drugs, and it was not disproportionate. This part of the decision, in respect of the defendant Lambert and s 28 of the Misuse of Drugs Act 1971, went to the House of Lords (*R v Lambert* [2002] AC 545).

By a majority of 4:1 (Lord Hutton dissenting), their Lordships dismissed Lambert's appeal based on the contention that s 28 was in contravention of Article 6 of the Convention, on the somewhat technical ground that the Human Rights Act 1998 could not be applied retrospectively, ie to take into account alleged breaches of the Convention before the Act came into force. However, in respect of s 28 itself, their Lordships accepted that the prosecution had only to prove that the accused had a bag with something in it in his custody and control, and that the something in it was a controlled drug. It was not necessary for the prosecution to prove that the accused had known that the thing was a controlled drug, let alone a particular controlled drug (see *R v McNamara* (1988) 87 Cr App R 246). The accused might then seek to establish one of the defences in s 5(4) or s 28.

Lord Steyn, giving judgment for the majority stated: 'It follows that legislative interference with the presumption of innocence requires justification and must not be greater than necessary. The principle of proportionality must be observed.' Whilst accepting that there was an objective basis for the justification, he went on to stress that any such justification must be proportionate. The burden, he noted, was on the state to show that the legislative means were not greater than necessary. Where there is an objective justification for some inroad into the presumption of innocence, the legislatures had to choose whether it was more appropriate to impose a legal burden or an evidential burden on the accused. A transfer of a legal burden amounted to a far more drastic interference with the presumption of innocence than the creation of an evidential burden on the accused, and necessarily involved the risk that the jury might convict where the accused had not dis-charged the legal burden resting on him but left them unsure on the point. Such a risk was not present if only an evidential burden was created.

In respect of s 28, his Lordship observed that the prosecution must establish that the pro-hibited drugs were in the possession of the defendant, and that he knew the package contained something. The accused must then prove, on a balance of probabilities, that he did not know the package contained controlled drugs. If the jury was in doubt on this issue, they must convict him. This might occur when the accused adduced sufficient evi-dence to raise a doubt about his guilt but the jury was not convinced on a balance of probabilities that his account was true. Indeed it obliged the court to convict if the version of the accused was as likely to be true as not. This is a far-reaching consequence: a guilty verdict may be returned in respect of an offence punishable by life imprisonment even though the jury might consider that it is reasonably possible that the accused has been duped. It would be unprincipled to brush aside such possibilities as unlikely to happen in practice. Moreover, there may be real difficulties in determining the real facts upon which the sentencer must act in such cases. In any event, the burden of showing that only a reverse legal burden can overcome the difficulties of the prosecution in drugs cases is a heavy one. Lord Steyn pointed out that some of the difficulties faced by the prosecution are already dealt with by the practicalities of procedure and the rules of evidence. Thus the relevant facts are peculiarly within the knowledge of the possessor of the container, and that presumptively suggests, in the absence of evidence to the contrary, that the person in possession knew what was in the container. This would be a complete answer to a submis-sion of no case to answer. It would also be a factor which the trial judge would put before the jury. After all, it is common sense that possession of a package containing drugs demands a full and adequate explanation.

Lord Steyn concluded that he was satisfied that the transfer of the legal burden in s 28 did not satisfy the criterion of proportionality and that in the current legal system s 28 was a disproportionate reaction to difficulties faced by the prosecution in drug cases. It was therefore sufficient to impose an evidential burden on the accused, and it followed that s 28 should be 'read down' in a way which is compatible with Convention rights by reading the words 'prove' and 'proves' as meaning giving sufficient evidence. Reading these words in such a way had the effect of imposing only an evidential burden on the accused.

The Insolvency Act 1986

The decision in *Lambert* was applied in *R v Carass* [2002] Crim LR 316. The defendant was charged with concealing debts in anticipation of a winding up, contrary to s 206(1)(a) of the Insolvency Act 1986. Section 206(4) provides that it is a defence for the accused to prove that he had no intent to defraud. On an interlocutory appeal under s 9 of the Criminal Justice Act 1987 against a finding by the trial judge that s 206(4) of the 1986 Act imposed a legal burden of proof on the accused, the Court of Appeal, Criminal Division, held that the word 'prove' in s 206(4) must be read as 'adduce sufficient evidence', impos-ing an evidential rather than a persuasive burden. Lord Justice Waller, giving the judgment of the court, stated that if a reverse legal burden of proof was to be imposed on an accused, it had to be justified and it had to be demonstrated why a legal or persuasive burden, rather than an evidential burden, was necessary. Their Lordships did not believe that a legal burden was justifiable or necessary. Common sense dictated that if conceal-ment of the debt was proved, the evidential burden itself would be quite difficult for the defendant to satisfy. Even the accused he did satisfy it, it would be less than satisfactory if he could still be convicted if the jury were not sure that he had intended to defraud. Nothing their Lordships had seen demonstrated a justification for that being a possible result in some cases brought under s 206 because of some 'threat faced by society' (*R v DPP, ex p Kebilene* [2000] 2 AC 326, 386). Their Lordships therefore declared that the judge was wrong in so far as he felt obliged to direct the jury that s 206(4) imposed a legal burden on the defendant. The burden was evidential only, and it was appropriate to read the word 'prove' in s 206(4) as 'adduce sufficient evidence'.

Conclusion

These decisions clearly indicate that, at least in relation to most serious offences, statutory reversals of the burden of proof will, if challenged under the 1998 Act, be interpreted as imposing only an evidential burden on the accused. It will be recalled (see p 78 above) that s 118 of the Terrorism Act 2000 makes almost all reversals of the burden of proof within that Act evidential burdens. This Act, together with the decisions in *Lambert* and *Carass*, suggests that Parliament and the courts accept that placing the legal burden of proof on the accused can rarely be justified under the European Convention on Human Rights. There are few more serious offences than those contained in the Terrorism Act, and few offences which are so serious a threat to society as the abuse of drugs; and if these offences do not justify the imposition of a legal burden of proof on the accused, it seems difficult to argue that a legal or persuasive burden of proof can be justified in relation to lesser offences. There may, however, be a difference of approach in relation to offences which, though seri-ous in their effect on society and in terms of the punishment imposed on conviction, are essentially regulatory and are not seen as truly criminal (see *R v S (Trademark defence)* [2003] 1 Cr App R 602 and *Davies v HSE* (2002) *The Times*, 27 December).

In *R v Johnstone* [2003] 1 WLR 1736, the House of Lords took the opportunity of clarifying the law on the burden of proof. Johnstone was convicted of an offence under s 92(1)(b) of the Copyright Act 1994 by infringing the copyright on CDs by Bon Jovi and others which he had copied. He had sought to rely, inter alia, on a defence provided in s 92(5), which stipu-lates that 'it is a defence for a person charged with an offence under this section to show that he believed on reasonable grounds that the use of the sign in the manner in which it was used, or was to be used, was not an infringement of the registered trademark'. The defen-dant's appeal was allowed by the Court of Appeal on other grounds, although the Court had read s 92(5) as imposing no more than an evidential burden on the defendant, and on this point (which was not in the end determinative of the appeal) the House of Lords disagreed.

Lord Nicholls, giving judgment with which the majority agreed, came to the conclusion that s 92(5) imposed a legal burden on the accused. The court took a variety of factors into account in reaching this decision:

> *A sound starting point is to remember that if an accused is required to prove a fact on the balance of probabilities to avoid conviction, this permits a conviction in spite of the fact-finding tribunal having a reasonable doubt as to the guilt of the accused ... This consequence of a reverse burden of proof should colour one's approach when*

evaluating the reasons why it is said that, in the absence of a persuasive burden on the accused, the public interest will be prejudiced to an extent which justifies placing a persuasive burden on the accused. The more serious the punishment which may flow from conviction, the more compelling must be the reasons. The extent and nature of the factual matters required to be proved by the accused, and their importance relative to the matters required to be proved by the prosecution, have to be taken into account. So also does the extent to which the burden on the accused relates to facts which, if they exist, are readily provable by him as matters within his own knowledge or to which he has ready access. In evaluating these factors the court's role is one of review. Parliament, not the court, is charged with the primary responsibility for deciding, as a matter of policy, what should be the constituent elements of a criminal offence.

In the instant case, his Lordship found a number of compelling reasons why the burden should be legal rather than evidential in nature, including the urgent international pressure to restrain fraudulent trading in counterfeit goods; the framing of offences against s 92 as offences of 'near absolute liability'; and the dependence of the s 92(5) defence on facts within the defendant's own knowledge. There were, in particular, clear policy reasons for imposing the burden on the accused, including that fewer investigations and prosecutions into counterfeit goods would occur where the burden of proving dishonesty fell upon the prosecution.

General guidance in determining a whether reverse legal burden is justified

It was recognised in *Attorney-General's Reference (No 1 of 2004)* [2004] 1 WLR 2111 that there appeared to be a significant difference in emphasis between the approach of Lord Steyn in *Lambert* and that of Lord Nicholls in *Johnstone*. Evidently, the former had a much more robust approach to the question of compatibility, which, if followed, would mean that a great number of legal burdens should be in future be read down so as to constitute an evidential burden only. In expressing a clear preference for the approach of Lord Nicholls, the Lord Chief Justice noted that his approach was considerably more flexible and reflective of the intention behind the Human Rights Act 1998, which aimed to strike a balance between the role of Parliament and that of the courts. It was also later in time and, unlike Lord Steyn's speech, was endorsed by all the other members of the House. Thus the decision in *Carass* was impliedly overruled.

In relation to each reverse burden it was necessary to consider, first, whether it contravened Article 6(2) of the European Convention on Human Rights. If so, it then needed to be considered whether it was possible to interpret the legislation in a way that made it compatible with Article 6, including, if that were possible, reading down the legislation under s 3 of the Human Rights Act 1998. In practice, that would usually involve determining:

(a) whether the particular provision placed an evidential or a legal burden on the defendant;

(b) if it did impose a legal burden, deciding whether the legal burden could be justified; and

(c) if it could not be justified, whether it could be read down so that it was an evidential burden.

The following guidance was intended to be of a general nature and would need to be applied lightly: the Court recognised that it might not be appropriate in all situations:

(a) Courts should strongly discourage the citation of authority to them other than Johnstone's case and this guidance. *Johnstone* was at present the latest word on the subject.

(b) The common law and the language of Article 6(2) had the same effect. Both permitted legal reverse burdens of proof or presumptions in the appropriate circumstances.

(c) Reverse legal burdens were probably justified if the overall burden of proof was on the prosecution, ie the prosecution had to prove the essential ingredients of the offence, but there was a situation where there were significant reasons why it was fair and reasonable to deny the accused the general protection normally guaranteed by the presumption of innocence.

(d) Where the exception went no further than was reasonably necessary to achieve the objective of the reverse burden (ie, it was proportionate), it was sufficient if the exception was reasonably necessary in all the circumstances. The assumption should be that Parliament would not have made an exception without good reason. While the judge must make his own decision as to whether there was a contravention of Article 6, the task of a judge was to review Parliament's approach, as Lord Nicholls had indicated in *Johnstone*.

(e) If only an evidential burden was placed on the defendant there would be no risk of contravention of Article 6(2).

(f) When ascertaining whether an exception was justified, the courts must construe the provision to ascertain what would be the realistic effects of the reverse burden. In doing that, the courts should be more concerned with substance than form. If the proper interpretation was that the statutory provision created an offence plus an exception, that would in itself be a strong indication that there was no contravention of Article 6(2).

(g) The easier it was for the accused to discharge the burden, the more likely it was that the reverse burden was justified. That would be the case where the facts were within the defendant's own knowledge. How difficult it would be for the prosecution to establish the facts was also indicative of whether a reverse legal burden was justified.

(h) The ultimate question was: would the exception prevent a fair trial? If it would, it must either be read down, if that was possible, or it should be declared incompatible.

(i) Caution must be exercised when considering the seriousness of the offence and the power of punishment. The need for a reverse burden was not necessarily reflected by the gravity of the offence; though from a defendant's point of view the more serious the offence, the more important it was that there was no interference with the presumption of innocence.

(j) If guidance was needed as to the approach of the European Court of Human Rights, that was provided by *Salabiaku v France* (1991) 13 EHRR 379, para 28: 'Article 6(2) does not regard presumptions of fact or of law with indifference. It requires states to confine them within reasonable limits which takes into account the importance of what is at stake and maintains the rights of the defence.'

As the law stood in the light of the decisions in *Johnstone* and *A-G's Reference (No 1 of 2004)*, it was considerably easier to persuade the court that Parliament knew what it was doing in enacting a reversal of the burden of proof and that imposing a reverse legal burden was necessary, reasonable and proportionate in the particular circumstances. However, the decision of the House of Lords in *Attorney-General's Reference (No 4 of 2002); Sheldrake v DPP (Conjoined Appeals)* [2005] 1 AC 264 has further modified the position. Lord Bingham of Cornhill (at para 30) made it clear that both *Lambert* and *Johnstone* were recent decisions of the House of Lords, binding on all lower courts for what they decided:

> *Nothing said in* R v Johnstone *suggests an intention to depart from or modify the earlier decision, which should not be treated as superseded or implicitly overruled. Differences of emphasis ... were explicable by the difference in the subject matter of the two cases. Section 5 of the Misuse of Drugs Act 1971 and s 92 of the Trade Marks Act 1994 were directed to serious social and economic problems. But the justifiability and fairness of the respective exoneration provisions had to be judged in the particular context of each case.*

In light of this, the guidelines laid down in *Attorney-General's Reference (No 1 of 2004)* were modified. *Lambert* or *Johnstone* can now be cited according to the particular context in which the provision under consideration operates. *Johnstone* is the latest word on economic offences which, though serious, may not be considered 'truly criminal'; *Lambert* is the latest word on 'truly criminal offences', and the court agreed with Lord Bingham's comments in *Attorney-General's Reference (No 1 of 2004)* that *Carass* had been wrongly decided. The assumption contained in guideline (d) above, that Parliament would not have made an exception without good reason, was also erroneous, since it might lead a court to give too much weight to the enactment under review and too little to the presumption of innocence and the obligation imposed on it by s 3 of the Human Rights Act 1998.

The combined effect of the Terrorism Act 2000 Act and the decisions in *Lambert* and *Carrass* appeared to be moving toward an endorsement of the recommendation of the Criminal Law Revision Committee, Eleventh Report, *Evidence (General)* (Cmnd 4991, 1971), that whenever a statute placed a burden of proof on the accused, it should be treated as an evidential burden rather than a legal burden. However, the decisions in *Johnstone* and in *Attorney-General's Reference (No 1 of 2004)* clearly put a brake on the movement toward replacement of legal burdens with evidential burdens and the restoration of the fundamental nature of the presumption of innocence. The latest decision of the House of Lords in *Attorney General's Reference (No 4 of 2002); Sheldrake v DPP* suggests not so much a brake on the movement, but an acceptance that there can be different approaches in relation to what may be termed 'real crime' and what may be termed 'regulatory offences' which are not truly criminal.

It can thus be confidently forecast that many statutes (eg, the Prevention of Corruption Act 1916, the Official Secrets Act 1989, and the Terrorism Act 2000) which create indictable offences in the mainstream of criminal offences, which are of a serious nature but contain a presumption against innocence, or place a reverse legal burden of proof on the defence, will be the subject of a challenge in the future. In considering whether these provisions are necessary, justified and proportionate one must apply the modified guidance set out in *Attorney-General's Reference (No 4 of 2002); Sheldrake v DPP*. It would also be prudent to bear in mind the questions suggested by Lord Hope in *Kebilene* (see p 77 above). On the basis of these principles, the likelihood is that many such statutes will be interpreted as imposing an evidential burden in order to avoid being in contravention of Article 6 of the European Convention on Human Rights.

While some statutory reversals of the burden of proof can be justified as being confined within reasonable limits given the importance of what is at stake, it is clear nonetheless that placing an evidential burden on the accused achieves the same purpose while better maintaining the rights of the defence. Placing an evidential burden on the accused requires him to raise the issue(s) that the prosecution must then rebut. This will still assist the prosecution by clarifying the issue(s) with which they must deal and, given the disclosure provisions which now apply to the defence, the prosecution can be made aware of those issues before trial, thus enabling them to deal with them at trial. It is fair to the accused since he, and sometimes he alone, knows what those issues are and has access to the evidence which will raise those issues. However, placing a legal burden of proof on the defence may lead to an unfair trial, and lead to the conviction of a defendant in circumstances where the jury harbour a doubt as to his guilt.

In *R v Brook* (2003) *The Times*, 3 March, it was, somewhat bizarrely, argued that being asked questions in cross-examination by the prosecution was tantamount to a reversal of the burden of proof. The defendant was charged with and convicted of seven counts of rape, six of indecent assault and three of attempted rape. During cross-examination, counsel for the prosecution applied to the judge to be allowed to ask the defendant whether he could think of any grounds why the complainants should lie. The judge gave permission and the question was put to the defendant. Following his conviction and sentence of 11 years' imprisonment, the defendant appealed. The grounds for appeal were, inter alia, that it was unfair and tantamount to a shifting of the (legal) burden of proof for the prosecution to have been permitted to ask that question.

Lord Justice Rose, giving the judgment of the court, said that the question under scrutiny was one which had been widely, if not invariably, put in such cases for at least 40 years without any recorded expression of disapproval from the courts. Indeed, in this jurisdiction there was no authority on the point. Having considered authorities from other jurisdictions, it was held that the question put at trial was not unfair and did not shift the burden of proof. It was an admissible question because it was relevant: for example, if something were known to the defendant which provided a reason for the complainant to lie, that would tend to undermine the complainant's credibility; and again, if a defendant unexpectedly gave a positive answer, that might be relevant to his own credibility.

Restoring the fundamental nature of the right?

The advent of the Human Rights Act 1998 and the incorporation of the European Convention on Human Rights into our domestic law have provided means by which the fundamental nature of the right to be presumed innocent can be restored. However, as the cases considered above make clear, the provisions of Article 6 are not absolute and can be displaced for good reason. It must be borne in mind that the European Convention on

Human Rights is a document prepared by European nations with diverse cultures, backgrounds and criminal processes. It was drafted by governments for governments, rather than by the people for the people. In order to obtain agreement, those who drafted the Convention tended to agree on the lowest common denominator, and almost all rights are qualified and can be displaced in the public interest when it is necessary and reasonable to do so. It follows that the Convention can provide only limited protection by requiring States to show that displacement of the fundamental right is necessary, justified and proportionate. It is, for example, unlikely that reverse burdens and presumptions in a majority of summary offences will be found to be in breach of Article 6, as some of the decisions already made under the Human Rights Act 1998 make clear (see *L v DPP* [2003] QB 137, *Parker v DPP* [2001] RTR 240, and *R v Sheldrake* [2005] AC 246). It is only the reverse burdens and presumptions which apply to serious indictable offences which are likely to contravene Article 6 (see, eg, the decision in *Lambert* and s 118 of the Terrorism Act 2000) and, as the guidance in *Attorney-General's Reference (No 1 of 2004)* makes clear, the seriousness of the offence and the punishment to be imposed are not the sole criteria. Courts are required to look to the realistic effect of imposing a reverse burden, and where the offence is regulatory in nature and intended to protect the public, reverse legal burdens are unlikely to be seen as incompatible with Article 6(2) if the effect of reading them down to evidential burdens is to make the investigation and prosecution of such offences more difficult. It may be that serious offences such as terrorism, and the possession of and dealing in prohibited drugs, will be seen as truly criminal and more deserving of the protection provided by the presumption of innocence.

The incorporation of the Convention provisions into our domestic law has obliged the courts to consider whether provisions which prima facie contravene Article 6 can be justified. In future Parliament will itself have to justify any new statutory provision which is incompatible with Article 6, and the courts must decide whether existing reverse burdens which place a legal burden of proof on the defence can be justified. The early promise of the Terrorism Act 2000 and the decisions in *Lambert* and *Carass*, that few such provisions in relation to the more serious offences can or will be justified, is now less likely to be realised. Rather the more realistic approach of Lord Nicholls in *Johnstone*, the House of Lords in *Sheldrake* and the Court of Appeal in *Attorney-General's Reference (No 1 of 2004)* will hold sway. This approach is likely to lead to an acceptance of reverse burdens in relation to a majority of regulatory offences where reverse burdens are prevalent despite the seriousness of the offence and punishment. There are few truly criminal offences containing reverse burdens, and it is in relation to such offences that one might expect the courts to read down legal burdens. Therefore it is likely that future researchers asking how many indictable or either way offences contain reverse burdens will find no significant reduction from the 40% found by researchers prior to the Human Rights Act 1998 and no great advance for the cause of the rights of the defence (A Ashworth and M Blake, 'Presumption of Innocence in English Criminal Law' [1996] Crim LR 30).

It will be recalled that the Criminal Law Revision Committee, which advocated that reverse burdens should be evidential only, also advocated the effective abolition of the right to silence along the lines of what are now ss 34 to 38 of the Criminal Justice and Public Order Act 1994. A consequence of placing an evidential burden on the accused is that the accused must adduce evidence of the particular defence or risk being found guilty. The right to remain silent, to decline to give evidence and require the prosecution to prove one's guilt, is no longer available to the accused where the offence-creating statute includes a reverse burden which requires the accused to adduce sufficient evidence. The accused is not required to prove his innocence, but is required to adduce sufficient evidence of a particular defence which will create a reasonable doubt unless the prosecution can disprove the defence beyond reasonable doubt. In doing so, he in theory he does not have to give evidence himself, but in practice he must almost always go into the witness box and give evidence, thus exposing himself to cross-examination which is likely to assist the prosecution in proving his guilt. As was indicated by Lord Justice Waller in *Carass* (see p 68 above), the evidential burden can be a difficult burden for the defence where, as in a case under s 206(1)(a) of the Insolvency Act 1986, the prosecution prove a concealment of the debt. Some would argue that in such a case it matters little whether the burden on the accused is the legal burden of proof or the evidential burden; both require him to give evidence and be exposed to cross-examination. There is, however, a significant difference. As was made clear by Lord Steyn in *Lambert*, placing a legal burden on the accused can result in conviction where the jury have a reasonable doubt, while placing an evidential burden does not carry that risk. The other difference is that imposing a legal burden may be incompatible with Article 6 of the European Convention on Human Rights, while imposing an evidential burden will not.

Some will argue that the imposition of the evidential burden is the lesser of two evils; that imposing an evidential burden on the accused is another means of requiring the accused to give evidence and may be seen as another attack on the accused's right to silence alongside that imposed by s 35 of the Criminal Justice and Public Order Act 1994 (which allows the jury to draw an inference from the failure to give evidence and is another means of pressurising the defendant into giving evidence). Others will argue that, like s 35, the imposition of an evidential burden does little to change the position of the accused. As is suggested in the discussion of s 35 (at pp 33–36 above), the section does nothing to change the common law position under which a jury, faced with a compelling case presented by the prosecution, and hearing no evidence from the accused, will conclude that the accused has not answered the case because he has no answer to it. Placing an evidential burden on the accused to adduce sufficient evidence to make the particular defence an issue which the prosecution must then prove beyond reasonable doubt is not true, adds nothing to the position of the accused who is faced with an overwhelming case against him. The pressure of the prosecution case is itself enough to require most defendants to give evidence or risk conviction by not doing so. Placing an evidential burden on the accused may often be seen by the accused as a statement of the obvious, that is, produce sufficient evidence of your defence to make it an issue which the prosecution must then rebut, or face conviction.

Whichever position is preferred, the fact remains that the fundamental principle, that it is for the prosecution to prove the guilt of the accused, and not for the accused to prove his innocence, is qualified by the imposition of a reverse burden of proof. It is less qualified by the imposition of an evidential burden, requiring the accused to adduce sufficient evidence to make the particular defence an issue which the prosecution must disprove, than by placing the legal or persuasive burden on the accused to prove the particular defence on the balance of probabilities, but it remains a qualified fundamental principle. One may argue that 'a qualified fundamental principle' is a contradiction in terms.

Thus the Human Rights Act 1998 ensures that the responsibility for maintaining such fundamental freedoms as the presumption of innocence will be placed on Parliament, using the circuitous route of a challenge to a statutory provision under the Human Rights Act 1998. Parliament will then be forced to take the burden of proof, and other fundamental freedoms, more seriously than it has in the past, but there remains much room for what the European Court of Human Rights describes as 'a margin of appreciation', which means that fundamental freedoms can be whittled down, but only 'within the reasonable limits' which take into account the importance of what is at stake and maintain the rights of the defence'. Fine words which justify the qualification of a fundamental right.

Further reading

Ashworth, A and Blake, M, 'The Presumption of Innocence in English Criminal Law' [1996] Crim LR 306.

Choo, A and Nash, S, 'Evidence Law in England and Wales: The Impact of the Human Rights Act 1998' (2003) 7 International Journal of Evidence and Proof 2.

Dingwall, G, 'Statutory exceptions, burdens of proof and the Human Rights Act 1998' (2002) 65(3) MLR 450.

Gillespie, A, 'Child Pornography: Balancing Substantive and Evidential Law to Safeguard Children Effectively from Abuse (2005) 9 International Journal of Evidence and Proof 29.

Healey, P, 'Proof and Policy: No Golden Threads' [1987] Crim LR 361.

Smith, J C, 'The Presumption of Innocence' (1987) 38 NILQ 223.

4 Examination and Cross-Examination

It was noted in **Chapter 2** that witnesses testifying in the modern English adversarial trial are orally examined and cross-examined under oath. The parties have a broad remit as to which witnesses they choose to call, and as to which questions they choose to ask. This was not always the case.

The way in which the parties question witnesses in the modern criminal trial is controlled by the trial judge, who has a duty to ensure that proceedings are conducted in accordance with the rules of evidence and procedure. Parties have traditionally enjoyed a broad latitude in the types of questions they are able to put to witnesses, and a witness can be questioned on any matter that is deemed to be relevant, either to the facts in issue or to the credibility of the witness. In recent years, however, concerns over the manner in which witnesses are questioned in court and a shift away from exclusionary rules of evidence towards increased judicial discretion have been instrumental in bringing about a number of changes to the regulation of examination and cross-examination in court. In particular, the Criminal Justice Act 2003 and the Sexual Offences Act 2003 have introduced major reforms to rules governing the examination and cross-examination of witnesses in court. This chapter sets out to analyse and evaluate the manner in which questioning in court is regulated under this new legislative regime.

Leading questions

A fundamental principle of good advocacy is that counsel must keep witnesses under tight control. Witnesses are not allowed to give their evidence in a simple narrative form. They will usually have made a statement to the police (if a prosecution witness), or to the defence solicitor (if a defence witness); at trial counsel will take the witness through that statement. In examination-in-chief, leading questions, which suggest the answer required or which suggest the existence of disputed facts to which the witness has not yet testified, are not permitted. Such questions usually require no more than a simple 'Yes' or 'No' from the witness. They are permissible where the evidence being elicited is purely formal and undisputed.

Thus it is permissible to set the scene by asking the witness questions such as 'Your name is ...?', 'And you work at ...?', to which the answers are 'Yes', but not a question such as, 'You saw the accused running from the house just after you heard a shot?'. The dangers of such questions are obvious. The witness may have seen someone run from the house. He may be sure it was the accused, or he may be less than sure; but a simple 'Yes' obscures this. Such questions must be put in a form which allows the witness to say what he saw without putting words into his mouth or suggesting the answer required. Thus, having placed the witness outside the house, he should be asked whether he heard anything. If he answers by saying he heard what he believed to be a gunshot, he should then be asked, 'And what happened next?'; the answer may be, 'I saw a man running from the house'. The next question would be, 'Can you identify this man?'. The answer then should be, 'Yes it was [the accused]'. Questions should then follow about how he was so sure it was the accused and the circumstances of the identification. This takes longer than the leading question but is better evidence. Leading questions may be used in cross-examination and on those rare occasions when a witness is declared to be hostile (see p 39 above).

Refreshing memory

Out of court

All witnesses may refresh their memories from statements or other documents made reasonably close to the events about which they are to give evidence. Both prosecution and defence witnesses are entitled to a copy of their statements and to refresh their memory from them at any time up to the point where they go into the witness box. The leading case in this area is *R v Richardson* [1971] 2 QB 484. At his trial in 1970, the defendant was charged with two counts of burglary. Shortly before giving evidence all five prosecution witnesses refreshed their memories from statements made to the police in July 1969. The Court of Appeal held that there was nothing improper in this:

> There can be no absolute rule that witnesses may not before trial see the statements they made at some period reasonably close to the event which is the subject of the trial. Indeed one can imagine many cases, particularly those of a complex nature, when such a rule would militate very greatly against the interests of justice (per Sachs LJ, at 490)

The interests of justice would not be served if the giving of evidence became a test of memory, particularly if months, or even years, pass between the events witnessed and the trial of the alleged offender. The Court in *Richardson* quoted with approval the comments of the Supreme Court of Hong Kong in *Lau Pak Ngam v R* [1966] Crim LR 443, that if a witness is deprived of the opportunity to refresh his memory, his testimony becomes more a test of memory than truthfulness; and to deprive witnesses of the opportunity creates difficulties for the honest witness while doing little to hamper dishonest witnesses. Such a rule would also make life impossible for the police officers who daily deal with many cases. In *Lau Pak Ngam*, the police read over the statements to the witnesses, who each heard what the others had to say. The Court of Appeal in *Richardson* expressed the view that it would be wrong to hand witnesses their statements in circumstances which enabled or encouraged them to compare what each had said.

In *Richardson*, the fact that witnesses had been shown their statements was revealed only during cross-examination. In *R v Westwell* [1976] 2 All ER 812, the Court of Appeal said it was desirable, though not essential, that the defence be informed when Crown witnesses had seen their statements, so that the defence might, when appropriate, draw attention to this in cross-examination. The Court of Appeal clearly thought that the fact that a witness has been able to refresh his memory is a matter that goes to the weight the jury might give to that evidence, the inference being that the witness who gives evidence without refreshing his memory may be a better witness. This comes close to endorsing the view of evidence as a test of memory rather than truthfulness. The reality is that the witness who refreshes his memory is likely to be more truthful than one who does not. The memory may fade or be distorted by the passage of time, hence the need to refresh it and recall what was said nearer the event in issue.

In court

The common law, with its emphasis on giving evidence orally, sought to restrict the use of documents to refresh the memory of a witness giving oral evidence in court. As a general rule, a witness was allowed to refresh his memory while giving evidence by reference to any writing made or verified by him when the facts were fresh in his mind. While this would often be a statement made to the police or defence, or, in the case of the police, entries made in their notebooks, it was not confined to such documents. A witness could refer to a diary, a receipt book or any other record that was relevant. For example, a witness recorded the registration number of a car that failed to stop after an accident on the back of a cigarette packet. Given that counsel usually led the witness through his statement made to the police, it made sense to allow the witness to read his statement before he testified. The courts, against the objection of most defence counsel, who preferred the witness to be less well prepared, approved of the practice.

The common law also required that a statement to which the witness referred must have been made by him, that is written by him or for him, as where he dictated it to a typist, and then verified by him by reading and signing it (though signing was not essential, the verification was); or the statement might be made by another in the presence and hearing of the witness but be verified by the witness while the facts were fresh in his memory. It was quite common for one police officer to make a note of what was being said and for the other to read it through and verify it as accurate. This was accepted as good practice by the Court of Appeal in *R v Bass* [1953] 1 QB 680, where officers referred to the same notebook in order to refresh their memories.

It was said to be essential that the witness who sought to refresh his memory while giving evidence must have made or verified the statement while the facts were still fresh in his memory or, in legal language, 'contemporaneously with the facts to which he testifies'. However, in *Richardson* it was said that this phrase provided a measure of elasticity and should not be taken to confine witnesses to an over-short period.

Nonetheless, the distinction between contemporaneous and non-contemporaneous statements has long been thought to be unsound. Outside the court a potential witness may refer to any statements, whether or not contemporaneous (see above). Why should those who wait until they are in court and about to give evidence be limited as to what material they use to refresh their memory by the rule on contemporaneity? The following cases suggest that the courts recognise that such a distinction is unsound, and went some way to removing it altogether.

In *R v Da Silva* (1990) 90 Cr App R 233, the Court of Appeal held that the trial judge had properly exercised his discretion to allow the witness, who had started to give evidence, to refresh his memory from a statement made one month after the events to which it related. It was not contemporaneous, neither was it made while the facts were fresh in his mind, but it would have been open to the witness to have read the statement before coming into court. The Court said it was equally proper to allow the witness to refresh his memory from that statement in court, though he should not be allowed to read from it. Four conditions must be satisfied if the judge is to allow a witness who has started to give evidence to refresh his memory:

(a) the witness must indicate that he cannot recall the details of events because of the lapse of time since they took place;

(b) he must have made a statement much nearer the time of the events so that the contents of his statement represented his recollection at the time he made it;

(c) he has not read the statement before coming into the witness box; and

(d) he wished to have an opportunity to read the statement before he continued to give evidence.

An even broader approach was adopted in *R v South Ribble Stipendiary Magistrate, ex p Cochrane* [1996] 2 Cr App R 544. Here, the witness had made three statements to the police. The first of these statements was made some two weeks after the events to which they referred. At committal proceedings, some 18 months later, the magistrate permitted the witness to refresh his memory from these statements, even though the witness had already spent 10 to 15 minutes reading them before he went into the witness box. The Queen's Bench Divisional Court dismissed a judicial review application to quash the decision to commit the defendant for trial in spite of the fact that the third condition laid down in *Da Silva* had not been satisfied:

> It seems to me that a judge has a real discretion as to whether to permit a witness to refresh his memory from a non-contemporaneous document. By a real discretion, I mean a strong discretion, a choice of alternatives of free binding criteria. I do not mean the so-called weak discretion which is not a true judicial discretion at all, but simply a binding rule of law to be followed by the judge. (per Henry LJ, at 551)

As Dennis notes, it would seem that this decision means that 'there appears to be nothing to stop a judge allowing a witness to refer repeatedly to a non-contemporaneous document in the course of testifying' and the appeal courts should be prepared 'to give the judge a generous margin of appreciation in applying the discretion' (I Dennis, *The Law of Evidence* (2002), 475).

The refreshing document as evidence

At common law the document used to refresh the memory was not evidence of the truth of its contents; the oral testimony given by the witness was the evidence, not the note or record to which he made reference. Thus if a witness used a diary or other record to recall dates or entries, the other party could require the production of that diary or record and could cross-examine on it without making it evidence in the case. If the cross-examination went further and introduced other dates or entries not referred to by the witness, the other party could insist on treating the document as evidence in the case. The document was then an exhibit in the case and the jury has a right to inspect it. Even then the evidential value was limited to showing that the witness's testimony as given in the witness box was consistent with those earlier entries. This rule, and the rules on allowing a witness to refresh his memory, have been the subject of legislative change.

Reform – the Criminal Justice Act 2003

The common law rules on the use of documents to refresh the memory while giving oral evidence have now been replaced by s 139 of the Criminal Justice Act 2003, which provides:

(1) A person giving oral evidence in criminal proceedings about any matter may, at any stage in the course of doing so, refresh his memory of it from a document made or verified by him at an earlier time if—

    (a) he states in his oral evidence that the document records his recollection of the matter at an earlier time, and

    (b) his recollection of the matter is likely to have been significantly better at that time than it is at the time of his oral evidence.

(2) Where—

    (a) a person giving oral evidence in criminal proceedings about a matter has previously given an oral account of which a sound recording was made, and he states in that evidence that the account represented his recollection of the matter at that time,

    (b) his recollection of the matter is likely to have been significantly better at the time of the previous account than it is at the time of his oral evidence, and

    (c) a transcript has been made of the sound recording,

    he may, at any stage in the course of giving his evidence, refresh his memory of the matter from that transcript.

The section creates a presumption that a witness in criminal proceeding may refresh his memory from a document subject to two conditions:

(a) that he indicates that the document represents his recollection at the time he made it; and

(b) that his recollection was likely to be significantly better at the time the document was made (or verified).

These requirements reflect the common law position as finally arrived at in *R v South Ribble Stipendiary Magistrate, ex p Cochrane* set out at p 94 above. It is to be hoped that the phrase in s 139(1) 'at an earlier time' will be interpreted more broadly than 'contemporaneously'.

There has been much criticism of the taking of witness statements by the police, who may, advertently or inadvertently, bias the statement toward a particular version of events. It has been suggested that tape-recordings or video-recordings could be made of the witness statement. As noted in **Chapter 2**, video-recorded evidence is much used in relation to children and other vulnerable witnesses, and is being used more widely by the police. Section 139(2) recognises the practical difficulties of refreshing one's memory from a tape- or video-recording, and acknowledges the trend toward the use of recordings of a witness's evidence by permitting the use of transcripts of such recordings as memory-refreshing documents. Although the section only mentions the use of such a document in court while giving oral evidence, the fact that the witness had the opportunity to refresh his memory before giving evidence will not affect the presumption created by s 139.

Section 120(3) of the 2003 Act is also relevant to documents used in this way. It provides that:

> *A statement made by a witness in a document—*
>
> *(a) which is used by him to refresh his memory while giving evidence,*
>
> *(b) on which he is cross-examined, and*
>
> *(c) which as a consequence is received in evidence in the proceedings,*
> *is admissible as evidence of any matter stated of which oral evidence by him would be admissible.*

The section preserves common law rule that the document used to refresh the memory was not evidence unless the cross-examination went beyond dates and entries to which the witness referred. However, while the common law permitted the document to be admitted if the cross-examination went further than the oral evidence, the refreshing document was only evidence of the consistency of the witness. The new statutory provision stipulates that it is admissible as evidence of the truth of the matter stated of which oral evidence by him would be admissible.

Thus, if a witness uses a diary or other record to recall dates or entries, the other party can require the production of that diary or record and cross-examine on it without making it evidence in the case. However, if the cross-examination goes further and introduces other dates or entries not referred to by the witness, the other party can insist on treating the document as evidence of the truth of the matters stated if the witness could have given oral evidence of those matters. The document is then an exhibit in the case and the jury have a right to inspect it.

Admissibility of previous statements

Previous consistent statements

At common law the general rule was that a witness might not seek to bolster his evidence by reference to the fact that he said the same thing out of court on an earlier occasion. Thus in *R v Roberts* [1942] 1 All ER 187, the accused, charged with murder, claimed that the gun had gone off accidentally. He was not allowed to call evidence that two days after the shooting he had told his father that it was an accident. Such statements were excluded because they were hearsay, that is, they were made otherwise than as oral evidence in court (see **Chapter 6**). There were exceptions to the rule against hearsay, which included previous consistent statements, but when admitted they were not seen as evidence of the truth of the matters in the statement but merely as evidence of the consistency of the witness. Another reason for not admitting them was the fear that such evidence could so easily be manufactured.

There were three main exceptional cases in which previous consistent statements were admissible. These were:

(a) statements made by complainants in sexual cases;

(b) statements forming part of the res gestae (see **Chapter 5**); and

(c) statements to rebut allegations of fabrication.

However, as indicated above, such statements were not evidence of the truth of the facts asserted in them, nor were they capable of corroborating the witness. The purpose in admitting such statements was merely to show the consistency of the witness, thus serving to bolster the witness's credibility (*R v Virgo* (1978) 67 Cr App R 323), or to rebut a charge that he had fabricated his evidence if it could be shown that the previous consistent statement was made before the allegations of fabrication. In *R v Benjamin* (1913) 8 Cr App R 146, a police officer was allowed to produce his notebook in evidence in order to rebut a charge of fabrication. The fact that the notes were in chronological order demonstrated that they were not fabricated as alleged. The previous statement was not evidence of the truth of the facts contained in it but was admitted simply for the purpose of rebutting the allegation of fabrication. The Law Commission, in its *Report on Hearsay Evidence* (1997, No 245) recommended that a recent complaint that satisfies the criteria set out in the recommendation should be admissible as evidence of the truth of any matter stated, provided oral evidence by that witness would be admissible. That recommendation has now been given legislative effect by s 120(2) of the Criminal Justice Act 2003.

Previous hearsay statements identifying persons, places or objects

Section 120(4) to (7) of the 2003 Act deals with the not uncommon situation where the witness has, in the past, made a statement to another person identifying a person, place or thing but cannot remember the detail when called to give evidence (such as a car registration number). Under the previous law, the witness would have been unable to rely on any document containing the relevant information if he had not verified it; and the person to whom any oral statement had been made could not give evidence in person unless it fell within an exception of the hearsay rule. Section 120(4) of the 2003 Act now stipulates that any such statement will be admissible as evidence of the facts contained within it, provided the witness states that he made the statement and believes it to be true, and one of the following conditions is met.

(5) The first condition is that the statement identifies or describes a person, object or place.

(6) The second condition is that the statement was made by a witness when the matters stated were fresh in his memory but he does not remember them, and cannot reasonably be expected to remember them, well enough to give oral evidence of them in the proceedings.

(7) The third condition is that—

(a) the witness claims to be a person against whom an offence has been committed,

(b) the offence is one to which the proceedings relate,

(c) the statement consists of a complaint made by the witness (whether to a person in authority or not) about conduct which would, if proved, constitute the offence or part of the offence,

(d) the complaint was made as soon as could reasonably be expected after the alleged conduct,

(e) the complaint was not made as a result of a threat or a promise, and

(f) before the statement is adduced the witness gives oral evidence in connection with its subject matter.

(8) For the purposes of subsection (7) the fact that the complaint was elicited (for example, by a leading question) is irrelevant unless a threat or a promise was involved.

Section 120(5) and (6) overlap and will be dealt with together, while bearing in mind that they can operate independently of each other.

Section 120(4) thus permits the person to whom the statement was made to give evidence of the detail, or for the document containing it to be admitted, provided the conditions of those subsections are satisfied. Thus a police officer in charge of an identification parade can give evidence that the witness who picked out the suspect but who cannot remember the 'number' of that person in the line-up, picked out 'number 5' (the number of the suspect) (see *R v Osborne and Virtue* [1973] QB 678). Similarly, the witness sees robbers leaving the scene of the robbery in a car, and gives the registration number of the getaway car to a traffic warden who makes a note of it but fails to get the witness to verify it. The witness cannot remember the registration number when called to give evidence, but while giving evidence he indicates that he made the statement and to the best of his belief it was true. The traffic warden can now give evidence that the witness gave him the registration number and relate that number to the court. (See the discussion of s 117(5) in **Chapter 6** for an alternative, if more cumbersome, means of introducing the registration number.)

A previous consistent statement was admissible at common law if it was part of the *res gestae*, that is, part of the transaction, story or event to which it related. This exception to the rule against hearsay is preserved by s 118 of the 2003 Act. Thus in *Fowkes* (1856) *The Times*, 8 March, the accused, also known as 'Butcher', was charged with murder. A witness gave evidence that he was in a room with a police officer and the victim, when the victim was killed by a shot fired through the window. Just before the shot was fired he saw a face at the window. He was allowed to give evidence that on seeing the face he had shouted, 'There's Butcher'. The police officer was permitted to give evidence to the same effect. The statement that the witness had shouted 'There's Butcher' would now be admissible under s 120(4) to (6) if he had forgotten the name.

A modern example of a previous consistent statement being admitted as part of the *res gestae* is to be seen in a news report of a trial in which a man was found guilty of the murder of his estranged wife (*The Times*, 15 September 2000). The man came to the house where the estranged wife was living with her two sons aged 11 and 15. He took a knife from the kitchen and pursued the wife to the bedroom of the youngest boy, where she sought refuge. He broke down the door and stabbed her to death before trying to stab himself. The 11-year-old boy saw his mother's mobile phone lying next to her. Pushing his father aside, he picked it up and dialled 999, and told the police that his mother had been stabbed. The 'harrowing' tape of the 999 call, on which the screams of the dying woman could be heard, was played to the jury. This was followed by a video-recording of the interview with the boy, made by the police the following day. Clearly the tape-recording of the 999 call was part of the event it described and, as we shall see when considering the *res gestae* exception to the hearsay rule (at pp 221–226 below), satisfied all the requirements of admissibility. However, if the boy were to suffer trauma which caused him to repress the memory of what he had seen, a transcript of his 999 call could be used by him to refresh his memory under s 139, or s 120(4) of the 2003 Act could be relied upon to enable the police officer who took the call to give evidence of what the boy told him. Note that this evidence, like evidence admitted under the *res gestae* exception, is admissible as evidence of the truth of what was said not simply as evidence of consistency, though it is also very good evidence of consistency. This exception to the rule against hearsay is discussed in more depth in **Chapter 6**.

Recent complaint

A complaint made by the victim of an alleged sexual offence was one of the longest-standing exceptions to the common rule against admitting previous consistent statements. The principle was at one time of more general application, possibly resulting from the need, before professional policing, to raise the hue and cry. An early complaint that one had been robbed, raped or was otherwise the victim of a crime was essential if there was to be any likelihood of catching the alleged offender. In *R v Wink* (1834) 6 Car & P 397, a police officer was allowed to prove that the witness had complained to him of robbery. This was only a few years after the creation of the Metropolitan Police in 1829, and there is no later case of a complaint being admitted other than in relation to sexual offences. That the practice continued in relation to such offences, particularly rape, is probably due to the requirement to prove lack of consent. An early complaint is said to be consistent with lack of consent; a late or no complaint may be inconsistent with the allegation that the act was not consensual. Neither assumption has any basis in fact and the practice was described by an Australian court as a 'perverted survival' which ought to be abolished. It is therefore somewhat surprising that rather than abolish the require-ment of an early complaint altogether, s 120(7)(d) extends it to any and all offences. The application of the principle to sexual offences has been the subject of numerous deci-sions which over the years developed the requirements for admissibility of a complaint that a sexual offence had been committed. Section 120(6) effectively reforms and codi-fies the former common law requirements (see *R v Lilleyman* [1986] 2 QB 167; *R v Osbourne* [1905] 1 KB 551).

Section 120(4) of the Criminal Justice Act 2003 makes it clear that a complaint is now admissible as evidence of any matter stated of which oral evidence by the witness would be admissible, that is, admissible as evidence of the truth of the matters stated. Section 120(8) of the 2003 Act removes a former restriction that the complaint must be voluntary and not made as the result of leading questions, while s 120(7)(e) requires that the complaint was not made as a result of a threat or promise. Thus if a mother sees her daughter in a distressed and dishevelled state and says, 'He raped you, didn't he?', the positive reply would be admissible. Questions such as 'Why are you crying?' or, as in *Osbourne*, 'Why are you going home?, will not affect the admissibility of the complaint. However, if a father threatened his daughter with violence unless she told him what had happened, the subsequent complaint would not be admissible.

At common law, it was the case that the complaint should be made at the first opportunity which reasonably offered itself after the alleged offence. This rule is largely preserved by the 2003 Act, s 120(7)(d) of which requires that, 'the complaint was made as soon as could reasonably be expected after the alleged conduct'. In *R v Valentine* [1996] 2 Cr App R 213, it was established that the complaint must be made at the first reasonable opportunity which reasonably offers itself after the alleged offence. The Court of Appeal held that what was 'the first reasonable opportunity' depended upon the particular circumstances, including the character of the complainant and the relationship between her and the person she complained to, and the person to whom she might have complained but did not. This is likely to be the interpretation put on the statutory phrase 'as soon as could reasonably be expected after the alleged conduct'. In that case the complainant was walking home at 11.30 pm, when she met the defendant, a complete stranger to her. She was persuaded to join him for a meal at a nearby Indian restaurant. They left the restaurant together at 12.30 am, and began to walk towards her home. The defendant suggested that they cut across a playing field and she agreed. When they got to the middle of the field he threatened her with a table knife (taken from the restaurant), and forced her first to fellate him and then to have intercourse against her will. The complainant arrived home at 2.30 am. Her parents and elder brother were at home but were asleep. The next morning she went into her brother's room and told him she had been attacked with a knife. She told him she did not want to tell her parents. She went to work during the afternoon, and in the evening told a friend she had been raped.

On appeal it was contended that the complaint made to the friend during the evening was inadmissible because it was not made at the first opportunity that reasonably presented itself. Dismissing the appeal, it was held that a complaint alleging rape can be recent and admissible even though it might not have been made at the first opportunity that presented itself. It is enough that it is the first reasonable opportunity (see above). It was also held that a complaint will not be inadmissible merely because there has been an earlier complaint, provided that the complaint was made as speedily as could reasonably be expected. However, it is not permissible for the prosecution to lead evidence that the complaint had been made by the complainant in substantially the same terms on several occasions soon after the alleged offence, where that would be prejudicial in that it might induce the jury to regard the reports of individual complaints as evidence of the truth of what was asserted.

Both the trial judge and the Court of Appeal showed a more understanding attitude to the victim of rape than, as we shall see later, has often been present. The trial judge remarked:

> *I do not think the law requires me to say that the evidence [of the second complaint]*
> *should be excluded in those circumstances [the circumstances being that the*
> *complainant had bottled up the matter for some 24 hours] if the first opportunity could*
> *be said to be that opportunity where she felt herself able to say [that she had been*
> *raped]. Not every woman can bring herself to say that a man has raped her, even if she*
> *has been most cruelly raped. I think we understand that in these courts these days,*
> *even if it was not appreciated by Victorian judges, who started laying down this*
> *principle toward the end of the last century.* (at 219)

Roch LJ, giving the judgment of the Court of Appeal, expressed similar sentiments when he observed:

> *We now have a greater understanding that those who are the victims of sexual*
> *offences, be they male or female, often need time before they can bring themselves to*
> *tell what has been done to them; that some victims will find it quite impossible to*
> *complain to anyone other than a parent or member of their family whereas others may*
> *feel it quite impossible to tell their parents or members of their family.* (at 224)

This case is likely to be followed in applying the requirement of s 120(7)(d) of the 2003 Act – that the complaint was made as soon as could reasonable be expected after the alleged conduct – to complaints not only of rape, but also of many of the other offences to which s 120 extends the concept of a recent complaint.

In *R v S (Evidence: Sex Abuse)* (2004) *The Times*, 11 June, questions arose as to whether evidence of recent complaint ought to be admitted where there were inconsistencies between the complainant's evidence of the complaint and that of the person to whom she complained. The defendant was charged with offences of buggery, rape, gross indecency and indecent assault. The prosecution case was that the defendant started sexually abusing the complainant, S, when she was 9 or 10 years old. The abuse took the form of indecent touching, which continued until she left home at the age of 19. In her evidence-in-chief S said that from the age of 10 or 11 she was also subjected to more serious sexual abuse, which included digital penetration and sexual intercourse. The prosecution applied to adduce evidence of her complaint to a schoolfriend, C, in whom she had confided when she was 13 or 14 years old. C's evidence was that S had told her about the defendant touching her. S's evidence at trial was that she had told C not just about the indecent assaults, but also about the more serious penetrative assaults. The defendant objected to C's evidence of the sexual conduct of which S complained. The trial judge permitted the evidence to be given. The defendant was convicted and sentenced to 12 years' imprisonment. He appealed against conviction on the basis that the evidence of the complaint was wrongly admitted given the inconsistency between the complainant and the person complained to.

The Court of Appeal held that provided the evidence of a recent complaint was sufficiently consistent with the complainant's evidence at trial to be capable of supporting the credibility of the complainant, it was both fair to the defendant and in accordance with established principles to admit it. Thomas LJ, giving the judgment of the court, said that the question of admissibility of evidence of recent complaint depended, applying the established principles, upon whether such evidence was sufficiently consistent that it could, depending on the view taken by the jury of the evidence, support or enhance the credibility of the complainant. The decision in each case as to whether such evidence was sufficiently consistent for it to be admissible must depend on the facts. It was not necessary that the recent complaint disclosed the ingredients of the offence; it would, however, usually be necessary that the complainant disclosed evidence of material and relevant unlawful sexual conduct by the defendant which would support the credibility of the complainant. It would not, therefore, usually be necessary for the complainant to have described the full extent of the unlawful sexual conduct alleged by the complainant in the witness box, provided that it was capable of supporting the credibility of the complainant's evidence given at trial. It was for the jury to assess any differences, which might be accounted for by a variety of reasons (for example, in cases of abuse by a family member, a complainant could not bring herself to disclose the full extent of the conduct at the time of her contemporaneous complaint). C's evidence was capable of supporting the credibility of S's evidence given in the witness box in relation to the more serious sexual conduct of penetration and rape. Accordingly, the testimony was properly admitted. However, the conviction was rendered unsafe because the judge's direction to the jury regarding the evidence was insufficient, in that he failed to draw attention to the inconsistencies between the evidence of C and that of S. The appeal was therefore allowed.

In *R v Birks* [2003] 2 Cr App R 7, the complainant, C, who was 19 at the time of trial, alleged that the defendant had sexually abused her when she was aged 5 or 6 and stopped when she was aged 6 or 7. She said she first complained to her mother some two months after the last incident. In cross-examination she admitted that it could have been up to six months later. She said it was while she was watching a programme on child abuse that she had been prompted to complain. Her mother gave evidence that she understood her daughter's complaint to refer to events that had stopped one year earlier. She then confronted the accused and warned him off. The judge ruled that in light of the C's young age at the time, the threats made to her by Birks and the manner in which the complaint had emerged spontaneously when watching a television programme, the complaint had been made at the first reasonable opportunity. Allowing the appeal and quashing the conviction, the Court of Appeal held that 'within a reasonable time' could not be understood to mean 'had to be made within a reasonable time of the alleged offence whether the complaint was recent or not'. In every case the court must be satisfied that the complaint was recent. Where, as here, the case depended on the credibility of the complainant vis-à-vis that of the appellant, the admission of C's evidence about the complaint she made to her mother about two to 12 months after the last offence assisted her credibility and should not have been admitted; or if admitted at the outset, the judge should have reviewed the decision and discharged the jury once evidence had emerged that the complaint might have been made six months or, according to the mother, a year after the end of the appellant's conduct. The conviction could not therefore be considered safe.

Per curiam, the Court noted that s 120 extended the concept of recent complaint, and said it would be helpful if these provisions could be considered in the light of this case with a view to defining a rule which would take account of the modern understanding of the difficulties facing young children in particular, speaking out to other people about the sexual abuse to which they have been subjected. Courts should be readier than they were in the past to accept that complaints had been made as soon as reasonably possible, and indeed within a reasonable time, even though the period of time between the incident and complaint extended not merely to days but even to weeks, months or years. The question for the court should be whether in all the circumstances, having regard to the characteristics of the complainant, her possible tender years, the threats she may have been subjected to and all other relevant circumstances, the fact remained that she made her complaint as soon as she could reasonably could do so. Subject to appropriate directions, it was undesirable that juries should be kept in the dark as to what happened between the time – sometimes many years, or even decades, in the past – of the alleged abuse and the time when they were trying the case. If complaints, in the existing sense of the term, had come forward in circumstances which were safe to put to the jury for their evaluation, they should be so put.

Even when the common law required that a jury be warned of the danger of relying on the uncorroborated evidence of the complainant in a case of rape, it was made absolutely clear that a recent complaint could not be independent corroboration since it came from the victim herself. This will remain the case even though the evidence of a recent complaint is now admissible as evidence of the truth of the matters asserted. The failure to make this clear to the jury has been, and doubtless will continue to be, a common ground for appeal.

At common law, evidence of a complaint was admissible only if the complainant gave evidence. Thus in *R v Wallwork* (1958) 42 Cr App R 153, the accused was charged with incest with his daughter, aged 5. The child was called to give evidence but said nothing. Her grandmother then gave evidence that the child complained to her about the accused's conduct. The Court of Appeal held that this evidence had been wrongly admitted because there was no evidence from the child with which it could be consistent. Section 120 does not change this common law rule. Section 120(1) stipultates that the provision applies only where the witness is called to give evidence in criminal proceedings, and s 120(4)(b) makes it clear that the previous statement is admissible only if the witness indicates that to the best of his belief he made the statement, and that to the best of his belief it states the truth.

It may be noted that, in the context of rape, the absence of an early complaint can be damaging to a complainant and will be used in cross-examination to suggest that if intercourse took place it was consensual. See the later discussion of cross-examination of rape victims and ss 41 to 43 of the Youth Justice and Criminal Evidence Act 1999, at pp 128–145 below. It remains to be seen whether, with the extension of the recent complaint to other crimes, victims of robbery, violence or any other crime suffer the same fate.

Previous statements by the accused in response to accusations

Statements made by the accused to the police or others, whether oral or written, are commonly adduced by the prosecution whether they contain admissions or denials. In so far as they contain admissions, they may amount to a confession (see the definition in s 82(1) of the Police and Criminal Evidence Act 1984). If they do, they are admissible as exceptions to the hearsay rule, subject to the test laid down in s 76 of the 1984 Act. Often they contain a mixture of statements that are incriminating and those which seek to exculpate, eg, 'Yes I was there [at the scene of the burglary] but I was looking for a hub cap which I lost off my car'. The first part is an incriminating admission and admissible as a confession; the second part is exculpatory and, if the defendant sticks to his story when he gives evidence, is a previous consistent statement. Since the one cannot be separated from the other without distorting what was said, both parts of the statement are admissible, but the trial judge will point out that the incriminating parts are likely to be true, whereas the excuses do not carry the same weight. Nevertheless, those excuses are admitted as evidence of the facts stated and not merely as evidence of consistency. Such matters are considered in detail in **Chapter 7**.

Unfavourable and hostile witnesses

Sometimes a witness will fail to give the evidence expected by the party calling him, ie the evidence he gives under oath at trial conflicts with, or substantially differs from, a previous statement. In these circumstances, the witness cannot be impeached, ie cross-examined as to the inconsistency between what he is saying, or not saying, in the witness box and what he said in his statement. However, one must distinguish between a witness who is merely unfavourable to the party calling him and one who by his conduct is positively hostile.

If the witness is unfavourable, not motivated by malice or dishonesty, but simply confused or unable to remember, the party calling him cannot treat him as hostile and cross-examine him. In modern times the problem may be resolved by allowing the witness to refresh his memory from the statement made nearer to the event to which he testifies (*R v South Ribble Stipendiary Magistrate, ex p Cochrane* (see p 94 above)). If that is not possible or does not resolve the problem, other witnesses can be called to give the evidence which the unfavourable witness was to give, or to contradict the evidence given.

Occasionally, a witness will be 'hostile', and will not give the evidence expected of him out of malice or dishonesty, or is for some other reason refusing to give evidence (such as through fear). It is for the judge to decide whether the witness is hostile. If he decides that he is the party calling the witness will be allowed to cross-examine him. He can be asked leading questions and any inconsistent statements can be put to him. Section 3 of the Criminal Procedure Act 1865 governs the use of previous inconsistent statements made by the witness.

Cross-examination

Introduction

Cross-examination has been described by Wigmore as 'the great engine for truth'. Biographies of famous barristers are replete with stories of their skilful cross-examination, which showed a witness to be mistaken or a liar and led to the demolition of the other side's (usually the prosecution) case. Courtroom dramas on film and television invariably depict the defence counsel pulling the prosecution case to pieces by skilful cross-examination, leading, inevitably, to the unmasking of the real villain (usually one of the prosecution witnesses). All this is fiction, as are most of the stories of effective cross-examination.

The purpose of cross-examination is said to be twofold: (i) to weaken the case for the other side; and (ii) to establish facts that are favourable to the case for the cross-examiner

(R Du Cann, *The Art of the Advocate* (1993), 114) (although it might be added that in modern times the first of these is achieved not by discrediting the *evidence* by demonstrating that it does not fit with other evidence before the jury, but by seeking to discredit the *witness* so that the jury will not believe, or give little credence to, any evidence given whether true or not). Parties have a right to cross-examine all witnesses on any relevant issue, or on any matter concerning a witness's credibility. Its importance to the trial is underlined by the consequences of failing to cross-examine a witness. In such an event, counsel may be deemed to have accepted the witness's version of events if the testimony has gone unchallenged (*R v Wood Green Court, ex p Taylor* [1995] Crim LR 879). If a party has been prevented from cross-examining a witness, that witness's testimony may be regarded as inadmissible, or may be afforded little weight, and there is the possibility that the defence may argue for the verdict to be overturned on appeal.

Occasionally the courts have been confronted with cases where only a partial cross-examination has taken place. In *R v Stretton* (1988) 86 Cr App R 7, the victim of an alleged rape and indecent assault was a chronically epileptic and mentally handicapped woman. After giving her evidence-in-chief and being cross-examined for some time, she became ill and was unable to continue. The trial judge directed the jury that if they felt the defence had been deprived of the opportunity properly to test her evidence, they should acquit the defendant. They convicted, and the Court of Appeal held that the trial judge has a discretion to allow the trial to continue in such circumstances. In that case cross-examination had proceeded for some time before the witness became ill, and the trial judge gave a clear warning and dealt carefully with the need for corroboration (no longer a requirement). Similarly, in *R v Wyatt* [1990] Crim LR 343, a 7-year-old child, the alleged victim of an indecent assault, gave her evidence-in-chief via a TV link and was cross-examined via that link for some 20 minutes before becoming too distressed to continue. There was no lengthy warning as in *Stretton*; nevertheless, the Court of Appeal was satisfied that the jury had been fairly directed on the girl's evidence and upheld the conviction. If little or no cross-examination takes place, an adjournment of the trial to enable the witness to recover might assist, or a new trial might be possible. However, in cases like those above, the witness is unlikely to be helped by an adjournment, and even less likely to be able to withstand the ordeal of another trial; the choice is then between continuing with the trial, or directing an acquittal.

In contrast to examination-in-chief, leading questions may be put to witnesses in cross-examination and the credibility of the witness will often be attacked. Strictly speaking, the cross-examiner should not 'suggest' matters to witnesses, but few barristers do not use the phrase 'I put it to you that ...'. Witnesses can easily be upset by suggestions that they are mistaken or, even worse, lying. Of course counsel will seldom call a witness a liar, but phrases such as 'I put it to you that what you have described never happened' have but one interpretation. The Code of Conduct for the Bar provides rules of guidance on cross-examination. They are not binding on the court but, since most judges will themselves have been guided by that Code, they have a certain status.

The nature of cross-examination

The idea that zealous and energetic cross-examination is an effective tool for uncovering the truth from witnesses has been subject to considerable criticism in recent years. The

Australian Law Commission has stated that 'so far as obtaining accurate testimony is concerned, [cross-examination] is arguably the poorest of the techniques employed at present in the common law courts' (Research Paper No 8, *The Manner of Giving Evidence* (1982), Ch 10, para 5) and John Langbein has described it as a 'flawed theory of truth-seeking' (J Langbein, *The Origins of Adversary Criminal Trial* (2003), 247). Cross-examination does not necessarily aim to elicit the truth, but to challenge or correct what has just been heard. Furthermore, aggressive questioning and the use of obscure language can confuse and frighten witnesses so that they agree with everything or become incoherent, or may be so discouraged from ever testifying; and the fact that a witness contradicts earlier evidence does not necessarily help fact-finders to decide which account to believe. As Louise Ellison has observed:

> [A]dvocates are attitudinally and ethically committed to winning the contest rather than to some other goal such as the discovery of truth or fairness to the opposing side. This standpoint has spawned a decidedly gladiatorial view of court-room advocacy, as evidenced in the metaphors lawyers select to describe litigation. Cross-examination is compared to a physical fight between advocate and witness with frequent references to 'verbal pugilism', 'forensic duels', and 'verbal combat'. Advocacy manuals speak candidly of 'butchering', 'breaking' and 'destroying' opposing witnesses. (L Ellison, The Adversarial Process and the Vulnerable Witness *(2001), 104)*

Why, then, do common law systems place so much importance on oral evidence given by witnesses in person? Historically, all questioning in criminal trials was initiated by the judge, which usually led to a 'freewheeling discussion' between the witnesses, the defendant and the judge. The practice of witnesses being called, examined and then cross-examined by the parties' counsel appears to have emerged in the 1730s, with the purpose being to 'supplement rather than supplant questioning by the court' (J Langbein, *The Origins of Adversary Criminal Trial* (2003), 291). During the nineteenth century, however, cross-examination underwent a sea-change. As the number of lawyers increased and litigation grew, the function of the judge as active inquirer was gradually usurped (ibid, 242–4). Lawyers began to assume ownership of the trial, which underlined the need for closer control of a system that was increasingly characterised by partisan advocacy. Cross-examination remains a central feature of the adversarial trial and Article 6(d) of the European Convention on Human Rights sets out the right of the defendant 'to examine or have examined witnesses against him'. There is no doubt that cross-examination properly conducted can lead to better evidence by disclosing deliberate lies or unintended errors and misconceptions. However, the reality is that cross-examination is a weapon that, though sometimes capable of unearthing the truth, is all too often used to hide or obfuscate it, usually by attacking the character of the witness rather than the evidence given.

Controlling abusive cross-examination

The experience of witnesses

Research has consistently shown that the cross-examination of complainants is often humiliating and distressing, and is largely uncontrolled. Usually such cross-examination is not concerned with the evidence given by the witness but with the character of the witness. If the witness can be shown to have a bad character, or otherwise be shown in a bad light, the jury may well give less credence to that witness's evidence. As noted at p 124 below, historically, victims of rape in particular have been the subject of abusive and intrusive cross-examination about their sexual history and lifestyle with a view to discrediting them. However, abusive and intrusive cross-examination is not confined to victims of rape. The point is well made by Ellison, 'Cross-Examination in Rape Trials' [1998] Crim LR 605, who asserts that few witnesses, regardless of the nature of the offence, escape being subjected to such cross-examination. Ellison cites the study by Paul Rock of one Crown Court, in *The Social World of the English Crown Court* (1993), which revealed that victims and prosecution witnesses in non-sexual cases often felt humiliated, degraded and frustrated by the process of cross-examination. Their treatment was described as 'traduced' and witnesses said that they were 'put on trial', being challenged about their veracity, disinterestedness, integrity, knowledgeability, way of life, reputation and associations.

According to Rock, defence counsel routinely transformed victims into villains and fools. In one assault case, the complainant was described by defence counsel in his closing speech as 'a spiteful, bitchy woman with a drink problem'. In another trial the complainant was cast as 'a deceitful, conniving, drug-pushing lesbian'. Rock reported as a matter of course that witnesses were 'vilified and shamed' under cross-examination, and that 'almost every cross-examination will contain a passage in which counsel puts on a mocking or stern face and presses the witness hard as if trying to drive him or her to anger' (at 268). Unsurprisingly, prosecution witnesses interviewed by Rock perceived cross-examination as an assault upon their identity and complained bitterly about their treatment in court. Rock's findings are confirmed by a study carried out by Brereton (D Brereton, 'How Different are Rape Trials? A Comparison of the Cross-examination of Complainants in Rape and Assault Trials' (1997) 37(2) BJ Criminol 242). He analysed the transcripts of 40 rape trials and 44 assault trials in Victoria in 1989–1991. Substantial similarities were found in the cross-examination strategies employed by defence counsel in both types of trial, and he found that the tactic of discrediting witnesses was used as a 'tool of the trade' rather than being unique to rape trials.

The cross-examination of complainants in rape trials will be examined in some depth at pp 124–146 below, but bear in mind that these studies show that the victim of rape is treated in much the same manner as complainants and witnesses in other trials. However, one should not dismiss the abuse of cross-examination to which they are subjected on the basis that all complainants and witnesses are treated (or mistreated) alike. The crux of the problem is that the treatment of rape complainants stems from the failure to regulate cross-examination as to credit in the criminal trial, and the way in which such cross-examination is all too often used as the last resort of defence counsel whose client has no defence. Indeed, in *The Adversarial Process and the Vulnerable Witness* (2001), Ellison advances the argument even further in contending that cross-examination can never be effectively regulated within an adversarial framework.

The role of the trial judge

The trial judge is seen as an impartial umpire whose overriding duty is to ensure a fair trial. He may call witnesses whom both parties have failed to call, and engage in limited examination and cross-examination if it is deemed necessary in the interests of justice (*R v Wallwork* (1958) 42 Cr App R 153). However, too much interference can be grounds for appeal, and the Court of Appeal has quashed a number of conviction where the judge's interventions have been seen as crossing the line between arbiter and inquisitor (see, eg, *R v Sharp* [1993] 3 All ER 225).

It is therefore unsurprising that empirical studies show a very limited degree of judicial intervention in cross-examination. Brown et al's study of Scottish sexual offence trials, *Sex Crimes on Trial* (1993), and Sue Lees's evaluation of English rape trials, *Carnal Knowledge: Rape on Trial* (1996) reported that there was widespread unwillingness amongst judges to prevent intimidating or unfair cross-examination in rape trials. Similar findings were made by Davies et al in respect of the cross-examination of child witnesses (*An Assessment of the Admissibility and Sufficiency of Evidence in Child Abuse Prosecutions* (1999)), and by Sanders et al with regard to witnesses with learning disabilities (*Victims with Learning Disabilities: Negotiating the Criminal Justice System*, Home Office Research Findings No 44, 1996). In their study of 'Diplock' courts in Northern Ireland where juries are not used, Jackson and Doran found that judges in Northern Ireland were 'acutely conscious of the danger of appearing partisan' (J Jackson and S Doran, *Judge Without Jury: Diplock Trials and the Adversary System* (1995), 113), a view commonplace among both judges and practitioners in Northern Ireland:

> It is the parties and not the judge who are perceived as being responsible for the development of the issues, and a judge's interference comes from an incomplete understanding of the overall picture which counsel wish to construct.

Jackson and Doran also state that where interventions did occur, 'the objection intruded very little on the questioning' (ibid, 112). For example, if counsel was required to clarify a line of questioning, he or she would simply rephrase the same question using different terms. The researchers concluded that although judges do not lack the power to intervene (see *R v Kalia and others* (1974) 60 Cr App R 200; *R v Milton Brown* [1998] 2 Cr App R 364), they do lack the authority to do so.

The problem of multi-defendants

The ordeal of complainants and witnesses is increased in those cases where there are several defendants, each of whom is represented separately. It is thought that there is little that a judge can do to lessen the ordeal of the complainant, since each defendant has a right to cross-examine prosecution witnesses. In a case in 1996, the complainant, who alleged that she was attacked and raped by a number of youths, endured the ordeal of being cross-examined over a number of days by individual counsel representing the separate defendants. The Government has indicated that it will consider means by which such extensive cross-examination may be controlled, but it is unlikely to be a matter for legislation, reliance instead being placed on counsel and judges to limit their cross-examination to prevent undue distress and trauma. *Speaking Up for Justice* (see **Chapter 2**) recommended as follows:

> In the case of multi-defendant cases in order to reduce the trauma of repeated examination on the same points we recommend that, once a particular point has been made during cross-examination counsel for the co-accused should be encouraged to consider saying, 'I adopt the challenge of previous counsel on points x but wish to question you on the additional point.' (Recommendation 44)

As at the time of writing, however, no attempt has been made to implement this recommendation.

The unrepresented defendant

Where a defendant is unrepresented the court has an inherent power to prevent the process being abused by the defendant, but in *R v Morley* [1988] QB 601 the Court of Appeal held that that power is to be exercised exceedingly sparingly. Thereafter, where a defendant was unrepresented, the trial judge tended to allow more latitude in cross-examination to avoid providing grounds for a successful appeal on the basis that the defendant was not permitted to defend himself adequately. As a result of this lenient approach, the complainants in two recent cases (*R v Edwards* (*Ralston*) (1996) *The Times*, 23 August 1996 and *R v Brown* (*Milton*) [1998] 2 Cr App R 364), were subjected to an ordeal when the defendant cross-examined in person; in *Edwards* (*Ralston*), the defendant even wore the same clothes it was alleged he had worn while committing the alleged rape. In both cases the trial judge allowed the defendant great latitude, which meant that the complainant was obliged to relive the ordeal by describing the events subject of the charge in great detail, and being subjected to repetitious and demeaning questioning over a long period. The publicity given to these cases caused the Government to set up a Working Party to consider these and other aspects of the way in which the criminal process treats vulnerable witnesses. The publicity also alerted the Court of Appeal to the problem and to reconsider the approach to the unrepresented defendant laid down in *Morley*.

In *Brown* (*Milton*) [1998] 2 Cr App R 364, a victim of rape was cross-examined for several hours by the defendant in person. The defendant had dispensed with the services of counsel and solicitors at an early stage of the trial and represented himself. In conducting the cross-examination of the complainants, he repeatedly asked repetitious and irrelevant questions designed to intimidate and humiliate them, in particular requiring one complainant to describe in evidence the ordeal to which she complained she had been subjected. The defendant was convicted. In dismissing his application for leave to appeal against conviction and the sentence of 16 years' imprisonment, the Lord Chief Justice, Lord Bingham, pointed out that while many continental jurisdictions obliged defendants to be represented, it was not the British tradition, which permitted individuals to represent themselves in civil and criminal proceedings, the only notable curtailment being that in s 34A of the Criminal Justice Act 1988 (see now ss 34 to 40 of the Youth Justice and Criminal Evidence Act 1999, considered at pp 111–112 below). The trial judge's duty was to ensure to the utmost of his ability that the defendant, even if unrepresented, or perhaps particularly if so, had a fair trial. Every defendant was not guilty until proved to be so. Where, for example, he was accused of rape, the trial could not be conducted on the assumption that he was a rapist and the complainant a victim, since the whole purpose of the proceedings was to establish whether that was the case.

His Lordship referred to the guidance given, in the context of s 34A, in *R v De Oliveira* [1997] Crim LR 600, to the effect that:

(a) the trial judge, without descending into the arena or acting on behalf of the defence, should ask such questions as he saw fit to test the reliability of the prosecution witnesses (see *R v Cameron* (2001) *The Times*, 3 May, considered at p 112 below);

(b) where appropriate the judge might ask the defendant whether there were matters he wished to put to a witness, although it would be for the judge to decide whether and how such matters might be put;

(c) it had to be borne in mind that a heavy duty lay on the prosecution to be scrupulously fair as to how the case was presented so as to avoid any prejudice to the defendant;

(d) in summing up it was desirable to direct the jury that it was open to a defendant to act in person, but that where he chose to do so they should bear in mind the difficulty of him doing so properly;

(e) a sensible course was for the judge to explain some or all of the matters to the jury at the outset of the trial to enable them to understand the course that the trial followed.

His Lordship expressed the court's full agreement with that guidance. The trial judge was obliged to have regard not only to the need to ensure a fair trial for the defendant, but also to the reasonable interests of other parties to the court process, particularly witnesses who were obliged to relive, by describing, an ordeal to which they said they had been subjected.

It was the trial judge's clear duty to do all he could, consistent with giving the defendant a fair trial, to minimise the trauma suffered by other participants. A trial was not fair if a defendant, by choosing to represent himself, gained the advantage he would not otherwise have had of abusing the rules in relation to relevance and repetition that applied when witnesses were questioned. Judges did not lack power to protect witnesses and control questioning. The trial judge was the master of proceedings in his court. He was not obliged to give an unrepresented defendant his head to ask whatever questions, at whatever length, he wished. In a case such as the present it would often be desirable, before any question was asked in cross-examination by the defendant of the complainant, for the judge to discuss the course of proceedings with the defendant in the absence of the jury. The judge could then elicit the general nature of the defence and identify the specific points in the complainant's evidence with which the defendant took issue and any points he wished to put to her. If he proposed to call witnesses in his defence, the substance of their evidence could be elicited so that the complainant's observations, so far as relevant, could be invited.

It would almost always be desirable in the first instance to allow a defendant to put questions to a complainant, but it should be made clear in advance that he would be required, having put a point, to move on, and if he failed to do so the judge should intervene to ensure compliance. If the defendant proved unwilling or unable to comply with the judge's instructions, the judge should, if necessary to save the complainant from avoidable distress, stop further questioning by the defendant and take over the questioning of the complainant. If the defendant sought by his dress, bearing, manner or questions to dominate, intimidate or humiliate the complainant, or if it was reasonably apprehended that he would seek to do so, the judge should not hesitate to order the erection of a screen in addition to controlling the questioning in the way indicated. If, however, exercising the best judgement they reasonably could in circumstances that were always difficult, judges intervened to ensure that witnesses were not subjected to inappropriate pressure, they were clearly to understand that the Court of Appeal would be extremely slow, in the absence of clear evidence of injustice, to disturb any resulting conviction. Where judges, responsible for the conduct of proceedings before them, made decisions with due regard to the interests of all involved, they would continue, as in the past, to be supported by the appellate court.

A news report in *The Times* on 29 March and on 5 April 2000 suggested that judicial control, as indicated above, was not sufficient. The reports stated that the accused, Camille Hourani, a former fiancé of the complainant, who was accused of soliciting to murder, rape and falsely imprison her, frequently reduced the complainant to tears during an extraordinary and highly charged cross-examination of her in person. During almost six days of questioning from 28 March to 4 April, filled with long pauses, ramblings and accusations that the complainant was lying, the defendant at one point exclaimed: 'Stop crying, you could not cry enough.' He accused her of being coached and claimed she was playing games with him. The report stated that the trial judge frequently interrupted the defendant to tell him to 'get on with it', but the rantings, accusations and delaying tactics of the defendant left the complainant physically sick each morning before she was forced into court.

The complainant, a nurse, was being cross-examined seven days after she had given her evidence-in-chief in open court, in which she alleged that after she broke off the affair the defendant held her prisoner for 24 hours, during which she was tied to a bed and subjected to a series of sexual indignities, raped and threatened with death. She had been called back to be cross-examined on two previous occasions, but the defendant refused to carry on after protesting about the conditions in he was being kept while on remand. The complainant had been told she would not be required to attend for cross-examination, but the trial judge agreed to the defendant's request for her to be recalled for that purpose.

Following the publication of *Speaking Up for Justice* (see p 50 above), ss 34 to 40 of the Youth Justice and Criminal Evidence Act 1999 were introduced to restrict the right of self-representation. From September 2000, unrepresented defendants have not been permitted to cross-examine child witnesses at all, neither may they cross-examine adult witness in certain types of cases. Furthermore, a broad discretion has been created to prohibit cross-examination by unrepresented defendants in other circumstances as the judge sees fit.

Under s 34 of the 1999 Act, no person charged with a sexual offence may cross-examine a witness who is the complainant in that offence. This section also replaces and extends the scope of s 34A of the Criminal Justice Act 1988, which had originally prohibited self-representation in cases concerning child violence or child sex abuse. Section 35 replaces and extends this provision to include kidnapping, false imprisonment and abduction.

The discretion contained in s 36 of the Act permits courts to issue directions prohibiting unrepresented defendants from cross-examining complainants in circumstances other than those covered in s 34. A direction may be given following application by the prosecution, or of the court's own motion, if the court is satisfied that the criteria set out in s 36(2) are met. This provides that the court may prohibit the accused from cross-examining any witness where it appears:

(a) that the quality of evidence given by the witness on cross-examination is likely to be diminished if the cross-examination is conducted by the accused in person, and would be likely to be improved if a direction were given under this section; and

(b) that it would not be contrary to the interests of justice to give such a direction.

Section 36(3) sets out a list of criteria which the court should take into account in assessing this:

(a) whether the witness has expressed any opinion as to whether or not he or she is content to be cross-examined by the accused in person;

(b) the nature of the questions likely to be asked;

(c) any behaviour on the part of the accused at any stage of the proceedings, both generally and in relation to the witness; and

(d) any relationship between the witness and the accused.

This section is likely to be used rarely in comparison with s 34, although it could operate where, for example, the charge is harassment or stalking that involves psychological trauma to the victim, or where an elderly lady was the victim of a burglary in which she was subjected to violence by the burglar(s). Sections 37 to 40 of the 1999 Act deal with practical matters relating to these directions, and include the power of the court under s 38 to appoint a representative for an accused in these circumstances where he declines to do so himself.

The tests laid down in the Act contain a number of safeguards for the accused, including the duty imposed on the trial judge under s 39 to give such a warning as he considers necessary to prevent prejudicial inferences being drawn against the accused by the jury in such circumstances.

The power of the judge to take over cross-examination of a witness

While a judge must generally remain impartial, there are circumstances when he may properly exercise his discretion to take over the cross-examination of particular witnesses. In *R v Cameron* (2001) *The Times*, 3 May, a girl of 14, the alleged victim of rape and indecent assault, after being cross-examined for some 15 minutes, refused to answer any more questions put to her by defence counsel. In the absence of the witness the judge discussed the matter with counsel. He asked counsel to provide him with the material that he wished to put to the witness. The judge then told counsel that he would put questions to the witness, though not where the proposed question was mere comment or would unproductively inflame the witness. After questioning the witness the judge told prosecuting counsel that, in the interests of fairness, she would have to forgo re-examination. The Court of Appeal said the judge was not wrong in principle to take over the cross-examination of the complainant. However, while approving the solution adopted by the judge, the Court said the solution adopted would not ordinarily be appropriate to the situation of an adult witness who, without good excuse, refused to answer questions put in cross-examination, though it might be appropriate in the case of a witness who was labouring under a mental disability, or a frightened or traumatised witness in the case of a sexual complaint.

Limitations on the cross-examination of non-defendant witnesses as to bad character

Cross-examination of a witness who has given evidence is seen as a central feature of all common law criminal justice systems. However, the gladiatorial nature of the adversarial trial can often produce a tendency to attack the witness rather than the evidence given by that witness.

Under the scheme proposed by the Law Commission (*Evidence of Bad Character in Criminal Proceedings* (2001, No 273)) and enacted by Pt 11, Ch 1 of the Criminal Justice Act 2003, witnesses will be protected against allegations of misconduct extraneous to the events that are the subject of the trial, and which have only marginal relevance to the facts of the case. For the purpose of deciding whether the evidence has sufficient relevance for leave to be granted, the same criteria apply to defendants and non-defendants. Defendants, however, have additional protection from the prejudicial impact of such evidence, to reflect the fact that it is their liability to criminal sanction which is at stake (see **Chapter 5**).

Under the proposed scheme, leave may be given to adduce evidence of the bad character of a non-defendant if it has substantial explanatory value, or if it has substantial probative value in relation to the matter in issue in the proceedings which is of substantial importance in the context of the case as a whole. 'Bad character' is defined by s 98 of the 2003 Act as 'evidence of, or a disposition towards, misconduct on his part, other than evidence which has to do with the alleged facts of the offence with which the defendant is charged, or ... evidence of misconduct in connection with the investigation or prosecution of the offence'. Under s 112, it is clear that 'misconduct' is intended to be defined broadly and to cover evidence that shows that a person has committed an offence, or has acted in a reprehensible way (or is disposed to do so), as well as evidence from which this might be inferred. This might include previous convictions, as well as evidence on charges being tried concurrently and evidence relating to offences for which a person has been charged, where the charge is not prosecuted, or for which the person was subsequently acquitted. This reflects the previous law: in the case of *R v Z* [2000] 2 AC 483 (see also **Chapter 6**), the House of Lords held that there was no special rule that required the exclusion of evidence that a person had been involved in earlier offences, even if he had been acquitted of those crimes, provided that the evidence was otherwise admissible (that is relevant to and probative of an issue).

Evidence not related to criminal proceedings might include, for example, evidence that a person has a sexual interest in children, even if he has not acted in a criminal way, or that he is a racist. This sort of evidence would have been admissible under the previous common law rules governing the admissibility of evidence of misconduct. Those rules are now abolished, but s 98 ensures that this evidence is admissible under the statutory scheme.

The admissibility of evidence of the facts of the offence(s) charged is not affected, neither are those facts that are closely related in time, place or circumstances to the offence. These are excluded from the definition by s 98(a) and (b), which also exclude evidence of misconduct in connection with the investigation or prosecution of the offence.

Section 100 sets out the circumstances in which, outside the alleged facts of the offence and its investigation and prosecution, evidence can be given of the previous misconduct of a person other than a defendant in the proceedings. This might be a victim of the alleged offence or a witness, but extends to any other person as well. Evidence of their bad character is not to be given without the permission of the court (s 100(4)), and under s 100(1) can be given only if it meets one of three conditions:

(a) if it is important explanatory evidence;

(b) if it is of substantial probative value to a matter in issue and that issue is of substantial importance in the case; or

(c) if the prosecution and defence agree that the evidence should be admitted.

Important explanatory evidence

The term 'explanatory evidence' is used to describe evidence that, while not going to the question of whether the defendant is guilty, is necessary for the jury to have a proper understanding of other evidence being given in the case by putting it in its proper context. An example is provided by the case of *R v M (T)* [2000] 1 WLR 42. Here, the Court of Appeal held that where daughters and sons had been raped and buggered by their father, and the sons were obliged to watch him abuse his daughters and later to abuse them themselves, evidence of 'introductory incidents' was correctly admitted as essential background or 'explanatory evidence'. This included evidence that the accused son was obliged to watch the abuse of his sisters by his father and later to take part (taught to abuse), and that when aged 16 he had gone on seriously to abuse his 10-year-old sister. The court said that such evidence was admissible not as evidence of propensity going to guilt, but as necessary background to enable the jury to understand what would otherwise be an incomplete and incomprehensible account. Similarly, in *R v Sawoniuk* [2000] 2 Cr App R 220, where the defendant was charged with war crimes in Belorussia during the Second World War, evidence of his role as a police officer under the occupying Germans was admitted.

For such evidence to be admissible it must be such that, without it, the magistrates or jury would find it impossible or difficult to understand other evidence in the case (s 100(2)). If, therefore, the facts or account to which the bad character relates are largely understandable without this additional explanation, the evidence will not be admitted. The explanation must also give the court some substantial assistance in understanding the case as a whole. In other words, it will not be enough for the evidence to assist the court to understand some trivial piece of evidence.

In the context of rape, the mere fact of a previous sexual relationship between the complainant and the defendant should be admissible as essential background (explanatory) evidence, but not as evidence of consent or a belief in consent unless there are special features to the relationship that make it relevant to an issue in the case (see the discussion at pp 124–146 below on the admissibility of previous sexual history evidence). If the evidence of the previous sexual relationship is before the court as important explanatory evidence, there would be no breach of the fair trial provisions of Article 6 of the European Convention on Human Rights; the trial would be fair to both defendant and complainant.

Evidence of substantial probative value

Evidence is of probative value, or relevant, to a matter in issue where it helps to prove that issue one way or the other. In respect of non-defendants, victims or witnesses, evidence of bad character is most likely to be relevant where a question is raised about the credibility of the victim or witness (as this is likely to affect the court's assessment of the issue on which the witness is giving evidence). It might also be relevant to support a suggestion by the defendant that another person may be responsible for the offence. Evidence that is of probative value is admissible if it meets an 'enhanced relevance' test set out in s 100(1)(b) of the 2003 Act. This basically means that the evidence must be of substantial probative value and the matter to which it relates must be of substantial importance in the context of the case. Thus evidence of no real significance to an issue, or of only marginally relevance, would not be admissible, neither would evidence that goes only to a trivial or minor issue in the case.

Section 100(3) directs the court to take into account a number of factors when assessing the probative value of evidence of a non-defendant's bad character. These include the nature and number of the events to which it relates and when those events occurred. When considering evidence that is probative because of its similarity with evidence in the case (which might be the case if the defendant were suggesting that that other person was more likely to have committed the offence), the court is directed by s 100(3)(c) to consider the nature and extent of the similarities and dissimilarities. Similarly, where the evidence is being tendered to suggest that a particular person was responsible, s 100(3)(d) requires the court to consider the extent to which the evidence shows, or tends to show, that the same person was responsible each time.

Under this scheme, attacks on the character of a witness would in all cases have to be justified in terms of substantial relevance to credibility. In its above-mentioned report, the Law Commission provided examples of how it saw the scheme in operation (at para 9.32):

> D is charged with theft. W, who was D's employee at the time of the alleged offence, is a witness who will give incriminating evidence which a jury could hardly accept without convicting D. The bad character evidence in question is the fact (not disputed by the prosecution) that, in her previous job, W was dishonest in her expenses claims. D says that the witness is incompetent and therefore mistaken. It is hard to conceive that the evidence would be admissible under our enhanced test.

> Alternatively, D is charged with theft, and wishes to ask W about an allegation that she was dishonest in her previous job. In this example, D's case is that W is lying not incompetent. The fact that in the relatively recent past she has been guilty of dishonesty at the workplace might well surmount the test of enhanced relevance.

> A third variation: D is charged with theft and wishes to ask W about an allegation of dishonesty 10 years previously, or in a non-work context. The court might well take the view that it did not pass the enhanced relevance test (applying s 100(3)(b)).

The Law Commission pointed out that, before the 2003 Act, the evidence of the victim's or witness's past might well be put in or allowed in all three of the above scenarios, or at least under the last two, on the basis that as there is a general dispute about the reliability of a witness's evidence, any evidence which might reflect on his credibility as a witness could be admitted, especially if the defendant did not himself have any previous convictions. Under the 'enhanced relevance' test, the court would force the advocate to consider and articulate why it is that that the evidence ought to be admitted as satisfying that test. The outcome might be that a witness will be saved a public humiliation for a cause which could not sensibly have been thought to advance the defendant's case. At the very least the defence will be forced to sharpen up the focus of their attack.

The enhanced relevance test would also assist in the case of a rape victim who was convicted of shoplifting some 10 years ago. The Law Commission suggested that if the defence is consent then evidence of the conviction would not substantially advance the defence case (in a Channel 4 *Dispatches* programme, 'Getting Away with Rape', which re-enacted a number of actual rape trials, the young victim of rape was cross-examined on a shoplifting conviction that took place *after* the alleged rape. The defence was consent. Under the proposed scheme, that conviction should not be adduced since it would not substantially advance the defence case, though it does damage the credibility of the complainant.

The distinction between evidence of substantial relevance and that of marginal relevance has not always been made in the past. It is noted at pp 126–128 below that, in the cross-examination of a victim of rape, one reason for the failure of a statutory attempt to limit cross-examination about her previous sexual history in s 2 of the Sexual Offences (Amendment) Act 1976, was the failure to distinguish between evidence of substantial relevance to the issue, usually consent, and evidence of only marginal relevance. In *R v A* [2002] 1 AC 45, the House of Lords, in considering s 41 of the Youth Justice and Criminal Evidence Act 1999, the successor to the 1976 Act, held that the exclusion of evidence of marginal relevance to the defence does not necessarily involve a breach of Article 6(2) of the European Convention on Human Rights. Similarly the exclusion of evidence of marginal relevance to the credibility of a witness will not affect the fairness of the trial (see below).

In the context of rape where consent is in issue, much is made of the manner in which the complainant was dressed or made up on the occasion of the rape: short skirts and bright red lipstick suggesting a woman of loose, if not bad, character among 'right-thinking people'. Clubbing, drinking and casual kissing were all presented by defence counsel as characteristics of a loose woman that should be disapproved of. The modern manner of dress, make-up and behaviour does not amount to bad character as defined by ss 98 and 112, and will not therefore be within the enhanced relevance test set out in s 100. It should, however, be subjected to a general test of relevance and judges should be more aware of modern attitudes to such dress and behaviour, and disallow cross-examination that uses such matters to suggest a lack of morality and (possibly) consent to the sexual intercourse subject of the trial.

Application to cross-examine as to bad character
Section 43 of the Youth Justice and Criminal Evidence Act 1999 requires an application for leave to adduce evidence of previous sexual history, in which counsel must specify the grounds on which it is asserted that leave should be given and particular instance(s) of sexual behaviour to which the application relates. As noted previously, the Criminal Justice Act 2003 places limitations on the adducing of the bad character of a witness, and the requirement for leave to adduce evidence of such bad character will necessitate a similar application. Previously counsel were allowed to cross-examine on the basis of unspecified

assertions, often based on no more than the 'client's instructions'. For example, in *R v Howes* [1996] 2 Cr App R 490, the basis of an attempt to cross-examine the victim of an alleged rape about an alleged previous act of intercourse, was that another witness had told the defendant that C had had intercourse with a boy. The Court of Appeal said that no cross-examination should be allowed to proceed unless counsel has instructions which provide 'reasonable grounds' for making the assertion; and it follows that the trial judge can properly ask what the proposed questions were and what support counsel has for them. That case has been overtaken by the procedure set out in s 43 of the Youth Justice and Criminal Evidence Act 1999. The requirement of leave before adducing evidence of bad character in s 100(4) of the 2003 Act, together with the approach in *Howes*, will create a similar reasoned argument approach.

Collateral questions and the finality rule

The fact that most evidence is required to be given orally, and that evidence-in-chief must be followed by cross-examination and re-examination, tends to make trials lengthy affairs. The requirement of relevance helps to prevent trials being too protracted. The rule that answers to collateral questions – that is questions that are not directly relevant to the issue(s) in the proceedings – must be regarded as final also assists in achieving this objective. One is not required to believe the answer to a collateral question, but one is prevented from calling further evidence to demonstrate that the answer is not true. Matters concerning the credit of a witness or the credibility of evidence given, are collateral matters because they do not bear directly on the issue(s) before the jury.

A less than helpful test of what is a collateral matter was put forward in *Attorney-General v Hitchcock* (1847) 1 Ex 91, 99:

> If the answer of a witness is a matter which you would be allowed on your own part to prove in evidence – if it has such a connection with the issues that you would be allowed to give it in evidence – then it is a matter on which you may contradict [the witness].

As a test of the distinction between collateral matters and matters going to the issue, this is tantamount to saying that a matter is in issue if it is in issue. This is of course something of a tautology. The true test, it is said, is whether the matter is relevant to the facts in issue, those facts that must be proved by the prosecution in order to obtain a conviction. If the answer relates to facts in issue, counsel may cross-examine the witness and adduce rebutting evidence to disprove the answer of the witness. If the answer relates to collateral issues, and is thereby not relevant to any material issue in dispute, no rebutting evidence is admissible and the witness cannot be contradicted in cross-examination. This 'Finality Rule' means that the witness's answer in these circumstances must be accepted as final, and that evidence in rebuttal may not be called. However, this does not mean that counsel concedes the answer is correct. This test is unhelpful in certain cases where the credit of the witness is seen as a relevant issue, as it often is in cases of rape.

In the *Hitchcock* case, the witness had been asked whether he had said in an out-of-court statement that he had been offered money to give evidence by excise officers. He denied having said this, and it was held that counsel could not call evidence to prove that he had because it was a collateral matter. Had the evidence been that he had received a bribe, or had been offered or had invited a bribe, the matter could have been pursued and evidence called to prove this. The fact of a bribe, or the offer or invitation of one, could be relevant to issues in the case by suggesting that the prosecution were manufacturing evidence and had no real case. Alternatively the existence of a bribe would suggest that the witness was biased, and that is always a matter which may be proved by other evidence. The question of a bribe is not directly related to the issue, which differs depending on the particular charge. It does nothing to prove that D, charged with theft, actually stole the goods subject of the charge, but is related to that issue in that it suggests a trumped-up charge or a biased witness prepared to lie for money. The true test may therefore be whether the matters that are the subject of the cross-examination are related to a relevant issue in the case in that the matters help to prove or disprove the issue(s) directly or indirectly.

There are a number of exceptions to the rule that the answers to collateral questions are final (see below). When these exceptions apply cross-examination was permitted, but the question whether or not such cross-examination will be permitted in the future depends on whether it seeks to introduce evidence of the bad character of the witness and, if so, whether, applying the enhanced relevance test set out in s 100 of the 2003 Act, the court will admit it.

Previous convictions

Section 6 of the Criminal Procedure Act 1865 provides that a 'witness may be questioned as to whether he has been convicted of an [offence] and upon being so questioned, if he either denies or does not admit the fact, or refuses to answer, it shall be lawful for the cross-examining party to prove such conviction'.

Prior to the Criminal Justice Act 2003, a witness, other than the defendant, could be asked about his previous convictions in accordance with the above provision on the basis that previous convictions were always relevant to the credibility of the witness. Previous convictions are clearly within the definition of 'bad character' in s 98 of the 2003 Act and will be subjected to the enhanced relevance test set out in s 100 (see p 115 above). Instead of the almost automatic admission of previous convictions as being relevant to the credibility of the witness, which was the situation before the 2003 Act, counsel seeking to introduce such convictions must now persuade the court that those convictions are of substantial probative value to an issue in the case which itself is of substantial importance in the context of the case.

The issue will usually be the credibility of the witness and, as indicated by the examples above, the probative value of the conviction and the importance of the witness's credibility in the context of the case will depend on the facts and circumstances of each case. However, if a previous conviction is to be probative the issue will usually have to be the honesty or otherwise of the witness. If the defence claim a prosecution witness is mistaken, a previous conviction is unlikely to meet the enhanced relevance test. If the defence claim that a prosecution witness committed the offence charged then previous convictions for that kind of offence might well be relevant. Thus if D is charged with causing grievous bodily harm to V, and D claims that it was V who attacked him and he only defended himself against that attack, the fact that V has convictions for violence may well be relevant to support that defence and could satisfy the enhanced relevance test (see also the discussion in **Chapter 5**, where it is noted that under s 101(1)(g) of the 2003 Act, the defendant's previous convictions and bad character may be admitted if he attacks another person's character).

The Rehabilitation of Offenders Act 1974 does not apply to criminal trials, but a *Practice Direction* [1975] 1 WLR 1065 gives judges a discretion to exclude spent convictions. Section 100(3) of the 2003 Act adds to that by requiring the trial judge to have regard a number of factors, including when those events happened or existed. Thus, as indicated in the example from the Law Commission at p 115 above, a 10-year-old conviction may not be seen as passing the enhanced relevance test.

Section 16(2) of the Children and Young Persons Act 1963 restricted the use of previous convictions when the defendant was a child. Section 108 of the Criminal Justice Act 2003 repeals that provision and provides for additional requirements for the admission of the defendant's convictions when under 14 (discussed at pp 182–183 below). This provision does not apply to a witness or victim, but the general principle that convictions when a juvenile are not normally relevant applies. It follows while such convictions may be the subject of cross-examination, they will be subjected to the enhanced test of relevance and, in particular, to s 100(3)(b), which requires the court to have regard to when the events occurred, or other things to which the evidence relates.

Convictions as a child, or spent convictions under the Rehabilitation Act 1974 may be seen as so stale as not to pass the enhanced relevance test. If the enhanced relevance test is satisfied a witness may be asked about his previous convictions and, if he denies them or refuses to answer, they may be proved, usually by a certificate of the court of conviction.

Bias or partiality

A witness may be questioned about matters that suggest bias or partiality and, if denied, the necessary facts may be proved in rebuttal. Such bias or partiality, though collateral in the sense that it goes to credibility, can go to the issue in the same way as the fact that the witness was bribed. It suggests manufactured evidence and no real case. In *R v Mendy* (1976) 64 Cr App R 4, the husband of the accused, who was to be called as a witness for her, was waiting outside the court, as all witnesses in a criminal case should before being called to give evidence. He was seen talking to a man who had been in court taking notes of the evidence. The implication was that, knowing what evidence had been given, he could tailor his evidence to assist his wife's defence. Under cross-examination he denied this, and the prosecution were allowed to bring evidence to rebut his denial. The Court of Appeal held that the rule of finality was not absolute and should not prevent the jury hearing evidence that suggested an attempt to pervert the course of justice. Similarly, in *R v Phillips* (1936) 26 Cr App R 17, the defendant was charged with incest and the defence wanted to pursue a line of questioning which suggested that his two daughters, the alleged victims, had been schooled by their mother and had admitted to others that the allegations against their father were not true. The children denied this and the trial judge refused leave to allow the defence to bring evidence in rebuttal. The Court of Appeal held that he was wrong to refuse leave. The questions and the evidence went to the heart of the issue in the case and were not collateral.

More recent cases involving police evidence have given a new twist to this line of authority. In *R v Busby* (1982) 75 Cr App R 79, it was alleged that police officers had threatened a defence witness to prevent him giving evidence for the accused. The officers denied this. It was held that this was not a collateral matter but went to the issue. If true, it showed an attempt to influence the outcome of the trial. Referring to *Mendy* and *Phillips*, the Court of Appeal held that the evidence in rebuttal of the denial was clearly admissible. This case has been described as a novel departure from precedent, but it is in line with the earlier cases, being concerned simply with a different way of seeking to pervert the course of justice.

R v Edwards [1991] 1 WLR 207 is more of a novel departure. The question for the Court of Appeal was whether the defence should be allowed to cross-examine the police officers in the case in order to show that they had given evidence in other cases, and that there had been reason to believe that evidence was dishonest and had been rejected by the jury who had returned verdicts of not guilty. The Court of Appeal held that the mere fact that an accused was acquitted in an earlier case in which the police officers gave evidence, did not provide a basis for cross-examining the officers on that evidence and outcome. However, where there was evidence that the officers had given evidence of an admission by the accused in a previous trial, and it could be demonstrated that the jury had disbelieved that evidence, and that the defence in the present case was fabrication, the jury were entitled to be made aware of what had happened in the earlier trial. The officers could therefore be asked about the earlier trials, but surprisingly the Court went on to say that in the unlikely event of the officers giving answers unfavourable to the defence, the defence would not be able to contradict those answers by calling evidence in rebuttal. This appears to contradict the Court's intention that the jury should be aware of facts which suggest that the officer is not the truthful witness he purports to be. There may be evidence to suggest that the police officer is dishonest, but we must rely on the honesty of the officer to ensure that the jury become aware of that evidence. Of course, a police officer will rarely deny facts that are in the public domain, or answer falsely and expose himself to a charge of perjury, but it seems strange that on the rare occasion when he does so, the defence will be unable to prove the truth unless the officer has a previous conviction for perjury, or violence to a prisoner if the accusation is of threats to obtain a confession (which may include conviction on disciplinary charges), or the defence can bring it within another exception to the Finality Rule.

The *Edwards* case arose out of the activities of the West Midland Serious Crime Squad, some members of which were proved to have used violence or threats of violence to obtain confessions or manufactured confessions. The police and prosecution feared that the opening up of the role of the police officers in other trials would lead to an overall loss of credibility and unjust acquittals. Where an officer's background is open to an attack on his credibility, the prosecutor's natural reaction is, where possible, not to call him as a witness. The proper course would be to call the witness and ask at the outset of the examination-in-chief whether he had been suspended, otherwise the court would assume he is a serving officer. Furthermore, the officer should be required to give evidence in accordance with his statement and not merely tendered for cross-examination, which is the practice when more than one officer is to give the same evidence (*R v Haringey Justices, ex p DPP* [1996] QB 351).

In *Haringey Justices*, ex p DPP, Stuart-Smith LJ held that a witness's credibility should be determined in relation to the content of his evidence and not in relation to his credit generally, unless the prosecution had reason to believe that the evidence he would give was or might be untrue because he had been found guilty of perverting the course of justice in other cases, or for some other reason. Some purely collateral act of dishonesty, whether proved or merely suspected, did not mean that a witness's evidence on a wholly unrelated matter was not credible. This is correct in theory, but in practice prosecution and defence counsel will seek expose a witness's bad character and any previous convictions with a view to suggesting to the jury that he is not worthy of belief. Convictions for dishonesty are used to suggest that a person who is dishonest in one respect is probably dishonest in another respect. Other convictions will be used to suggest that the witness is of poor moral character and for that reason less worthy of belief. The adduction of bad character evidence is now subject to the enhanced relevance test set out in s 100 of the 2003 Act. If counsel believes that this test will be satisfied in relation to a particular witness, he might put the character of that witness before the jury themselves, rather than allowing the other side to expose it and suggest an attempt to hide it from the jury and deceive them.

In *R v Edwards (Maxine)* [1996] 2 Cr App R 345, the Stoke Newington Drugs Squad, whose members had been the subject of an inquiry into planting of evidence and perjury (known as Operation Jackpot), arrested Edwards on suspicion of possessing crack cocaine with intent to supply. The police alleged that when they searched her they discovered eight foil wraps, later found to contain crack cocaine, and £175 cash. They said that she had admitted that the wraps contained cocaine while in the car on the way to the police station. She refused to sign a note of this admission and at her trial said she had never been in possession of the foil wraps. The police, she said, had found them in a parked car she was standing next to. She was convicted and her application for leave to appeal was refused by a single judge and the full court. However, following the inquiry into the Drug Squad's activities, and the acquittal of a number of persons arrested and charged by the Squad, the Home Office referred the case to the Court of Appeal under s 17(1)(a) of the Criminal Appeal Act 1968.

Allowing the appeal, the Court held that the appellant was one of a number of persons convicted on very similar evidence from officers of the Stoke Newington Drug Squad and who had complained that the evidence was fabricated. An investigation, Operation Jackpot, was launched in 1991. One of the officers had been involved between 1991 and 1993, along with others who had been investigated, in cases that had resulted in acquittals after allegations of fabrication, or in which police prosecutions were dropped or the Crown had not contested the case. The prosecution had argued that because no charges had been made or disciplinary proceedings taken against the officers who had arrested the appellant, the conviction could not be said to be unsafe. However, the fact remained that in 1993 the degree of suspicion of the trustworthiness of the evidence of one of the arresting officers, and of others with whom he was working, was such that the Crown conceded that convictions based on that evidence could not be supported:

> *Once the suspicion of perjury starts to infect the evidence and permeate cases in which the witnesses have been involved, and which are closely similar, the evidence on which such convictions are based becomes as questionable as it was in the cases in which the*

appeals have already been allowed. It is impossible to be confident that had the jury which convicted this appellant known the facts and circumstances in the other cases in which [the witness] had been involved, that they would have been bound to convict this appellant. (per Beldam LJ, at 350)

The above test was applied in *R v Whelan* [1997] Crim LR 353, where the accused had been convicted of possessing cannabis. The arresting officers in the case were arrested and suspended from duty after an investigation into their conduct in other cases of alleged possession of drugs. This had led the prosecution to offer no evidence in other cases in which the arrested officers were involved. On appeal, the prosecution in this case conceded that had they known at the time of trial that the officers were under investigation, they would not have relied on the officers' evidence. The Court of Appeal allowed the appeal and held that the prosecution were right to make the concession.

These cases involving bias or corruption fall within the definition of bad character in ss 98 and 112 of the 2003 Act as reprehensible behaviour. As such, the enhanced relevance test in s 100 must be applied, but is likely to be satisfied in the cases mentioned above.

Previous inconsistent statements

If under cross-examination a witness denies a previous oral or written statement made by him that is relevant to an issue in the case and is inconsistent with his testimony, s 4 of the Criminal Procedure Act 1865 allows that statement to be proved against him. The provision refers to statements which 'are relative to the subject matter of the indictment or proceedings'. Whether the statement is or is not 'relative' (relevant) is a matter for the trial judge. Under s 5 of the 1865 Act, the witness may be cross-examined on any document containing a previous inconsistent statement without showing it to the witness, but, because the judge has the right under s 5 to call for the document and make such use of it as he thinks fit, the party cross-examining must have it with him even if he does not intend to contradict the witness with it. If he does intend to contradict the witness with it, he must show it to the witness, draw attention to the contradictory parts, ask him to read those parts and then ask whether he still wishes to stand by what he has said in court. If he declines to do so and adopts what is said in the previous statement, that statement becomes part of the evidence, replacing any earlier testimony. If he sticks to the evidence given in court, the cross-examiner may wish to use the document to contradict what the witness said. If so, he must prove the document and put it in evidence. The court and jury may then inspect the whole document, though the trial judge may direct that the jury see only the parts referred to in cross-examination.

When a previous inconsistent statement was adduced into evidence in this way, it was not evidence of the truth of its contents but went only to the consistency and credit of the witness, and the judge had to make this clear to the jury. Following a recommendation by the Law Commission in its *Report on Hearsay Evidence* (1997, No 245, at para 10.92), that rule has now been changed by s 119(1) of the Criminal Justice Act 2003, which provides that such a statement will be evidence of any matter stated in it of which oral evidence by that person would be admissible. Section 119(2) makes a similar provision when a previous inconsistent statement is admitted to attack the credibility of a witness who does not give oral evidence but whose statement is admitted under one of the exceptions created or preserved by the 2003 Act.

Evidence of physical or mental disability affecting reliability

Almost all witnesses who give identification evidence will be cross-examined about their eyesight and whether they wear glasses – American trial dramas on television are replete with examples of the trial lawyer testing the eyesight of a witness in court and dramatically showing that he or she is unable to see how many fingers are being held up. The effect is to totally destroy the credibility of the witness. Such theatrics are seldom used in English criminal courts, but the effect of proving that the witness, who claims to have positively identified the accused from a distance of 50 yards, has defective vision and cannot see clearly beyond 30 yards, even wearing his spectacles, is the same. Such an example was given in the leading case on this area of law, *Toohey v The Metropolitan Police Commissioner* [1965] AC 595. Here, the accused was convicted of assault with intent to rob. The defence was that the alleged victim had been drinking and, while the accused and his friends were trying to help him by taking him home, he became hysterical and accused them of trying to rob him. The trial judge allowed evidence from a doctor that the victim had been drinking and was hysterical when examined, but refused to allow the witness to state his opinion that the drink exacerbated the hysteria and that the victim was more prone to hysteria than the average person. The Court of Appeal dismissed the appeal but the House of Lords quashed the conviction, holding that the doctor should have been allowed to give his opinion. The evidence was admissible to show that the witness was unreliable, whether or not it affected his credibility:

> *Medical evidence is admissible to show that the witness suffers from some disease or defect or abnormality of mind that affects the reliability of his evidence. Such evidence is not confined to a general opinion of the unreliability of the witness but may give all matters necessary to show, not only the foundation of and the reasons for the diagnosis, but also the extent to which the credibility of the witness is affected.* (per Pearce LJ, at 609)

The opposing party may call expert evidence in rebuttal, but such evidence should be confined to the issues raised by the medical evidence and should not usurp the role of the jury in determining whether V is a credible witness. This was emphasised by Lord Pearce in *Toohey*, where he said (at 608):

> *Human evidence ... is subject to many cross-currents such as partiality, prejudice, self-interest and above all, imagination and accuracy. These are matters with which the jury, helped by cross-examination and common sense, must do their best. But when a witness through physical (in which I include mental) disease or abnormality is not capable of giving a true or reliable account to the jury, it must surely be allowable for medical science to reveal this vital hidden fact to them.*

The point is further illustrated by the decision of May J in *R v Mackenney* (1981) 72 Cr App R 78, where he refused to allow a psychologist, who had studied the main prosecution witness while he gave evidence, to give evidence that the witness was a psychopath who was likely to be lying. A distinction was drawn between the witness who suffers from a mental disability that makes him incapable of giving evidence, and the witness who is capable of giving reliable evidence but may not be doing so. The jury may need help with the former, but it is for them, assisted by cross-examination and common sense, to determine whether the witness who is capable of giving reliable evidence is doing so.

Evidence of a reputation for untruthfulness

It has long been the case that a witness may be called to give evidence that in his opinion a witness called by the other side is not to be believed on his oath. The rule was restated in *R v Richardson* [1969] 1 QB 299 at 304–5:

1. A witness may be asked whether he has knowledge of the impugned witness's general reputation for veracity and whether (from such knowledge) he would believe the witness's sworn testimony.

2. The witness called to impeach the credibility of another witness may also express his individual opinion (based upon his personal knowledge) as to whether the latter is to be believed on his oath, and is not confined to giving an opinion based merely on general reputation.

3. But whether his opinion as to the impugned witness's credibility be based simply upon the latter's general reputation for veracity or upon his personal knowledge, the witness cannot be permitted to indicate during his examination-in-chief the particular facts, circumstances or incidents that formed the basis of his opinion, although he may be cross-examined as to them.

There are more arguments against allowing such evidence than there are for it. Despite this, s 118(1) of the Criminal Justice Act 2003 preserves the common law rule that evidence of a person's reputation is admissible for the purposes of proving his good or bad character. The danger is that poor reputations may be unearned and the product of malicious gossip. The usual rule is that witnesses give evidence of facts and only experts in the particular field express opinions. If the witness is not allowed to give evidence of particular facts on which his opinion is based, how are the jury to determine what weight to give to such an opinion? If a witness is called for this purpose, it is open to the other side to call witnesses as to that witness's reputation and so on, thus unnecessarily prolonging trial. Fortunately, it is rare to call such witnesses (but see *R v Bogie* [1992] Crim LR 302, where a number of defence witnesses, male and female, testified as to the general reputation for untruthfulness of the complainant in a case of alleged rape).

Cross-examination of rape complainants

Evidence of previous sexual history

Many of the problems experienced by rape complainants in court discussed earlier in this chapter arise from the defence seeking to adduce previous sexual history evidence. It might be assumed that since questions concerning previous sexual history were not directed to proving a fact in issue, these should be regarded as being collateral, and therefore subject to the finality rule. This, however, is not the case. The common law has traditionally accepted that in crimes of rape, attempted rape, and assault with intent to commit rape, acts of intercourse between the victim and the accused were relevant to the issue and could thus be the subject of cross-examination and rebuttal of any denials (see *R v Riley* (1887) 18 QBD 481). The common law also permitted the complainant to be cross-examined about acts of intercourse with men other than the accused, but, because this was a collateral matter, her denial of such acts could not be contradicted by calling evidence of such acts of intercourse (*R v Holmes* (1871) LR 1 CCR 334). However, the fact that one could not call contradictory evidence did not prevent counsel asking the questions that, regardless of the answer, were designed to cast doubt on the complainant's moral character and her credibility by suggesting that she was a 'loose woman'.

In *R v Bashir and Manzur* [1969] 1 WLR 1303, it was held that evidence that the complainant in a case of rape was a prostitute was admissible to contradict a denial, because it went to the issue of consent. Similarly, in *R Krausz* (1973) 57 Cr App Rep 466, the accused, charged with rape, alleged that he met the complainant in a pub for the first time and she agreed to sleep with him. After intercourse she demanded money, and complained of rape only when he refused to pay. The Court of Appeal held the judge was wrong to refuse to allow the defence to call evidence of previous similar conduct by the complainant to rebut her denial.

Even in 1973 it was questionable whether the fact that a woman was promiscuous was of any relevance to the question whether she consented to intercourse on a particular occasion. The *Report of the Advisory Group on the Law of Rape (Heilbron Report)* (1975, Cmnd 6352) led to statutory changes to the law on cross-examination of victims of rape and related offences. The Report recognised that the existing procedure, which permitted much exploration of the woman's previous sexual history, tended unjustly to stigmatise the complainant and suggest that she was the type of woman who either should not be believed, or who deserved no protection from the law, or was likely to have consented anyway. It came to the conclusion that unless some restrictions were placed on cross-examination, 'questioning can take place that does not advance the cause of justice but in effect puts the woman on trial' (para 91). The Report recommended that no evidence of the previous sexual history of the complainant with persons other than the accused should be admitted unless (i) the judge is satisfied that the evidence relates to behaviour on the part of the complainant which was strikingly similar to her alleged behaviour on the occasion of, or in relation to, events immediately preceding the alleged offence; and (ii) the degree of relevance of that evidence to issues arising in the trial is such that it would be unfair to the accused to exclude it.

Section 2 of the Sexual Offences (Amendment) Act 1976 (now replaced by s 41 of the Youth Justice and Criminal Evidence Act 1999, considered at pp 128–146 below) placed restrictions on the cross-examination of a complainant in cases of rape and other sexual offences, but not in the way the Heilbron Report recommended. The provision stipulated:

(1) If at any trial any person is for the time being charged with a rape offence to which he pleads not guilty, then, except with the leave of the judge, no evidence and no question in cross-examination shall be adduced or asked at the trial, by or on behalf of any defendant at the trial, about any sexual experience of a complainant with a person other than the defendant.

(2) The judge shall not give leave in pursuance of the preceding subsection for any evidence or question except on an application made by him in the absence of the jury by or on behalf of a defendant; and on such an application the judge shall give leave if and only if he is satisfied that it would be unfair to that defendant to refuse to allow the evidence to be adduced or the question to be asked.

The test Heilbron proposed was taken from the then test for the admission of evidence of previous misconduct by the accused. At the time of the Report the test was that the evidence had to be relevant to an issue in the case, but not merely relevant but so very relevant that its probative value outweighed the prejudicial effect of admitting it. The fact that the previous conduct was strikingly similar to the conduct complained of in the present case was seen as giving it relevance, but then the trial judge had to balance the prejudicial effect of that evidence against its probative value. However, s 2 of the 1976 Act preserved the common law view that evidence of previous sexual experience of the complainant with the defendant is relevant to consent, and excluded such evidence and questioning from the ambit of s 2. It followed that all the common law cases, except *R v Riley*, were to be read in the light of s 2.

The statutory test under s 2(2) of the 1976 Act was whether 'it would be unfair to that defendant to refuse to allow the evidence to be adduced or the question to be asked', and though the court had to attempt to balance justice for the accused with fairness to and the protection of the complainant, the statutory emphasis was on whether it was fair to the accused to exclude such evidence, not whether its admission might be unfortunate for the complainant. It was clear that only if the evidence was relevant to the issue(s) in the trial (usually consent) could it be unfair to the accused not to admit it, but there are degrees of relevance and there was no consideration of how relevant the evidence was to that issue. The result was that once it was determined that the evidence was relevant, it must be unfair to the accused not to admit it. Section 2(2) not only gave the trial judge the power to restrict prejudicial questions in cross-examination, it also gives him the power to override the finality rule. This was one of the major problems with the 1976 Act.

The distinction between questions going to credit and questions going to the issue had effectively disappeared in rape trials. The previous behaviour of the complainant was almost always seen to be relevant to the issue, usually consent, with the result that the finality rule was overridden, and a statute passed to restrict the use of sexual history, which was thought to go only to credit, in fact allowed its use just as often as, if not more often than, the common law had.

In *R v Funderburk* [1990] 2 All ER 482, the defendant alleged that the complainant, who described in graphic detail losing her virginity to him, was lying as she was already sexually experienced. He wished to adduce evidence that the girl had told him, and others, on a number of occasions, that she was sexually experienced. If such evidence was relevant to the credibility of the witness alone, it could not be adduced; if it was relevant to the facts in issue, it could be heard. The trial judge refused permission, although his refusal was overturned by the Court of Appeal. As the Court saw it, these facts were intimately connected with the facts in issue.

In *R v Nagrecha* [1997] 2 Cr App R 401, the Court of Appeal took the same view. The accused was convicted of indecent assault, which he had denied. The only evidence was that of the complainant, C. She was cross-examined to the effect that she had made allegations of sexual misconduct against others, which she denied. The defence sought leave to call a witness, L, to say that C was a difficult woman who had made allegations of sexual misconduct against him. The judge refused to allow the evidence to be adduced because the cross-examination was to C's credit, therefore a collateral matter, and her answers were final. The Court of Appeal quashed the conviction, holding that the defence should have been allowed to call the rebutting witness. The evidence of that witness went to the heart of the case, which depended on C's credibility. Since she had denied making a complaint against the witness, it was possible to call him on the issue of whether she had done so without going into the peripheral matter of whether the allegation was true. The jury might have taken a different view of C's credibility had the evidence been adduced.

Dennis comments that the decision in *Funderburk* was defensible on the basis of the facts, but notes that it has been interpreted as 'authority for a wide principle that in sexual cases generally the court should not draw too fine a line between matters going to the issue and matters going to credit'. He contends that this interpretation was also evident in *Nagrecha*, which he argues gave 'a green light to the defence to investigate any and all inconsistencies in a complainant's evidence', where the case centred on whether or not she is telling the truth (*The Law of Evidence* (2002), 485). Since many rape cases turn on the issue of consent, complainants in such cases were particularly vulnerable to having their past behaviour admitted in evidence at court under s 2 of the 1976 Act.

Research by Zsuzsana Adler (*Rape on Trial* (1989)) found that an application to admit sexual history evidence was made under s 2 in 40% of the cases studied, and was admitted in 75% of such applications. The research further suggests that the use made of such evidence seems to go beyond that demanded in the interests of relevance to the issues in the trial, being used, contrary to the intention of s 2, in an attempt to discredit the victim's character in the eyes of the jury. This goes beyond the need for fairness to the defendant, who is protected from exposure to questioning on his own previous misconduct (*Speaking Up for Justice*, para 9.63). More recently, Lees's study, *Carnal Knowledge: Rape on Trial* (1996), found that over half of all female acquaintance rape complainants in her study were questioned about their sexual history with men other than the defendant. She found that in some cases such questions were asked without application under s 2 either because judges and counsel are unaware of the prohibition imposed by the section, or because, though aware of the prohibition, counsel ignore it and judges fail to prevent them doing so. The fact that 75% of applications (when made) to adduce evidence of the complainant's previous sexual history succeeded, lent credence to the criticism that s 2 contained no requirement that the sexual history evidence should be of a high degree of relevance to the issue in the case, and that the Act was overly concerned with fairness to the defendant at the expense of the complainant.

The principal problems with s 2 of the 1976 Act were twofold. First, the emphasis on fairness to the accused to the exclusion of any detriment to the complainant, and the failure to require a high degree of relevance to an issue in the trial before the evidence could be admitted, allowed evidence of past sexual history to be adduced or question(s) to be asked about such history. Ultimately, the decision whether or not to grant leave to allow the defence to cross-examine the witness about previous sexual history was a matter for the trial judge. The Court of Appeal made clear in *R v Viola* [1982] 3 All ER 73 that this was not a matter of judicial discretion. The judge had to determine, first, whether the evidence was relevant to the issue of consent, then whether or not it would be unfair to the accused to disallow such questioning. The second problem was the failure to control cross-examination about previous sexual history between the accused and the complainant, the section applying only to 'persons other than the defendant'. Given that a majority of alleged rapes involve an acquaintance, and many of these involve previous acts of intercourse between the parties, the section failed to control cross-examination as to sexual history in the majority of cases.

Reform: the Youth Justice and Criminal Evidence Act 1999, ss 41–43

In 1998, *Speaking Up for Justice* (see p 50 above) paved the way for a major overhaul of the law regulating sexual history evidence. The subsequent Youth Justice and Criminal Evidence Act 1999 ('the 1999 Act') repealed s 2 of the 1976 legislation, replacing it with a new provision in an attempt to put an end to such cross-examination. The new provision, contained in s 41 of the 1999 Act, is not the easiest to interpret, but the first point to note is that the restriction on questioning the complainant about any of his or her sexual behaviour without leave of the court applies to any sexual behaviour or experience, including any with the accused. Section 2 of the 1976 Act did not apply to sexual experience with the accused. The new law applies to trials for sexual offences, whereas the 1976 Act applied only to rape offences. 'Sexual behaviour' means any sexual behaviour or other sexual experience, whether or not involving any accused or other person, but excluding (except in s 41(3)(c)(i) and (5)(a)) anything alleged to have taken place as part of the event which is subject matter of the charge against the accused (s 42(1)(c)).

In *R v T; R v H* [2002] Crim LR 73, in two separate cases T was charged with rape on his niece, and H with indecent assault on his stepdaughter. The trial judge had refused to allow cross-examination directed by the defence to one of the complainants alleging past fabrication of such an assault, and the other complainant's failure to mention the alleged assault when complaining of other such assaults. In T's case it was submitted that the proposed questions were about the failure to mention the allegations and not about 'sexual behaviour'. In H's case it was argued that the questions were about lies, albeit about sexual matters.

The Court of Appeal, allowing the appeal in both cases, held that the questions were relevant to the issues in the trial and were not automatically inadmissible under s 41, not being evidence of sexual behaviour or experience within s 42(1)(c). The courts had in the past drawn a distinction between questions about sexual behaviour itself and questions concerning statements about such behaviour by the complainant. The Court held, per curiam, that it would be open to the trial judge to prevent abuse of questioning where there was not an evidential basis for the defence asserting that a previous statement had been made and that it was untrue. It would be profoundly improper to elicit details of a complainant's previous sexual experience under the guise of previous false complaints. The withdrawal of a complaint of rape or other sexual assault in the past, or the failure to proceed with a prosecution, may be seen as outside that definition, but the relevance of such withdrawal or failure depends very much upon the circumstances. The withdrawal of a complaint of rape or sexual assault is relevant only if the complaint was not true. A complaint withdrawn because the complainant could not face the prospect of a trial is of no relevance to the issues in the case. Adopting a purposive approach in interpreting the statute, the Court noted that the mischief at which s 41 was aimed was to prevent evidence of the complainant's sexual behaviour being admitted and presented to the jury with the invitation to infer from it that a person with a colourful sexual history is more likely to tell lies, or to have consented to the sexual intercourse subject of the charge.

In *R v Mukadi* [2004] Crim LR 373, the complainant, C, met the defendant at a Tesco store where he worked as a security guard. C entered the store wearing a short, tight skirt, transparent in places, and a vest top. C and M got into conversation and, since the defendant was about to finish his shift, they went to a park where they drank a bottle of wine. Afterwards they travelled by tube to the defendant's flat, where they kissed and oral sex took place. However, full intercourse followed, which C said was without consent. When the defendant went to the bathroom, C tried to escape via a window but fell, fracturing both wrists and a kneecap. The issue was consent; in support M sought to adduce evidence that before C entered the Tesco store, she was standing on the pavement when a large and expensive car drew up driven by a much older sole male. C got in to the car and they drove to a filling station. Presently she left the car, having exchanged telephone numbers. The trial judge refused to admit this evidence because it had no bearing on the issue of consent.

On appeal it was held that the judge was wrong to conclude that the behaviour had no bearing on the issue of consent. It would have been possible for the jury to draw the proper inference that when C got into the car she anticipated some sexual activity with the occupant. By contrast, C said that when she went to M's flat, she merely intended to get to know him with a view to becoming friends. If the jury heard about the car incident, that would have been relevant when assessing that part of her evidence. If it was sexual behaviour it was admissible under s 41(3)(b), and a refusal of leave under s 41(2)(b) would have had the effect of rendering unsafe a conclusion of the jury on the issue of consent. If it was not sexual behaviour it was not within s 41 and was relevant and admissible. In the circumstances, C's behaviour shortly before 'picking up' M probably was 'sexual behaviour' coming close to acting as a prostitute picking up clients for sex, and was clearly relevant to the issue of whether C consented to intercourse with M.

Refusal of leave

As under s 2 of the 1976 Act, the court can give leave under s 41 of the 1999 Act to allow questions about any sexual behaviour with the accused or anyone else, but only on an application by or on behalf of the accused, and then only if the court is satisfied 'that a refusal of leave might have the result of rendering unsafe a conclusion of the jury or (as the case may be) the court on any relevant issue in the case'. This is an improvement on the test under the 1976 Act and the interpretation of that test in *R v Lawrence* [1977] Crim LR 492, which based the test around the likelihood that the jury might take a different view had the evidence been adduced or the questions asked. The problem was that juries, hearing about the complainant's sexual history, often did take a different view based on bias or prejudice resulting from the debasement of her character.

The question whether the conclusion of a jury might be unsafe is inevitably based on guesswork as to what the basis of that conclusion was, given that we cannot ask the jury why they came to a particular conclusion. However, the judgment as to whether a conclusion of the jury might be unsafe if the evidence is not adduced or the questions not asked, will again be based on the relevance of the evidence or question to the relevant issue(s) in the case. The difficulty is that once again there is no requirement of a substantial degree of relevance to the issue. The phrase in s 41(2)(b), 'the refusal of leave *might* have the result', suggests a low degree of relevance, allowing sexual history evidence more readily than if the section said 'refusal of leave *would* have the result'. Section 41(4) (considered below) may help to raise the level of relevance.

The distinction between matters going to credit and matters going to the issue

There also remains the problem, identified in relation to the 1976 legislation, of the blurring of the distinction between matters going to credit and matters going to the issue. Unless that problem is addressed, the admissibility decisions under s 41 may not be all that different from those taken under the former regime. However, s 41(4) attempts to restore the distinction between credit and the issue, providing that 'no evidence or question shall be regarded as relating to a relevant issue in the case if it appears to the court to be reasonable to assume that the purpose (or main purpose) for which it would be adduced or asked is to establish or elicit material for impugning the credibility of the complainant as a witness'.

Much will depend on whether the courts are prepared to accept this distinction. The subsection may be interpreted as a means of excluding evidence of low relevance to an issue in the case that is highly prejudicial to the complainant. The fact that it is of low relevance but very damaging to the complainant makes it reasonable to assume that the purpose (or main purpose) is to impugn credibility, rather than assist in proving or disproving the relevant issue. On the other hand, if the evidence is highly relevant and highly prejudicial, it cannot be reasonable to assume that the purpose (or main purpose) of adducing the evidence is to impugn credibility, though that is an inevitable consequence of allowing the evidence to be adduced. In *R v Martin (Durwayne)* [2004] 2 Cr App R 22, the Court of Appeal emphasised the distinction between the main purpose of adducing the evidence and one of the purposes. The defendant alleged that the complainant had pestered him for sex and that it was his rejection of her advances which led to her making a false allegation against him. The trial judge refused to permit cross-examination of the complainant as to the alleged sexual acts, on the basis that the main purpose of the cross-examination was to impugn the credibility of C. The Court of Appeal took the view that the judge's ruling was wrong. One purpose of the proposed questions was to impugn the credibility of C, but it could also realistically be said that one purpose was to strengthen the defence case. It was one purpose, but not the main purpose, to impugn the credibility of the complainant. Accordingly the judge's ruling was wrong. However, the defendant did not give evidence and the judge would have directed the jury that the question, if allowed, did not result in any evidence on which the jury could act. The conviction was therefore safe.

This briefly reported case suggests that s 41(4) will not be the safeguard against the adduction of evidence intended to blacken the character of the complainant that it was intended to be. One presumes the trial judge had received an application for leave to adduce the evidence of the alleged sexual advances which, in accordance with the rules of court made under s 43, requires specific particulars of the grounds on which it was asserted that leave should be given. Section 41(6) also requires that the evidence or questions relate to specific instances of alleged sexual behaviour on the part of the complainant. If the defendant is to be permitted to cross-examine C on the basis of an allegation which the defendant is not prepared to support by giving evidence, and for which there appears to be no other support, the complainant's character will be impugned and a direction to the jury that the questions did not result in any evidence upon which they can act is unlikely to repair the damage done.

The application for leave to adduce sexual history evidence

The provision in s 42(3) of the 1999 Act for rules of court requiring application to be made for leave, which must specify particular grounds upon which leave should be granted, together with the requirement in s 40(6) that the evidence or question relate to a specific instance (or instances) of alleged sexual behaviour, will help to avoid the use of generalisation. Section 41(2) provides that the court may not give leave for evidence to be adduced or questions to be asked about the complainant's sexual history unless the court is satisfied that the evidence or questioning relates to an issue in the case and falls within one of the four exceptions:

(a) *if it is relevant to an issue in the case other than consent (s 41(3)(a));*

(b) *if it concerns sexual behaviour at or about the time of the incident in question (s 41(3)(b));*

(c) *if it relates to previous behaviour which is 'so similar … that the similarity cannot be explained by coincidence' (s 41(3)(c)); or*

(d) *if the evidence is required to rebut prosecution evidence (s 41(5)).*

Each of these exceptions is explored in further detail below.

Section 41(3)(a) – an issue other than an issue of consent

Section 42(1)(b) of the 1999 Act defines 'issue of consent' as meaning any issue whether the complainant in fact consented to the conduct constituting the offence with which the accused is charged (and accordingly does not include any issue as to the belief of the accused that the complainant was consenting). Under s 41(3)(a), the court may grant leave if the evidence or questioning relates to any issue that has to be proved other than an issue as to whether the complainant consented. By virtue of s 42(1)(b), the defendant's belief that the complainant was consenting falls into this category as relevant to an issue other than consent.

In *R v Y* (2001) *The Times*, 13 February, one of the first cases in which s 41 applied, the defendant, accused of raping a woman, alleged that she had consented to intercourse or, if not, that he believed that she had consented. At a preparatory hearing, the judge ruled that on neither issue could the defendant cross-examine the complainant about a consensual sexual relationship between them, which, he said, had begun about three weeks before the events subject of the charge. In his ruling the trial judge said that where the defence was the defendant's belief in the complainant's consent, the defence were precluded by s 41(1) and (3)(a) and (b) from adducing evidence that the defendant and the complainant had recently taken part in consensual sexual activity with each other, unless under s 41(3)(b) the sexual behaviour had occurred at or about the same time as the event subject of the charge against Y, or was so similar that it might be said to be part of a pattern of sexual behaviour under s 41(3)(c).

The defence challenged this ruling by an interlocutory appeal to the Court of Appeal under s 35 of the Criminal Procedure and Investigations Act 1996, alleging that s 41 prima facie offended against the principle that the defendant had a right to a fair trial under Article 6 of the European Convention of Human Rights. It was conceded by the prosecution in the course of argument that questioning and evidence in relation to the complainant's prior sexual activity with the defendant was admissible under s 41(3)(a) in relation to his belief as to the complainant's consent, but not under s 41(3)(b) or (c). Arguably this concession should not have been made. As suggested above, there is a distinction between the belief, based on the known character of the complainant, that he/she will consent to sexual inter-course if approached, and the belief that the person is consenting to the sexual intercourse which is taking place. While the known character of the complainant may jus-tify the approach, it cannot by itself support a belief that the complainant is in fact consenting, and still more so so if the complainant resists and protests.

The Court of Appeal, without making a final determination as to whether s 41(3)(b), if it precluded evidence of previous consensual sexual activity between the complainant and the defendant, was incompatible with the fair trial provisions of Article 6, found it impos-sible to construe the words 'at or about the same time as the event which is the subject matter of the charge' in s 41(3)(b) as applying to events days, or weeks or months prior to the events said to have given rise to the alleged rape. Their Lordships had 'no doubt that the previous sexual activity of the complainant had no relevance to credit and that sexual intercourse with persons other than the defendant had no relevance to the question whether she consented on the occasion said to give rise to the charge', but they took issue with the view that previous recent sexual intercourse between the complainant and the defendant was irrelevant as to whether she had consented on this occasion.

In their Lordships' judgment, provisional though it was, it was common sense that a person, whether male or female, who had had previous sexual intercourse with the defen-dant might, on the occasion in dispute, have consented to sexual intercourse with the defendant. Their Lordships did not accept that such an approach stemmed from a sexist view of women; rather, it reflected human nature. It seemed to reflect human nature:

> The trial process would be unduly distorted if the jury were precluded from knowing, if it were the case, that the complainant and the defendant had recently taken part in sexual activity with each other and it might be that a fair trial would not be possible if there could not be adduced in support of the defence of consent, evidence as to the complainant's previous consensual recent sexual activity with the defendant. (per Rose LJ at para 31)

However, it was held that the trial judge was correct to conclude that such cross-examina-tion was not permissible under s 41(3)(b). He was not correct, however, in excluding such questions and evidence entirely. The Crown had therefore rightly conceded that such ques-tions and evidence were permissible under s 41(3)(a) in relation to the defence of belief as to consent.

One may respectfully disagree with Lord Justice Rose's view of human nature expressed above, and with a similar view expressed by Lord Steyn on appeal to the House of Lords (see p 138 below). The entire purpose of the restriction on the use of sexual history is to deny the relevance of the complainant's previous sexual history except in the circum-stances indicated in s 41(3). It may well be necessary for the jury to know of the previous relationship, but not for the purpose of inferring that because the complainant consented to intercourse on previous occasions she might well have consented on this occasion. If a wife complains of rape within marriage, it would be a nonsense to hide from the jury the fact that the defendant and complainant are married and have engaged in sexual activity within that marriage. However, it does not follow that the complainant must have consented on the occasion in question. There are many cases in which the jury are told of possibly prejudicial matters so that they may see the evidence in its proper context.

For example, in *R v Sawoniuk* [2000] 2 Cr App R 220, where the defendant was charged with the murder of Jews during the Nazi occupation of Belorussia, it was held that evidence of witnesses relevant to prove that S was a policeman involved in search and kill operations was admissible. The Court said that criminal charges cannot be heard in a factual vacuum. Evidence describing the context and circumstances in which the offences were said to have been committed might often be necessary. Provision is now made by s 101(1)(c) and s 102 of the Criminal Justice Act 2003 for the admission of 'important explanatory evidence' (see discussion in **Chapter 5**).

Considering the decision of the Court of Appeal in *R v Y*, the decision, or acceptance by the parties, should not be seen as making previous sexual activity between the complainant and the defendant automatically admissible under s 41(3)(a). It remains prohibited under s 41(1), and is admissible under s 41(3)(a) only if it is relevant to the defendant's belief that the complainant was consenting. This very much depends upon the particular facts of the case in question.

The Court of Appeal accepted that the sexual history of the complainant has no relevance to her credit as a witness, and sexual intercourse with persons other than the defendant has no relevance to the question whether she consented on the occasion in question. Arguably the past sexual behaviour of the complainant with the defendant is rarely, if ever, relevant to the question whether she actually consented on the occasion in question. It is now recognised that a wife can say 'No' to her husband, making rape within marriage a possibility. It follows that a person can say 'No' to a man with whom she or he has had a previous sexual relationship. While it may be nonsensical to prevent the jury hearing about the previous relationship, whether as man and wife or an unmarried relationship, it does not follow that the relationship is relevant to the issue of whether the complainant consented on the occasion in question. It must be admitted as part of the surrounding circumstances that enables the jury to put the evidence in a context, but not necessarily as evidence going to the issue in the case, be it consent or a belief in consent.

However, it is submitted that the sexual behaviour of the complainant with the defendant can be relevant to support a belief in consent if, and only if, it is closely proximate to the act of intercourse. The woman's past history may be evidence justifying the belief, and may explain why the accused approached her seeking sexual intercourse, but it will have no bearing on the belief that she was consenting at the time of the act of intercourse. In other words, knowledge of the woman's past history may explain why the accused approached her rather than another, but it is not sufficient to ground a belief in the fact that she was consenting to the intercourse that took place later and which is subject of the charge. There must, it is submitted, be some conduct reasonably close to the act of intercourse that he says he believed to be consensual, which may be added to the previous history, and which may provide a reasonable basis for the belief that the woman was consenting. This effectively creates a smaller time frame than s 41(3)(b), given that the sexual behaviour evidence must have been at the time of the act of intercourse or immediately preceding it. It follows that, as in *R v Y*, the fact that the accused had recently had a sexual relationship with the complainant may give rise to a belief that she will consent to sexual intercourse and may explain why he approached her in the first place, but the previous relationship will not by itself provide grounds for a belief that she was consenting to the intercourse that is the subject of the charge.

Additional circumstances may make previous sexual activity between the defendant and the complainant relevant to, and provide reasonable grounds for, belief that the woman was consenting. For example, if the previous sexual activity took place in circumstances very similar to the circumstances in which the alleged rape took place. Suppose the defendant and the complainant have had consensual sexual intercourse in the past in circumstances in which the defendant pretended to force himself upon her and the complainant pretended to resist, which included vocal protests and allowing her panties to be torn off before appearing to be overcome. If the alleged rape involved the accused forcing himself upon the complainant despite her vocal protests and tearing off her panties, the accused might well have believed that she was consenting when in fact she was not. In such circumstances, the time gap between the previous sexual activity and the alleged rape could be days, weeks, months or years, the central issue for the jury being whether the defendant believed she was consenting. As s 1(2) of the Sexual Offences Act 2003 makes clear, the jury must determine whether the belief was reasonable having regard to all the circumstances, including any steps taken by the defendant to ascertain whether the complainant was consenting. The fact that she was behaving exactly has she had behaved in the past when the intercourse was consensual, is a circumstance providing a reasonable basis for the defendant's belief that she was consenting on this occasion.

However, the fact that the complainant and defendant have engaged in what may be called ordinary consensual sexual intercourse in the past, with no violence or other extraordinary circumstances, is unlikely to be relevant to the defence of belief in consent. As indicated above, the fact that they have been intimate in the past may lead the accused to believe that she will consent to intercourse on this occasion, but it cannot support a belief that she was consenting to the intercourse subject of the charge.

There are other scenarios that could arise where the issue is not consent. For example, in *R v Elahee* [1999] Crim LR 399, a decision based on s 2 of the Sexual Offences (Amendment) Act 1976, a 13-year-old girl, C, alleged that she was walking past a takeaway restaurant when the accused, a 43-year-old man, led her into a lobby and raped her. The accused in his evidence said that the complainant had introduced herself and, without invitation on his part, had touched his genital area. He said he had pushed her away and no sexual intercourse took place, the allegations being a complete fabrication. Medical evidence was that complainant displayed no injury and that her hymen was not intact. She had told the doctor that she had had full sexual intercourse some 12 months previously with her boyfriend, but that had been edited out of the doctor's statement and the jury were not made aware of what the complainant had said. Counsel for the accused sought leave under s 2 of the 1976 Act to elicit that evidence from the complainant, arguing that it was relevant to show that, contrary to her outward appearance, the complainant was a person capable of the conduct alleged by the accused. The trial judge refused leave and the accused was convicted.

Somewhat predictably, in the light of the approach of the Court of Appeal to s 2, the appeal was allowed. It was held that where the issue in a case was not one of consent but of who had made an improper approach to whom, the evidence of the complainant's previous sexual experience was a matter that was relevant to an issue in the trial and therefore one that the jury could properly take into account – not to assess credit, but to assess the plausibility of the account given by the defendant. In that situation the evidence had to be admitted unless there was a strong reason not to. The danger for the appellant, in the present case, was that if the jury knew about the complainant's sexual activity on a previous occasion, they might take a different view of the case.

This is a good example of how s 2 failed to protect the complainant in rape cases. The doctor's evidence was that the complainant's hymen was broken. The prosecution, after discussion with the judge, put it on the basis that the hymen was already broken lest the jury assume that the accused was responsible. The defence were not satisfied with that and made application under s 2 to allow the complainant to be questioned about the previous act of intercourse because, without that evidence, the jury might think it unlikely that a 13-year-old would approach and touch a 43-year-old man as alleged. It was also alleged that it would also have been unfair, once the jury had been told that the complainant's hymen was already broken, for them not to be told the details. They might have speculated as to other ways in which it might have been broken.

This is a spurious argument. In truth, the evidence of one act of intercourse with a boyfriend 12 months earlier is of no relevance to the issue of who made the approach. It may be that young virgins do not go up to middle-aged men and grab their testicles, but neither do the vast majority of teenage or any age girls. Recent statistics on teenage pregnancies show that many teenagers have some sexual experience, and many have a great deal, but sexual experience does not suggest a tendency to approach middle-aged men in the manner suggested. As for the suggested speculation, given that the jury had been told that the hymen was already broken it would have been clear to them that the accused was not responsible. If they did speculate as to the cause, it would not have been prejudicial or unfair to the accused. It would have been better to tell the jury not to speculate rather than to introduce C's previous sexual history. It is possibly true, as the Court of Appeal suggests, that 'if the jury knew about the complainant's sexual activity on a previous occasion they might take a different view of the case'; but why would they do so? Simply because she was not a virgin? If so, this is precisely the sort of prejudicial reasoning which s 2 of the 1976 Act was supposed to prevent.

It is doubtful, however, whether s 41 would have made any difference in this kind of case. If the courts see the complainant's previous sexual behaviour as relevant to the issue of who made the first approach then the refusal of leave to allow C to be questioned about the previous act of intercourse might have the result of rendering unsafe a conclusion of the jury on the relevant issue of who made the first approach. It follows that the same result will be reached under s 41 and the supposed reform will have made no difference.

Section 41(3)(b) – sexual behaviour at or about the time of the incident in question

This provision places a severe constraint on the adduction of evidence or questions about any sexual behaviour. In the first draft of the Bill, it was expressed as 24 hours either side of the offence. The 1999 Act itself adopts the phrase 'at or about the same time', which certainly provides a greater degree of flexibility, but is intended generally to be interpreted no more widely than 24 hours before or after the offence. It would permit evidence such as that in *Viola* (see pp 127–128 above), where the complainant was seen to be drinking and flirting with men before the alleged rape, and afterwards a man, naked but for his socks, was seen sleeping on her couch. The obvious inference the court was invited to draw was that she was drunk and looking for sex, and therefore was likely to have consented to the intercourse that took place some little time later. Many would argue that this is the kind of character assassination that, though permitted under the 1976 Act, ought to be prevented, and demonstrates how the 1976 Act failed to provide the protection of the complainant that the framers intended. However, it would seem that such questioning would be permitted under s 41(3)(b) of the 1999 Act.

The House of Lords in *R v A* [2002] 1 AC 45 (discussed at pp 137–142 below) refused to assign a specific temporal limit to the phrase, but were unanimous in holding that a sexual relationship between the defendant and the complainant some three weeks before the alleged rape fell outside the scope of s 41(3)(b). While holding that the test was a flexible one to be determined in the light of the particular circumstances of a case, their Lordships offered confusing guidance. Lord Slynn thought the words should be given a narrow meaning, which would restrict evidence and questions to sexual behaviour of the complainant that was 'really contemporaneous' with the event subject of the charge. Lord Steyn thought that the complainant's invitation to the defendant to have sex with her made earlier in the evening would be within the subsection, but he thought the temporal restriction would not extend to days, weeks or months. Lord Hope of Craighead referred to the *Notes of Guidance*, which expected that the phrase should not be interpreted more widely than 24 hours before or after the offence. Lord Hutton was clear that an act one week before the offence was outside the subsection, and Lord Clyde thought it would be difficult to extend the provision to include a period of several days.

Section 41(3)(c) – previous behaviour which is 'so similar ... that the similarity cannot be explained by coincidence'

Until a very late stage in the passage of the Bill that is now the 1999 Act, s 41(3) contained only paras (a) and (b). Various commentators pointed out that to limit the evidence which could be adduced to a 24-hour period either side of the alleged rape would be unfair to the accused in a case such as *R v Cox* (1986) 84 Cr App R 132, where the accused was permitted to adduce evidence that the complainant, who claimed he had raped her while her boyfriend was in police custody, had intercourse with another man on another occasion when her boyfriend was away, and there too she had claimed she had been raped in order to hide her infidelity. The previous sexual behaviour fell well outside the 'at or about the same time' period required under s 41(3)(b).

Judge Andrew Geddes has argued that there was little evidence that s 2 of the 1976 Act was not working and that the radical change effected by s 41 was unjustified (A Geddes, 'The exclusion of evidence relating to a complainant's sexual behaviour in sexual offence trials' (1999) 149 NLJ 1084). He described 'a not uncommon case' in which a former cohabitee of the accused alleges that he came to the house where the complainant lived (often the former matrimonial home) and raped her, and the accused says that sexual intercourse took place with her consent. The accused will often wish to support that defence by alleging (as may be the case) that although the relationship had been a stormy one (particularly since his departure), nevertheless the complainant had frequently allowed him back in the house and that sexual intercourse had taken place on virtually every occasion with her consent. It is often further alleged that the reason why the complainant is alleging rape on this occasion is that there is a bitter dispute over who is to occupy the house, or who is to have custody of the children, and she is using the accusation to support her case in those respects. If the jury are unaware that there has been a long history of the complainant consenting to sexual intercourse with the accused after they had separated, before the sexual intercourse in question (as would be the case if the restriction imposed by s 41(3)(b) were to apply), there must be a real danger that they would convict where otherwise they would acquit.

The response to these criticisms was s 41(3)(c), which also applies when the issue is one of consent. The purpose of the subsection is to allow the defence to cross-examine the complainant about his or her previous sexual behaviour which, although it may not be alleged to have taken place 'at or about the same time' as the event that is the subject of the charge, is so similar to the defence's version of the complainant's behaviour at the time of the alleged offence that it cannot reasonably be explained as a coincidence. This will, in effect, act as supporting or corroborative evidence for the defence who say, or will say when they give evidence, that on a previous occasion sometime before the event subject of the charge (or at or about the time of the event or some time afterwards), the complainant acted in a particular way. The fact that very similar behaviour took place as part of, or about the same time as, the event subject of the charge against the accused, lends credence to the defence version of events.

R v A – The *R v Y* case before the House of Lords

The case of *R v Y* (see pp 131–132 above) was taken on appeal to the House of Lords by the Director of Public Prosecutions, who sought to reverse the decision of the Court of Appeal that evidence of a previous consensual sexual relationship was admissible under s 41(3)(a) and to uphold the ruling of the trial judge that it was not admissible under s 41(1)(b) and (c). The House of Lords decision was reported as *R v A* [2002] 1 AC 45, but it is the same case that came before the Court of Appeal as *R v Y*.

It will be recalled that the accused wanted to cross-examine the complainant on the sexual relationship he claimed they had been having before the alleged rape, which had continued for three weeks prior to the alleged rape, the last act of sexual intercourse between them having taken place approximately one week before the alleged rape. The respondents maintained their argument that in restricting cross-examination on the prior consensual sexual relationship between the complainant and the defendant, s 41 of the 1999 Act infringed the defendant's right to a fair trial under Article 6 of the European Convention on Human Rights. The House of Lords dismissed the Crown's appeal and concluded that a prior consensual sexual relationship between a complainant alleging a sexual offence and the defendant might in some circumstances be relevant to the issue of consent and the absence of evidential material relating to it might infringe the right to a fair trial under Article 6. Lord Steyn commented that in the aftermath of the sexual revolution of the 1960s, the autonomy and independence of women in sexual matters had become an accepted norm. But it had to be acknowledged that in the criminal courts, here and elsewhere, outmoded beliefs about women and sexual matters lingered on. In Canadian jurisprudence they had been described as the 'discredited twin myths': that unchaste women were more likely to consent to intercourse and, in any event, were less worthy of belief (see *R v Seaboyer* (1991) 83 DLR (4th) 193).

Sections 41 to 43 of the 1999 Act imposed wide restrictions on evidence and questioning about a complainant's sexual history, and s 41 imposed the same exclusionary provisions in respect of the complainant's sexual history with the accused as with other men. That was the genesis of the problem before the House. There were great differences which needed to be explored. The blanket exclusion of prior sexual history between the complainant and the accused in s 41(1), subject to narrow categories of exception in the remainder of s 41, posed an acute problem of proportionality. As a matter of common sense, such a prior relationship between them might, depending on the circumstances, be relevant to the issue of consent. It was a species of prospective evidence which might throw light on the complainant's state of mind. It could not, of course, prove that she consented on the occasion in question: relevance and sufficiency of proof were different things. Each decision to engage in sexual activity was always made afresh. But the mind did not always blot out all memories; what one had been engaged on in the past might influence what choice one made on a future occasion. Accordingly, a prior relationship between a complainant and an accused might sometimes be relevant to what decision was made on a particular occasion. When a question arose as to whether Parliament adopted a particular legislative scheme which made an excessive inroad into the right to a fair trial, the court was qualified to make its own judgment and had to do so. The correct approach was for the court to ask itself first: did the legislation interfere with a Convention right?

It was well established that the guarantee of a fair trial under Article 6 was absolute. A conviction obtained in breach could not stand. The only balancing permitted was in what the concept of a fair trial entailed. Here account might be taken of the familiar triangulation of interests of the accused, the victim and society. In that context proportionality had a role to play. In determining whether a limitation was arbitrary or excessive, a court should ask itself whether:

(a) the legislative objective was sufficiently important to justify limiting a fundamental right;

(b) the measures designed to meet that objective were rationally connected to it; and

(c) the means used to impair the right were no more than necessary to accomplish the objective.

The critical matter was the third criterion. Given the centrality of the right to a fair trial in the scheme of the Convention and giving due weight to the important legislative goal of countering the twin myths, the question was whether s 41 made excessive inroads into the guarantee of a fair trial.

Subject to narrow exceptions, s 41 was a blanket exclusion of potentially relevant evidence. It had to be construed in order to determine its precise exclusionary impact on alleged previous sexual experience between the complainant and the accused. Two processes of interpretation had to be distinguished. First, ordinary methods of purposive and contextual interpretation might yield ways of minimising the prima facie exorbitant breadth of the section. Secondly, the interpretative obligation in s 3(1) of the Human Rights Act 1998 Act might come into play. It provided that so far as it was possible to do so, primary legislation had to be read and given effect in a way that was compatible with the Convention rights. It was a key feature of the 1998 Act.

Lord Slynn considered s 41(3)(b), where leave might be given to admit evidence or questioning about the complainant's sexual behaviour where consent was an issue and the behaviour was alleged to have taken place at or about the same time as the event which was the subject matter of the charge. In his view, on neither the ordinary method of interpretation nor the interpretative obligation under s 3 could the temporal restriction be extended to days, weeks or months. The subsection acknowledged by its own terms that previous sexual experience between a complainant and the accused might be relevant, but then restricted the admission of the evidence by an extraordinarily narrow temporal restriction. With regard to s 41(3)(c), leave might be given where consent was an issue and 'the sexual behaviour of the complainant to which the evidence or question relates is alleged to have been, in any respect, so similar ... to any sexual behaviour of the complainant which ... took place as part of the event which is the subject matter of the charge ... that the similarity cannot reasonably be explained as a coincidence'.

The interpretative obligation under s 3 of the Human Rights Act 1998

Looking at the ordinary methods of interpretation, one could say that s 41(3)(c) was a statutory adoption of the 'strikingly similar' tests enunciated in *R v Boardman* [1975] AC 421; so interpreted, it was a narrow gateway which would be available only in rare cases. Alternatively, one could argue that the subsection involved the test of high probative force which made it just to admit the evidence: see *R v P* [1991] 2 AC 447. Even if that approach was consistent with the language of s 41, the threshold requirement would be too high. Often the evidence would be relevant but not capable of being described as having high probative value. Those ways of interpreting s 41(3) could not solve the problem of the prima facie excessive inroad on the right to a fair trial.

In *R v A* their Lordships found that ordinary methods of purposive construction could not cure the problem of the excessive breadth of the section read as a whole so far as it related to previous sexual experience between a complainant and the accused. While the statute pursued desirable goals, the methods adopted amounted to legislative overkill. However, the interpretative obligation under s 3 of the Human Rights Act 1998 was a strong one. It applied even if there was no ambiguity in the language in the sense that it was capable of two different meanings (see *R v DPP, ex p Kebilene* [2000] 2 AC 326, 366, 373). The obligation went far beyond the rule which enabled the courts to take the Convention into account in resolving any ambiguity in a legislative provision. Parliament specifically rejected the legislative model of requiring a reasonable interpretation. Section 3 of the Human Rights Act 1998 placed on the court a duty to strive to find a possible interpretation compatible with Convention rights. Under ordinary methods of interpretation, a court might depart from the language of the statute to avoid absurd consequences; s 3 went much further. Undoubtedly a court had always to look for a contextual and purposive interpretation: s 3 was more radical in its effect and required a court to find an interpretation compatible with Convention rights if it was possible to do so.

It was realistic to proceed on the basis that the legislature would not, if alerted to the problem, have wished to deny the right to an accused to put forward a full and complete defence by advancing truly probative material. It was therefore possible under s 3 to read s 41 of the 1999 Act, and in particular s 41(3)(c), as subject to the implied provision that evidence or questioning which was required to ensure a fair trial under Article 6 should not be inadmissible. The result of such a reading would be that sometimes logically relevant sexual experience between a complainant and an accused might be admitted under s 41(3)(c), although there would be cases where such previous sexual experiences were irrelevant, and it would be left to the judgment of trial judges as to where the line ought to be drawn.

The effect of the House of Lords' decision in *A* was to restore to the trial judge some degree of control over the ambit of cross-examination in relation to previous sexual history evidence. The test of admissibility was whether the evidence, and questioning in relation to it, was nevertheless so relevant to the issue of consent that to exclude it would endanger the fairness of the trial under Article 6. If that test was satisfied, the evidence should not be excluded. Lord Slynn, Lord Hope, Lord Clyde and Lord Hutton delivered speeches concurring in the result.

Lord Hutton gave an example of the broadening effect on s 41(3)(c) which an application of the special interpretative obligation would have:

> *A defendant wishes to give evidence that for a number of months prior to the date of the alleged offence he had a close and affectionate relationship with the complainant and that he had had frequent consensual intercourse with her during that period. Before intercourse he would kiss her and she would return his kisses. At the time of the alleged offence, before having intercourse, affectionate behaviour took place between them as it had done on the earlier occasions. Is this evidence admissible under s 41(3)(c)? (at para 159)*

His clear answer was that, according to ordinary canons of interpretation, it would not be admissible, since the (alleged) earlier incidents would not be so similar as not to be reasonably explicable as coincidental. However, because it was possible to interpret s 41(3)(c) as rendering such evidence admissible, and because the accused would otherwise be deprived of his fair trial right, s 3(1) of the Human Rights Act 1998 would render it admissible. This example, if it is correct, indicates the extent of the change to the section wrought by the application of the interpretative obligation. Kissing is an ordinary prelude to an act of sexual intercourse and does not meet the criteria set out in the section of being 'so similar ... that the similarity cannot reasonably be explained as a coincidence'.

Parliament did not intend to make evidence of such ordinary behaviour admissible as being relevant to consent, but s 3(1) of the Human Rights Act 1998, as interpreted by the House of Lords, ignores that lack of intention. One may note the acceptance by their Lordships that while excluding evidence of substantial relevance would endanger the fairness of the trial and breach Article 6, excluding evidence of marginal relevance would do neither. Under the 1976 Act, evidence of previous sexual behaviour was admissible if it was relevant, and there was no mention of degrees of relevance. Under the 1999 Act, such evidence, if of marginal relevance, can be excluded without affecting the fairness of the trial. Arguably the kissing example given by Lord Hutton, if deemed relevant by the application of s 3(1) of the Human Rights Act 1998, could be seen as being of minor relevance.

The decision of the Court of Appeal in *R v Y* was therefore reversed in so far as it said that previous sexual experience with the accused is admissible only under s 41(3)(a), where it might be admissible as relevant to a belief that the complainant was consenting. However, the House of Lords, in holding that such evidence might be admissible as relevant to consent under s 41(3)(c), does not exclude the possibility that such evidence might be admissible under s 41(3)(a) – as relevant to an issue other than consent (see the discussion of s 41(3)(a) above). The House of Lords does not mention this possibility, perhaps because it was accepted by all sides that previous sexual experience between complainant and accused could be relevant under s 41(3)(a). The appeal therefore concentrated on the argument that such evidence was not admissible under s 41(3)(b) and (c).

The decision in *R v A* may be seen as a neat solution to the tricky problem facing their Lordships, who obviously thought s 41 could be interpreted as going too far in restricting the admissibility of sexual history evidence. However, in holding that s 41(3)(c) of the 1999 Act must be interpreted subject to the implied provision that evidence or questioning which was required to ensure a fair trial under Article 6 of the European Convention on Human Rights should not be inadmissible, their Lordships have provided a measure of flexibility which avoids the suggestion of incompatibility. Some argue that, contrary to the intention of Parliament, the judgment increases the likelihood that evidence of previous sexual experience between the complainant and defendant will be admitted as relevant to consent, that is where the defence allege that C actually consented to the sexual intercourse subject of the charge. However, it may also be argued that while providing the necessary flexibility to avoid incompatibility with Article 6 and the Human Rights Act 1998, the judgment continues the restrictive approach Parliament intended.

A prior consensual sexual relationship between a complainant alleging a sexual offence and the defendant might in some circumstances be relevant to the issue of consent, and the absence of evidential material relating to it might infringe the right to a fair trial under Article 6. Accordingly, where the material in question was so relevant to the issue of consent that its exclusion would endanger the fairness of the trial, evidence and questioning of such a relationship between the defendant and the complainant was admissible under s 41(3)(c) of the Youth Justice and Criminal Evidence Act 1999, construed, where necessary, by applying the court's interpretive duty under s 3 of the Human Rights Act 1998, and always giving proper regard to the protection of the complainant.

Section 41(2) of the 1999 Act provides that despite the prohibition contained in s 43(1) on the adduction of evidence or questions about the sexual behaviour of the complainant:

> *The court may give leave ... and may not give such leave unless it is satisfied:*
>
> (a) *that subsections (3) or (5) applies; and*
>
> (b) *that refusal of leave might have the result of rendering unsafe a conclusion of the jury ... on any relevant issue in the case.*

As the judgment in *R v A* recognises, the question of admissibility is not, then, simply a question of relevance. The material in question must be so relevant to the issue of consent that its exclusion would endanger the fairness of the trial. While the failure to admit evidence that is very relevant or highly relevant to an issue, be it consent or any other issue, might well have the effect of rendering unsafe a conclusion of the jury on that issue, refusing to admit sexual history evidence that is only of marginal relevance is not likely to have that effect. As Lord Steyn observed (at 61–2), 'relevance and sufficiency of proof are different things'.

The fact that the complainant and the accused have had a consensual sexual relationship in the past may throw light on the complainant's state of mind, but will rarely be of significant relevance to the issue of whether she consented to the sexual intercourse which is subject of the charge. There must be something more than the mere fact of a sexual relationship. Section 41(3)(c) requires that 'something more' to be a similarity between the conduct of the complainant on the night in question and his/her conduct on the previous occasion(s) which cannot be reasonably explained as coincidence.

If there is such a similarity, there is no need to expand the terms of the subsection by reference to the interpretative obligation of s 3 of the 1998 Act. If there is no such similarity, the mere fact of a previous sexual relationship it is not relevant to the issue of consent; or if it is of relevance, it is of such little relevance, that to refuse to admit it would not be likely to render unsafe a conclusion of the jury on that issue. As indicated below, such evidence should always be available to the jury as essential explanatory evidence, enabling them to see the whole picture and to put the other evidence in context. One cannot, for example, hide from the jury that the complainant who alleges rape was married for some years to the accused, that theirs was a stormy marriage which recently broke up and that the alleged rape took place while they were legally separated. This would not, as suggested by the Court of Appeal, give a 'Lewis Carroll' feel to proceedings, the jury being directed that such evidence is merely explanatory and not relevant to the issue of consent.

An alternative to the above is that judges will, rather than face the possibility of being appealed, take the broader interpretation of s 41(3)(c) advocated by the House of Lords and admit evidence of a previous sexual relationship much more freely than was intended by the legislature. This will make it more difficult to gain convictions in such cases, resulting in even fewer convictions for 'acquaintance rape' than there already are. Should that happen, there will be pressure for a change in the law, not necessarily to restore Parliament's intention to restrict the admissibility of such evidence, but to change the law to create a gradation of offences, three degrees of rape, in the hope that juries will convict more readily on the lesser offence. However, juries convict – or should convict – on the evidence, not on the degree of punishment likely to be awarded.

The overlap between s 41(3)(b) and (c)
There appears to be an overlap between s 41(3)(b) and s 41(3)(c), both of which apply to an issue of consent. The difference is that s 41(3)(c) is concerned with the similarity of the complainant's sexual behaviour on a previous occasion outside the temporal limitation imposed by s 41(3)(b), that is so similar to his conduct on the occasion in question that it cannot be explained as coincidence. Thus, to take the facts in *R v Cox* (1986) 84 Cr App R 132, where the complainant claimed that Cox had raped her while her boyfriend was in police custody. When her boyfriend discovered that she had been intimate with one of his friends while he was helping the police with their enquiries, she claimed that she had not consented, that Cox had in fact raped her. The defence had evidence that on a previous occasion when the complainant had been unfaithful, having slept with another man in the

absence of the boyfriend, she had also cried rape, falsely. Such evidence would not be admissible under s 41(3)(b) because the previous sexual behaviour took place well outside the 24-hour period either side of the alleged rape subject of the present charge; but would be admissible under s 41(3)(c), since it is an issue of consent and the similarity of the sexual behaviour of the complainant on both occasions cannot be explained as a coincidence. However, if the same conduct took place 'at or about the same time as the event subject of the charge', it would also be admissible under s 41(3)(b). Similarly, in the example given by the circuit judge in *Cox* of the cohabiting couple where, after breaking up, the woman cried rape, evidence that the couple had consensual sexual intercourse on numerous previous occasions when the accused had revisited the former matrimonial home would be admissible under s 41(3)(c) and under s 41(3)(b) if the last previous act of consensual intercourse had taken place within a day (possibly two) of the intercourse alleged to be rape.

Rebutting prosecution evidence – s 41(1)(5)

The other occasion when the judge can give leave for sexual behaviour evidence to be admitted is when the evidence the defence wish to introduce is intended to dispute evidence that the prosecution has introduced about the complainant's sexual behaviour (s 41(5)). This is based on the principle that there should be equality of arms between the parties: the defence must be able to challenge the prosecution's evidence. It must go no further than directly to contradict or explain claims made by or on behalf of the complainant. Thus if the prosecution evidence states or suggests that the complainant was a virgin before the alleged rape, evidence that she previously had had intercourse with another or others could be adduced. It follows that the prosecution should take care that the way they present their case does not expose the complainant to cross-examination about her previous sexual history which may damage their case. One may note that s 41(6) provides that any evidence or questioning about sexual behaviour must relate to a specific instance, or instances, of such behaviour. Fishing expeditions will not be permitted.

Refusal to admit relevant evidence for the purpose of attacking the credibility of the complainant – s 41(4)

Section 41(4) of the 1999 Act provides that the court can refuse to allow evidence or questions that the defence claim are relevant to an issue and admissible under s 41(3), if the court considers that the real main purpose is to undermine or diminish the complainant's credibility. This brings us back to the supposed distinction between matters going to the issue and matters going only to credibility (see p 130 above). If there is no such distinction in rape cases then the subsection will be of little help. It might be better if the court was required, before admitting evidence of sexual history, to consider the prejudicial effect the admission of such evidence might have on the complainant, and balance that against the relevance of the sexual history evidence to the issue to which it is relevant. Only if that relevance outweighs the possible prejudice should the evidence be admitted (see the discussion of *R v Martin (Durwayne)*, at p 130 above).

Procedure on application under s 41

It may be useful briefly to note the procedure that is used on an application under s 41 of the 1999 Act. Section 43 provides that there must be an application to the court by or on behalf of the defendant. That application will be heard in the absence of the jury, any witnesses (other than the defendant), the public and the press. Rules of court will require the applicant to specify, in relation to each item of evidence or question to which they relate, particulars of the grounds on which it is asserted that leave should be granted. The court will be able to require from the parties to the proceedings any information it considers will assist in making the decision whether or not to grant leave. Reasons for giving or refusing leave must be stated in open court (but in the absence of the jury), and if leave is granted the court must indicate the extent to which evidence may be adduced or questions asked in pursuance of the leave. This will give the trial judge more time to consider the application (under the previous law such applications were made orally during the course of trial) and will require a reasoned argument, in writing from the defence, to which counsel for the prosecution can respond. It may also put an end to the improper practice of asking questions about the complainant's sexual behaviour that should not be asked, unless and until leave has been given. Research suggests that under the old law questions about the complainant's previous sexual history were asked without application to the trial judge either because judge and counsel were unaware of the requirement for leave, or perhaps deliberately to avoid the restriction on such questions. The fact that there is new law and new procedures should ensure that all the legal participants in rape trials are aware of the restrictions on questions about the complainant's sexual behaviour and of the need to make application for leave, and to support it in writing with reasoned argument.

The defendant's past history

While the complainant's sexual history may be open to scrutiny, the defendant's sexual history is generally not. However, the common law and previous statutory rules restricting the admissibility of evidence of the bad character of the defendant are repealed and replaced with statutory provisions contained in Pt 11 of the Criminal Justice Act 2003. This is discussed in the next chapter, although it is worth noting at this point that the Criminal Evidence Act 1898 allowed the previous convictions of the defendant to be put to him in cross-examination if he put his own character in issue, or if he attacked the character of the prosecutor or prosecution witnesses. However, in rape cases where the defendant alleged consent, this was not seen as an attack on the character of the complainant, therefore the defendant in a rape case did not place himself in peril of cross-examination as to his bad character (*R v Turner* [1944] KB 463). Section 101(1)(a) to (g) of the 2003 Act provide for the admissibility of evidence of the bad character of the defendant. In particular, s 101(1)(g) makes such evidence admissible if the defendant has made an attack on another person's character. Section 106(2) defines 'evidence attacking the other person's character' as including evidence to the effect that he has committed an offence (whether a different offence from the one charged, or the same one), or evidence that he 'has behaved, or is disposed to behave, in a reprehensible way'.

Alleging that the complainant is promiscuous, sleeps around or is otherwise of a sexually bad character may fall within that definition, allowing evidence of previous convictions or other reprehensible behaviour to be adduced by the prosecution. However, this is subject to the discretion to exclude under s 101(3) if the admission of the evidence would have such an adverse effect on the fairness of the proceedings that the court ought not to admit it. It is possible, if not likely, that the courts may accept, as did the court in *Turner*, that given that lack of consent is a part of the definition of the offence, it would be unfair to the defendant to allow his bad character to be admitted simply because he denies a central aspect of the offence.

Section 101 provides for several other circumstances in which evidence of the bad character of the defendant may be admitted. These are considered in **Chapter 5**.

Further reading

Birch, D, 'Untangling sexual history evidence: a rejoinder to Professor Temkin' [2003] Crim LR 370.

Durston, G, 'Previous (in)consistent statements after the Criminal Justice Act 2003' [2005] Crim LR 206.

Kibble, N, 'Judicial perspectives on the operation of s 41 and the relevance and admissibility of prior sexual history evidence: four scenarios: Part 1' [2005] Crim LR 190.

Kibble, N, 'Judicial discretion and the admissibility of prior sexual history evidence under section 41 of the Youth Justice and Criminal Evidence Act 1999: sometimes sticking to your guns means shooting yourself in the foot: Part 2' [2005] Crim LR 263.

Temkin, J, 'Sexual history evidence – beware the backlash' [2003] Crim LR 217.

5 Evidence of Character in Criminal Proceedings

Background

This chapter examines the admissibility of the accused's previous good or bad character in evidence. The common law refused to allow bad character to be adduced generally as part of the prosecution case for two main reasons. First, it was believed that evidence of bad character might have a disproportionate prejudicial effect on the jury. The common law test of admissibility of evidence of the bad character of the defendant involved a balancing exercise, in which the trial judge weighed the relevance (or probative value) of the evidence of bad character to an issue in the case against the possible prejudice to the defendant of admitting it. If the relevance of that evidence to an issue in the case outweighed the prejudicial effect the evidence was admitted, otherwise it was not. The Law Commission Consultation Paper, *Evidence in Criminal Proceedings: Previous Misconduct of a Defendant* (Law Com No 141, 1996), took 'prejudicial effect' to mean that a verdict is reached not as a valid conclusion from a logical line of reasoning, but either by giving too much weight to the evidence of bad character ('reasoning prejudice'), or by convicting otherwise than on the evidence ('moral prejudice') (at para 7.2). This was refined in the Law Commission Report, *Evidence of Bad Character in Criminal Proceedings* (Law Com No 273, 2001), and in cl 17(2) of the Draft Bill attached to the Report, 'prejudice' is defined as 'a risk that the court or jury would attach undue weight to the evidence, or ... the nature of the matters with which the evidence deals is such as to give rise to a risk that the court or jury would find the defendant guilty without being satisfied that he was'.

The above definition clearly demonstrates a mistrust of the lay jury, a mistrust that, despite the supposedly revered status of that institution, is shared by a majority of the legal professionals operating within the criminal justice system. The Criminal Justice Act 2003, discussed at pp 157–184 below, does not enact that definition of prejudice. Section 101(3) provides a discretion to exclude evidence of bad character which the prosecution seek to adduce, similar to that in s 78 of the Police and Criminal Evidence Act 1984, requiring exclusion if 'it appears to the court that the admission of such evidence would have such an adverse effect on the fairness of the proceedings that the court ought not to admit it'. This suggests a move away from the common law test based on prejudicing the jury, but the *Notes of Guidance*, which accompany and explain the provisions of the Act, assume the court will apply the common law test that required the trial judge to balance the probative value (the relevance) of the evidence of bad character against the prejudicial effect to the defendant of admitting it. There is no hard evidence of either form of prejudice. Section 8 of the Contempt of Court Act 1981 prevents research into the deliberations and decisions of juries. Resort has therefore been made to shadow juries, members of the public acting as jurors having been presented with the facts of cases with more or less information about the character of the defendant. Research conducted into shadow juries by Cornish and Sealey ('Juries and the Rules of Evidence, The LSE Jury Project' [1973] Crim LR 208) found that the admission of previous convictions did increase the chance of a guilty verdict, but only if those convictions were for offences similar to that charged. If they were dissimilar, it was possible for them to have an effect that was positively favourable to the accused. The research also found that a previous conviction for indecent assault on a child tended to produce a markedly adverse effect on the conviction rate. In *R v Bills* [1995] 2 Cr App R 643, the jury brought in a verdict of guilty on a charge of unlawful wounding under s 20 of the Offences Against the Person Act 1861 and a verdict of not guilty on a s 18 charge of wounding with intent; but when the jury heard the defendant's previous convictions, which included assault occasioning actual bodily harm and robbery, they told the judge that they had brought in the wrong verdict. They were reconvened and they convicted on the s 18 charge. The Court of Appeal reinstated the original verdict, it being obvious that hearing about the previous convictions had influenced the jury (see also *R v Follen* [1994] Crim LR 225).

Research directed by Sally Lloyd Bostock for the Law Commission ('The Effect on Juries of Hearing about the Defendant's Previous Criminal Record' [2000] Crim LR 734) also provides some support for the belief that hearing evidence of bad character can prejudice a jury. 'Prejudice' here, as in other studies, is assumed on the basis that the simulated jury convicted more readily when told that the defendant had previous convictions for an offence similar to that for which he was being tried. The study found that mock jurors were less likely to believe a defendant's evidence and more likely to convict if told that he had previous convictions of indecent assault on a child, regardless of the nature of the offence with which he was charged. Such convictions are understandably viewed with a greater degree of revulsion than most previous convictions and it is probably dangerous to draw wider conclusions about the ability of juries to deal with potentially prejudicial evidence. The study also confirmed that evidence of previous convictions for similar offences led to a higher conviction rate. Whether this constitutes 'prejudicial effect', as claimed in the study, or is simply the result of a greater weight of evidence is unclear (Appendix A to the report of the Law Commission, *Evidence in Criminal Proceedings: Previous Misconduct of a Defendant* (Law Com No 141, 1996)). However, contrary to common supposition, Lloyd Bostock's survey suggests that juries do give real weight to an instruction to disregard relevant previous convictions wrongly admitted.

The second reason why the common law traditionally excluded evidence of bad character was that it was often considered irrelevant. It is arguable that while dissimilar convictions are relevant to credit only, ie whether the defendant is to be believed, similar convictions may be relevant to credit and to the issue in the case, on the basis that a person who has done the acts charged before is more likely to have committed the offence charged. The Criminal Law Revision Committee (Eleventh Report, *Evidence (General)* (Cmnd 4999, 1972) stated (at para 72):

Evidence of other misconduct of the accused tending to show that he has a disposition to commit the kind of offence charged may clearly be highly relevant in the sense of making it more probable that he committed the offence charged; and this is the sense in which relevance must be understood for the purpose of the law of evidence. Obviously if there is no other evidence at all to connect the accused with the offence charged, the fact that he has a disposition to commit this kind of offence, then evidence of disposition must be of greater or lesser value according to the circumstances.

As the Criminal Law Revision Committee emphasises, there must be evidence linking the defendant to the crime with which he is charged, the previous similar conviction being only a part of the prosecution case. The studies which speak of juries being 'prejudiced' do not appear to appreciate that previous convictions, particularly when they are similar to the offence charged, can be evidence which, when added to the other evidence in the case, creates a stronger prosecution case. The prospect of conviction will then be increased not because the jury are prejudiced by hearing of the previous conviction(s), but because of the increased weight of the evidence of the defendant's guilt.

The common law recognised this fact but looked for a high degree of relevance in the previous convictions which outweighed any possible prejudice resulting from the admission of the convictions. Arguably, the use of the term 'prejudice' in relation to evidence which is highly relevant to an issue in the case is inappropriate. The fact that it increased the likelihood of the defendant being found guilty is not prejudice; all prosecution evidence is directed to this end. 'Disposition evidence' is part of the general evidence in inquisitorial systems, where juries can be guided by the judges who retire with them (eg, in France), but is not generally permitted in this country, even if relevant, because it is believed that the jury cannot be trusted to handle such evidence without undue prejudice to the accused. The relevance of such evidence is admissible only if the degree of relevance is so high that it outweighs any prejudicial effect. Until recently the scandal of jury service was that so many professional people were exempt from it, meaning that juries were often extremely unrepresentative of society at large. However, the Criminal Justice Act 2003 removes most of the previous exemptions, making jury service compulsory for a wide range of professionals, including those connected with the legal system such as judges, barristers, solicitors and police officers. Whether this broadening of representation will lead to a greater trust in the ability of future juries to handle potentially prejudicial material remains to be seen.

In addition, 'character' in this context means the tendency of a person to act, think or feel in a particular way. 'Disposition' and 'propensity' are alternative terms with the same meaning, and are often used in the cases and academic commentary on the subject. Thus a man with previous convictions for violence may be described as being of a 'violent disposition'; a person of good character may be described as 'a man of integrity'.

There a many ways in which a person's character may be revealed, although it is most commonly revealed through reference to any previous convictions. However, not all convictions carry the same stigma: a minor motoring offence, for example, is unlikely to prejudice a jury in the same way as a serious sexual offence. Bad character can also be acquired by the commission of criminal acts for which a person has been acquitted, though this may depend upon the manner of the acquittal, by being charged with a criminal offence that does not proceed to prosecution for lack of evidence, by association with other known criminals and in many other ways. Similarly, good character can be shown by the absence of convictions, or by association with good people or causes, such as being a churchgoer or member of voluntary or charitable organisations. Much of the evidence of good or bad character stems from a reputation that may or may not be a true reflection of the person's character. The priest may appear to be of good character, having a very good reputation, but may be abusing choirboys. The bank employee may appear to be the epitome of respectability, but may be stealing from his bank. A local sporting hero may have an excellent reputation, but may be abusing and battering his wife. Nevertheless, such people are treated as being of good character until the contrary is proved.

The previous law

Until very recently, the admissibility of evidence of bad character was governed both by common law and by the rules laid down in the Criminal Evidence Act 1898. Each of these will now be examined in turn before we consider the new regime contained in the Criminal Justice Act 2003.

The 'similar fact' rule at common law

The main exception to the exclusion of bad character evidence at common law was known (somewhat misleadingly) as the 'similar fact' rule, which was first laid down in *Makin v The Attorney-General* [1894] AC 57:

> It is undoubtedly not competent for the prosecution to adduce evidence tending to show that the accused has been guilty of criminal acts other than those covered by the indictment, for the purpose of leading to the conclusion that the accused is a person likely from his criminal conduct or character to have committed the offence for which he was being tried.

> On the other hand, the mere fact that the evidence tends to show the commission of other crimes does not render it inadmissible if it be relevant to an issue before the jury, and it may be so relevant if it bears upon the question whether the acts alleged to constitute the crime charged in the indictment were designed or accidental, or to rebut a defence which would otherwise be open to the accused.

The first paragraph sets out the general rule that one cannot adduce evidence of previous criminal conduct in order to show that the defendant is a person likely from his criminal conduct or character to have committed the offence charged. The second paragraph sets out the exception to that rule, which would admit such evidence if it is relevant to an issue in the case, such as rebutting a defence of accident or any other defence open to the accused. Over the years the rule was refined so that the basis of the admissibility of evidence of previous convictions or other bad character was that such evidence was relevant to an issue in the case, but not merely 'relevant' but *so* relevant that its relevance outweighed any prejudice that might arise from admitting the evidence. One basis for relevance (or probative value) was the similarity between the manner and circumstances in which the previous offences were committed and the manner and circumstances in which the offence charged had been committed. This led to the description of such evidence as 'similar fact evidence', but in *Boardman v DPP* [1975] AC 42, there was a shift in emphasis in the criterion for admitting similar fact evidence from the purpose of the evidence to the amount of relevance it bore to the matter in issue.

The notion that the similar fact evidence should have 'striking similarity' to be admissible was developed by their Lordships. This was interpreted as imposing a mandatory require-ment upon the prosecution to show how any evidence they sought to adduce under this head bore a 'striking similarity' to the manner and circumstances in which the offence charged was committed. Merely committing the same offence in a manner which was the 'stock in trade' of persons committing such an offence, was not sufficient to make evi-dence of the previous offences admissible. There had to be some 'unique and striking similarity' in the manner in which the previous offences had been committed, and evi-dence that the offence charged was committed in the same unique and strikingly similar way. Thus, in time, the courts began to refuse to admit such evidence unless it was strik-ingly similar to the way in which the offence charged had been committed. This led to the failure of many prosecutions because similar fact evidence was ruled inadmissible, or the quashing on appeal of convictions based on similar fact evidence which the Court of Appeal held should not have been admitted (see *R v Inder* (1977) 67 Cr App R 143).

The House of Lords sought to remedy this problem in *DPP v P* [1991] 2 AC 447. In this case, a father was accused of rape and incest with his two daughters. Like *Boardman*, the question was whether the evidence in relation to each daughter was cross-admissible. The common features were that in each case there was evidence to indicate that the father had exercised dictatorial power over each girl, and that in each case he had paid for an abortion. The Court of Appeal had held that although the cases bore similarities, they could not be said to be striking. This decision was reversed by the House of Lords, which concluded that striking similarities ought not to be the determining criteria of admissibil-ity. Striking similarities could be used as one way of establishing the probative force of the evidence, particularly in cases where the identity of the accused was at issue; but here the issue was not identity but whether an offence had actually been committed, and as such their Lordships held that there were other ways of deriving probative force. The essence of the judgment is contained in the following passage (at 462):

> When a question of the kind raised in this case arises I consider that the judge must first decide whether there is material upon which the jury would be entitled to conclude that the evidence of one victim, about what occurred to that victim, is so related to the evidence given by another victim, about what happened to that other victim, that the evidence of the first victim provides strong enough support for the evidence of the second victim to make it just to admit it notwithstanding the prejudicial effect of admitting the evidence. This relationship, from which the support is derived, may take many forms and while these forms may include 'striking similarity' in the manner in which the crime was committed, consisting of unusual characteristics in its execution the neces-sary relationship is by no means confined to such circumstances. Relationships in time and circumstances other than those may well be important relationships in this connection. Where the identity of the perpetrator is in issue, and evidence of this kind is important in that connection, obviously something in the nature of what has been called

in argument a signature or other special feature will be necessary. To transpose this requirement to other situations where the question is whether a crime has been committed, rather than who did commit it, is to impose an unnecessary and improper restriction on the principle.

This decision led to a broader interpretation of the law and the admissibility of more similar fact evidence, particularly in cases involving sexual abuse of children by carers or parents.

Similar fact evidence and the jury

The traditionally narrow scope of the similar fact rule was based primarily on a lack of trust in the ability of a lay jury to deal properly with evidence of bad character. However, this paternalistic attitude towards the function of the jury led to much relevant evidence being excluded and possible injustice. For example, in August 1992, the jury at the Central Criminal Court (The Old Bailey) acquitted Simon Berkowitz of the burglary of a solicitor's office and the theft of personal documents belonging to Paddy Ashdown, the then leader of the Liberal Democrats. Mr Berkowitz was caught in possession of the stolen documents, which he was trying to sell to the media. He admitted possession of them but claimed they had been given to him by a man in a pub. What the jury did not know was that Mr Berkowitz had 240 previous convictions, 230 of them for burglary and a majority of these for burglary of solicitors' offices and the theft of documents. The prosecution had applied to the trial judge to allow these convictions to go before the jury as evidence of the guilt of Mr Berkowitz on the charge of burglary. The judge refused on the ground that it would be too prejudicial to the accused (although he was convicted of the alternative charge of handling the stolen documents).

In 1989, one William Beggs was convicted of murder, but the conviction was quashed on the grounds of insufficient similarity between the killing (which he admitted whilst pleading self-defence) and a number of woundings that indicated an unusual tendency to attack sleeping young men and inflict grievous wounds with sharp instruments. In 2001, Beggs was found guilty of sexually assaulting and murdering a young man whose body had been dismembered and decapitated. The police continued to investigate the possibility of 17 other murders committed by Beggs. We may never know how many deaths could have been prevented had the Court of Appeal taken a less restrictive view of the evidence of his disposition to violence. More recently, a trial judge refused to allow the jury to hear that two Russian sailors, charged with rape, had tried to abscond two days before their retrial. They were acquitted, but the jury had not been allowed to hear of their attempt to jump bail, which was evidence tending to suggest guilt, on the basis that it would prejudice the trial (even the trial judge thought the law was 'too fair' to the defendants).

There is no doubt that the fact that a person has a disposition to commit particular offences can be highly relevant evidence in a case which alleges that he committed that offence. See the remarks of the Criminal Law Revision Committee (Eleventh Report, *Evidence (General)* (Cmnd 4999, 1972) at p 149 above.

It is at the very least arguable that a man found in possession of goods stolen in the burglary of a solicitor's office, who has some 200 convictions for burglary of a solicitor's office, committed the burglary in question. That is not to say that one merely jumps from the fact of previous convictions to conviction on the present charge – there must be other evidence linking the defendant to the present burglary, as there was in the *Berkowitz* case where the stolen documents were found in his possession – but the evidence of previous convictions for burglaries then becomes part of the relevant evidence before the jury.

The fact that a man charged with the kidnapping, sexual assault and murder of a young girl has kidnapped and sexually assaulted a young girl previously is highly relevant evidence of his guilt, with which a jury should be trusted to deal as part of the evidence against the defendant. Similarly the fact that an accused charged with rape tries to flee the jurisdiction before trial is evidence of his guilt: and should be made known to the trier of fact. If there is evidence that real juries make decisions based on moral prejudice, perhaps we should be asking whether we should continue with the jury as a means of trial. Justice is certainly not done if juries convict out of prejudice; but equally it is not done if, because we do not trust the jury to deal with previous convictions or bad character, the accused is allowed to present himself as a man of good character, when in truth he has committed similar offences in the past that are relevant to his guilt, or the jury are prevented from hearing of other relevant matters that are proof of guilt.

The similar fact rule has now been abolished by s 99 of the Criminal Justice Act 2003, although s 101(d) provides for the admissibility of 'bad character' evidence if it is relevant to an important matter in issue between the defendant and the prosecution. Such an issue may include a propensity to commit the kind of offence charged or to be untruthful, and such a propensity may be established by evidence that the defendant has been convicted of offences of the same description as, or in the same category as, the offence with which he is charged. Thus, although the formulation of the rule has entirely changed, the new statutory provision should envelope those types of cases where the similar fact rule would previously have been applied.

The Criminal Evidence Act 1898

Alongside the similar fact rule at common law, the Criminal Evidence Act 1898 also permitted evidence of bad character to be adduced in certain circumstances. Until the 1898 Act the defendant was not permitted to give evidence in his own defence; thereafter he was able to do so 'upon his own application', which meant that he could choose to give evidence but could not be compelled to do so. The framers of the 1898 Act were faced with two problems resulting from the decision to make the accused a competent witness in his own defence:

(a) whether the accused should be entitled to claim the privilege against self-incrimination in respect of the offence charged; and

(b) whether, and to what extent, the accused should be open to cross-examination about his previous bad character or previous convictions for the purpose either of proving his guilt on the offence charged, or of attacking his credibility as a witness.

The Act represented a compromise by providing that while the defendant could be cross-examined as to any matter concerning the offences with which he was charged (s 1(2)), he was also given a 'shield against cross-examination as to his bad character' which prevented such cross-examination unless the shield was lost in one of the circumstances set out in s 1(3) of the 1898 Act.

Section 1(2) of the Criminal Evidence Act 1898

Section 1(2) provided that: 'A person charged in criminal proceedings who is called as a witness in those proceedings may be asked any question in cross-examination notwithstanding that it would tend to criminate him as to any offence with which he is charged in those proceedings.' This meant that the accused who gave evidence could be cross-examined about his part in the offence(s) charged and had no privilege against self-incrimination as to those offences, and could not therefore refuse to answer questions relating to the offence(s) with which he was charged on the ground that the answers might incriminate him.

Section 1(3) of the Criminal Evidence Act 1898

Section 1(3)(a)

Section 1(3)(a) stated that 'the proof that he has committed or been convicted of such other offence is admissible evidence to show that he is guilty of an offence with which he is then charged'; it allowed the accused to be cross-examined about his previous bad character when it was exceptionally admissible at common law (as similar fact evidence) or by statute to prove his guilt on the offence charged. It was the least used of the subsections, because when such evidence is admissible it will almost always be part of the prosecution case and form part of their evidence-in-chief. Having been admitted as similar fact evidence as part of the prosecution evidence-in-chief, it could then be the subject of cross-examination without reliance on s 1(3)(a). Only when the defence raised a defence which was not anticipated and made evidence of bad character or previous conviction relevant would the prosecution rely on that section, but since the imposition of onerous disclosure requirements upon the defence in the Criminal Justice Act 1994 and the Criminal Procedure and Investigations Act 1996, the section was, to all intents and purposes, redundant. When such evidence was admitted under s 1(3)(a) it illustrated the accused's bad character. Evidence admitted under paras (b) or (c) (below) was intended to go only to the credibility of the accused, and the trial judge had to direct the jury to this effect.

Section 1(3)(b)

Section 1(3)(b) of the 1898 Act stated that where the accused 'has personally or by his advocate asked questions of the witnesses for the prosecution with a view to establish his own good character, or has given evidence of his own good character, or the nature or conduct of his defence is such as to involve imputations on the character of the prosecutor or the witnesses for the prosecution, or the deceased victim of the alleged crime', he might be cross-examined as to his own bad character. The accused could thus be treated as any other witness and be fully exposed to cross-examination as to his bad character, or he could be totally protected. The subsection shielded him from such cross-examination unless the accused asserted his own good character by giving or calling character evidence, or gave evidence and attacked the character of prosecution witnesses or the deceased victim of the offence charged (see *R v Becouarn* [2005] UKHL 55).

The basis of admitting the previous convictions or bad character of the accused when he had cast imputations on prosecution witnesses was described as 'tit-for-tat', in that it was intended to be an automatic response so that the jury, who had to decide whom they were going to believe, knew the character of the person casting the imputations. The result was that comparatively minor imputations resulted in a long history of previous convictions being admitted, even when the imputation was seen as necessary to the defence. For example, in *R v Bishop* [1975] QB 274, the defendant, charged with burglary, sought to explain the presence of his fingerprints in the burgled premises by alleging a homosexual relationship between himself and the occupier. This was seen as an imputation on the character of a prosecution witness, entitling the prosecution to cross-examine the defendant on his previous convictions. Some judges thought this was unfair and developed a discretion to prevent such cross-examination where to allow such cross-examination would unfairly prejudice the accused and be too severe an application of the section. Later it was suggested that where the nature of the defence involved an imputation, the discretion should, as a general rule, be exercised in favour of the defendant. However, the House of Lords in *Selvey v DPP* [1970] AC 304 rejected what it described as a fetter on the exercise of the discretion and held that the fact that the imputation was a necessary part of the defence was merely one factor to be taken into account in exercising the discretion.

The Court of Appeal in *R v Burke* (1986) 82 Cr App R 156 set out guidelines to assist in the exercise of the discretion. In two raids on premises occupied by Burke, police seized small quantities of cannabis, plastic bags containing traces of cannabis, scales and £3,263. Burke later made admissions and pleaded guilty to possession of cannabis in connection with the first raid, but he pleaded not guilty to a charge of supplying and possessing cannabis. At his trial he alleged that the police had concocted the evidence, and maintained that there had been no drugs, bags or scales and denied making any admissions. The trial judge allowed cross-examination on the guilty plea to possession and an earlier conviction of possession with intent to supply. Burke was convicted and appealed against the decision to allow cross-examination on his previous convictions. Dismissing the appeal, the Court of Appeal set out four cardinal principles to be applied when deciding whether to permit cross-examination under this section:

(a) The trial judge must weigh the prejudicial effect of the questions against the damage done by the attack on the prosecution witnesses, and must generally exercise his discretion so as to secure a trial that is fair both to the prosecution and the defence (approving observations of Devlin J, in *Cook* [1959] 2 QB 340, 348).

(b) Cases must occur in which it would be unjust to admit evidence of a character gravely prejudicial to the accused, even though there may be some tenuous grounds for holding it technically admissible. Thus, although the position is established in law, still the putting of the question as to character of the accused person may be fraught with results which immeasurably outweigh the result of questions put by the defence and which make a fair trial of the accused almost impossible.

(c) In the ordinary and normal case the trial judge may feel that if the credit of the prosecutor or his witnesses has been attacked, it is only fair that the jury should have before them the material on which they can form their judgement whether the accused person is any more worthy to be believed than those he has attacked. It is obviously unfair that the jury should be left in the dark about an accused person's character if the conduct of his defence has attacked the character of the prosecutor or the witnesses for the prosecution within the meaning of s 1(3)(b) of the Act of 1898.

(d) In order to see if the conviction should be quashed, it is not enough that the Court think it would have exercised its discretion differently. The Court will not interfere with the exercise of a discretion by a judge below unless he has erred in principle, or there is no material on which he could properly have arrived at his decision (*per* Viscount Dilhorne in *Selvey v DPP* [1970] AC 304, 342).

The third of these rules is the most important in suggesting that only in exceptional cases was the discretion to be exercised in favour of the defendant. In the ordinary and normal case it was only fair that the jury be made aware of the character of the person making the attack on the character of the prosecution witness. When the defendant gave evidence of good character or asked questions, or called witnesses in order to do so, thus presenting the jury with a false impression of his character, the discretion did not apply; it was obviously right that where the accused set up a false or misleading character, the prosecution should be able to set the record straight by cross-examining the defendant about his previous convictions or bad character. In both cases the judge was required to warn the jury that the purpose of the cross-examination was to enable them properly to assess the credibility of the defendant as a witness and that they were not to use the previous convictions for the purpose of determining the defendant's guilt. This was always asking a lot of a jury, but when the previous convictions were for the same offence as that charged it became an impossibility, as was recognised by judges, academics and the Law Commission. In *R v Watts (Idwal)* [1983] Crim LR 541, where the defendant charged with indecent assault on a woman was cross-examined on his convictions for indecent assault on his nieces aged 5 and 3, Lord Lane CJ spoke for many in stating that: 'The jury were warned that the previous convictions were not to be taken as making it more likely that he was guilty of the offence charged (which it did) but only as affecting his credibility (which it almost certainly did not). It was an intellectual impossibility to disregard the previous convictions except as to the question of credibility.'

As noted at pp 176–181 below, s 101(1)(f) and (g) of the Criminal Justice Act 2003 permit evidence of the defendant's bad character to be adduced if he gives a false impression of his character, or if he attacks another person's character. The intention is that while such evidence will go primarily to the credibility of the defendant, it can also be used by the jury in the determination of his guilt. Given that the subsection replaces s 1(3)(b) of the 1898 Act and has the same purpose, the discretion under s 101(3) of the 2003 Act is likely to be applied in the same way as suggested by the decision in *R v Burke*.

Section 1(3)(c)

Section 1(3)(c) of the 1898 Act provided a similar shield against cross-examination as to the bad character of an accused by a co-accused unless that accused gave evidence against the co-accused. When the co-accused was permitted to cross-examine another co-accused as to his previous convictions, the trial judge had no discretion to prevent the cross-examination but (as under s 1(3)(b)) he was obliged to direct the jury that the cross-examination went only to the credibility of the co-accused and was not to be used in order to determine his guilt. However, in *R v Randall* [2004] 1 WLR 56, the House of Lords held that where two defendants are jointly charged with a crime, and each blames the other for its commission, thus permitting both to cross-examine the other as to his previous convictions under s 1(3)(c) of the 1898 Act, one accused may rely on the criminal propensity of the other. Furthermore, the trial judge was not required to direct the jury that the bad character revealed went only to the credibility of the other accused.

The road to reform

There were other criticisms of the operation of the 1898 Act, in particular that it was much abused by corrupt police officers, who made up confessions or planted evidence which they knew the defendant could not dispute without being seen to cast imputations on them, leading to the defendant's often lengthy list of convictions being put before the jury with the obvious result. There also remained difficulties in the operation of the similar fact rule that led to the reference to the Law Commission, which resulted in the Report referred to at p 150 above. That Report took a radical approach by proposing a scheme to deal with the admissibility of evidence of the bad character of defendants and non-defendants. Thus, for the first time there were to be constraints on the admissibility of evidence of the bad character of witnesses, victims and defendants. The Law Commission believed that the similar fact rule worked fairly well and needed only a clearer statutory formula to regulate the admissibility of evidence of bad character, and to clarify the difficult borderline between similar fact evidence and background or explanatory evidence. The 1898 Act was to be repealed and reworked to enable the defendant more readily to challenge the central features of the case against him, without making his previous convictions or bad character admissible.

While broadly accepting the Law Commission's recommendations, the Government issued a White Paper, *Justice for All* (Cmnd 5563, 2002), which outlined its legislative proposals. It was clear that the Government intended to go further and admit the defendant's bad character and previous convictions more often than the previous law allowed and the Law Commission proposed. The White Paper's proposals were expanded upon in Pt 11, Ch 1 of the Criminal Justice Act 2003 (ss 98 to 113), which governs the admissibility of evidence of the bad character of a defendant and non-defendant. The adduction of the bad character of a witness or victim (dealt with in s 100 of the 2003 Act) is considered in **Chapter 4**. Here we are concerned only with the admissibility of evidence of the bad character of the defendant. Although the Act adopts most of the recommendations of the Law Commission Report, it also goes further by taking a more inclusionary approach than that which was recommended.

Reform: Criminal Justice Act 2003, Pt 11, Ch 1

The Court of Appeal, in *R v Bradley* (2005) 169 JP 73, has accepted that the bad character provisions in the Criminal Justice Act 2003 have now come fully into force. This is restricted to trials that commenced after 15 December 2004, and it means that nearly all of the previous common law and statutory rules have now become redundant.

What constitutes 'bad character'?

Section 98 of the 2003 Act defines the sort of evidence the admissibility of which is to be determined under the new statutory scheme. The definition covers 'evidence of, or a disposition toward misconduct'. The term 'misconduct' is further defined in s 112 as 'the commission of an offence or other reprehensible behaviour'. This is intended to be a broad definition and to cover evidence that shows that a person has committed an offence, or has acted in a reprehensible way (or is disposed to do so), as well as evidence from which this may be inferred. The definition includes evidence such as previous convictions, as well as evidence on charges being tried concurrently, and evidence relating to offences for which a person has been charged, where the charge is not prosecuted, or for which the person was subsequently acquitted.

Non-criminal acts

The *Notes of Guidance* state that the definition of misconduct also includes evidence that a person has behaved or is disposed to behave in a reprehensible way, even if this has not amounted to an offence. This might include, for example, evidence that a person has a sexual interest in children, even if he has not acted on it in a criminal way. It may include, for example, the previous history of Ian Huntley, convicted in 2004 of the murder of Holly Wells and Jessica Chapman in Soham in 2002.

Between 1995 and 1999, Huntley had been investigated for four alleged rapes, four cases of sex with under-age girls and one indecent assault on an 11-year-old girl. A charge was preferred in respect of only one of these allegations, the alleged rape of an 18-year-old girl, but the Crown Prosecution Service discontinued the prosecution because there was no reasonable prospect of conviction. No charges were preferred in respect of the other allegations and no record was kept of them (in some cases the alleged victims did not want to be involved in criminal proceedings and withdrew the allegations so the police took no further action). Even if records had been kept, the allegations would have remained unproven. The phrase 'the commission of an offence or other reprehensible behaviour' in s 112 of the 2003 Act is wide enough to include the nine allegations of sexual misconduct, but it seems that the intention was to exclude matters not resulting in a charge. An investigation followed by a charge suggests that the police (and now the Crown Prosecution Service, who have the final say on whether a charge is to be preferred) were satisfied that there was a case to answer. The charge may not result in a prosecution, particularly where young children are involved, but adds substance to the allegation and is intended to be within the definition of 'misconduct'. In the future the police will investigate such allegations, and the Crown Prosecution Service will decide whether a charge is to be preferred. If they decide not to proceed against the suspect, that would tend to imply that there is no substance, or insufficient substance, to the allegations, suggesting that the allegation cannot be described as 'other reprehensible conduct'.

Previous acquittals

The inclusion of acquittals reflects the previous law and preserves the effect of the decision of the House of Lords in *R v Z (Prior Acquittal)* [2000] 2 Cr App R 283. There, the House of Lords held that there was no special rule that required the exclusion of evidence that a person had been involved in earlier offences, even if he had been acquitted of those crimes, provided that that evidence was otherwise admissible. *Z* was charged with a single count of rape committed in 1998. The prosecution sought leave to adduce evidence of four previous incidents involving Z and four different women who complained of rape in 1984, 1985, 1989 and 1993. Z was tried on a charge of rape in respect of each of these incidents. In each case it was common ground that intercourse had taken place and the central issue was whether the complainant consented. Only in one case was Z convicted; in the other three he was acquitted by verdict of the jury. The trial judge accepted the Crown's case that the four incidents involved circumstances sufficiently similar to those of the present case for them to have been admissible under the principles established in *Boardman* and *DPP v P* (see pp 151–152 above). However, the judge held that the fact of the prior acquittals in respect of three of the complainants meant that the Crown could not adduce evidence involving those incidents as similar fact evidence in respect of the present charge of rape. Standing by itself, one conviction did not present a sufficiently cogent   picture of similar incidents to be admissible.

The Court of Appeal, dismissing the Crown's appeal from that decision, expressed its regret at having reached that conclusion, but certified that a question of general public importance was involved in their decision, namely:

> Other than in cases of autrefois acquit, (a) is evidence admissible on behalf of the Crown in a trial of offence A which also proves guilt in respect of one or more prior incident (B, C and D) in respect of each of which the defendant has been tried and acquitted; and (b) is evidence so admissible if its nature and purpose is to show guilt in respect of offence A on the basis that offence A was not an isolated offence, but one in a series of similar incidents (including those in respect of which the defendant was tried and convicted)?

The House of Lords allowed the Crown's appeal. Lord Hutton, giving a judgment with which all their Lordships agreed, cited (at 283), in relation to the plea of *autrefois acquit*, the words of Lord MacDermott in *Sambasivam v Public Prosecutor, Federation of Malaya* [1950] AC 458, 479:

> The effect of a verdict of acquittal pronounced by a competent court after a lawful trial is not completely stated by saying that the person acquitted cannot be tried again for the same offence. To that it must be added that the verdict is binding and conclusive in all subsequent proceedings between the parties to the adjudication ... provided that a defendant was not placed in double jeopardy in the way described evidence that was relevant on a subsequent prosecution was not inadmissible because it showed, or tended to show, that he was, in fact, guilty of an offence of which he had earlier been acquitted.

Having considered the authorities, Lord Hutton came to the following conclusions:

(a) The principle of double jeopardy operated to cause a criminal court in the exercise of its discretion to stop a prosecution where the defendant was being prosecuted on the same or substantially the same facts as had given rise to an earlier prosecution that had resulted in his acquittal or conviction.

(b) Provided that a defendant was not placed in double jeopardy in that way, evidence that was relevant on a subsequent prosecution was not inadmissible because it showed or tended to show that the defendant was, in fact, guilty of an offence of which he had earlier been acquitted.

(c) It followed from that that a distinction should not be drawn between evidence that showed guilt of a previous offence of which the defendant had been acquitted and evidence that tended to show guilt of such an offence or that appeared to relate to one distinct issue rather than the issue of guilt of such an offence.

In this instance, the defendant was not placed in double jeopardy because the facts giving rise to the present prosecution were different from those that had given rise to the earlier prosecution. The evidence of the earlier complainants was accepted to be relevant and to come within the ambit of the similar facts rule, and therefore it was not inadmissible because it showed that the defendant was, in fact, guilty of the offences of which he had earlier been acquitted. The admissibility of previous acquittals would be subject to the judge's discretion to exclude them after weighing the evidence's prejudicial effect against its probative force, or under s 78 of the Police and Criminal Evidence Act 1984. (See *R v Becouarn* [2005] 1 WLR 2589.)

The principle on the admissibility of prior acquittals in s 101(3) applies to any offence. Thus if there was a series of robberies and the defendant was acquitted of involvement in them, evidence tending to show that he had committed those earlier robberies could be given in a later case involving a similar charge, particularly if it went to show that if the previous incidents took place in similar circumstances to those alleged in the case at hand.

Evidence of the facts of the offence charged – s 98(a) and (b)

Section 98 does not affect the admissibility of evidence of the facts of the offence, or facts that are closely related in time, place or circumstances to those facts. These are excluded from the definition of bad character evidence by s 98(a) and (b), which also exclude evidence of misconduct in connection with the investigation or prosecution of the offence. Thus, if the defendant were charged with burglary, the prosecution evidence of the facts of the offence – any witnesses to the crime, forensic evidence, etc – would be admissible outside the terms of these provisions. So too would evidence of an assault that had been committed in the course of the burglary (if not separately charged), as evidence to do with the facts of the offence. Many offences include within them a number of other offences – for example, a person committing robbery may have a weapon in his possession; a burglar may commit criminal damage in the course of the burglary. These are all facts which are evidence which has to do with the alleged facts of the offence with which the defendant is charged. Evidence that the defendant had tried to intimidate prosecution witnesses would also be admissible as evidence of misconduct in connection, as appropriate, with the investigation or the prosecution of the offence, as would allegations by the defendant that the evidence had been planted. However, evidence that the defendant had committed a burglary on another occasion, or that a witness had previously lied on oath, would not be evidence to do with the facts of the offence or its investigation or prosecution, and would therefore not be excluded by s 98(a) and (b).

Trials involving multiple victims

As indicated at pp 150–153 above, many cases involving similar fact evidence were cases in which the defendant was charged with the commission of the same type of crime against several victims. In such a case, several counts (charges) are joined in the same indictment and all are tried in one single trial rather than several separate trials. The normal rule applying to such trials was that the jury must consider the evidence on each count separately, and in determining the defendant's guilt on one count they were not permitted to take into account the evidence on the other counts. The similar fact principle operated to override this rule and permit the evidence of each of the other victims to be taken into account by the jury when considering the evidence on a charge against another victim. The practical effect was that each victim became a witness for the other victims, greatly increasing the likelihood of conviction on all charges.

The exclusion from the definition of 'bad character' of evidence of the facts of the offence charged (see above) would seem at first sight to put trials involving multiple victims outside the framework of the new law. However, s 112(2) of the 2003 Act provides that 'where a defendant is charged with two or more offences in the same criminal proceedings, this Chapter (except section 101(3)) has effect as if each offence were charged in separate proceedings; and references to the offence with which the defendant is charged are to be read accordingly'.

The effect of this subsection is that in trials in which the defendant is charged with a number of offences each of which is joined in the same indictment and tried together, the evidence of the alleged facts of each individual offence, together with evidence of misconduct in connection with the investigation or prosecution of that offence, is admissible without seeking leave under s 101. However, if the prosecution want the jury, when considering the guilt of the defendant on one count, to take into consideration the evidence of the witnesses and victims of other counts, they must seek the leave of the court under s 101. Put more simply, the evidence of the facts of each individual offence is not evidence of bad character, but evidence of other offences that are charged concurrently and which are to be applied to that offence is.

The intention is that this Part of the Act will provide a new basis for the admissibility of previous convictions and other misconduct. Accordingly, s 99 abolishes the common law rules governing the admissibility of such evidence. Statutes dealing with admissibility are repealed by Pt 5 of Sch 37, although this abolition does not extend to the rule that allows a person's bad character to be proved by his reputation. At common law it was held, in *R v Rowton* (1865) Le & Ca 520 CCR, that character evidence should be confined to reputation in the community. 'Reputation' referred to the accused's reputed disposition or propensity to act, think or feel in a given way, as opposed to his actual disposition or propensity to act, think or feel in a given way. Evidence of opinion, or of particular acts or other examples of conduct, should not be given, but the decision in *Rowton*, though never overruled, was often ignored in practice and, as an indulgence to the accused, such evidence is often admitted. This common law rule is preserved as a category of admissible hearsay in s 118(2) (see **Chapter 6**).

Collusion between alleged victims/witnesses – contamination of the evidence

At common law, collusion between the alleged victims was capable of contaminating their evidence and destroying its corroborative effect. In *R v H* [1995] 2 AC 596, the House of Lords clarified the law, holding that the admissibility of similar fact evidence should be approached on the basis that the evidence is true. The defendant was charged with a number of sexual offences against his adopted daughter and stepdaughter between 1987 and 1989. At the defendant's trial, the judge directed the jury that they had to consider whether the girls had collaborated and concocted a false story against their father, and whether they, as the defence claimed, might have fantasised about the assaults. He further directed that it was for the prosecution to satisfy the jury that the girls were in fact telling the truth, and that the evidence of one girl could support the evidence of the other only if the jury were sure that the girls had not collaborated to concoct a false story against the defendant. The defendant was convicted and appealed, contending that the judge had misdirected the jury on the risk of collusion. The House of Lords dismissed the appeal and advocated a two-stage approach where the question of witness collusion arose. First, the judge should consider whether the similar fact evidence, if true, was so probative of the crime of which the defendant was accused that it ought to be admitted notwithstanding the prejudicial effect of disclosing that the defendant had committed other crimes. If the evidence was admitted, it was then for the jury to determine its credibility as a question of fact, after being directed by the judge that they could not properly rely on the evidence as corroboration unless they were satisfied that it was reliable and true and not tainted by collusion or other defects. Only when it was obvious that no reasonable jury could accept the evidence as free from collusion or contamination should the judge direct the jury that they should not rely on the evidence for any purpose adverse to the defence, effectively excluding it. These matters are now dealt with by s 107 and s 109 of the Criminal Justice Act 2003, discussed at pp 181–183 below.

Admissibility of the defendant's bad character

Section 101(1)(a) to (g) of the 2003 Act set out seven circumstances in which the prosecution, or in certain cases a co-defendant, can adduce evidence of bad character:

(a) where all the parties agree to the evidence being admissible;

(b) where the evidence is adduced by the defendant himself, or is given in answer to a question asked by him in cross-examination and intended to elicit it;

(c) where it is important explanatory evidence;

(d) where it is relevant to an important matter in issue between the defendant and the prosecution;

(e) where it has substantial probative value in relation to an important matter in issue between the defendant and a co-defendant;

(f) where it is evidence to correct a false impression given by the defendant; or

(g) where the defendant has made an attack on another person's character.

Each head of admissibility is then expanded upon by a number of sections which provide additional definitional material (ss 102 to 106). Section 107 provides an important safeguard where evidence of bad character may be contaminated by collusion or is otherwise contaminated, and s 108 repeals the previous prohibition on the use in evidence of offences committed by the defendant while a child. It should also be noted that two of these heads of admissibility, ss 101(1)(d) and 101(1)(g), are subject to a judicial discretion to refuse to admit the evidence if, on application by the defendant, the trial judge is of the opinion that it would have such an adverse effect on the fairness of the proceedings that it ought not to be admitted.

Section 101(1)(a) and (b)

So far as s 101(1)(a) is concerned, of the parties who agree to the bad character evidence being given in evidence the most important will be the defendant and his counsel. They will rarely agree to such evidence being admitted, unless it is part of the defence strategy to reveal previous convictions or other bad character. This may be the case when the defence are about to launch an attack on the character of prosecution witnesses. Such an attack would lead to evidence of the defendant's bad character being admitted under s 101(1)(g) (see pp 179–181 below). As previously noted, under the Criminal Evidence Act 1898, an attack on the character of a prosecution witness led to the loss of the shield against cross-examination on the defendant's bad character. Although the court had a discretion to prevent such cross-examination, it was accepted that the basis of the provision was tit for tat, and if a defendant made a deliberate attack on the character of a prosecution witness it was seen as only fair that the jury know of the character of the person making that attack. They would then be better placed to assess the credibility of the defendant. The same approach is likely to be taken under s 101(3), which gives the court a discretion to refuse to admit evidence of bad character where the defendant has made an attack on another person's character. However, it should be noted that though evidence of bad character admitted under s 1(3)(b) of the 1898 Act went only to credibility, the position under the 2003 Act is different. While such evidence is primarily relevant to the defendant's credibility, it is not intended that the jury would put out of their minds knowledge of the defendant's bad character in deciding whether he is guilty of the offence charged. The judge may, however, direct the jury that care should be taken about the level of weight to be placed on such evidence when considering issues other than the credibility of the accused.

Other defence strategies which might lead to the disclosure of bad character evidence would include the situation where the defendant, who is charged with an offence involving violence, has convictions for non-violent offences. For example, the defendant is charged with armed robbery, but his previous convictions are for shoplifting and theft from cars. Those previous convictions might well be disclosed to the jury in an effort to persuade them that the defendant is a small-time criminal and not into major league crime involving violence of the kind charged. In *R v Shaw* [2003] Crim LR 278, the accused pleaded self-defence to a charge of assaulting police officers. He sought to adduce evidence of his bad relationship with the police, including an arrest for murder, in order to show his state of mind as being more likely to imagine he was under threat from police officers in support of his defence. The Court of Appeal held that the bad character of the defendant was properly admitted on behalf of the defendant for that purpose. Once bad character evidence is properly revealed to the jury the prosecution can cross-examine the defendant on that bad character, though the trial judge will prevent them from dwelling on it too much lest the jury be given the impression that it is of greater importance than is the case. However, cross-examination may also follow bad character evidence revealed by the defendant indirectly or more directly by other witnesses, provided such evidence is properly adduced.

In *Jones v DPP* [1962] AC 655, a decision under the Criminal Evidence Act 1898, the accused had been arrested following the rape of a girl guide and the murder of a second girl just one month later. He was first tried for the rape and was convicted. He was then tried for the murder. The circumstances of the murder resembled those of the rape in many respects, but the prosecution made no attempt to prove the facts of the rape case as similar fact evidence in the murder case, apparently because they did not wish to put the victim of the rape through the ordeal of giving evidence again. When giving evidence at his trial for murder, Jones attempted to explain a false alibi he had given to the police by stating that he had been in trouble with the police on a previous occasion. He then put forward a new alibi, in which he said he had been with a prostitute in London at the time. He gave an account of his return home and an account of a conversation with his wife, in which he assured her that his late return home had nothing to do with the crime which had been reported in the newspapers. The prosecution were then given leave to cross-examine him about a previous occasion on which he had claimed to have had exactly the same conversation with his wife, again after supposedly visiting a prostitute in London. The prosecution did not indicate what that previous occasion was, but it must have been obvious to the jury, given the notoriety of the case, that it was the occasion on which he had been charged with the rape of the girl guide. The cross-examination was directed at discrediting the new alibi given by Jones, emphasis being placed on how unlikely it was that Jones and his wife should repeat an earlier conversation word for word. However, the cross-examination inevitably indicated to the jury that Jones had previously been suspected of committing a crime serious enough to be reported in all the newspapers. The appeal against conviction, which argued that leave should not have been given to cross-examine, went to the House of Lords. Their Lordships interpreted the words of s 1(3) of the 1898 Act, which prohibited questions 'tending to show that he has committed or been convicted of or been charged with any offence', as meaning 'tending to show the jury for the first time matters which had not been already disclosed to them'. Since Jones himself had revealed the facts upon which the cross-examination was based, the cross-examination was properly allowed.

In an earlier case, *R v Chitson* [1909] 2 KB 945, Chitson was convicted of unlawful sexual intercourse with an under-age girl. The girl was allowed to give evidence that the defendant had boasted to her of his sexual relationship with another girl. The Court of Appeal held that he was properly cross-examined on that boastful statement on the basis that if he had made that statement, it would strongly corroborate the young girl's evidence that he had had sexual intercourse with her. The Court of Appeal's decision that it was admissible under s 1(2) of the 1898 Act was disapproved of by the House of Lords in *Jones v DPP*, but the cross-examination would appear to be admissible under the principle enunciated by their Lordships that the statement was already before the court and therefore the prohibition in s 1(3) did not apply. In *Chitson*, the defendant's statement made to the girl was properly admitted as an exception to the rule against hearsay as part of the *res gestae* (that is, it was part of the event to which it related). That exception is preserved by the 2003 Act (see **Chapter 6**). However, given that s 99 of the Criminal Justice Act 2003 abolishes the common law rules governing the admissibility of evidence of bad character, the prosecution must seek leave to admit the evidence of bad character under s 101. The *Jones* case is likely to fall under s 101(1)(b), but if *Chitson* were tried under the new rules the previous conviction for under-age sexual intercourse might not be admissible under s 101(1)(b) given that the defendant did not directly adduce the evidence. However, it might well be admissible under s 101(1)(d) as relevant to an important matter in issue between the defendant and the prosecution, which includes the question whether the defendant has a propensity to commit the kind of offence charged (see the discussions at pp 166–171 below considering s 101(1)(d) and s 103).

Section 101(1)(c) – important explanatory evidence

For evidence to be admissible as 'important explanatory evidence', it must be such that, without it, the magistrates or jury would find it impossible or difficult to understand other evidence in the case (2003 Act, s 102). If, therefore, the facts or account to which the bad character evidence relates are largely understandable without this additional explanation, the evidence should not be admitted. The explanation must also give the court some substantial assistance in understanding the case as a whole. In other words, it will not be enough for the evidence to assist the court to understand some trivial piece of evidence: an example would be a case involving the abuse by one person of another over a long period of time. For the jury properly to understand the victim's account of the offending and why he did not seek help from, say, a parent or guardian, it would be necessary for evidence to be given of a wider pattern of abuse involving that other person.

At common law this area of admissibility was originally known as *res gestae*, a Latin phrase meaning part of the facts surrounding an event. Evidence falling within this description was seen as an exception to the rule against the admissibility of hearsay evidence. More recently it became known as 'background evidence'; and for the future, 'explanatory evidence'. The basis of the admissibility of facts surrounding the event in question was that it is often impossible to understand and deal with an event in isolation without knowing more about the surrounding circumstances and the general background. In an Australian case, *O'Leary v R* (1946) 73 CLR 566, a number of men employed at a timber camp went on a drunken rampage for several hours, during which time several serious assaults were committed. After the rampage one of the men, who had been seriously assaulted, was found dying. At the trial for murder it was held that the episode should be treated as one event, including the other assaults that had occurred:

> The evidence disclosed that, under the influence of the beer and wine [the prisoner] had drunk and continued to drink, he engaged in repeated acts of violence which might be regarded as amounting to a connected course of conduct. Without evidence of what, during that time, was done by those men who took any significant part in the matter and especially evidence of the behaviour of the prisoner, the transactions of which the alleged murder formed an integral part could not be truly understood and isolated from it, could only be presented as an unreal and not very intelligible event. The prisoner's generally violent and hostile conduct might well serve to explain his mind and attitude and, therefore, to implicate him in the resulting homicide. (per Dixon J, at 577)

The difficulty in providing the essential background information is contained in the phrase 'to implicate him in the resulting homicide'. As in *O'Leary*, it could include evidence of other offences committed by the defendant, or evidence of other misconduct on his part. Some critics saw this as a backdoor means of admitting evidence of the defendant's previous convictions or other bad character. However, it was later made clear that necessary background evidence without which the account placed before the jury would be incomplete or incomprehensible, was not to be excluded simply because it involved establishing the commission of an offence with which the defendant was not charged.

In *R v Sidhu* (1994) 98 Cr App R 59, the defendant was charged with conspiracy to possess explosives in England. It was held that the trial judge had rightly admitted a videotape, which appeared to show the defendant leading a band of armed rebels in Pakistan. Although the evidence suggested to the jury that the defendant had been involved in other criminal activities, it was justified as being necessary to explain the background to the defendant's activities in England and the motives for his activities. One can readily see that such evidence is also useful to the prosecution in proving the guilt of the defendant. Similar reasoning was applied in *R v Sawoniuk* [2000] 2 Cr App R 220, where Sawoniuk was charged with the murder of Jews during the Nazi occupation of Belorussia in 1942. Evidence was admitted that during that period the accused had been a member of a group of police officers who had carried out search and kill operations for Jewish survivors of an earlier massacre. In this case broadly-based background evidence was necessary to enable the jury properly to understand the circumstances which prevailed such a long time ago in a foreign country, in an atmosphere in which ethnically based war crimes were committed. The Court held that criminal charges cannot fairly be judged in a factual vacuum. Evidence describing context and circumstances (important explanatory evidence) in which the offences were said to have been committed might often be necessary.

In *R v M (T)* [2000] 1 WLR 421, the Court of Appeal held that a long history of sexual and physical abuse suffered by M and his sister was rightly admitted at the trial of M for the rape of his sister, as essential background evidence to explain why the victim had not turned to her parents for help when her brother allegedly raped her. The evidence was that daughters and sons were raped and buggered by the father, and the sons were forced to watch him abuse their sisters and later to abuse them themselves. This included evidence that M was forced to watch the abuse and later made to take part (taught to abuse), and that when aged 16 he had gone on seriously to abuse his 10-year-old sister. The Court said such evidence was admissible as necessary background (important explanatory evidence) to enable the jury to understand what would otherwise be an incomplete and incomprehensible account, not as evidence of propensity going to guilt.

Section 101(1)(d) – relevance to an important matter in issue between prosecution and defendant

This subsection roughly equates with the similar fact principle applied at common law. Under the 2003 Act, evidence of bad character will be admissible if it is relevant to an important matter in issue between the defendant and the prosecution. Section 103(1) states that for the purposes of s 101(1)(d), matters in issue between the defendant and the prosecution include the question 'whether the defendant has a propensity to commit offences of the kind charged, except where his having such a propensity makes it no more likely that he is guilty of the offence'. Section 103(2) provides that such a propensity can be established by evidence that the defendant has been convicted of offences of the same description, or of the same category.

There has so far been very little guidance from the courts as to how to assess whether a defendant has a propensity to commit offences of the kind with which he is charged, but in *R v Hanson* [2005] 2 Cr App R 21, the Court of Appeal stated that essentially there are three questions to be considered (although the Court made it clear that this was not a comprehensive treatise on the new provisions):

(a) Did the history of his convictions establish a propensity to commit offences of the kind charged?

(b) Did that propensity make it more likely that the defendant had committed the offence charged?

(c) Was it just to rely on the convictions of the same description or category; and, in any event, would the proceedings be unfair if they were admitted?

Therefore, such evidence might be relevant to a number of issues in the case. For example, it might assist the prosecution to prove the defendant's guilt by establishing his involvement or state of mind, or by rebutting a defence or explanation of his conduct. Previous conviction for offences which are of the same description or category as those charged are admissible to prove a propensity to commit that kind of offence, or to be untruthful when either of these matters is in issue.

Examples of s 101(1)(d) and s 103 in operation

Subject to the exercise of the discretion of the court to exclude bad character evidence under s 101(3) and s 103(3), which states that evidence of a conviction of the same description or category is not to be admitted 'if the court is satisfied, by reason of the length of time since the conviction or for any other reason, that it would be unjust for it to apply in his case', the following examples may assist in understanding the application of the section. One should note that s 103(1) states that matters in issue between the defendant and the prosecution 'include' the question whether the defendant has a propensity to commit offences of the kind charged or to be untruthful. The issue(s) in the case will differ according to the circumstances and are not confined to the issue of a propensity to commit particular offences or to be untruthful.

Consider the following scenarios:

EXAMPLE 1

The defendant is charged with obtaining property by deception having sold a necklace, which he said he had inherited from his grandmother, which he falsely represented to be a diamond necklace when in fact it was glass. His defence is that he honestly believed it was a diamond necklace, and whether he held that belief is the issue in the case. He had been arrested and charged with a similar offence in which he sold a necklace inherited from a relative, which he represented as a diamond necklace, which was also glass. He was acquitted, the jury accepting his defence that he knew nothing about diamonds and honestly believed that it was a diamond necklace. The similarity of the offences and the fact that he had made the same false representation previously suggest that he now knows the difference between diamonds and glass, and would be admissible to prove that, contrary to his defence, he knew the necklace was glass. The previous acquittal is relevant to an important matter in issue between the defendant and the prosecution, and is admissible under s 101(1)(d) and s 103, subject to the exercise of the discretion in s 101(3).

EXAMPLE 2

The defendant had two previous convictions, one for obtaining property by deception and one for obtaining a pecuniary advantage by deception. In the first instance, he had used a cheque drawn on a closed account to obtain goods, and he claimed he did not know the account had been closed. In the second case, he used a credit card to purchase goods after being told by the credit card company that he was overdrawn and was not to use the card. Here the convictions are relevant to the issue of whether the defendant was dishonest and has a propensity to commit the kind of offence charged (s 103(1)(a)). The convictions are for offences of the same description (the offence of dishonestly obtaining property by deception) or of the same category (the offence of dishonestly obtaining a pecuniary advantage by deception), and would be admissible under s 101(1)(d) and s 103(2) to establish the propensity to commit an offence of the kind charged.

EXAMPLE 3

The defendant is charged with rape, during which the victim was threatened with a knife. The victim's description of her assailant fitted that of the accused. He denied being in the area, claiming to have been far away at the time of the rape. He was arrested the day after the rape while trying to sell items stolen from a car parked near the scene of the rape, which had been broken into shortly before the rape took place. He was convicted of the offence of theft from the car, and has previous convictions for violence involving the use of a knife and a number of convictions for theft from cars. The issue in this case is whether the defendant was the rapist, or whether, as he states, he was elsewhere at the time. His previous convictions would be admissible under s 101(1)(d), the issue being not whether he has a propensity to commit an offence of rape but whether he has a propensity to be untruthful. The evidence of his possession of items stolen from the car parked near the scene of the rape just before that offence took place, together with his convictions which show a disposition to commit acts of violence while using a knife, are all capable of being admitted under this head. The possession of the stolen items and his convictions for theft from the car put him at the scene of the rape and rebut his story that he was elsewhere at the time, and his propensity to violence using a knife assists in identifying him as the rapist.

EXAMPLE 4

The defendant is charged with the murder of two 11-year-old girls, whose bodies were discovered in a shallow grave in a country park after an attempt to burn them. The prosecution case is that the defendant sexually assaulted the girls, and killed them to prevent them exposing him. He then took the bodies to a country park and tried to burn them to dispose of any forensic evidence before burying them. The defendant says the deaths were accidental. One girl had fallen down stairs and struck her head. When the other girl realised her friend was dead, she started screaming and the defendant panicked. He placed his hand over her mouth to stop her screaming and inadvertently suffocated her. He later hid the bodies. The defendant was acquitted of having sexual intercourse with an under-age girl in 1995, and in the following five years had been charged on two occasions with rape and once with an offence of indecent assault on a 12-year-old girl. In all cases the charges were not proceeded with because the complainants did not want to be involved in a criminal prosecution. The issue in the case is whether the defendant intentionally killed the girls having sexually assaulted them, or whether their deaths were accidental.

The acquittal of under-age sex is admissible as evidence of bad character (*R v Z*; see p 158 above) and the charges are evidence of bad character as defined in s 112 'other reprehensible behaviour', which together prove a propensity to commit offences of a sexual nature against young girls which is the basis of the offence charged, ie sexual assault followed by murder to hide the fact of the sexual assault. Section 103 does not exclusively define 'matters in issue between the defendant and the prosecution', although s 103(1) states that matters in issue 'include' propensity to commit offences of the kind with which the defendant is charged and propensity to be untruthful. Thus, in the present case, while the defendant's prior record does not show a propensity to violence leading to death, it does show a propensity to sexually assault young girls that goes to the heart of the prosecution case and tends to rebut the defendant's defence of accident. The acquittal and charges may also be relevant to the question whether the defendant has a propensity to be untruthful if he denies the propensity to commit sexual offences against young girls, as he might in denying the prosecution case that he sexually assaulted the girls before killing them.

EXAMPLE 5

An example of bad character which was not criminal conduct being admitted is to be found in the case of *R v Barrington* (1981) 72 Cr App R 280. Barrington was convicted of indecently assaulting three young girls. They gave evidence to the effect that they had been invited into Barrington's house on separate occasions to baby-sit, and were shown pornographic pictures and persuaded to pose nude. It was during this posing that the indecent assaults were alleged to have taken place. Barrington's defence was that the girls were lying and had got together to concoct the charges. Three other young girls were permitted to give evidence of being induced to enter Barrington's house to baby-sit, being shown pornographic picture and of being invited to pose nude. All three had refused and no offence was committed against them. The Court of Appeal noted (at 290) that:

> That they did not include evidence of the commission of offences similar to those with which the appellant was charged does not mean that they are not logically probative in determining the guilt of the appellant. Indeed we are of the opinion that taken as a whole they are inexplicable on the basis of coincidence and that they are of positive probative value in assisting to determine the truth of the charges against the appellant, in that they tended to show that he was guilty of the offences with which he was charged.

Applying s 101(1)(d) and s 103 to this scenario, the issue between the defendant and the prosecution would be whether the defendant had indecently assaulted the young girls, or whether they had concocted a false story. The evidence of the approach to the other girls that came close to an attempt to indecently assault serves to rebut the allegation of concoction and strongly supports the allegations of the alleged victims. The fact that the conduct (though within the definition of 'bad character' as some form of misconduct or reprehensible behaviour under s 112) is not criminal (though in this case it was not far short of an attempt to indecently assault) means that it is easier to admit, given that any adverse effect from its admission is likely to be less than if the conduct was criminal (see the similar case of *R v Butler* (1987) 84 Cr App R 12). If in the above case the defendant had previous convictions for indecent assault, those convictions would be admissible under s 101(1)(d) and s 103(2)(a) where the issue between the defendant and the prosecution would include the question whether he has a propensity to commit the kind of offence charged.

EXAMPLE 6

The defendant is charged with conspiracy to defraud Customs and Excise by smuggling cigarettes and selling them without paying duty. He denies knowing or being involved with the men alleged to be his co-conspirators. He has a conviction for affray, in which three of the four co-conspirators were involved and were also convicted. That conviction would be admissible to prove that the defendant did know the co-conspirators – an important matter in issue between the defendant and the prosecution. Section 103(1)(b) makes it clear that the matters in issue include the question whether the defendant has a propensity to be untruthful. The prosecution will suggest that the defendant's case is untruthful, and his conviction for affray, which involved three of his co-conspirators, is admissible to prove that the defendant has a propensity to be untruthful.

EXAMPLE 7

The defendant is charged with causing grievous bodily harm to V. Following an incident during a local football match, the match referee, V, sent the defendant off for violent conduct, ie punching an opponent. The following day the defendant approached V in his local public house and, after berating him for the sending off, struck V with a beer glass, fracturing V's cheekbone. The defendant has a number of previous convictions for assault, ranging from common assault to assault occasioning actual bodily harm. In addition, he has been sent off in football matches for violent conduct on seven previous occasions. The defendant pleaded not guilty, claiming it was an accident; he says he was gesticulating and forgot he had the glass in his hand.

The issue between the defendant and the prosecution is whether the defendant intended to cause V serious bodily harm, or whether it was, as the defendant alleges, an accident. The convictions for violence would be admissible under s 101(1)(d) and s 103. Convictions for assaults ranging from common assault to assault occasioning actual bodily harm may not be of the same description as defined by s 103(4), since the statement of the offence in the indictment would be different, but there can be little doubt that they will be of the same category, though at the time of writing the Secretary of State has not made an order prescribing such offences. The previous convictions will therefore be admissible to show a propensity to commit offences of the kind charged.

The history of violence need not involve criminal convictions and in this case can include the defendant's disciplinary record, that is bad character as defined by s 98, being evidence of, or of a disposition towards, misconduct on his part. At common law the disciplinary record of a rugby player, accused of assaulting an opponent during a match, was admitted. He had no previous convictions but the Court of Appeal held he was properly cross-examined on his disciplinary record, which included being sent off a number of times, otherwise the jury might be misled (*R v Marsh* [1994] Crim LR 52). The disciplinary record showing a propensity to violence will also be admissible under this head. Similarly, in many cases of domestic violence, the police may have attended the home following a complaint from a wife that her husband had assaulted her. A relatively commonplace scenario may be that the wife is taken to hospital for treatment and the husband is arrested. Next day the wife withdraws her complaint and no prosecution follows. That history of violence, together with any witness accounts of the husband assaulting the wife in the past, will be admissible if the husband is tried for causing grievous bodily harm to his wife and, possibly, on a charge of causing grievous bodily harm to anyone else. One should note that evidence of a propensity to act in a particular way is not admissible if the existence of such a propensity makes it no more likely that the defendant is guilty of the offence charged (s 103(1)). It follows that the trial judge must determine that the particular propensity evidence is sufficiently relevant to make it more likely that the defendant is guilty of the offence charged.

The distinction between important explanatory evidence admissible under s 101(1)(c) and evidence of disposition admissible under s 101(1)(d)

The above example of a history of violence in the domestic setting demonstrates that there is a fine line between important explanatory evidence, admitted to assist the court or jury to understand other evidence or the case as a whole, and evidence of a propensity to commit the kind of offence charged. There is an important but difficult distinction to be made between 'important explanatory evidence' and 'evidence of propensity'. Explanatory evidence is intended to enable the court and jury better to understand the evidence and the case as a whole. It is not intended to demonstrate a propensity to commit the kind of offence charged, but it is questionable whether juries are capable of using such evidence only for the intended purpose.

The difficulty is illustrated by the decision in *R v Dolan* [2003] Crim LR 41, where the defendant was charged with the murder of his $3\frac{1}{2}$-month-old son by shaking him to death. Evidence of the defendant's tendency to lose his temper with inanimate objects and react violently toward them was wrongly admitted as what we now call important explanatory evidence, because it did not show a tendency to lose his temper with human beings. As such it did not inform the court and was prejudicial, and it diverted the jury from the real and important issue before them. It would seem to follow that had there been evidence of the defendant's tendency to lose his temper with human beings, and of his violent reaction toward them, that would have been admissible as important explanatory evidence. However, had the defendant's loss of temper resulted in violence toward persons, it could well be admissible under s 101(1)(d) and s 103 (see above).

Suppose, for example, that the defendant has been charged with the murder of his young child by shaking him to death. Suppose further that there is evidence that he is quick to lose his temper when criticised or on the losing side of an argument, that he has convictions for assault occasioning actual bodily harm and there is a history of violence toward his wife, as evidenced by numerous calls to the police from the wife and her hospitalisation on two occasions following such assaults. If the defendant pleads not guilty and says the death was accidental, such evidence of bad character would appear to be admissible under s 101(1)(d) as relevant to an important matter in issue between the defendant and the prosecution, the issue being accident or deliberate assault. That issue would include, as s 103(1)(a) makes clear, the question whether the defendant has a propensity to commit an offence of the kind charged. His tendency to lose his temper without provocation, his convictions for assault and his violence toward his wife combine to suggest that D has a propensity to commit the kind of offence charged (murder is an assault resulting in death). As such, the evidence of bad character is likely to be admitted under s 101(1)(d) and is unlikely to be excluded under s 101(3). If evidence of bad character is to be admitted as important explanatory evidence, the emphasis must be on the explanatory nature of the evidence rather than its tendency to suggest a propensity to commit the kind of crime charged.

A propensity to be untruthful

Section 103(1)(b) provides that evidence relating to whether the defendant has a propensity to be untruthful (in other words, is not to be regarded as a credible witness) can generally be admitted if it is suggested that the defendant's case is untruthful. This is intended to cover evidence such as a conviction for perjury or offences involving dishonest deception (for example, obtaining property or a pecuniary advantage by deception). It is not, however, intended that a conviction for any criminal offence should be admissible by virtue of this provision, only those which show a propensity to be untruthful where it is suggested that the defendant's case is untruthful in any respect. Evidence will not be admissible under this head where it is not suggested that the defendant's case is untruthful in any respect. As with evidence of a propensity to commit the kind of offence charged, this is likely to be the case where the defendant and the prosecution are agreed on the facts of the alleged offence and the question is whether all the elements of the offence have been made out. For example, the defendant is charged with burglary and theft of a CD player from a flat occupied by V. The defendant admits that he entered the flat and took the CD player, but claims that it belongs to him. The only issue in the case is whether the property alleged to have been stolen 'belonged to another' as required by the definition of 'theft' in the Theft Act 1968.

Co-accused taking advantage of bad character evidence once admitted

Section 103(6) makes it clear that only prosecution evidence is admissible under s 101(1)(d), therefore a co-accused cannot take advantage of this section to adduce evidence of the bad character of a co-accused and must rely on s 101(1)(e), discussed below. However, once the bad character evidence has been admitted, there is no reason why a co-accused should not take advantage of its admission by cross-examining the co-accused on that bad character or previous convictions. At common law, where evidence of the propensity of a co-accused to commit the kind of offence was relevant to a fact in issue between the prosecution and a co-accused, the trial judge was required to direct the jury that they were to ignore that evidence in considering the case against another co-accused. However, in *R v Randall* [2004] 1 WLR 56, Lord Steyn stated (at 67):

> For the avoidance of doubt I would further add that in my view where evidence of the propensity of a co-accused is relevant to a fact in issue between the Crown and the other accused it is not necessary for the trial judge to direct the jury to ignore that evidence in considering the case against the co-accused. Justice does not require such a direction to be given. Moreover, such a direction would needlessly perplex a jury.

Thus D1 and D2 are charged with robbery. D2 denies that he was involved in the robbery, claiming that if D1 was involved he was acting on his own. D1's convictions for robbery are admitted to prove a propensity to commit offences of robbery. The jury, when considering D2's liability, can take account of the fact that D1 has previous convictions for robbery, which might assist in persuading them that D2 was not involved.

Section 101(1)(e) – substantial probative value in relation to an important matter in issue between defendant and co-defendant

The question as to what constitutes an 'important matter in issue' between co-defendants will differ according to the circumstances of the case. Often it will simply be which one of them committed the offence charged. In *Randall*, Randall and one Glean were jointly charged with murder. Each raised what is known as 'a cut throat defence', in which each claimed the other had killed the deceased victim. Each had given evidence of his own bad character during his evidence-in-chief. Randall had minor convictions for driving offences and disorderly behaviour. Glean, on the other hand, had convictions for theft and nine separate convictions for burglary, the most recent of which involved burglary of a dwelling house by a gang armed with hammers and screwdrivers, the occupier being threatened with a hammer. Glean carried a screwdriver on that occasion. At the time of the murder, Glean was on the run from the police following a robbery committed by a gang armed with knives. One of the robbers held a knife to the victim's throat and Glean admitted threatening a witness, saying 'If they get me for this I will get you'. Counsel for each defendant told the jury that the propensity of the other accused to use violence was relevant to the likelihood of that accused having attacked the deceased. However, the trial judge directed the jury that the previous convictions were relevant only to the credibility of each defendant and were irrelevant to the likelihood of his having attacked the deceased. Randall was convicted of manslaughter and Glean was acquitted. Randall appealed, arguing that evidence of Glean's bad character was relevant to the issue of who, as between Randall and Glean, was more likely to have inflicted serious violence on the deceased.

The Court of Appeal agreed that on the facts of the present case the evidence of propensity was relevant and ordered a retrial of Randall. However, the Court certified a question of law for the House of Lords as follows: 'Where two accused are jointly charged with a crime, and each blames the other for its commission, may one accused rely on the criminal propensity of the other?' Their Lordships unanimously answered the question in the affirmative, and agreed with Kennedy LJ in the Court of Appeal ([2003] 2 Cr App R 442) when he stated (at 451) that

> in the particular circumstances of the present case, where there was a cut throat defence, the antecedent history of Glean was relevant not only in relation to the truthfulness of Glean's evidence but also because of the imbalance between that history and the antecedents of Randall ... the evidence tended to show that the version put forward by one co-accused was more probable than that put forward by the other.

Now that the 2003 Act is in force the previous convictions of Glean and Randall could be admitted under s 101(1)(e), the important matter in issue between them being which of them was more likely to have been responsible for the death of the deceased. Glean's propensity to commit crimes that involved violence would make it more likely that he killed the deceased. Randall could, as he did in the above case, adduce his own bad character under s 101(1)(b) with a view to demonstrating the lack of a propensity to violence. If Glean had convictions for offences of the same description or of the same category, the prosecution could adduce them under s 101(1)(d), but offences of burglary, or aggravated burglary and robbery, are not of the same description or category as murder, which was not committed in the course of either of those offences.

Section 104 also limits the admissibility of evidence of the defendant's propensity to be untruthful (but only such a propensity) to circumstances in which the defendant has undermined his co-defendant's evidence. Under s 1(3)(c) of the Criminal Evidence Act 1898, a co-defendant was permitted to cross-examine another defendant on his previous convictions or bad character when that defendant gave evidence against the co-defendant. This was interpreted as evidence that directly supported the prosecution case against the co-defendant, or indirectly undermined the co-defendant's defence. Section 101(1)(e) and s 104 replace that provision. These sections relate to evidence that is relevant to an issue between the defendant and a co-defendant. Section 104(1), while including within the definition of 'matter in issue between a defendant and a co-defendant' evidence which is relevant to the question whether the defendant has a propensity to untruthful, states that such evidence is only admissible if 'the nature and conduct of his defence is such as to undermine the co-defendant's defence'. Under the Criminal Evidence Act 1898, a co-accused gave evidence against another co-accused when he said in evidence that the co-accused had been in sole control and possession of a box containing stolen goods which were the subject of the charge against them (*Murdoch v Taylor* [1965] AC 574). In *R v Varley* [1982] 2 All ER 519, the Court of Appeal, building on guidance given in *Murdoch v Taylor*, gave the following guidance as to the meaning of 'evidence against a co-defendant':

> *(1) If it is established that a person jointly charged has given evidence against a co-defendant that defendant has a right to cross-examine the other as to previous convictions and the trial judge has no discretion to refuse an application.*

> *(2) Such evidence may be given either in chief or during cross-examination.*

> *(3) It has to be objectively decided whether the evidence either supports the prosecution case in a material respect or undermines the defence of the co-accused. A hostile intent is irrelevant.*

> *(4) If consideration has to be given to the undermining of the other's defence care must be taken to see that the evidence clearly undermines the defence. Inconvenience to or inconsistency with the other's defence is not of itself sufficient.*

> *(5) Mere denial of participation in a joint venture is not of itself sufficient to rank as evidence against a co-defendant. For the [provision] to apply such denial must lead to the conclusion that if the witness did not participate then it must have been the other who did.*

> *(6) Where the one defendant asserts or in due course would assert one view of the joint venture which is directly contradicted by the other such contradiction may be evidence against the co-defendant.*

These cases would now be seen as falling within s 101(1)(e) as a matter in issue between the defendant and a co-defendant, and the courts are likely to take a similar view of the meaning of words 'the nature and conduct of his defence is such as to undermine the co-defendant's defence'. However, unlike the provisions of the Criminal Evidence Act 1898, which allowed cross-examination on any aspect of the co-defendant's bad character only if the co-defendant had given evidence against the other co-defendant, the requirement that the co-defendant undermines the defence of the other co-defendant is confined to the situation in which a co-defendant seeks to adduce evidence of the other defendant's propensity to be untruthful. Other evidence that is of substantial probative value in relation to an important matter in issue between the defendants is admissible whether or not the nature or conduct of the other's defence is such as to undermine the co-defendant's defence.

Evidence of a propensity to be untruthful may include offences of dishonesty and convictions for perjury which suggest that the defendant is not a credible witness, but it is not confined to such convictions. The above-mentioned Law Commission Report, *Evidence of Bad Character in Criminal Proceedings* (see p 147) gave the following example:

> D1 (who has previous convictions for robbery) and D2 are jointly charged with robbery. D1's defence is that D2 did it on her own. In order to get D1's criminal record admitted under the co-defendant exception (now ss 101(1)(e) and 104) on the basis that D1 has undermined D2's case, D2 must show that his convictions show that he is likely to lie on oath. What is in issue is D1's propensity to tell the truth not his propensity to rob. (para 14.49)

The Law Commission accepted that such evidence is less likely to be admitted as being relevant to credibility than under the then existing law, and recognised that previous convictions for robbery will be more directly relevant to the issue of who committed the robbery. In such circumstances the prosecution will seek to adduce those convictions under s 101(1)(d). However, if the trial judge were to exclude those convictions under s 101(3), D2 in the above scenario could seek to adduce them under s 101(1)(e). The discretion to exclude does not apply to s 101(1)(e), but D2 must demonstrate that the convictions are of substantial probative value in relation to an important issue between her and D1.

'Important issue' and 'substantial probative value'
Under s 101(1)(e), evidence is admissible only if it has substantial probative value in relation to an important issue between a defendant and co-defendant. The two conditions, 'substantial probative value' and 'an important issue', make it clear that evidence that has marginal or trivial value will not be admissible; neither will it be admissible if the issue to which it relates is marginal or trivial in the case as a whole. Under the 1898 Act, a denial of guilt by one defendant was not evidence against the other unless the circumstances were such that in denying guilt the defendant was inevitably accusing the other. For example, in *R v Davis* (1974) 60 Cr App R 157, the circumstances were such that the necklace, subject of a charge of theft, could only have been stolen by the defendant or his co-accused. The defendant's denial that he had taken the necklace was then inevitably evidence against the co-accused. Such circumstances are rare, and an ordinary denial of guilt was not evidence against the other defendant and would not raise an issue between the defendants under this head. In *R v Bruce* [1975] 1 WLR 1252, Bruce, M and another were charged with robbery. The prosecution case was that they had frightened a passenger in a train into giving them money. M gave evidence that there had been an agreement to rob. They had been looking for a Pakistani to rob but, finding none, they boarded a train and found a victim there. However, M said he played no part in the robbery. In his evidence Bruce said there had been no plan to rob anyone. The trial judge ruled that this was evidence against his co-defendants, who were permitted to cross-examine Bruce on

his past record. The Court of Appeal disagreed with the trial judge. Although Bruce had contradicted part of M's evidence, he had not contradicted M's statement that he took no part in the robbery. Indeed, Bruce's evidence did more to contradict the prosecution case and gave M an additional line of defence. Similarly, if the defendant contradicts his co-defendants but gives the co-defendant a better defence, it is not evidence against the co-defendant and is unlikely to be seen as undermining a co-defendant's defence under the new provisions. At common law, and under the 1898 Act, the courts had no discretion to exclude defence evidence. Their task was confined to ensuring the defence evidence was relevant and, in the context of the 1898 Act, that the defendant had 'given evidence against a co-defendant'. Similarly under the new scheme, the discretion under s 101(3) being confined to s 101(1)(d) and (g). The task of the trial judge under s 101(1)(e) is then confined to determining that the evidence has substantial probative value in relation to an important issue in the case.

Section 101(1)(f) – evidence to correct a false impression given by the defendant

For this provision to apply, the defendant must have been responsible for an assertion that gives a false or misleading impression about himself. This might be done expressly, for example by claiming to be of good character when this is not the case, or impliedly, for example through his conduct in court, such as his appearance or dress (s 105(4) and (5)). This may be done verbally or non-verbally.

The provision largely reflects the old law contained in s 1(3) of the Criminal Evidence Act 1898, which permitted the prosecution to cross-examine a defendant about his previous convictions or bad character if 'he has personally or by his advocate asked questions of the witnesses for the prosecution with a view to establish his own good character or has given evidence of his good character'. In *R v Samuel* (1956) 40 Cr App R 8, the defendant, charged with stealing by finding, gave evidence of having restored lost property. The Court of Appeal held that he had given evidence of his good character. That evidence is likely to be seen as implying a good character under this head. The cases under the 1898 Act suggest that, inter alia, an accused gives evidence of his good character if he:

(a) gives evidence that he is a religious man who has attended church services for years (*R v Ferguson* (1909) 2 Cr App R 250);

(b) asserts that for the past four years he has been carrying on an honest living (*R v Baker* (1912) 7 Cr App R 252);

(c) asserts that he is a married man, with a family and in regular work (on a charge of indecency with small boys – the stable family relationship suggesting he was unlikely to commit the offence) (*R v Coulman* (1927) 20 Cr App R 106).

These cases are likely to be seen as examples of a direct assertion of good character which, if true, may be rebutted by evidence admissible under s 101(1)(f) of the 2003 Act.

However, under the 1898 Act the defendant did not give evidence of his good character by:

(a) asserting innocence or a repudiating of guilt (*R v Rouse* [1904] 1 KB 184);

(b) giving evidence of general relations with and conduct toward customers with a view to negativing fraud (*R v Ellis* [1910] 2 KB 746);

(c) wearing a regimental blazer in court (*R v Hamilton* [1969] Crim LR 486).

While the cases of *Rouse* and *Ellis* would likely be decided in the same way, the case of *Hamilton* might now be decided differently given that s 105(5) makes it clear that 'conduct' in s 105(4) includes appearance or dress. It would, of course, be only a *false* impression if the defendant is not *entitled* to wear that regimental blazer.

The Criminal Law Revision Committee (Cmnd 4991, 1971) gave an example of an implied assertion of good character drawn from a case tried at the Central Criminal Court in the late 1960s (at para 135). One of two men charged with conspiracy to rob (both of whom had long criminal records) went into the witness box wearing a dark suit and looking every inch the respectable businessman. Asked by his counsel when and where he met his co-defendant, he replied: 'About eighteen months ago at my golf club. I was looking for a game and the secretary introduced us.' The Committee had no doubt that this was an imputation of good character, as was the suggestion in another case that the defendant, who lived on crime, was negotiating the purchase of a substantial property. Whether in modern times these statements would be seen as an assertion of good character is a moot point. The Criminal Law Revision Committee appear to assume that golf clubs only accept persons of good character as members. This might have been the case in the 1960s, but in the twenty-first century persons of all characters join golf clubs and buy substantial properties. The *Notes of Guidance* to the 2003 Act suggest, as an example of asserting good character by dress or conduct, a defendant wearing a clerical collar to which he was not entitled. Such extreme examples are likely to be rare.

In a television re-enactment of a rape trial for the Channel 4 documentary *Dispatches*, involving the defendant subject of the decision in *Z (Previous Acquittals)* (see p 150 above), the defendant stood in the dock dressed in a dark suit, white shirt and tie, clutching a bible with both hands as though in prayer. That might now be seen as asserting a false good character, given that he had a conviction for rape and had been acquitted of rape a number of times. Section 105(4) allows the court to treat the defendant as responsible for an assertion which is apt to give a false impression, where it appears to the court that his conduct in the proceeding (other than the giving of evidence) is seeking to give the court or jury a false impression about himself. The exception of conduct while giving evidence would appear to include the circumstances in *R v Robinson* [2001] Crim LR 478, where the defendant was a rather difficult witness. He gave evidence at his trial for theft holding a small Bible in his hand and gesticulating, so that it could be clearly seen by the jury. The trial judge accepted a prosecution argument that by doing so the defendant had put his character in issue. The trial judge said that this was a cynical and manipulative action calculated to make the jury think he was a religious person and likely to tell the truth. The Court of Appeal disagreed and held that he did not put his character in issue by taking the oath, or by reminding the jury of the oath he had sworn on the Bible. The conviction was unsafe and a re-trial was ordered. Section 105(4) suggests that such conduct will not be seen as an assertion of a false or misleading character under the new scheme.

Section 105(2) sets out the circumstances in which a defendant is to be treated as being responsible for an assertion. These include the defendant making the assertion himself, either in his evidence or in his representative's presentation of his case, or, if used in evidence, when being questioned under caution or being charged with the offence. This last circumstance changes the previous law, which took the view that the assertion had to be made by the defendant in evidence. Thus in *R v Holman* (1992) *The Times*, 9 September, the accused was charged with stealing two necklaces which were found in his possession. He told the police he had found them in the garden of a house when he went to recover a car, and intended to telephone the police and tell them. It was held that he had given evidence of his good character and the prosecution were allowed to cross-examine him under s 1(3)(b) of the 1898 Act. The Court of Appeal held that the judge should not have allowed them to do so. Although the explanation suggested he was honest, though not as clearly as in *Samuel* (above), the evidence of his explanation was admitted as an exception to the hearsay rule as part of the *res gestae* and was not evidence given by the defendant. The position will be different under s 101(1)(f). If the defendant gave the explanation on being questioned under caution before charge, or on being charged with the offence, and that explanation was given in evidence, he would now be seen as being responsible for it under s 105(2)(b)(i) and (ii). If the defendant has convictions for dishonesty, that explanation, suggesting that he was honest, would be seen as misleading and rebuttable by evidence of his convictions (one may note, however, that if the defendant is charged with theft, convictions for theft would also be admissible under s 101(1)(d) if his defence was that he had found and intended to return the necklaces). The defendant will also be seen as responsible for assertions made by defence witnesses, those made by any witness in response to questions by the defendant which were intended (or likely to) elicit them, and out-of-court assertions made by anybody if adduced in evidence by the defendant.

In correcting the impression, the prosecution (and only the prosecution – see s 105(7)) may introduce evidence of the defendant's misconduct that has a probative value in correcting it, in other words, evidence which is relevant to correct the false impression. Exactly what evidence is admissible will turn on the facts of the case, in particular the nature of the misleading impression he has given. Evidence is admissible under s 105(6) only if it goes no further than is necessary to correct the false impression. This reverses the common law rule that character was indivisible. Thus where a defendant is charged with theft, and asserts his reputation for honesty, convictions for offences of dishonesty will be admissible to correct that false impression but not a conviction for a sexual offence. If, however, the defendant gives the impression, either verbally in evidence or by his conduct and dress, that he is an upstanding citizen, convictions for any offence will be admissible as necessary to correct that false impression. Thus if the accused sits in the dock wearing dark clothing, a white collarless shirt, piously holding a Bible as if in prayer, giving the impression that he is either a cleric or a god-fearing and upright citizen, any and all convictions will be admissible to correct that false impression.

A defendant may withdraw or disassociate himself from a false or misleading impression by, for example, correcting the impression himself through presentation of his case or cross-examination of witnesses (s 105(3)). Evidence to correct the false impression is not then admissible. Given that the defendant can prevent bad character evidence being admitted by such withdrawal or disassociation, the opportunity to apply under s 101(3) to have such evidence excluded does not apply to this subsection.

Section 101(1)(g) – attacks on another person's character

Under this provision, a defendant's own bad character will become admissible when there has been an attack on another's person character. A defendant makes an attack on another person's character when he gives evidence that that person committed an offence (either the one charged, or a different one), or has behaved or is disposed to behave in a way that might be disapproved of by a reasonable person (s 106(1)(a) and s 106(2)). This is similar to the definition of bad character in s 98, but this definition includes evidence relating to the facts of the offence charged and its investigation and prosecution. Thus, a defendant would be attacking a prosecution witness if he claimed that she was lying in her version of events, or adduced evidence of her previous misconduct to undermine her credibility. A defendant also attacks another person's character if he or his representative asks questions that are intended (or are likely) to elicit evidence of this sort, or if the defendant makes an allegation of this nature when questioned under caution or on being charged with the offence (s 106(1)) and this is heard in evidence, as it usually is when a police officer gives evidence of an interview with the defendant or of his response on being charged. Section 106(1)(b) stipulates that that includes an attack by counsel who has been appointed under s 38(4) of the Youth Justice and Criminal Evidence Act 1999 to cross-examine when the defendant is prevented from doing so. Given that such counsel is not responsible to the defendant (s 38(5)), an unauthorised attack on another person should not result in the admission of the defendant's bad character. However, unlike s 101(1)(f) and s 105(3), there is no provision to allow the defendant to withdraw or disassociate himself from the attack. Nonetheless, the discretion under s 101(3) applies and may be relied upon to exclude evidence of bad character when the attack was unauthorised. Attacks on the character of another person could include an allegation that the other person committed the crime, adducing the previous convictions of a witness in order to attack his credibility, or suggesting bias or animosity toward the defendant as a reason for the witness's false evidence.

It might be asked whether it matters if the attack or imputation is true or false. Under the 1898 Act, the veracity of such an attack did not affect the loss of the shield. In *R v Bishop* (1974) 59 Cr App R 246 it was said 'an imputation on character covers charges of faults or vices whether reputed or real'. Similarly, in *R v Wainwright* [1998] Crim LR 665, the court rejected the submission that there can only be an imputation if the facts are disputed. Cross and Tapper suggest that 'it is immaterial whether the matter alleged is accepted to be true, as it normally is when previous convictions are alleged; or is denied, as it usually is when improper conduct is alleged' (*Cross and Tapper on Evidence*, 10th edn (2004), 438). The dictionary definition of 'imputation', as accepted by the Court, is simply 'attributing a fault to someone'. It would seem to follow that the attack on another person's character, or an imputation about the other person, need not be untrue for the purposes of s 101(1)(g).

Under the 1898 Act, the attacks on the character of the prosecution witnesses often involved claims that a confession was not made, was false or had been obtained by threats. Unfortunately, before the Police and Criminal Evidence Act 1984, such claims were all too often true, and corrupt police officers used the 1898 Act as a shield for their misconduct. The introduction of tape-recording of interviews, and now video-recording, put an end to such allegations, which then switched to police conduct outside the police station, for example planting evidence during a search of premises or during a stop and search. Similar attacks on the conduct of the police will be seen as an attack on their character within s 106(2)(b). However, an assertion of innocence or emphatic denial of guilt did not trigger s 1(3)(b) of the 1898 Act, and is unlikely to be seen as an attack on another person under s 101(1)(g). There is, though, a thin line between an emphatic denial of guilt and attacks on the veracity of the prosecutor or his witnesses. Denying a confession, or disclaiming knowledge of an article found during a search by police, is one thing; to claim that the police concocted the confession or planted the evidence is another. Whether it is an emphatic denial or an attack on veracity depends on the facts of each case.

Where a defendant has attacked another person's character, evidence of his own bad character becomes generally admissible (but only by the prosecution (s 106(3)). This is a continuation of the 'tit for tat' rule which applied under s 1(3)(b) of the Criminal Evidence Act 1898, under which the shield against cross-examination was lost if a defendant cast imputations on the character of the prosecution, prosecution witnesses or the deceased victim of the alleged crime. Section 101(1)(g) appears to widen that provision by applying the 'tit for tat' rule when the defendant launches an attack on any other person's charac-ter – there is no limitation to the prosecutor, witnesses for the prosecution or deceased victims. One can understand why an attack on the character of someone involved in the trial should result in the defendant's bad character being put before the court or jury: in determining whether a witness or the defendant is to be believed, it is only right that the character of the person who has attacked the credibility of the witness or deceased victim be known so that his credibility can be properly judged. But does this apply if the person attacked is not a witness or the deceased victim? Suppose the defendant says that his brother, who is not a witness in the trial, committed the crime. On what basis is the admission of his bad character to be admitted? If he has a propensity to be untruthful, evidence to show that is admissible under s 101(1)(d) and s 103.

The discretion to exclude evidence of bad character under s 101(3) applies to s 101(1)(g). At common law, the purpose of the discretion was to prevent too harsh an application of s 1((3)(b) of the 1898 Act, but it was accepted that the basis of the rule was the 'tit for tat' principle under which it was seen as only fair that the jury be made aware of the character of the person casting imputations on the prosecution or its witnesses. In *R v Burke* (1986) 82 Cr App R 156, while the Court of Appeal accepted that 'cases must occur in which it would be unjust to admit evidence of a character gravely prejudicial to the accused, even though there may be some tenuous grounds for holding it technically admissible', it nonetheless concluded (at 161) that:

> In the ordinary and normal case the trial judge may feel that if the credit of the prosecutor or his witnesses has been attacked, it is only fair that the jury should have before them the material on which they can form their judgement whether the accused person is any more worthy to be believed than those he has attacked. It is obviously unfair that the jury should be left in the dark about an accused person's character if the conduct of his defence has attacked the character of the prosecutor or the witnesses for the prosecution within the meaning of section 1(3)(b) of the Act of 1898.

The same approach is likely to be taken under the 2003 Act. The discretion could be used to limit the extent of the subsection, so that in the case of an attack on the character of a person not involved in the trial, admission of the defendant's bad character, though tech-nically admissible, might be seen as having such an adverse effect on the fairness of the trial that it ought not to be admitted. However, if the defendant makes a deliberate attack on a prosecution witness, the court is likely to take the view that it is 'obviously unfair that the jury should be left in the dark about [the] accused person's character'.

Guilt and credibility

Under the 1898 Act, the evidence of the defendant's bad character went only to his credibility, and juries were directed that they should not use the bad character in determining the defendant's guilt. This was the subject of much criticism, the reality being that such evidence went to both issues, and where the previous convictions were for the same offences as those charged, they probably went more to the issue of guilt than credibility. However, while evidence admissible under s 101 of the 2003 Act will primarily go to the credit of the defendant and allow his character to be known by the jury, it is not intended that the jury should be expected to put all knowledge of these matters out of their minds when considering other issues in the case, such as the guilt of the defendant. Nonetheless, the trial judge may consider directing the jury that care should be taken about the level of weight to be placed on the evidence in any other respect. The decision of the House of Lords in *R v Randall* [2004] 1 WLR 56, to the effect that bad character adduced under s 1(3)(c) of the 1898 Act was admissible both as to the credibility of the co-defendant and as to his propensity to commit the kind of offence charged (see pp 172–173 above), endorses the correctness of this approach.

Other 'bad character' provisions of the 2003 Act

Section 107 – stopping the case where evidence is contaminated

Section 107 deals with the circumstances in which bad character evidence has been admitted but it later emerges that the evidence is contaminated, that is, affected by an agreement with other witnesses or by hearing the views of other witnesses, so that it is false or misleading. Such allegations were commonplace in cases involving multiple victims of sexual abuse, particularly when the victims were known to each other, for example pupils at the same school or resident at the same children's home. Police and prosecutors are well aware of the possibility of collusion in such cases and would rarely prosecute if there was a real possibility of contamination. Witnesses who have yet to give evidence are not allowed in the court while others give evidence, but they often sit together outside the courtroom, and there have been cases in which a witness who has given evidence has been seen talking to a witness who has yet to do so. It follows that while such collusion or contamination is rare, it is not entirely unknown.

Ordinarily it is for the jury to decide whether or not to believe evidence and decide on the weight to be placed on it. In a case where the question of contamination had arisen, the common law position was that the judge must decide on the admissibility of the similar fact (bad character) evidence on the basis that it was true, and decide whether the probative value of that evidence was such that it was fair to admit it despite its prejudicial effect. The question of collusion or contamination was then to be left to the jury as a question of fact. If the jury had a reasonable doubt whether the evidence was free of collusion or contamination, they should not use it as corroborative or for any purpose adverse to the defence. Only if it was obvious that no reasonable jury could accept the evidence as untainted by collusion or contamination should the trial judge direct the jury that they could not use it for any purpose adverse to the defence (see *R v H* [1995] AC 596). However, there may be cases where it is not possible for the jury to put this evidence out of their minds. Common law powers for the judge to withdraw a case from the jury at any time following the close of the prosecution case already exist (see *R v Galbraith* [1981] 1 WLR 1039).

Section 107 builds on these powers by conferring a duty on the judge to stop the case if the contamination is such that, considering the importance of the evidence to the case, a conviction would be unsafe. This is intended to be a high test, and if the judge were to consider that a direction along the lines described above (*R v H*) would be sufficient to deal with any potential difficulties, the question of safety of the conviction does not arise and the case would not be withdrawn from the jury. Having stopped the case the judge may consider that there is still sufficient uncontaminated evidence against the defendant to merit his retrial, or may consider that the prosecution case has been so weakened that the defendant should be acquitted. Section 107(1) provides for the judge to take either of these courses. If, however, an acquittal is ordered then the defendant is also to be acquitted of any other offence for which he could have been convicted, if the judge is satisfied that the contamination would affect a conviction for that offence in the same way (s 107(2)). Section 107(3) extends the duty to the situation where a jury is determining, under the Criminal Procedure (Insanity) Act 1964, whether a person, who is deemed unfit to plead, did the act or omission charged. Section 107(4) makes it clear that s 107(3) does not affect any existing court powers in relation to ordering an acquittal of discharging a jury.

Section 108 – offences committed by defendant when a child

As indicated in the discussion of the definition of 'bad character' (see pp 157–160 above), convictions while a child (under the age of 14), previously excluded as evidence of previous convictions, are now within that definition and may be admitted as evidence of bad character under the general scheme for admitting such evidence under this Chapter of the 2003 Act (s 108). However, before convictions as a child are admitted, two further requirements must be satisfied. These requirements under s 108(2)(a) and (b) are:

(a) that the offence for which the defendant is being tried and the offence for which the defendant was convicted are triable only on indictment; and

(b) that the court is satisfied that the interests of justice require the evidence to be admissible.

Thus if a defendant aged 22 years is charged with the rape and indecent assault on a girl aged 15 years, and has a conviction for attempted rape and indecent assault on a young girl when aged 13 years, and further convictions for indecent assault on a young girl when aged 16 and 19, all these convictions are admissible under s 101(1)(d). However, the defendant's conviction when aged 13 is also subject to s 108. In this example, s 108(2)(a) and (b) are likely to be satisfied. The convictions show a propensity to commit the kind of offence charged and demonstrate that the defendant is a danger to young woman, and has been since he was a child.

One may also note that s 101(4) provides that on an application to exclude evidence under s 101(3), the court must have regard, in particular, to the length of time between the matter to which that evidence relates and the matters which form the subject of the offence charged. If, then, the defendant is an adult, offences committed as a child might be considered to be of no relevance, or of only minor relevance to the case, and it might be thought unfair to the defendant to admit them. A similar approach is taken to 'spent convictions' under the Rehabilitation of Offenders Act 1974. Though admissible in criminal proceedings, *Practice Note* [1975] 2 All ER 1072 requires that leave be obtained before cross-examining on these, and the judge will then exercise his discretion to ensure that there is no unfairness to the defendant.

Section 109 – assumption of truth in assessment of relevance or probative value

Section 109 requires a court, when considering the relevance or probative value of bad character, to assume that the evidence is true. This reflects the distinction between the roles of the judge and the jury: it is for the jury to form a view on matters of fact, such as the reliability of evidence; it is for the judge to rule on issues of law. However, there may be occasions where evidence is so unreliable that no reasonable jury could believe that it was true. In these circumstances, intended very much to be exceptional cases, s 109(2) makes it clear that the judge does not have to assume the evidence is true. In such a case, the court should normally make its decision based on the papers before it, but there may be circumstances in which a separate hearing on the issue (a trial within a trial in the absence of the jury) might be necessary. This reflects the common law position as established in *R v H* (see pp 161–162 above).

Section 110 – court's duty to give reasons for rulings

Section 110 requires a court to give reasons for its rulings under these provisions. These must be given in open court (in the absence of the jury) and, in magistrates' courts, entered into the register of proceedings, ensuring that a record is kept. This applies to rulings on whether an item of evidence is evidence of bad character, on questions of admissibility and exclusion, and to any decision to withdraw a case from the jury.

Section 111 – rules of court

This section provides for rules of court to be made which may, and in the case of the prosecution must, contain provisions requiring a party who wishes to adduce evidence of a co-defendant's bad character (or elicit it from a witness) to serve on the defendant notice of the intention to do so (s 111(2)). The rules may provide for the court or defendant to dispense with any notice requirement (s 111(3)). The court cannot simply refuse to allow the bad character evidence to be admitted, but it is empowered to take a failure to give the required notice into account in considering the exercise of its powers with respect to costs (s 111(4)).

Section 112 – interpretation of Pt 11, Ch 1

Section 112 defines terms employed in this Part of the Act. Section 112(2) makes it clear that where the defendant is charged with two or more offences, the provisions of this Part refer to each charged as separate proceedings. This means that bad character evidence that is admissible in relation to one charge in the proceedings is not automatically admissible in relation to another charge in the same proceedings, but must instead meet the provisions laid down in this chapter of the Act. The impact of this provision on the situation in which a defendant is charged in the same proceedings with the same crime against multiple victims, is discussed (at pp 160–161) above.

Further reading

Law Commission, Report No 273, *Evidence in Criminal Proceedings: Previous Misconduct of a Defendant* (2001).

Lloyd Bostock, S, 'The effects on juries of hearing about the defendant's previous criminal record: a simulation study' [2000] Crim LR 734.

Munday, R, 'What constitutes 'other reprehensible behaviour' under the bad character provisions of the Criminal Justice Act 2003?' [2005] Crim LR 24.

Munday, R, 'Bad character rules and riddles: 'explanatory notes' and true meanings of s 103(1) of the Criminal Justice Act 2003' [2005] Crim LR 337.

Munday, R, 'Cut-throat defences and the "propensity to be untruthful" under s 104 of the Criminal Justice Act 2003' [2005] Crim LR 625.

Roberts, P, 'Acquitted Misconduct Evidence and Double Jeopardy Principles – From *Sambasivam* to Z' [2000] Crim LR 952.

6 Hearsay Evidence

Hearsay evidence may be defined as an oral or written statement, made by a person other than while testifying at a trial, which is offered in evidence to prove the truth of the matter asserted. Put more simply, it is evidence that aims to establish the existence of a fact not through the witness's first-hand knowledge, but through what a third party has stated out of court. The rule against the admissibility of hearsay evidence has traditionally been regarded as one of the defining features of the Anglo-American trial. Until recently, such statements were inadmissible at common law unless they fell within a common law or statutory exception. Judges had no discretion to admit hearsay evidence, though over the years the courts grafted on a large number of exceptions or evaded the rule by interpreting the evidence as real evidence rather than hearsay. Add to these common law exceptions the statutory exceptions and there was little left of the rule by the end of the last century, though what little was left had important consequences until it was finally abolished and replaced with a new statutory regime contained in the Criminal Justice Act 2003.

Identifying hearsay

In *Subramaniam v Public Prosecutor* [1956] 1 WLR 965, it was said:

> *Evidence of a statement made to a witness by a person who is not himself called as a witness may or may not be hearsay. It is hearsay and inadmissible when the object of the evidence is to establish the truth of what is contained in the statement. It is not hearsay and is admissible when it is proposed to establish by evidence, not the truth of the statement, but the fact that it was made.*

It follows from the above statement that in order to identify evidence as hearsay, one had to establish the purpose for which it was to be adduced. This remains true under the new statutory framework. It often proved difficult to determine whether the evidence was hearsay, and there are many cases in which the courts treated evidence as hearsay when it was not and vice versa. Thus in *Woodhouse v Hall* (1980) 72 Cr App R 39, the defendants were charged with managing a brothel at premises described as a sauna and massage parlour. Magistrates refused to allow police officers who had posed as customers to give evidence of conversations between them and the women employed as masseuses, giving details of the availability and cost of sexual services, stating that the conversations were hearsay. The Divisional Court allowed the prosecution appeal against this refusal.

Donaldson LJ had some sympathy with the magistrates, who he thought had been misled by *Subramaniam*, believing they had to be satisfied as to the truth of what the ladies had said, or were alleged to have said. But this was not a matter of truth or falsity. There was no question of the hearsay rule applying to these conversations. The relevant issue was whether the offers of sexual services were made, and the officers were entitled to give evidence of the oral offers made to them.

Similarly, in *Roberts v DPP* [1994] Crim LR 926, the question arose as to whether certain documents were hearsay. The accused was charged with assisting in the management of a brothel and running an unlicensed massage parlour. He had been seen entering the premises, and a search of the office of the company of which he was the managing director revealed a number of documents relating to the company's ownership of the premises used as a brothel, including a telephone account for the premises in the accused's name; documents relating to goods and services supplied to the premises; and adverts placed for the premises, invoiced to the company. A search of the accused's home revealed other documents relating to the premises, including a gas bill. He was convicted and appealed, arguing that these documents should not have been admitted.

Dismissing the appeal, the Court accepted that the documents were not admissible to show the truth of their contents but were admissible as circumstantial or 'real' evidence, to which the hearsay rule did not apply. The prosecution did not seek to rely on the truth of the contents of the documents but on the fact that they were in the accused's possession, from which the inference could be drawn that he was involved in the management of the premises. That inference was irresistible. His knowledge that the premises were being used as a brothel was an easy inference to draw from the fact that he had visited the premises, plus the letter requesting adverts in a magazine. There was therefore ample evidence to convict.

Direct and indirect hearsay (first- or second-hand hearsay)

Hearsay may be direct (or first-hand), or indirect (second-hand or multiple hearsay). For example, Witness A sees a robbery taking place; he notes the registration number of the getaway car and a description of one of the robbers who removed his mask. He immediately makes a statement to the police in which he states what he saw. Witness A dies before trial. The purpose of adducing the statement of the deceased Witness A is to prove the truth of the facts asserted, that the person described was one of the robbers and the car bearing the registration number seen was the getaway car. This is then hearsay, direct or first-hand hearsay, because the witness perceived the events directly before communicating them to B.

If the dead witness, A , saw the above, but this time told B, a bystander, what he had seen and B told the police officer, C, the statement is second-hand or multiple hearsay, being one or more remove from the witness who perceived the events. Multiple hearsay is seen as the least reliable form of hearsay given the possibility of distortion, which increases the further down the chain of communication one goes. For that reason oral multiple hearsay was inadmissible at common law, and is inadmissible under s 23 of the Criminal Justice

Act 1988 if contained in a document. However, multiple hearsay is commonplace in business, and s 24 of the 1988 Act (and now s 117 of the Criminal Justice Act 2003) allowed such a statement in a document to be admitted provided that the statement was created or received by a person in the course of a trade, business, profession, etc, and the information contained in the statement was received by each person in the chain of communication in the course of a trade, business, profession, etc. Under the 2003 Act, multiple hearsay remains inadmissible if it is in oral form but is now subject to discretionary admissibility under s 114(1)(d) (see pp 194–195 below).

Given that direct hearsay involves the perception of the events by the witness who is unable to give oral evidence of what he saw, made directly to the witness who repeats it in court, it is the more reliable form of hearsay. Even so, in the above example of direct hearsay, the police officer could not give evidence of what Witness A told him unless it came within a common law exception to the rule against hearsay. In these circumstances it might have fallen within the common law exception known as *res gestae* (preserved by s 118(1) of the 2003 Act). This exception is based on the idea that if the event witnessed was a startling and dramatic event, and the statement was made before there was time to think about it, there was unlikely to be any concoction or distortion and the statement was therefore likely to be reliable. If the statement had been in writing, it would have been admissible under s 23 of the Criminal Justice Act 1988, which created an exception for written statements in a document where the maker has died (or other conditions explaining the absence of the witness applied), but not for oral statements. Its replacement, s 116 of the 2003 Act, includes both oral and written statements. As we shall see, this creates an overlap between ss 116 and 117 (which is concerned with the admissibility of business documents) and s 118 (which preserves some of the common law exceptions).

Reliable hearsay excluded

The common law rule against hearsay operated to exclude evidence no matter how reliable. In *Myers v DPP* [1965] AC 1001, the prosecution wished to adduce evidence of the vehicle identification numbers (VINs) placed on various motor vehicles, in order to prove that the vehicles subject of the charge had been stolen. The manufacturer operated a system under which the number passed through several hands before being recorded. It was, however, impossible to determine who those persons were. The House of Lords, while accepting that the evidence of the VINs was reliable and recommending major statutory change to the law, upheld the decision of the trial judge to refuse to admit the evidence because it was hearsay. It was not until the enactment of s 68 of the Police and Criminal Evidence Act 1984 (later replaced by s 24 of the Criminal Justice Act 1988, and now covered by s 117 of the Criminal Justice Act 2003) that such evidence became admissible as a statutory exception to the hearsay rule.

As indicated, the rule against hearsay applied equally to oral statements, statements in a document, or evidence of conduct. There were a number of suggested reasons for the rule. One was the likely unreliability of second-hand evidence. If you have played the game known as 'Chinese Whispers', it is clear how distorted a statement can become as it is passed down the chain. Yet there were examples of reliable evidence being excluded under the rule (eg *Myers v DPP*), which suggested that the facts that the evidence is not given on oath and that it is not subject to cross-examination are the main reasons for excluding such evidence. This links up with the reliance of the adversarial system on oral evidence given on oath before a jury, who are thus able to observe the demeanour of the witness and see and hear his evidence being tested under cross-examination. Admitting hearsay evidence contradicted and undermined the basic tenets of the system, and was therefore excluded whether reliable or not (see Lord Normand in *Teper v R* [1952] AC 480, at 486). The rule often proved inconvenient, excluding evidence that was clearly reliable.

In *Sparks v R* [1964] AC 964, S, a white man aged 27, was convicted of indecently assaulting a girl under 4 years of age. The child did not give evidence and the trial judge ruled that a statement by the girl shortly after the alleged assault that 'it was a coloured boy' was inadmissible hearsay. The Privy Council upheld this ruling, despite the obvious injustice. Similarly, in *R v Thompson* [1912] 3 KB 19, the accused was charged with using an instrument to procure an abortion. The woman died before trial from an unrelated cause. The trial judge ruled that two statements from the woman – the first, made before the operation by the defendant, that she intended to operate on herself, and the second, made after the operation, that she had in fact done so – were inadmissible hearsay. The Court of Appeal upheld this ruling as correct. In *Ratten v R* [1972] AC 378, the defendant was convicted of murdering his wife by shooting her. His defence was that the gun had gone off accidentally while he was cleaning it. The time of death was put at between 1.12 and 1.20 pm. A telephonist was permitted to give evidence that at 1.15 pm she had received a telephone call from Ratten's house made by a sobbing and hysterical woman, who had said, 'Get me the police please'. The Privy Council held that this was correctly admitted. Holding that there was no element of hearsay, the Board held that the evidence was relevant, first, to show that, contrary to Ratten's evidence denying that his wife had made the call, the call had been made, and, secondly, to show the state of mind of the wife as being a state of fear at an existing or pending emergency, which was capable of rebutting the accused's defence that the shooting was an accident. (Note, however, that the House of Lords in *R v Kearley* [1992] 2 All ER 345 took the view that the evidence of the telephonist was hearsay, but that it was admissible as an exception to the rule as being part of the *res gestae*. Evidence of the state of mind of a person is admissible as an exception to the rule against hearsay under the *res gestae* principle, discussed at pp 221–226 below.)

R v Hussain [1998] Crim LR 820 demonstrates the esoteric nature of the rule against hearsay and the inconvenience to the criminal justice system. Here, the accused was convicted of the murder of his sister-in-law. It was alleged that he drove over her several times, killing her. Four men, including the defendant, were regular drivers of the car that killed her. A witness, X, identified the accused as the driver at the time and as a person he had seen driving the car previously. He knew him as H, because the deceased had told him in the past that the person he recognised as H was her brother-in-law. H's appeal against conviction was allowed on the basis that X's evidence was hearsay and should not have been admitted. The Crown was seeking to rely on X's evidence to prove two facts: (i) X recognised the man he had previously seen; and (ii) the man X had previously seen was H. The only basis on which they could establish the second fact was by relying on the hearsay statement of the deceased. The Court of Appeal expressed some sympathy with the trial judge in that this ought to be a matter of weight rather than admissibility, but it was not for the court to seek to legislate in relation to the long-established hearsay rule, to which the present situation was not an exception. A re-trial was ordered, at which H pleaded guilty to manslaughter.

A more modern example of the rule against hearsay, and an example of the more flexible approach to the application of the rule, is provided by *R v Ward, Andrews and Broadley* [2001] Crim LR 316. Ward and others were convicted of conspiracy to steal, and appealed on the ground that the trial judge had admitted evidence of Ward's identity, which was in fact inadmissible hearsay (following *R v Hussain*, above). Police officers had given evidence that on three occasions involving two cars, when the cars had been stopped and the passengers were asked to identify themselves, a passenger in the car had given his name as 'Michael Kevin Ward'. The passenger had also given his address and date of birth, which were those of Michael Kevin Ward. However, the police officers could not independently identify Ward as the passenger on those occasions. Lord Justice Waller, giving the judgment of the court and dismissing the appeal, accepted that the evidence was prima facie hearsay. He pointed out that the difficulty could not be overcome by contending that the purpose of admitting the statement was to prove that it was made, since that was simply not the case and the evidence was clearly being put in by the prosecution to establish that Ward was in the car at the relevant time. It was an unattractive proposition that, where someone identified himself as compellingly as was done here, objection could be taken to the evidence going before the jury and then the maker of the statement could refrain from giving evidence so as to avoid exposing himself to cross-examination in relation to the question whether he was present in the car on the particular day.

Equally, however, the application of the hearsay rule and the dangers from which it protected a defendant must be borne in mind at all times. Thus if, as here, a man was giving his full name, a date of birth (which was the date of birth of the person with that full name) and an address (which was also the address of the person with that full name), the evidence was strong to establish an admission. If, additionally, there was evidence, as here, which supported part-ownership of the car by the appellant Ward, then further support was given to the evidence. In such a case the trial judge should give a direction to the jury along the lines that only if the jury were sure, from the contents of the statement and such surrounding evidence as there was, that it was the defendant giving an accurate identification, should they rely on the statement as an admission of his presence in the car by the defendant. There was no such direction here, but no prejudice had resulted.

In *R v Blastland* [1986] AC 41, the accused was convicted of the buggery and murder of a 12-year-old boy. He gave evidence that he had attempted to bugger the boy but stopped when the boy said it was too painful. Shortly afterwards he had seen M nearby and, afraid that he had been seen trying to commit a serious offence, he had run off and gone home. He sought to adduce evidence from a number of witnesses that M had, before the death of the boy had been made public, told them that the boy had been murdered. M had also confessed to the police that he had killed the boy, but later withdrew that statement, so the defendant applied to call M and treat him as a hostile witness. Both applications were refused and the accused was convicted on both counts. His appeals to the Court of Appeal and to the House of Lords were both dismissed, both courts holding that the evidence had been correctly excluded. Lord Bridge pointed out that to admit statements of third parties, not called as a witness, confessing to the crime for which the defendant was being tried, would be to create a significant and (many may think) a dangerous new exception to the hearsay rule.

Bending the rule

The cases discussed thus far indicate that the hearsay rule can mean that cogent and reliable evidence may be excluded. Over the years judges developed exceptions to the rule, and hearsay in document form was made admissible by ss 23 to 30 of the Criminal Justice Act 1988 subject to judicial discretion. Judges and counsel often sought ways to sidestep what was left of the rule. In *Glinski v McIver* [1962] AC 726, Lord Devlin roundly condemned the practice of attempting to evade the rule by disguising the nature of the evidence being adduced. He was particularly scathing about the common device which involves counsel in asking not what the conversation or content of the document was, but the witness to answer 'Yes' or 'No' to a series of questions. For example: 'Did you go to see X?' Answer, 'Yes'; 'Do not tell us what he said, but as a result of what he told you did you do something?' Answer, 'Yes'; 'What did you do?' Such questioning thinly disguises the fact that the witness is responding to what a third party not a witness told him, but it is just as inadmissible as repeating what the third party actually said.

In *R v Saunders* [1968] 1 QB 490, the prosecution sought to prove that the defendant, charged with obtaining by deception, had not carried on a genuine business, by asking a witness whether he had made enquiries as to whether any trade had been done by the defendant. The witness replied that he had made the enquiries. Counsel then asked whether, as a result of those enquiries, he had found that any trade had been done, to which the witness had replied that he had not. The Court of Appeal quashed the conviction because the line of questioning was intended to circumvent the hearsay rule, which rendered inadmissible the answer to the direct questioning of others as to whether S had done any trading by asking 'What was said in response to your questions?'.

Jones v Metcalfe [1967] 1 WLR 1286 is a more blatant attempt at evasion or ignoring of the rule. An eyewitness to a road accident memorised the number of the lorry he thought responsible, and later dictated it to a police officer. The officer made a note of it, but the witness did not verify the note as correct. At trial the witness could not remember the number and, because he had not verified the note made by the officer, he was not permitted to refresh his memory from that note. However, another officer, not the one to whom the witness had dictated the note, was allowed to give evidence that he had interviewed the accused and put to him the allegation, including the registration number of the lorry which belonged to the accused. Quashing the conviction, Diplock LJ pointed out that although the inference that the appellant was the driver of the lorry at the time of the accident was irresistible as a matter of common sense, what the witness had said to the police was inadmissible hearsay and the inference was based on that hearsay.

Hearsay fiddles

Hearsay 'fiddles' arise when the court says that evidence which is plainly hearsay is not, in order to avoid an inconvenient result, that is excluding clearly reliable and relevant evidence when there is no hearsay exception which fits the circumstances. An example can be found in *R v Rice* [1963] 1 QB 857. Part of the prosecution case on a charge of conspiracy was that Rice had taken a flight to Manchester on a particular date, in the company of a co-accused, H, who had given evidence to this effect. The defendant denied this. The prosecution produced an airline ticket to Manchester on the date in question in the names of Rice and another co-accused, M (the prosecution case was that H took the place of M on the flight). Rice denied all knowledge of the ticket, but the ticket was admitted in evidence and shown to the jury as an exhibit. On appeal, it was argued that the ticket should not have been admitted; it was tendered by the prosecution as evidence that Rice had flown to Manchester on the date in question with a co-accused, and as such it was hearsay. The Court of Appeal rejected that argument, holding that the ticket was relevant and admissible circumstantial evidence on the issue of whether Rice had flown to Manchester with another. The Court of Appeal doubted that the ticket had been booked by a person called Rice: for that purpose it was hearsay. However, it was permissible for the jury to draw the inference that the ticket had been used by someone called Rice, because of 'the balance of probability recognised by common sense and common knowledge that an air ticket which had been used on a flight and which had a name upon it has more than likely been used by a man of that name'. The ticket was a fact from which the jury might infer that probably two people had flown on the particular flight and that they might or might not have been the defendants, by applying their common knowledge of such matters that the passengers bore the surnames which were written on the ticket. Such an inference can be drawn only if one assumes that the statement on the ticket is true; it follows that the purpose of adducing the ticket was to prove the truth of the facts asserted and that the ticket was therefore hearsay.

The distinction between the two uses of the ticket seems artificial: it was no more likely that the ticket had been used by someone called Rice than that it had been issued to someone of that name. If it was admissible on the one issue, it should have been admissible on the other (airline tickets, or any other tickets, together with documentation on their purchase (eg, credit card payments), have been admissible as business documents since 1988, and will be so admissible as considered at pp 216–221 below in the discussion on s 117 of the 2003 Act).

In *R v Shone* (1983) 76 Cr App R 72, the evidence of a stock clerk and a sales manager that workers would have made an entry on record cards if certain items had been disposed of lawfully, that there were no such entries, and that those items must therefore have been stolen, was held not to be hearsay but direct evidence of that fact. It seemed that if an inference was drawn from what a document said, the document was hearsay; but if an inference was drawn from what it did not say (or from the fact that no document existed), that was direct evidence. Similarly, in *R v Lilley* [2003] All ER (D) 143, the Court of Appeal held that a notebook bearing the inscription 'Sharon's notebook', containing practice signatures, was not hearsay when used to connect S with a conspiracy to obtain benefits using stolen benefit books.

The above cases demonstrate that the rule against hearsay can operate to exclude reliable evidence and lead to possible injustice. The introduction of ss 23 to 30 of the Criminal Justice Act 1988 made most hearsay statements contained in a document admissible, subject to certain conditions and judicial discretion (see below). Thus the airline ticket would have been admissible under s 24 of the 1988 Act and will be admissible under s 117 of the 2003 Act. However, until the 1988 Act, much reliable evidence was inadmissible if the rule against hearsay was strictly applied. The common law judges recognised this and either ignored the rule or bent it, or created exceptions to the rule. These exceptions may be grouped under the following heads:

(a) Admissions and confessions of parties and their agents.

(b) Statements by deceased persons:
    (i)   declarations against interest;
    (ii) declarations in the course of duty;
    (iii) declarations as to public interests;
    (iv) dying declarations (in the case of homicide);
    (v) declarations as to pedigree;
    (vi) declarations by testators as to their wills;
    (vii) testimony given in a previous trial.

(c) Reputations (and, in all but (i), family tradition):
    (i)   of bad character;
    (ii) of pedigree;
    (iii) of the existence of a marriage;
    (iv) of the existence or non-existence of any public or general rights;
    (v) to identify any person or object.

(d) Public documents.

(e) Statements admitted as part of the *res gestae* (part of the transaction or story).

(f) Statements made by a party to a common enterprise, admitted against another party to the enterprise as evidence of any matter stated.

Parliament had originally created an exception for statements in a document made for the purposes of criminal proceedings, such as a statement made by a witness to a crime, in ss 23 to 30 of the Criminal Justice Act 1988. The written statement was admissible if the maker of the statement was unable to give oral evidence because he was dead, mentally or physically unable to give oral evidence, out of the country or who was in fear. In addition, business documents not made for the purposes of criminal proceedings were admissible without proof that the maker was unavailable for one of the above reasons. Admissibility was subject to judicial discretion, but that discretion was seen as being overly concerned with whether admitting the document would be unfair to the defendant, who could not cross-examine on it, and failed to take account of the interests of the prosecution.

There were also wide powers under the Criminal Procedure and Investigations Act 1996 to admit at trial depositions taken by magistrates from witnesses at committal proceedings or statements admitted at such proceedings. They were inadmissible if either party to the trial objected, but the objection could be overridden if the court considered it to be in the interests of justice to do so. There was, however, no guidance as to how this wide discretion should be exercised.

Reform of the hearsay rule
The need for reform

The Royal Commission on Criminal Justice (Cmnd 2263, 1993) considered the law on hearsay in criminal cases to be 'exceptionally complex and difficult to interpret'. Those who have studied this area of law will heartily agree. The Royal Commission recommended major reform in concluding that:

> *In general, the fact that a statement is hearsay should mean that the court places less weight on it, but not that it should be inadmissible in the first place. We believe that the probative value of relevant evidence should in principle be decided by the jury for themselves, and we therefore recommend that hearsay evidence should be admitted to a greater extent than at present.* (Ch 8, para 26)

At the suggestion of the Royal Commission, the Law Commission considered this area of law and made recommendations in its report on *Evidence in Criminal Proceedings: Hearsay and Related Topics* (Law Com No 245, 1997). These recommendations formed the basis of legislative reform proposals which the Government first outlined in the White Paper, *Justice for All* (Cmnd 5563, 2002):

> *Another area ripe for change is the principle that evidence must be given by witnesses in person to the court. This is based on the idea that seeing and hearing the evidence of a witness in the witness box is the best means of getting at the truth. Whilst reported evidence or 'hearsay', is generally less satisfactory than first hand, there may be some cases where this is not so and others where it is all that is available and should therefore be considered by the court. The strict application of the rules also means that the previous statements of witnesses are not admissible as evidence even on long forgotten issues of detail, and that video recorded evidence is only admissible in a limited range of specified cases.*

> *We believe that the right approach is that, if there is a good reason for the original maker not being able to give the evidence personally (for example, through illness or death) or where records have been properly compiled by businesses, then the evidence should automatically go in, rather than its admissibility being judged. Judges should also have a discretion to decide that other evidence of this sort can be given. This is close to the approach developed in civil proceedings.*

> *We believe it is important to ensure that when witnesses are testifying, rules of evidence do not artificially prevent the true and full story from being presented to the court. Justice is not served if important information is excluded for no good reason. Therefore we propose to legislate to make it easier for witnesses to give their evidence*

by making their previous and original statements, often made at the time or shortly after the incident, more widely admissible at trial and allowing witnesses to refer to them when they give their evidence in court. We also propose to extend the scope for witnesses to give evidence on tape or by TV link. (paras 4.60–4.62)

The Criminal Justice Act 2003

The reforms were enacted in Ch 2 of the Criminal Justice Act 2003. With the exception of eight of the common law exceptions to the rule against hearsay which are preserved, the common law rules governing the admissibility of hearsay evidence are abolished. Sections 23 to 30 of the Criminal Justice Act 1988, which made much documentary evidence admissible subject to judicial discretion, are repealed and replaced with similar but improved statutory provisions.

Section 114: admissibility of hearsay

Under s 114 of the 2003 Act, a statement which is not made in oral evidence during criminal proceedings can be used as evidence of the facts stated within it, provided it comes under one of the following heads:

(a) it is admissible under a statutory provision;

(b) it is admissible under a common law rule preserved by this Chapter of the Act;

(c) the parties agree that it can go in; or

(d) the court gives leave to admit the statement.

Section 114(1) to (3) set out the circumstances in which a statement which is not made in oral evidence during criminal proceedings can be used as evidence of the facts stated within it. For example, if B was charged with robbery of a jewellers, the prosecution might want A to testify that B told her that he was 'outside the jewellers at midday on Monday' in order to prove that B was outside the jewellers at the relevant time. As these subsections remove the common law rule against the admission of such hearsay evidence, this out-of-court statement would be admissible in A's testimony, provided it comes under one of the heads set out in s 114(1)(a)–(d).

Section 114(1)(d) provides what one may describe as a long-stop, allowing the court to admit a hearsay statement that is not admissible by agreement of the parties or under any statutory provision (ss 116 or 117), nor one of the exceptions preserved by s 118. However, before the court can grant leave to admit such a statement under s 114(1)(d), it must be satisfied that, despite the difficulties there may be in challenging the statement, it would not be contrary to the interests of justice to admit the evidence. The intention, therefore, is that the court should be able to admit an out-of-court statement which does not fall within any of the other categories of admissibility, where it is cogent and reliable. The discretion extends to multiple hearsay (where the statement passes through more than one person before it is recorded) as well as first-hand hearsay (where a statement is made by a person who directly perceived the facts of which the evidence is being given).

Section 114(2) sets out a number of factors that the court must consider when deciding whether to grant leave under the discretion in s 114(1)(d):

(a) how much probative value the statement has (assuming it to be true) in relation to a matter in issue in the proceedings, or how valuable it is for the understanding of other evidence in the case;

(b) what other evidence has been, or can be, given on the matter or evidence mentioned in paragraph (a);

(c) how important the matter or evidence mentioned in paragraph (a) is in the context of the case as a whole;

(d) the circumstances in which the statement was made;

(e) how reliable the maker of the statement appears to be;

(f) how reliable the evidence of the making of the statement appears to be;

(g) whether oral evidence of the matter stated can be given and, if not, why it cannot;

(h) the amount of difficulty involved in challenging the statement;

(i) the extent to which that difficulty would be likely to prejudice the party facing it.

This list is intended to focus attention on whether the circumstances surrounding the making of the out-of-court statement indicate whether it can be treated as reliable enough to admit it as evidence, despite the fact that it will not be subject to cross-examination.

Section 114(3) provides that out-of-court statements may still be excluded even if they fulfil the requirements of this Chapter. For example, confessions must meet the additional requirements of ss 76, 76A and 78 of the Police and Criminal Evidence Act 1984 (see **Chapter 7**). If the out-of-court statement includes evidence of the bad character of a witness or defendant, the statement must also satisfy the requirements of s 100 or s 101 of the Criminal Justice Act 2003, and may be excluded under s 101(3) of that Act (see **Chapter 5**).

One may note that s 126 of the 2003 Act provides a general discretion to refuse to admit a hearsay statement where the court is satisfied that the case for excluding the statement, taking account of the danger that to admit it would result in undue waste of time, substantially outweighs the case for admitting it, taking account of the value of the evidence.

Section 130 of the 2003 Act repeals para 5(4) of Sch 3 to the Crime and Disorder Act 1988, which provided that a judge could overrule an objection to a deposition, a witness statement made in committal proceedings, being read as evidence if he considered it to be in the interests of justice to do so. In future such depositions will be admissible under this section (and s 116 if the witness is absent for one of the reasons set out there – see pp 201–216 below)

Section 115: assertions and direct evidence

Section 115 of the 2003 Act is concerned with the distinction between assertions and direct evidence, and seeks to resolve the difficulties created by some common law decisions. There are two basic ways of proving a fact in issue. First, it may be proved by proving some other fact which renders it more likely to be true; the other fact is directly probative of the fact to be proved. Secondly, it may be proved by a person's assertion that it is true. The hearsay rule applied only to the latter form of proof.

An assertion can consist of words, or conduct or both. Nonetheless, merely because a person's words or conduct are relied upon as evidence of a fact, it does not follow that they are an assertion of that fact. For example, a person's words may betray guilty knowledge without amounting to a confession of that person's guilt. Often it will be clear whether a person's words or conduct are adduced as proof of a fact on the basis that they are directly probative of it – in other words, if it were not true then that person would not have spoken those words or acted in that way – or on the basis that they amount to an assertion of it. However, it is sometimes doubtful which of these is the case.

For example, in *Wright v Doe d Tatham* (1837) 7 Ad & E 313, the issue was whether letters written to a man in which the writers appeared to assume the sanity of the recipient, could be evidence of his sanity. It was held that the letters were hearsay (and inadmissible) because they were not directly probative of the facts to be proved, but only an assertion of it. The decision was explained by the example of a sea captain who boards his ship and sets sail, from which a court might be tempted to infer that the ship was seaworthy. It was said that the hearsay rule would apply to such conduct, and evidence of it would be inadmissible.

Similarly, in *R v Harry* (1986) 86 Cr App R 105, the accused and his flatmate P were charged with possession of a controlled drug with intent to supply. The accused's defence was that P was the sole supplier. He sought to prove this by calling police officers to give evidence that while they were at the flat after arresting Harry and P, the police officers had answered a number of telephone calls from persons who could not be traced, but who had asked for P and enquired whether P had drugs for sale. The trial judge refused to allow evidence of the content of the calls to go before the jury because it was hearsay and inadmissible, on the ground that the callers impliedly alleged P to be the supplier (he did allow counsel for Harry to establish by cross-examination that there had been calls, none of which asked for Harry). Harry was convicted and P acquitted. The Court of Appeal upheld the judge's ruling, while recognising that Harry felt a justifiable grievance.

That decision was approved of by a bare majority of the House of Lords in *R v Kearley* [1992] 2 AC 228. The issue here was whether, on a charge of possessing drugs with intent to supply, a prosecutor could rely on evidence by the police that they had been to the home of the defendant when he was not there, and had received telephone and personal calls from people (who were not called as witnesses) asking about drugs that the defendant had for sale. A majority held that the hearsay rule applied where it was sought to draw an inference of a fact from words or conduct which were intended to be assertive of some other fact, or not intended to be assertive at all. As evidence of the fact that the defendant dealt in drugs, the callers' words were hearsay; and, being unable to find any applicable exception to the rule, the majority of the House held them inadmissible.

Lord Browne-Wilkinson and Lord Griffiths dissented on the basis that while a single call asking for P and requesting drugs would be of little probative value and would cause great prejudice to P's case if the jury drew the wrong inference, they saw no reason why the evidence of multiple calls should not be admitted. Lord Browne-Wilkinson thought that *Harry* had been wrongly decided; the words 'Can I have some drugs?' were not, in his view, a statement making an assertion, but a fact and direct evidence. It was common ground that the flat was being used to supply drugs, the only issue was whether it was Harry or P who was the supplier. Those words directed at P were direct evidence that P was supplying drugs. Lord Browne-Wilkinson thought that the inference to be drawn by the jury was not from the words used by the callers but from the fact that there were callers who (from the words used) were shown to be seeking to acquire drugs.

Evidence of the kind that was excluded in *Wright* and *Kearley* was referred it to as an 'implied assertion'.

Closely associated with the problem of 'implied assertions' was that of 'negative assertions'. The kind of case said to fall within this description is illustrated by *R v Patel* [1981] 3 All ER 94. The issue here was whether the defendant was an illegal immigrant. An immigration officer looked up the register of persons granted leave to stay in the UK. If the defendant's name did not appear on the register he had no permission to stay and was, it was argued, an illegal immigrant. The Court of Appeal agreed with the conclusion but held, applying *Myers v DPP* [1965] AC 1001 (see p 187 above), that the officer's testimony was hearsay on the basis that he was not the compiler of the records and the assertion that the records were accurate could not be relied upon. The compiler of the record was the only one who could give evidence of the fact that, since the defendant's name did not appear on the record, he was an illegal immigrant.

These borderline cases are not precisely analogous to one another. But they do have one feature in common, and one which is absent in the case of statements to which the hearsay rule clearly applies. That is that, while the words or conduct relied upon may in fact cause others to draw certain inferences, it is not the intention of the person whose words or conduct are in question that they should have that effect. The Law Commission took the view that a person's words or conduct should not be regarded as asserting a fact, and therefore should not be caught by the hearsay rule, if adduced as evidence of that fact, unless the person intends to assert that fact.

Section 115(3) seeks to resolve the difficulties experienced by the common law and gives effect to the Law Commission's recommendation that a person's words or conduct should not be caught by the hearsay rule unless the purpose, or one of the purposes, of that person appears to be to cause the hearer to believe that the matter stated is true, or to act on the basis that it is true. Thus the evidence of police officers in *Kearley* that they received 17 calls from persons asking for drugs, would not be a matter to which Ch 2 of the 2003 Act applies unless it could be shown that the purpose, or one of the purposes, of the callers was to cause the police officers to believe that K was a drug-dealer. Given that they would not have known they were talking to police officers and they were only concerned to get their usual supply of drugs, that would not be their purpose. Evidence of the calls will then be admissible as direct evidence and will not be caught by the hearsay rule.

The Law Commission believed that a statement should fall within the hearsay rule only where it is made with the intention that some action be taken on the basis that the facts stated are true, where that statement is made to a human person, and even if the taking of that action involved no human intervention but only the operation of a machine. The Commission offered the following examples:

> *Suppose A's job is to reimburse travelling expenses claims made by colleagues. It is sought to prove that his colleague B travelled to Glasgow on a particular date, by adducing her claim form in which she stated that she had done so. This should fall*

within the hearsay rule because it might be fabricated. A may not apply his mind to the question whether or not it is true, but B does intend that he should act on the basis that it is true. Her purpose would then be to cause another person to believe the matter and it is therefore within s 108(3)(a).

Alternatively, suppose that the processing of B's expenses claim is carried out not by A but by a computer system, which had been programmed to print a cheque for the amount claimed if the information provided by the claimant appears to meet the specified criteria. The risk of fabrication is as great as if the information were given to a human. B's purpose is to cause a machine to operate on the basis that the matter is as stated. Both claim forms would be a matter stated to which Chapter 2 applies and such matters would be subject to the rules of admissibility set out in s 114.

Section 114(3)(b) preserves the common law position whereby statements which are not based on human input fall outside the ambit of the hearsay rule. The previous law drew a distinction according to whether the statement consisted of, or was based upon, only what the machine itself had observed; or whether it incorporated, or was based upon, information supplied by a human being. The hearsay rule did not therefore apply to tapes, films or photographs which record disputed incidents actually taking place, or to documents produced by machine (usually computers) which automatically recorded an event or circumstances. Thus surveillance cameras in stores or streets, which record a person shoplifting or committing a robbery in the street, were seen as direct evidence and not hearsay. Section 108 continues this approach.

In *Taylor v Chief Constable of Cheshire* [1987] 1 All ER 225, a video cassette recording made by a security camera in a store, which showed a person stealing items from the shop, was shown to two police officers who recognised the accused as the thief. The cassette was returned to the shop where it was mistakenly erased. The officers were, however, allowed to give evidence of recognising the defendant on the video. His appeal against conviction, based on the wrongful admission of this evidence, was dismissed, the court holding that what the officers had seen on video was no different to the evidence of a bystander who had seen the incident directly. Since it was identification evidence it was subject to the rules laid down in *R v Turnbull* [1977] QB 224, which recognise the dangers of mistaken identification, but was no different from other forms of identification evidence (see **Chapter 1**).

In *Attorney-General's Reference (No 2 of 2002)* [2003] Crim LR 192, the defendant was identified as one of a number of rioters from a video film of the riot taken by the police. The Court of Appeal noted that there were at least four circumstances when, subject to judicial discretion, the jury could be invited to conclude that the defendant committed the offence on the basis of photographic evidence:

(a) when the photographic evidence was sufficiently clear the jury could view it and compare the image with that of the defendant in the dock;

(b) where the witness knew the defendant sufficiently well to recognise him, he could give oral evidence of this;

(c) when the witness who did not know the defendant had spent time viewing and analysing the video evidence, he could give evidence on the identification based on a comparison between D and the images;

(d) where the witness was suitably qualified in facial mapping, he could compare the photo image with a recent photograph of the defendant.

Computer-generated statements

Whether evidence produced by a computer is, or is not, hearsay depends on the process by which the statement is produced. If the computer produces the evidence automatically and without human input, it is not hearsay but direct evidence. Thus the analysis of breath or blood taken for the purposes of determining the blood alcohol level of a driver alleged to have committed the offence of driving with excess alcohol in the blood, is real evidence (*Castle v Cross* [1984] 1 WLR 1372). Similarly, the recording and analysis of telephone calls made from a hotel room, which prints out the details of the call, duration and cost, is not hearsay but is real evidence (*R v Spiby* (1990) 91 Cr App R 186). The same process is used by mobile telephone operators in order to charge their customers. The absence of any human input is seen as confirming their reliability. In *R v Robson, Mitchell and Richards* [1991] Crim LR 362, the defendants were convicted of armed robbery. The prosecution linked the second defendant with the crime by means of a computer printout of telephone calls made by the second defendant on his mobile phone to that of the first defendant. It was held that the printout was not hearsay but real evidence, following *Spiby*, because the printout was produced by a computer which operated automatically and independently without human intervention.

In *R v Golizadeh* [1995] Crim LR 232, a forensic scientist tested a substance (which proved to be opium) by a gas chromatography masspechtromotry process. The machine produced a printout of the results. The scientist simply used the resultant analysis in order to frame an opinion, which he then gave in evidence. The defence contention that the evidence of the expert was hearsay was misconceived, as *Spiby* (above) makes clear.

In *R v Wood* (1982) 76 Cr App R 23, the prosecution sought to prove that metal found in the possession of the accused was of the same type as a stolen consignment, by adducing evidence of tests, the results of which were produced by a computer which had analysed the results of tests carried out by a number of chemists. It was held that this was not hearsay because the chemists could have given oral evidence of the results. In the absence of such evidence the computer analysis would not have been admissible, the computer merely being used as a calculator or collator of information put into it by humans. In *R (O) v Coventry Magistrates Court* (2003) *The Times*, 22 April, the Queen's Bench Divisional Court held that a computer printout recording successful and unsuccessful attempts to enter a website was admissible as real evidence, applying *Spiby* and the above line of cases. The case involved attempts to download child pornography from an American company. The printout in question was obtained from the database of the company running the website, and contained a breakdown of the defendant's successful and unsuccessful attempts to access the website, and charges made to his credit card.

It is also worth noting that s 129 of the 2003 Act provides that where a statement generated by a machine is based on information implanted into the machine by a human, the output of the device will be admissible only where it is proved that the information was accurate, and s 129(2) preserves the common law presumption that a mechanical device has been properly set or calibrated.

Photofit identification

Witnesses to a crime are often asked to provide a description of the criminal. This used to be done by a sketch artist, who drew a likeness of the person based on the description given. Today computer-generated images replace the artist, but the process remains the same – the witness describes the person (his hair, eyes, nose, etc), and the operator selects the facial characteristics most closely fitting the description. Photofit evidence was traditionally regarded as an exception to the hearsay rule.

Thus in *R v Smith (Percy)* [1976] Crim LR 511, a sketch of the person alleged to have committed the crime, drawn by a police artist under the direction of the witness, was admitted as part of the witness's testimony. It was held that the sketch was not hearsay because the court was not relying on the conversation between the witness and the artist; the sketch had effectively been made by the witness who merely directed the artist's hand. The more advanced photo-fit process was similarly treated in *R v Okorodu* [1982] Crim LR 747. The photo-fit picture constructed by a witness was very similar to the accused. The witness failed to pick out the accused at an identification parade. The photo-fit picture was then admitted at trial on the ground that in all cases based on identification, the jury should have access to all relevant information. This applies also to the even more advanced computerised process of creating an identifiable image.

The Court of Appeal held in *R v Cook* [1987] QB 417 that sketches, photo-fits and photographs (and computer-generated images) are in a class of evidence on their own to which the rule against hearsay and the rule against previous consistent statements do not apply. Watkins LJ described the sketches and photo-fit pictures made in accordance with the witness's recollections as 'manifestations of the seeing eye, translations of vision onto paper through the medium of the officer's skill of drawing or composing which a witness does not possess'. He continued (at 425):

> We regard the production of the sketch or photo-fit by a police officer making a graphic representation of the witness's memory as another form of the camera at work, albeit imperfectly and not produced contemporaneously with the material incident but soon or fairly soon afterwards. As we perceive it the photo-fit is not a statement in writing made in the absence of the defendant or anything resembling it in the sense that this very old rule against hearsay has ever been expressed to embrace. It is we think sui generis, that is to say the only one of its kind. It is a thing apart, the admissibility to evidence of which would not be in breach of the hearsay rule.

Section 115(2) appears to contradict the above decision that the photofit is not a statement within the hearsay rule when it defines a statement as 'any representation of fact or opinion made by a person by whatever means; and it includes a representation made in a sketch, photofit or other pictorial form'. Since the photofit, when completed, is intended to cause another person to believe that it depicts the person alleged to have committed the crime, it falls within s 115(3) and is hearsay to which Ch 2 applies. Such photofits do not appear in the common law exceptions preserved by s 118, and since s 118(2) abolishes all other common law rules governing the admissibility of hearsay evidence, it would appear that photofits are now to be considered as hearsay. However, s 120 provides that 2003 Act makes a previous statement by the witness admissible under certain conditions. Section 120(4) provides as follows:

A previous statement by the witness is admissible as evidence of any matter stated of which oral evidence by him would be admissible, if

(a) *any of the following three conditions is satisfied, and*

(b) *while giving evidence the witness indicates that to the best of his belief he made the statement, and that to the best of his belief it states the truth.*

The first condition, as laid down in s 120(5) is that the statement identifies a person, an object or a place.

The photofit statement (and s 115(2) makes it clear that it is a statement) identifying the person seen by the witness is a previous statement made by the witness which satisfies the terms of s 120(4) and the condition in s 120(5). At common law it was a previous consistent statement that, if admissible, was admissible only as evidence of consistency. Under s 120, it is admissible as evidence of the truth of the matters stated.

Section 116 – cases where a witness is unavailable

Section 116 of the 2003 Act replaces ss 23 and 26 of the Criminal Justice Act 1988, and is primarily concerned with statements made by persons who would have been witnesses in criminal cases but are unable to attend court. Section 117, considered at pp 216–221 below, is concerned with statements made by persons in the course of a trade or business, etc, which were not normally intended to be statements in criminal proceedings.

Section 23 of the 1988 Act made a statement by a person in a document admissible in criminal proceedings as evidence of any fact of which direct oral evidence by him would have been admissible if any of the conditions set out in the section were satisfied. Those conditions were similar to those set out in s 116(4) of the 2003 Act. The essential difference is that while s 23 of the 1988 Act applied only to statements in a document, s 116 applies to any first-hand hearsay statement, oral or in a document. In contrast, s 117, which replaces s 24 of the 1988 Act, applies only to statements in a document.

Where a statement in a document is involved, the statement may be admissible under both ss 116 and 117, but where the statement was prepared for the purposes of criminal proceedings (usually a witness statement) there will seldom be any advantage in arguing for admission under s 117. Where the statement was made orally, it may be admitted only under s 116 or one of the exceptions preserved by s 118 (principally the exception known as *res gestae*). Circumstances will dictate which head of admissibility is best argued.

A statement made out of court may be admissible under s 116 (subject to the additional conditions to be considered below) if the person who made the statement (the relevant person):

(a) is dead;

(b) is physically or mentally ill;

(c) is outside the United Kingdom;

(d) cannot be found despite taking reasonably practicable steps;

(e) does not give oral evidence through fear (s 116(2)).

These are discussed in further detail at pp 205–215 below.

Section 116(1) requires that two conditions be satisfied in addition to any of the above five conditions, as follows.

Admissibility of the relevant person's oral evidence

Section 116(1)(a) requires that oral evidence given in the proceedings by the person who made the statement would be admissible as evidence of that matter. It follows that one must ask whether the person who made the statement (the relevant person) which one seeks to admit under s 109 would have been able to give oral evidence if he or she had been available to do so.

There are three reasons why oral evidence by the person who made the statement would not be admissible. First, evidence of the matter contained in the statement is not relevant to any issue in the case. Relevance to an issue is a requirement of all admissible evidence and no further discussion is required.

Secondly, the person who made the statement was not a competent witness. It will be recalled that s 53 of the Youth Justice and Criminal Evidence Act 1999 states that a person is not competent to give evidence in criminal proceedings if it appears to the court that he is not a person who is able to understand questions put to him as a witness and give answers to them which can be understood. This requirement will rarely be called into question, but if the condition in s 116(2)(b) is relied upon – that the relevant person is unfit to be a witness because of his mental condition – his competence may be called into question if the mental illness preceded the making of the statement. Section 116(1)(a) provides that an out-of-court statement cannot be admitted under this section if the person who made the statement was not legally capable of making a statement at the time the statement was made. Section 123 (Capability to make statement) confirms this by stating that:

> (1) Nothing in ss 116, 119 or 120 makes a statement admissible as evidence if it was made by a person who did not have the required capability at the time when he made the statement ...

> (3) For the purposes of this section a person has the required capability if he is capable of—

> (a) understanding questions put to him about the matters stated, and

> (b) giving answers to such questions which can be understood.

(Section 119, which deals with previous inconsistent statements, and s 120, which deals with other previous statements of a witness, are dealt with in **Chapter 4**.)

Section 116(3) restates in positive form s 53(3) of the Youth Justice and Criminal Evidence Act 1999, which defines competence of witnesses to give evidence, while s 116(4) provides for the same means of determining competency as is set out in s 54 of the 1999 Act. In *R v Sed* [2004] 1 WLR 3218, the trial judge admitted the video statement of an 81-year-old woman suffering from Alzheimer's disease, under ss 23 and 26 of the Criminal Justice Act 1988, in which, although her answers were confused, she stated that a man had had sexual intercourse with her without her consent. Expert medical evidence indicated that at the time of her interview she was not fit to give evidence in court owing to her dementia. The trial judge anticipated the test of competence set out in s 53 of the 1999 Act (at the trial in January 2003) and ruled that she was competent, and admitted the video statement.

The Court of Appeal dismissed the appeal by Mr Sed against that decision. The question was what test of competence was appropriate to evidence in the form of a documentary statement admissible under s 23 and s 26 of the 1988 Act (now s 116) before s 53 of the 1999 Act came into force? Lord Justice Auld said that even before s 53 came into force, its formulation of a new notion of competence was a reasonable, though not obligatory, approach for the judge to adopt when considering whether to admit the hearsay evidence, that is the degree of mental illness at the time of the making of the statement or at trial. Section 123(3) (above) makes it clear that consideration of s 53 of the 1999 Act is now obligatory when considering the admissibility of a hearsay statement under s 116.

The third reason why the person who made the statement cannot give oral evidence of the matters stated, is that the matters stated are themselves hearsay. Thus if the statement of an unavailable witness sought to prove a fact by reference to what another person had told him, he would not have been able to give oral evidence of that fact unless a common law exception applied. First-hand hearsay is admissible under s 116, as where A makes a statement about a fact that he perceived but dies or is otherwise unavailable at trial. However, where the unavailable witness could only have given evidence of a fact under a common law exception, that is seen as a cumulative or multiple use of hearsay and would not be admissible under s 116. Thus if A was stabbed when he answered his door, staggered to his next door neighbour, B, and told him that it was D who had stabbed him, the unavailability of A will permit B to give evidence of what A told him under s 116. These circumstances also fall within the common law exception to the hearsay rule known as *res gestae* (preserved by s 118(1),(4)(a) and discussed at pp 221–226 below). However, if B is also unavailable, the cumulative use of a hearsay exception will not permit B's statement to be admitted under s 116. Thus if A, having been stabbed, tells B that D stabbed him, and B tells C, and both A and B are unavailable to give evidence, C cannot give evidence that B told him that A said it was D who stabbed A.

The Law Commission recommended (Law Com 245, 1997 at para 8.23) that the unavailability exception 'should not apply if the declarant's oral evidence would itself have been hearsay, and would have been admissible only under the unavailability exception or one of the common law exceptions we recommend should be preserved'. Section 121 implements this recommendation and lays down additional requirements for admissibility of multiple hearsay, in providing as follows:

> *(1) A hearsay statement is not admissible to prove the fact that an earlier hearsay statement was made unless—*
>
> *(a) either of the statements is admissible under s 117, 119 or 120,*
>
> *(b) all parties to the proceedings so agree, or*
>
> *(c) the court is satisfied that the value of the evidence in question, taking into account how reliable the statements appear to be, is so high that the interests of justice require the later statement to be admissible for that purpose.*
>
> *(2) In this section 'hearsay statement' means a statement, not made in oral evidence, that is relied upon as evidence of the matter stated in it.*

Explaining the refusal to admit multiple hearsay under the unavailability exception that is now s 116 of the 2003 Act, the Law Commission noted, at para 8.19–8.22 of its Report:

Suppose, for example, that A said that event x had occurred, and that A knew this because B had seen it happen and had told A about it immediately afterwards, in such circumstances that A could have given oral evidence of B's statement under the res gestae rule. But A is dead. Should A's statement be admissible as evidence of x?

The statement is multiple hearsay, since A has no personal knowledge of the fact stated. The unavailability exception should not apply if, because A had no such knowledge, A would have been unable to give oral evidence of that fact. But in this case A could have given such evidence – by virtue not of personal knowledge, but of the res gestae exception. The question is: should it be sufficient for the purposes of the unavailability exception that the declarant could have given oral evidence of the fact stated, even if that evidence would have been (admissible) hearsay? Or should it be necessary that the declarant could have given oral evidence without resort to a hearsay exception?

We have concluded that the answer should depend on which hearsay exception would have rendered A's oral evidence admissible – in other words, how B's statement (the statement on which the statement of the unavailable declarant A is based) itself comes to be admissible. If B gives evidence the fact that B is available for cross-examination is in our view sufficient to compensate for the fact that A's statement is multiple hearsay. And if B's statement is admissible on the ground that it was made in a business document, we think the presumed reliability of such documents is again sufficient to outweigh the drawbacks of multiple hearsay.

If, however, B's statement is only admissible on the basis that B is unavailable to testify, or under one of the common law exceptions (such as res gestae) that we recommend should be preserved (section 118), we think it would be going too far to permit B's statement to be proved by another hearsay statement merely because the maker of that other statement is unavailable to testify. Our reasons are essentially those that we have given for excluding multiple hearsay in general from the unavailability exception – namely that with each additional step in the chain, the risk of error or fabrication increases.

It is worth noting here the reasoning given by the Law Commission for refusing to allow multiple hearsay (ie, that with each additional step in the chain the risk of error or fabrication increases) Note also that if such a statement made in the non-business context is relevant to an issue before the court and is considered reliable, the trial judge may give leave to admit it applying s 114(1)(d) and (2).

Identifying the person who made the statement

Section 116(1)(b) requires that the person who made the statement (the relevant person) is identified to the satisfaction of the court. This will enable the opposing party to challenge the absent witness's credibility under s 124, which allows the opposing party to put before the jury any evidence relevant to the credibility of that witness which he could have put had he been able to cross-examine the witness in person.

Section 116 requires that any of the various conditions 'is satisfied', or, in the context of s 116(1)(b), that the person be identified 'to the court's satisfaction'. The 1988 Act used similar terminology, but the courts required that the conditions be strictly proved, by the prosecution beyond reasonable doubt and by the defence on the balance of probabilities. Given that these matters are not strictly speaking evidence, the issue of the admissibility of a statement being made either in a preliminary hearing or in a trial within a trial in the absence of the jury, there is no reason why there should be the variable standards which apply in the trial proper. On the issue of competence, s 54(2) of the Youth Justice and Criminal Evidence Act 1999 states that it is for the parties to satisfy the court that a witness is competent to give evidence, on the balance of probabilities. It remains to be seen whether the courts will impose the variable standards, or apply the lower standard to both parties, or simply accept that 'satisfied' does not require proof to either standard.

Conditions for admission under s 116(2)

Relevant person is dead

Section 116(2)(a) stipulates that such a statement may be admitted if the relevant person is dead. This is largely self-explanatory. A death certificate (itself admissible as a public document – a common law exception to the hearsay rule preserved by s 118(1)(b) or as a business document under s 117) will be necessary to prove that the witness is dead.

Relevant person is physically or mentally ill

Section 116(2)(b) applies where the relevant person is unfit to be a witness because of his physical or mental condition. Medical evidence will be necessary to prove the unfitness to attend by reason of physical or mental condition, and this may also be in documentary form if such evidence is uncontested. However, in *R v Elliott and others* (2003) *The Times*, 15 May, it was held that when the prosecution sought to rely on a written statement rather than his oral testimony on the ground that the witness was unfit through illness, the defence should ordinarily be given an opportunity to cross-examine the relevant doctor who was providing support for the application. In a disputed case it would not be sufficient for the prosecution merely to provide a written statement recording the doctor's views.

A physical disability will not affect the competence of the witness but a mental condition might, depending on whether that condition was present before the statement was made or occurred only afterwards. In *R v Setz-Dempsey* (1994) 98 Cr App R 23, an important identification witness was mentally unfit to give evidence at the time of trial and his written statement was admitted under s 23 of the Criminal Justice Act 1988. Allowing the appeal, the Court of Appeal held that the trial judge should not have admitted the written statement. He had failed to take into account the effect of medical evidence about the witness's state of mind on the quality of the identification evidence, and the unfairness to the defendant in being unable to cross-examine the witness. This suggests that the witness was mentally incapable when the identification and subsequent statement were made. If so, the witness was not competent to give evidence and would not have satisfied the requirements of s 23, and would not now satisfy the condition in s 116(2)(b).

Relevant person is outside the UK

Section 116(2)(c) deals with the scenario where the relevant person is outside the United Kingdom and it is not reasonably practicable to secure his attendance. It is worded in almost exactly the same terms as the previous provision under s 23(1)(b)(i) and (ii) of the 1988 Act. These provisions were considered in *R v Case* [1991] Crim LR 192. Here, two police officers saw the defendant take a purse from the bag of a Portuguese tourist, S, who was accompanied by another tourist, G. The accused admitted the theft in the police station in the presence of the custody officer, and signed the custody record as accurate.

However, he denied this at trial, where the prosecution relied on the evidence of the arresting officers but not that of the custody officer. The defendant's defence was that S and G were mistaken or lying and that he was put under pressure to admit the offence to secure the release of his companion. The prosecution sought leave to admit in evidence the statements of the two tourists, relying on s 23(1) and (2)(b) (now s 116(2)(c)). G had given a Portuguese address but had made no mention of where she normally lived, nor of the length of time she had been living in Britain or how long she intended to stay here. S's statement made it clear that she was staying temporarily in a hotel. That was the only evidence that the witnesses were outside the UK, and there was no evidence that any attempt had been made to find out if either was willing to attend court. The trial judge inferred from the statements that they would be unwilling to attend and that it would not be reasonably practicable to secure their attendance given the expense involved. He therefore admitted the statements and the defendant was convicted.

The Court of Appeal quashed his conviction and found that there was no evidence before the court that the witnesses were outside the UK. Even if it had been permissible to look at the contents of the statements, in the circumstances of this case, there was still insufficient evidence. While the word 'reasonably' implied that financial implications could be considered, there was no evidence whatsoever as to whether it was practicable for them to attend court on the day. Given that the criminal standard of proof had to be satisfied, there was no evidence upon which the trial judge could have been satisfied that the conditions had been made out. This amounted to a material irregularity requiring the quashing of the conviction (even if the lesser burden of proof is applied to s 116, it is suggested that there would still be insufficient evidence to satisfy the trial judge that the condition had been satisfied).

It should normally be possible for a party to prove the existence of a condition under s 116(2) by another document admissible under s 116 or 117. In *R v Castillo* [1996] Crim LR 193, the Court of Appeal, applying s 23(2)(b) of the 1988 Act, held that it was permissible to prove that a witness was unable to attend by using a statement of another person admitted under s 23. The case involved the importation of cocaine from Venezuela and the prosecution sought to admit the statement of M, an airline official, about tickets from a destination in Venezuela which had been issued to Castillo. A trial within a trial was held in which evidence was given about enquiries made of a Mr Tyler, the drugs liaison officer in Venezuela, as to the ability of M to attend. The judge ruled that it was not reasonably practicable for Mr Tyler to attend and admitted his statement under s 23(2)(b). He also ruled that having admitted Mr Tyler's statement, it revealed that it was not practicable for M to attend, so that M's statement was also admissible under s 23(2)(b).

It was argued on appeal that it was not open to the trial judge to apply s 23 twice, first as to the statement of M and second as to the statement of Mr Tyler that it was not practicable for M to attend. Section 23, it was argued, applied to first-hand hearsay (see the marginal note), and this was in fact second-hand hearsay. This argument was rejected. In their Lordships' judgment, it was not second-hand hearsay. They saw no reason why the inability of M to attend should not be proved by the statement of Mr Tyler, whose inability to attend had been proved and whose statement had been admitted in evidence under s 23(2)(b).

The Court also pointed out that the fact that it was possible for a witness to attend did not answer the question whether it was reasonably practicable for him to do so. The judge had to consider a number of facts. First, he had to question the importance of the evidence the witness could give and whether or not it was prejudicial, and how prejudicial, to the accused if he did not attend. In this case the evidence of Mr Tyler was concerned only with what M had told him, and it was M's evidence with which the court was concerned. Secondly, there were considerations of expense and inconvenience. That should not be a major consideration, but in this case it would be a matter of considerable expense for Mr Tyler to travel from Venezuela simply to give evidence which could not seriously be challenged in cross-examination. Thirdly, the judge had to consider reasons put forward as to why it was not reasonably practicable for the witness to attend. Those were findings of fact with which their Lordships would not lightly interfere, and they had not been persuaded in this case that the judge's ruling was wrong.

It is likely that the courts would take a similar approach if the above facts were to occur under the 2003 Act. The statement of the airline official and that of the drug liaison officer would be admissible either under s 116, or as a business document under s 117.

In *R v French (Lee Ernest); R v Gowhar (Walid Mohammed)* (1993) 97 Cr App R 421, the Court of Appeal approved the statement in *R v Bray* (1988) 88 Cr App R 345, 347, where it was said that '[w]hether it is reasonable [to secure the attendance of a witness] or not is not to be examined at the moment the trial opens but must be examined against the whole background of the case'. The Court then proceeded to ask whether there was any necessity for the judge to have regard to the future, and answered its own question in stating that '[i]t would be difficult to apply s 23 with any certainty if one could look to the future. The right way to approach it was to consider it as at the date of the application' (at 425). It is therefore likely that the court will look at all that was done up to the date of the application to admit the statement of the relevant person, including the cost of bringing the witness to the court. Even if one is convinced that the witness will not attend, steps must be taken to confirm this, and if nothing is done the court will almost certainly refuse to admit the written statement, as was the case in *Bray*.

In *R v Maloney* [1994] Crim LR 525, the trial judge admitted the written statements of two Greek cadets after hearing that the police enquiries had been met by the statement that the cadets were at sea, at the Naval Academy in Piraeus or in Cyprus on leave. The Court of Appeal held that there was evidence from which the judge could find that it was not reasonably practicable to secure their attendance. 'Practicable' was not equivalent to physically possible. It must be construed in the light of the normal steps which would be taken to arrange the attendance of a witness at trial. 'Reasonably practicable' involved a further qualification of the duty, to secure attendance by taking the reasonable steps which a party would normally take to secure a witness's attendance having regard to the means and resources available to the parties.

In *R v Jiminez-Paez* [1993] Crim LR 596, the appellant was arrested at Heathrow en route from Colombia, where she lived, to Italy. Customs officers found 564 grammes of cocaine, with a street value of £50,000, secreted on her person. At her trial she admitted that she was involved in smuggling, but said that she thought she was smuggling emeralds, which she had illegally exported from Colombia before. She sought to introduce in evidence a letter from the Colombian Embassy's adviser in charge of consular affairs. The letter stated that there was a black market in emeralds in Colombia and that they were frequently illegally exported, and one method of concealment was the type used in the appellant's case. The defence sought to rely on a provision similar to s 116(2)(c), arguing that the consular official, who had diplomatic immunity and was therefore immune from process, was effectively outside the United Kingdom, despite the fact that she was physically present but unwilling to give evidence. Not surprisingly, the trial judge rejected the argument and excluded the letter as hearsay. The Court of Appeal held that he was right to do so. The defence contention would not give effect to the two distinct requirements that the person was outside the UK and that it was not reasonably practicable to secure his attendance. Had the letter been sent from an official in Colombia it would have satisfied the subsection, and would satisfy s 116(2)(c) of the 2003 Act.

Relevant person cannot be found
Under s 116(2)(d), a statement may be admissible where the relevant person cannot be found although such steps as it is reasonably practicable to take have been taken. The above discussion of 'reasonably practicable' applies here. Witnesses often leave the area in order to avoid having to give evidence. Some simply move on to another area leaving no forwarding address. Exceptionally, a witness will be kept out of the way by persons acting for the defendant, and it is not unknown for police officers to persuade a defence witness to leave the area. What steps it is reasonably practicable to take to find such witnesses will depend on the circumstances, and it will be for the party seeking to have the statement admitted to satisfy the court that they have taken all such steps as are reasonable in the particular circumstances.

Relevant person fearful
Section 116(2)(e) may apply where a person is reluctant to give oral evidence (or does not continue to give oral evidence) through fear. For the purposes of this provision, 'fear' is to be widely construed and (for example) includes fear of the death or injury of another person, or fear of financial loss. Section 116(4) stipulates that the court may give leave for a statement to be admitted under s 116(2)(e) only if it considers that the statement ought to be admitted in the interests of justice, having regard:

(a) to the statement's contents;

(b) to any risk that its admission or exclusion will result in unfairness to any party to the proceedings (and in particular to how difficult it will be to challenge the statement if the relevant person does not give oral evidence);

(c) in appropriate cases, to the fact that a direction under s 19 of the Youth Justice and Criminal Evidence Act 1999 (special measures for the giving of evidence by fearful witnesses, etc) could be made in relation to the relevant person; and

(d) to any other relevant circumstances.

The intimidation of witnesses was commonplace throughout the twentieth century and numerous attempts were made to deal with it, including making such intimidation a criminal offence and making provision for the admission of the written statement of such witnesses who were unable or too fearful to attend court and give oral evidence. Prior to its repeal by the Criminal Procedure and Investigations Act 1996, s 13(3) of the Criminal Justice Act 1925, in conjunction with s 102(7) of the Magistrates' Courts Act 1980, permitted the written statements of witnesses to be read out in cases where the witness was proved to have been 'kept out of the way by means of the procurement of the accused or on his behalf'. These provisions were not all that helpful to the prosecution whose witness had disappeared. Even if it could be proved that the witness had been abducted by friends of the accused, the section did not come into play unless it could also be proved that they had done it 'at the instigation of or with the accused's knowledge and approval' (*R v O'Loughlin* [1988] 3 All ER 431).

Section 23 of the Criminal Justice Act 1988 introduced a much wider provision that gave the trial judge discretion to allow a written statement to be used where a witness would 'not give oral evidence through fear'. This section avoided many of the difficulties associated with the 1925 Act, but carried certain problems of its own. It was not confined to statements which had been used at committal proceedings, but it was confined to written statements. It was also confined to prosecution statements, it being a condition of admissibility that 'the statement was made to a police officer or other person charged with the investigation of offences or charging offenders; and that the person who made it does not give oral evidence through fear or because he is kept out of the way'. It will be noted that s 116(2) separates these conditions, 'kept out of the way' being replaced by the condition under s 116(2)(d), 'cannot be found'. The new section also applies to written or oral statements, and is available to defence and prosecution witnesses.

Section 17 of the Youth Justice and Criminal Evidence Act 1999 makes witnesses in fear or distress eligible for special measures, which may enable them to give oral evidence (see pp 52–53). In determining whether the witness was in fear under s 23(3) of the 1988 Act, the courts took into account the availability of special measures and, where the witness appeared in court but refused to give evidence through fear, the trial judge was required to consider whether special measures would enable the witness to give oral evidence. If he did not attend court in person, the police were required to bring the availability of special measures to the attention of the witness in the hope that he could be persuaded to give oral evidence. Section 116(4)(c) now requires the court to consider the possibility of special measures when determining if it would be in the interests of justice to admit the statement of the fearful witness.

Section 23(3) of the Criminal Justice Act 1988 raised a number of questions about the fearful witness which were subsequently answered by the courts. In *R v Acton Justices, ex p McMullen* (1991) 92 Cr App R 98, it was argued that the fear of the witness had to be reasonable. Rejecting this argument, the Court stated that it was 'not helpful in the context to speak of the objective or subjective approach. It would be sufficient that the court, on the evidence, was sure that the witness was in fear, as a consequence of the material offence or of something said or done subsequently in relation to it and the possibility of the witness testifying as to it' (at 105).

A similar approach is likely to be taken under s 116(2)(e), requiring a connection between the fear and the offence or the giving of evidence in relation to that offence. The fact that the average witness would not be in fear, or that his/her fear is wholly unreasonable, is irrelevant. The fact that the witness is timid or vulnerable because of age or other factors is relevant, but the test is not subjective. It is simply that it is easier to prove that such witnesses are in fear as a result of the crime or the possibility of testifying as to it. For example, a fragile lady of 82 who was burgled and beaten by the burglars, may well be psychologically damaged by the crime and fearful of giving evidence in open court when she might be faced with her attackers.

Under s 23(3), 'fear' had been construed as including fear of death or injury to one's family, and would doubtless have included others close to the witness. Section 116(3) makes it clear that for the purposes of s 116(2)(e), 'fear' is to be widely construed to include not only the fear of death or injury to oneself but also the fear of death or injury of another person, or the fear of financial loss. Whether financial loss would have sufficed for the purposes of the 1988 Act was never raised, but one can readily see that the threat to fire bomb a witness's business or home could be as effective as, if not more effective than, a threat to his person. How much financial loss will be sufficient to satisfy the sub-section and justify the admission of a statement instead of oral evidence by the witness, remains to be seen.

The wording of s 23(3) of the 1988 Act, 'does not give evidence through fear', raised the question whether a person who came to court, took the oath and started to give evidence but refused to go on, or took the oath and refused to give any evidence, was within the section. It was argued in *ex p McMullen* that the wording of the subsection meant that it did not apply when a witness who had started to give evidence stopped through fear. As soon as the witness uttered one word of evidence the section ceased to apply. The court rejected this argument, holding that the better interpretation of the section was that the witness 'should not have given evidence of any significant relevance to the case'. The wording of s 116(2)(e), 'does not give (or does not continue to give) oral evidence', ensures that the wide interpretation placed on the old wording continues to apply.

If the witness attends court the court can determine the issue for itself; that the witness is in fear can be inferred from his/her demeanour. In *R v Ashford and Tenterden Justices, ex p Hilden* (1993) 96 Crim App R 92, the accused was committed for trial on a charge of causing grievous bodily harm to his girlfriend, after the magistrates allowed the written statement of the girlfriend to be admitted under s 23 of the 1988 Act. The girlfriend went into the witness box and took the oath, but instead of giving evidence in accordance with her statement to the police, she said she could not remember or had no comment to make. The prosecution applied to the magistrate to have the statement admitted under s 23 because the girl was in fear. The magistrate saw for herself that the girl was in fear and, since she had given no evidence of any significance, admitted the statement. The Divisional Court refused the application for judicial review and upheld the magistrate's decision, holding that the magistrate had satisfied herself from the demeanour of the witness and her responses that the witness was refusing to give evidence through fear.

In *R v James Greer* [1998] Crim LR 572, there had been a serious assault by three men on C and G, both employees in a kebab shop. The sole issue in the case was identification. The Crown sought leave to admit statements of three witnesses, C, D, and G, under s 23 of the 1988 Act on the basis that they were afraid to give live evidence. The recorder dismissed the application in respect of D, but, having heard from C and G, who were both present in court and explained, without being sworn, why they could not give evidence, and having noted that their evidence was crucial, he concluded that they both fell within s 23 and allowed their statements to be read. On appeal it was argued that the recorder had erred because in the circumstances C and G did not fall within s 23; rather than refusing to give evidence or relying on secondary evidence of their fear, they had attended court to tell the recorder why they were not going to give evidence. Dismissing the appeal, the Court of

Appeal held there was no reason, either as a matter of practice or on the wording of the statute, why the recorder should not hear from the persons concerned of their actual fear. C and G were not in fact giving evidence as they were not sworn, and what they said was not evidence in the case. It was helpful and sensible for the court to determine the matter before the time came for the witness to give evidence; if the circumstances then changed, the matter would be reviewed.

When the witness is not present in court at all there is a major difficulty. One can only rely on admissible evidence to prove that the witness is in fear. In *Neill v North Antrim Magistrates' Court* (1993) 97 Crim App R 121, police officers recounted what the two witnesses, who did not give evidence through fear, had told their mother. This was clearly hearsay, being a third-hand account of the witnesses' apprehension. Since there was no other evidence given of their fear, the House of Lords held that the statements should not have been admitted. However, Lord Mustill, giving a judgment which was adopted by all of their Lordships, pointed out that the police officers could have given evidence of what the witnesses had said about their fear, it being long-established law that a person's declaration as to his contemporaneous state of mind is admissible to prove the existence of that state of mind (*R v Blastland* [1986] AC 41, 54). It was emphasised that the evidence must *not* be that the witnesses were afraid (that is an inference for the court to draw), but that the witnesses said they were afraid and that their demeanour was consistent with what they had said.

In *R v H, W and M* (2001) *The Times*, 6 July, the Court emphasised the need for up-to-date evidence of fear and the need to consider the provisions of the Youth Justice and Criminal Evidence Act 1999. As noted in **Chapter 2**, the Act provides for special measures to assist witnesses to give evidence, or better evidence. Under s 17, witnesses are eligible for assistance if the court is satisfied that the quality of evidence given by the witness is likely to be diminished by reason of fear or distress on the part of the witness in connection with testifying in those proceedings. Section 17(2)(a),(b) and (c) set out the factors the court must take into account in determining whether a witness qualifies. If the witness does qualify, the special measures in ss 23 to 28 are available. These measures must now be considered by the court, in appropriate cases, before giving leave under s 116(2)(e), the emphasis being on allowing the opportunity to cross-examine the witness whenever possible, s 116(2)(e) being seen as something of a last resort.

In that case, the Court of Appeal allowed the appeal of the defendants against convictions for kidnapping and possession of firearms with intent to endanger life, because the trial judge had wrongly admitted the statement of a witness who was said to be unwilling to give evidence through fear. The witness had made three statements to the police. On 29 June, the police took a short statement from the frightened witness to the effect that he would not give evidence because he feared repercussions against himself and his family. The trial started on 1 September and the prosecution had no contact with the frightened witness between those dates. The trial judge accepted the evidence of the police that the witness said he was in fear, and admitted the statements under s 23(3) and s 26 of the 1988 Act. On appeal it was held that the evidence of fear was out of date. The question for the trial judge was whether the witness would not give evidence through fear on 1 September when he made his ruling, not whether he was in fear on 29 June when he gave a statement to the police:

In their Lordships' judgment, before the court could be satisfied that a witness did not give oral evidence through fear, the court should be informed of any, and if so what efforts had been made to persuade the witness to attend or to alleviate his fears, by, for example, an offer of witness protection, or of screens at court. Another aspect of the inquiry was to establish what might be done to enable the court to know directly from the witness why he was in fear. The best possible source of this information was likely to be the witness himself, giving oral testimony to the judge.

If that was not practical, the Court recommended that the prosecution should interview any witness asserting fear on a video link, or indeed to have a tape recording of the actual conversation, in order for the judge fully to appreciate that proper efforts had been made to secure his or her attendance. Such information would allow the court to assess as the level of the determination of the witness not to give evidence, and the reasons on which it was founded. Whether information of that kind bore strictly on the issues arising under s 23(3)(b), if that paragraph was given a restricted interpretation, it would in most cases normally be relevant to the court's decision whether the statement ought to be admitted in the interests of justice.

In summary, therefore, if the witness is present in court the trial judge can directly determine the degree of fear and determination not to give oral evidence, and is required, in appropriate cases, by s 116(4)(c), to have regard to the provisions of the 1999 Act to see if the measures available under that Act will enable the witness to overcome his fear and to give oral evidence. If the witness does not appear in court the prosecution must consider the possibility that such measures might persuade the witness to give evidence, or, if he is determined not to give evidence, provide the court with up-to-date and reliable evidence of the fact that he is in fear. Though not a requirement of the 2003 Act, the courts are likely to follow the above decision and require that the statement of the fearful witness be recorded on tape or video, so that the court can properly determine that he is in fear and assess his determination not to give evidence.

Section 116(4) provides that the court should give leave under s 116(2)(e) only if it is of the opinion that the statement ought to be admitted in the interests of justice. In making this assessment, it should have regard:

(a) to the statement's contents;

(b) to any risk that its admission or exclusion would result in unfairness to any party to the proceedings (and in particular to how difficult it will be to challenge the statement if the relevant person does not give oral evidence);

(c) to whether, in appropriate cases, a special measures direction could be made under s 19 of the Youth Justice and Criminal Evidence Act 1999; and

(d) to any other relevant circumstances.

It will be noted that s 116(4) applies only to s 116(2)(e), the statement of a fearful witness. Under s 26 of the 1988 Act, the court had a discretion to admit a statement when a witness was unavailable for any of the five reasons referred to in s 109(2), using terminology similar to that set out in s 116(4)(a) and (b), though the 1988 Act required the court to have regard to the 'contents of the statement' and 'to any risk, ... that its admission or exclusion will result in unfairness to the accused'. Section 116(4)(a) is largely the same, but s 116(4)(b) refers to any risk that the admission or exclusion of the statement will result in unfairness to any party to the proceedings (not simply the defendant), and in particular to how difficult it will be to challenge the statement if the relevant person does not give oral evidence. In both cases, the underlying concern would seem to be the possibility of unfairness resulting from the absence of the witness and the inability to cross-examine in the traditional way. Decisions under the 1988 Act may thus throw some light on how the courts will interpret s 116(4).

In the leading case on the exercise of the discretion under the 1988 Act, *R v Cole* [1990] 1 WLR 866, Cole was convicted of an assault on a security guard. The prosecution applied for the statement of a deceased witness to be admitted under s 23. The defence, who disputed the circumstances of the assault as described in the witness's statement, resisted the application. The trial judge ruled that in relation to s 26(b)(ii), which refers to the possibility of 'controverting' the statement (s 116(4)(b) of the 2003 Act refers to inability to 'challenge' the statement), the defendant might, if he chose, controvert (challenge) the statement by his own evidence or that of other witnesses. On appeal it was contended that the trial judge had erred in ruling that the defendant might controvert the statement by his own evidence or that of other witnesses. This, it was said, had the effect of putting improper pressure on the defence to call witnesses. The trial judge should have had regard to the words 'any risk' of unfairness arising from the inability to cross-examine the witness, particularly given the importance of the statement in the proceedings.

Dismissing the appeal, the Court of Appeal noted that in exercising the discretion under s 26, the court was not required to disregard the likelihood of the possibility of controverting the statement by the evidence of the accused or of witnesses called on his behalf. The overall purpose of the provisions in ss 25 and 26 was to widen the power of the court to admit documentary hearsay evidence, while ensuring that the accused received a fair trial. In judging how to achieve fairness, a balance had on occasions to be struck between the interests of the public in enabling the prosecution case to be properly presented, and the interests of a particular defendant in not being put in a disadvantageous position, for example by the death or illness of a witness. The point of balance was set out in the sections. The matters to which the court must have regard included any risk of unfairness, having regard to the possibility of controverting the statement. Counsel for the appellant had argued that the words should be restricted to the possibility of it being controverted by cross-examination of prosecution witnesses. However, there was no reason to imply any such restriction upon the plain meaning of the words. The meaning of 'controvert' included that of 'dispute' or 'contradict'. The court was entitled to have regard to such information as it had at the time that the application to admit was made. It could not require to be told whether the accused intended to give evidence or to call witnesses, but it was not required to assess the possibility of controverting the statement upon the basis that the accused would do neither. The decision of an accused whether or not to give evidence or call witnesses was to be made by him by reference to the admissible evidence put before the court, and he had no right, for the purposes of the provision, to be treated as having no possibility of controverting the statement because of his right not to give evidence or to call witnesses. If Parliament had intended the question to be considered on that basis, express words would have been used to make the intention clear. Thus a complex balancing exercise had to be performed whereby the court must consider the contents of the statement, which might leave relevant questions unanswered and appear to provide evidence of greater certainty than is warranted having regard to the absence of those answers.

As Lord Griffith had observed in *R v Scott* (1989) 89 Cr App R 153, it was the quality of the evidence in the statement that was the crucial factor that should determine the exercise of the discretion. Thus the weight to be attached to the inability to cross-examine, and the magnitude of any consequential risk that admission of the statement would result in unfairness to the accused, would depend in part on the court's assessment of the quality of the evidence shown by the contents of the statement. Here the court was entitled, indeed required, to consider how far any potential unfairness, arising from the inability to cross-examine on the statement, might effectively be counterbalanced by a proper warning, which was given by the judge in the present case. The court would also, for example, consider whether, having regard to other evidence available to the prosecution, the interests of justice would be properly served by excluding the statement. The judge had asked himself whether it had been shown that it was in the interests of justice that the statement be admitted. He had clearly thought that the risk of unfairness, having regard to the availability of other witnesses for cross-examination and of other evidence, was minimal. In his view, it was in the interests of justice for the jury to be given the fuller picture provided by the statement, subject to the necessary warning. He was entitled to reach that conclusion.

If this decision is followed, as it is likely to be given the similarity between the sections, the courts will seek to achieve a balance between the contents of the statement and the risk of unfairness to any party from the inability to cross-examine if the statement is admitted or excluded. The quality of the evidence in the statement, will be the crucial factor. The higher the quality of the evidence in the statement, the less risk there will be of unfairness to any party resulting from the inability to cross-examine. The degree of quality will also impact on the question whether it is in the interests of justice to admit the statement: the higher the quality, the more important the statement will be to the issues in the case, and the interests of justice would demand that such evidence be admitted. It will be noted that the Court of Appeal approved the warning given to the jury by the trial judge that the statement admitted instead of the oral evidence of the witness had not, as other evidence had, been subjected to cross-examination. This was seen as a counterbalance to any possible unfairness, and became a standard requirement in all cases where a such a statement was admitted. It is likely that a similar warning will become a standard requirement when statements are admitted under s 116.

Where the accused is responsible for any of the conditions in s 116(2)

Section 116(5) of the 2003 Act provides as follows:

> *(5) A condition set out in any paragraph of subsection (2) which is in fact satisfied is to be treated as not satisfied if it is shown that the circumstances described in the paragraph are caused—*
>
> *(a) by the person in support of whose case it is sought to give the statement in evidence, or*
>
> *(b) by a person acting on his behalf,*
>
> *in order to prevent the relevant person giving oral evidence in the proceedings (whether at all or in connection with the subject matter of the statement).*

While it is not necessary to show that a particular person was responsible for bringing about the circumstances leading to the satisfying of one of the five conditions, if one is satisfied the evidence will not be admissible if the person in support of whose case the admission of the statement is sought, or someone acting on his behalf, can be shown to be responsible for the absence of the person who made the statement (the relevant person). Thus if the defendant has an alibi witness whom he thinks will not stand up to cross-examination, he may cause him to be absent, possibly by sending him abroad or causing him to stay out of the way during the trial. The subsection applies to both prosecution and defence, and is intended to prevent abuse of the provisions for admitting the statements of witnesses who are unavailable to give oral evidence by deliberately causing the condition of their unavailability. It will be for the party opposing the admission of the statement to satisfy the court that the other side is responsible for the operation of the particular condition.

Although it is not mentioned in the Act, the fact that the defendant is responsible for the condition of an important prosecution witness may be a factor in determining whether the statement of that witness should be admitted. It would, for example, be difficult for a defendant to argue against the admission of the statement of a witness who is physically unable to attend if he had been shown to be responsible for the attack on the witness which caused the condition to be satisfied. In *R v Moore* [1992] Crim LR 882, the appellant challenged his conviction on the ground that the trial judge had erred in admitting the statement of an 82-year-old woman who was not fit to attend court. The witness had let a garage to the defendant, who used it to store a car which he claimed had been stolen. He then claimed for its loss on his insurance. The trial took place five years after the committal because the defendant had absconded before trial. He argued that the statement of the elderly woman was crucial and was the foundation of the prosecution case. The only way to challenge it was for the defendant to give evidence, and it was unfair to force him to give evidence in this way. Applying *R v Cole* (see p 213 above) and dismissing the appeal, the Court of Appeal held that the more important the evidence the greater the damage it may do to the defendant, but it did not follow that it was always unfair to the defendant to admit such evidence. There was no general principle that it will be unfair and contrary to the interests of justice to admit a statement if the only way of controverting the statement is for the defendant to go into the witness box. One of the circumstances taken into account by the Court was the fact that the defendant had evaded trial for so long that the prosecution's elderly witness was no longer fit to give evidence. As was stated in *Cole*, fairness required a balance between the prosecution and the defence, and the prosecution should not be put in a disadvantageous position by the illness of a witness, more particularly when the defendant's conduct contributed to such illness.

In *R v M (KJ)* [2003] 2 Cr App R 21, the accused was charged with murder but found unfit to plead, and a hearing was held to determine whether he had committed the acts alleged, which the jury determined that he had. The prosecution witness whose statement was admitted under ss 23 and 26 of the 1988 Act (now s 116(2)(e) and (4) of the 2003 Act) because he was in fear, was the sole witness. M appealed, arguing that the statement should not have been admitted and that its admission was incompatible with Article 6(3)(d) of the European Convention on Human Rights (the right to examine or have examined all witnesses). The Court of Appeal held that there was no invariable rule that a conviction might not be based solely, or to a decisive degree, on the statement of a witness who does not give oral evidence. Although the accused had no opportunity to cross-examine during investigation or trial, a conviction based on such evidence will not necessarily violate Article 6(3)(d). Otherwise s 23 and s 26 of the 1988 Act would never apply, where the essential or only witness was kept out of the way or put in fear. This would be an encouragement to criminals. Where the witness gave evidence that he would not give evidence because threats had been made, and the judge drew the inference that the threats were made by or at the instigation of the accused or with his approval, that would normally be conclusive as to how the discretion under s 26 of the 1988 Act (s 116(4) of the 2003 Act) should be exercised. In considering whether the defence could controvert the statement, the court should not limit itself to the question of whether the defendant could give effective evidence but should also consider the reality of his opportunity to cross-examine as to events, or to put the statement maker's credibility in issue by other means. In the present case the trial judge had failed to attach sufficient weight to the inability of the defendant to go into the witness box (having been found unfit to plead). The suspect nature of the statement was apparent at the outset, therefore the jury's decision was quashed.

It should be noted that the discretion under s 116(6) and (7) to make a direction that a statement is not admissible, is in addition to the statutory and common law power of the court to exclude unfair or prejudicial evidence (see s 78 of the Police and Criminal Evidence Act 1984 and *R v Sang* [1980] AC 402, discussed in **Chapter 7**).

Section 117 – business and other documents

Section 117 of the 2003 Act replaces ss 24 and 25 of the Criminal Justice Act 1988. It provides that documents created or received in the course of a trade, business, profession, etc are admissible if three conditions are satisfied:

(a) oral evidence given in the proceedings would be admissible as evidence of any matter stated;

(b) the requirements of s 117(2) are satisfied; and

(c) the requirements of s 117(5) are satisfied, in a case where s 117(4) requires them to be.

Section 24 of the 1988 Act was worded in similar terms, and it was broadly accepted that statements in business documents which were created or received for the purposes of the business and not for the purposes of criminal investigations or proceedings, were likely to be reliable and less susceptible to challenge by cross-examination. Section 24(4) contained a provision similar to that in s 117(4) and (5), which requires one of the conditions in s 116(2) (ie, where the witness is unavailable to give oral evidence – see pp 205–215 above) to be satisfied if the statement had been made for the purposes of criminal investigations or proceedings.

It must be emphasised that while s 116 is concerned with both oral and written statements, s 117 is concerned only with written statements. Section 117(1) refers to 'a statement contained in a document' and s 117(2)(b) refers to 'information contained in the statement'. The three terms used – 'document', 'statement' and 'information' – need to be clarified. As defined by s 134(1), a 'document' means 'anything in which information of any description is recorded'. A 'document' is therefore merely a container for a statement which has been reduced to writing or another form, such as a tape-recording or any other form of recording. As noted at p 200 above, 'statement' is widely defined by s 115(2) as 'any representation of fact or opinion made by a person by whatever means; and it includes a representation made in a sketch, photofit or other pictorial form'. The Court of Appeal in *R v Carrington* [1994] Crim LR 438 held that a document may contain more than one statement, and this is impliedly accepted by s 117(2)(a), which refers to 'the document or part containing the statement'. Every statement contains 'information', and in this context the supplier of the information contained in the statement which is contained in the document must have had, or be reasonably supposed to have had, personal knowledge of the matters dealt with. The supplier of the information is the 'relevant person' for the purposes of s 117(5), in respect of whom one of the conditions set out in s 116(2) must be satisfied.

The requirements of s 117(2)

A statement contained in a document will be admitted under s 117(2) provided that three conditions are satisfied:

(a) the document was created or received by a person in the course of a trade, business, profession or other occupation, or by the holder of a paid or unpaid office; and

(b) the person who supplied the information in the statement (the relevant person) had or may reasonably be supposed to have had personal knowledge of the matters dealt with in the statement; and

(c) each person through whom the information was supplied received the information in the course of a trade, business or profession, or as the holder of a paid or unpaid office.

It had been argued that since s 24 of the 1988 Act applied to documents received or created by a person in the course of a trade, business, etc, it was capable of applying to all those documents admitted under s 23 of that Act, rendering that section unnecessary (see further J C Smith, 'Sections 23 and 24 of the Criminal Justice Act 1988: (1) Some Problems' [1994] Crim LR 426). Thus a statement dictated to a police officer by a witness was a statement in a document 'created' by the police officer. A statement written by a witness and handed to a police officer is 'received' by the police officer in the course of his profession, from information given by the witness, and was prima facie admissible under s 24. Similarly, if the witness dictated his statement to a solicitor, or wrote his own statement and passed it to his solicitor. The statement would have been 'created' or 'received' by the solicitor in the course of his profession and the literal terms of s 24 were satisfied.

Section 117(2)(a) uses exactly the same terminology, therefore, as with the previous law, there will be circumstances in which a statement in a document will be admissible under either s 116 or s 117. However, all statements admitted under s 116 must satisfy one of the conditions in s 116(2). Under s 117(4) and (5), a statement in a document prepared for the purposes of pending or contemplated criminal proceedings, or for a criminal investigation, must also satisfy one of the five conditions in s 116(2), or the additional condition in s 117(5)(b), if it is to be admitted. If the statement was not prepared for the purposes of criminal proceedings then none of those conditions need be satisfied. In practice there will rarely any advantage to be gained in using s 117 rather than s 116. The rare occasion when it might be advantageous to use s 117 is when one seeks to rely on s 117(5)(b), which is discussed at pp 219–221 below.

It is also doubtful whether the court, applying s 117(6) and (7), will allow unreliable or undesirable evidence to be admitted where the party seeking to rely on it uses the 'device' of handing the document to a person who receives it in the course of his trade or business, etc. If the statement in a document is a purely business document, it matters, little whether reliance is placed on the document being 'received' or 'created' in the course of a trade, business, etc. If it was prepared for criminal proceedings or a criminal investigation, one is thrown back on s 116(2), and in such a case one might as well proceed under s 116, unless one seeks to rely on s 117(5)(b) (see the example given in the discussion at p 220 of *R v Carrington*).

Where the creator, recipient of the document and the supplier of the information are the same person

Section 117(3) states that the persons mentioned in s 117(2)(a) and (b) may be the same person. This will be the case where A puts the information he has into a written form, or otherwise records it. He is then the creator of the document and the supplier of the information it contains. If he then posts it to himself, in the manner of the best spy novels, he would, in due course, become the recipient of the document he created which contains information supplied by him. It may also be noted that while s 117(2)(a) requires that the document was created or received by a person in the course of a trade, business, profession, etc, that trade, business, profession, etc need not have any connection with the statement in the document, nor with the maker of that statement or the supplier of the information. For example, a robbery occurs which is witnessed by A, a shop assistant. He tells the driver of a delivery truck what he saw, and the driver writes it down. The driver passes the statement in a document to a police officer. The shop assistant has left the area and cannot be found. Section 117 is prima facie satisfied. The truck driver created the document in the course of a trade or business. The police officer received it in the course of his trade or business. A, the person who supplied the information in the statement, had personal knowledge of the matters dealt with. However, in this case s 117(4) requires that the additional requirements of s 117(5) must be satisfied (ie, one of the conditions in s 116(2) must be satisfied), as it will be if A cannot be found. Therefore, though the statement could be admitted under s 117, there is no advantage in seeking to admit it under that section given that s 116 applies.

If A was a passer-by who, having given the information without identifying himself, has not been found, s 116(1)(b) would not be satisfied (see pp 204–205 above), the person making the statement not being identified to the court's satisfaction. The identification of the statement maker, though a requirement of s 116, is not a requirement of s 117, but s117(6) and (7) allow the trial judge to refuse to admit a statement under the section if the judge is not satisfied as to its reliability given its contents, the source of the information contained in it, the way in which or the circumstances in which the information was supplied or received, or the way in which or the circumstances in which the document was created or received.

Multiple hearsay under s 117

Section 123(2) provides that a statement may not be admitted under s 117 if any person who supplied or received the information, or created or received the document, did not have the required capability or, where that person cannot be identified, cannot reasonably be assumed to have had the required capability. It follows that if anyone who supplied or received the information that is the subject of an application to admit under s 117 was not at the time competent to give oral evidence, the information cannot be admitted.

Although multiple hearsay is not admissible under s 116, s 116(1)(a) of that section refers to 'oral evidence given in the proceedings by the person who made the statement'. Section 117, however, does not require that a particular person should have been able to give oral evidence, but simply that 'oral evidence given in the proceedings would be admissible as evidence of that matter'. It follows that it does not matter that the facts are inadmissible hearsay if the informant sought to give evidence of those facts. The facts themselves could be the subject of direct evidence by the person who perceived those facts. Therefore multiple hearsay, if relevant, which is contained in a statement in a document, is admissible under s 117, provided the other conditions of admissibility are satisfied under s 121.

As noted at pp 203–204 above, the reason for excluding multiple hearsay from the unavailability exception in s 116 was the belief that with each additional step in the chain of communication the risk of error or fabrication increases. That risk is considerably reduced where the chain of communication is contained within a business context, therefore multiple hearsay will be admissible under s 117 provided that the requirements of s 117(2) are satisfied, particularly that in s 117(2)(c). A safeguard is provided by s 117(6) and (7), so that if the trial judge becomes aware that the relevant person received the information second- or third-hand in circumstances of unreliability, he can make a direction that the statement is not admissible.

This provides for the chain of communications which may exist in a business environment. Suppose a workman on a production line allocates a number to a cylinder block. He tells his foreman, who tells the line manager, who tells the records clerk, who enters the information onto a computer. The document containing the statement which contains the information (the computer disk or print out) was created in the course of a trade, business, etc, by the clerk from information supplied by the man on the production line, who had personal knowledge of the matters dealt with, indirectly through the agency of the foreman and line manager, each of whom received the information in the course of their trade or business. Thus s 117(2)(c) is satisfied and the evidence would be admissible.

The 'relevant person' in this chain of communication is the workman who allocated the number to the cylinder block, who passed the information to the foreman. Under the previous legislation there was much confusion as to who was the maker of the statement who had to be shown to be dead, ill, etc. In *R v Deroda* [2000] 1 Cr App R 41, it was finally made clear that it was the person who made the statement as a representation of facts that had been placed in a document. Thus where A passes information to B, who passes it to C, who writes it down or otherwise records it, A is the person who made the representation of fact that had been placed in the document and is the relevant person for the purposes of these sections (it may be noted that since the document above was a purely business document, s 117(4) and (5) do not apply and none of the requirements of s 116(2), nor the additional requirement in s 117(5)(b), need be satisfied).

The additional condition in s 117(5)(b)
Where none of the requirements laid down in s 116(2) can be met, an alternative condition is provided by s 117(5)(b) where the statement was made for the purposes of criminal

proceedings or investigation. This may apply if 'the relevant person cannot reasonably be expected to have any recollection of the matters dealt with in the statement (having regard to the length of time since he supplied the information and all other circumstances)'.

The facts of *R v Carrington* [1994] Crim LR 438 provide an example of the circumstances in which this provision might apply. A man attempted to use a stolen credit card in a supermarket. The cashier called a supervisor, B, who called another supervisor, S, who was about to go off duty. B told the customer that she was going to check on the card, and S left the store on the way to her car. The man left the supermarket and S saw the man, whom she recognised as the customer tendering the suspect credit card, driving a white Peugeot car at high speed out of the car park. She made a note on a magazine of the make of the car, the registration number and a brief description of the man. She went back into the store and, using the internal telephone, passed the description of the man and the car to B, who noted it on her memo pad. S then went home without checking that the memo was correct, and did not keep the magazine.

The accused, the owner of the white Peugeot seen by S, was arrested. He, as was the customer, was black. He said that someone else, whom he declined to identify, had borrowed his car on the day in question. An identification parade some two and a half months after the offence proved inconclusive; the cashier could not identify the defendant and S only thought it was number 5 (the defendant's number). The memo was admitted as exhibit MB1 as a business document under what would now be s 117 (formerly s 24 of the Criminal Justice Act 1988). The appellant challenged his conviction, arguing that the memo MB1 should not have been admitted in evidence.

Dismissing the appeal, the Court of Appeal held that s 24(4) of the Criminal Justice Act 1988 applied and the issue was whether the requirements of s 24(4)(iii) (now s 117(5)(b)) were satisfied, ie that the person who made the statement could not reasonably be expected, having regard to the time which had elapsed since he made it and to all the circumstances, to have any recollection of the matters dealt with in it. The parties had wrongly agreed that B was the maker of the statement (the relevant person) contained in memo MB1; it should have been S. She could remember passing on the information about the man and the car and giving the registration number, but could not recall the registration number when giving evidence in court. The fact that S was available to give direct evidence, and did give direct evidence, was the basis of the defence objection to the admissibility of the memo under s 24. The argument was essentially that if a person was present and did give evidence, he or she should not fall within s 24. Rejecting that argument, the Court held that a document consists of a number of statements, therefore parts of the document may be admissible as independent statements notwithstanding that the maker has a clear recollection of some parts of the document. The prosecution were therefore entitled to treat the part of document MB1 which contained the registration number of the car as an independent statement for the purposes of s 24. The condition in s 24(4)(iii) was satisfied, since the witness could not reasonably be expected to recollect the details of the registration number given the length of time since she saw it and all other circumstances.

It will be noted that in the above scenario, supervisor B received the information during the course of her trade or business and the statement in the document was created by her from information supplied by supervisor S, who clearly had personal knowledge of the matters dealt with. In this case the statement was prepared for the purposes of a criminal investigation, therefore s 117(4) requires that a condition in s 116(2), or the additional condition in s 117(5), be satisfied. Since S was present and able to give evidence, none of the conditions in s 116(2) could be satisfied. However, s 117(5)(b) would apply.

Section 118 – preservation of certain common law categories of admissibility

The common law originally developed a number of exceptions to the rule against hearsay, arguably because it was recognised that too strict an application of the rule denies to the court and jury what might well be relevant and cogent evidence. Those exceptions concerning documentary evidence, such as public documents and works of reference such as maps and plans, are now of less importance given that they are admissible under s 110 of the 2003 Act, while matters of reputation or family tradition, and evidence of reputation as to character, are extremely rare in criminal cases. They will not therefore be considered here.

Formal and informal admissions, and declarations against interest, were admitted at common law on the basis that a person is unlikely to speak falsely against himself. In criminal proceedings, such admissions are seen as confessions (as defined by s 82(1) of the Police and Criminal Evidence Act 1984) and have traditionally constituted an exception to the hearsay rule at common law (their admissibility is now governed by ss 76 and 78 of that Act – see **Chapter 7**). Therefore, only *res gestae*, common enterprise and expert evidence will be considered in this chapter. Before doing so, it should be borne in mind that all common law exceptions were decided on a case-by-case basis and, inevitably, some are more developed than others. For that reason, some of them are uncertain in their scope and await further development.

Res gestae

This exception, preserved by s 118(1) 4, is in fact a label covering a number of exceptions. The expression *res gestae* is a corruption of a larger Latin phrase which simply means that it is part of the story. The basis of the exception is that the human action consists of words and actions, and often the actions cannot be understood without the words. Looking at the actions in isolation may give a false impression. Looking at the actions and hearing the accompanying words which were spoken at or about the same time should, in theory at least, assist discovery of the truth. It should also be pointed out that because s 116 of the 2003 Act provides for the admissibility of oral statement and statements in a document where the maker of the statement is unavailable (see pp 205–215 above), reliance may be placed on that section rather than one of the *res gestae* exceptions where, as will often be the case, the maker of the statement is dead or otherwise unavailable. There is thus a potential overlap between s 116 and the exceptions preserved by this section.

There are three categories of statements admissible under this head:

(a) statements made by a person so emotionally overpowered by an event that the possibility of concoction or distortion can be disregarded;

(b) statements accompanied by an act that explain the act of the maker;

(c) statements of a person's own contemporaneous state of mind.

Section 118(1) 4 (a) – Statements made by a person so emotionally overpowered by an event that the possibility of concoction or distortion can be disregarded

This is the most important application of the *res gestae* principle – at least, it has been the subject of more judicial decisions than the other two categories. American lawyers sometimes describe it as the 'Excited Utterance Rule', because the statement must be made spontaneously and contemporaneously with the events subject of the trial. The basis of the admissibility of spontaneous statements made contemporaneously with the events making up or connected with the offence, which is usually a serious and violent offence but need not be so, is that the instinctive and spontaneous reaction to sudden and unusual events effectively rules out the possibility of fabrication or concoction by the maker. Many cases involve statements by the deceased person about the cause of his injuries, but the exception is not confined to statements about the cause of the victim's injuries, neither is it a necessary condition of admissibility that the declarant be dead.

A good example of the exception is found in *R v Fowkes* (1856) *The Times*, 8 March. There a witness to a murder was heard to shout, 'There's Butcher!' (the name by which Fowkes was known), just as a face appeared at the window from which the fatal shot had been fired. The policeman who had heard this was allowed to give evidence of doing so. In *Ratten*, considered at p 188 above, the Privy Council held that if, contrary to their decision, the telephone call from the victim had been hearsay, it was admissible as part of the *res gestae*.

The requirement that the statement be made contemporaneously with the relevant act does not mean that the statement and act must exactly coincide in point of time. At one time the common law did require exact contemporaneity. For example, in *R v Bedingfield* (1879) 14 Cox CC 341, the victim staggered out of a room in which she had been with B, with her throat cut. Pointing to the wound, she said to her aunt, 'Oh dear Aunt, see what Harry [Bedingfield] has done to me'. This was excluded because '[i]t was not part of anything done, nor something said while something was being done, but something said after something was done'. (The trial judge contrasted this with a cry such as 'Don't Harry!' uttered while the act was done which, if heard by the aunt, would have been admissible.) However, this decision no longer represents the law.

The leading case in this area is now *R v Andrews* [1987] AC 281. A was charged with murder. The victim had been stabbed and fatally wounded. Immediately after the attack he staggered downstairs to the flat of a neighbour, seeking assistance. Shortly afterwards the police arrived, and the victim made a statement identifying A and another as his assailants. He died some two months later of his injuries. The police officers were allowed to give evidence of what the victim told them as part of the *res gestae*. The House of Lords held that this evidence had been properly admitted as evidence of the truth of the facts asserted. Lord Ackner, with whom all of their Lordships agreed, summarised the relevant principles to be applied when admitting evidence under the *res gestae* doctrine, as follows:

(1) The primary question which the judge must ask himself is: can the possibility of concoction or distortion be disregarded?

(2) To answer that question the judge must first consider the circumstances in which the particular statement was made, in order to satisfy himself that the event was so unusual or startling or dramatic as to dominate the thoughts of the victim, so that his

utterance was an instinctive reaction to that event, thus giving no real opportunity for reasoned reflection. In such a situation the judge would be entitled to conclude that the involvement or pressure of the event would exclude the possibility of concoction or distortion, providing that the statement was made in conditions of approximate but not exact contemporaneity.

(3) In order for the statement to be sufficiently `spontaneous' it must be so closely associated with the event which has excited the statement that it can fairly be stated that the mind of the declarant was still dominated by the event. Thus the judge must be satisfied that the event which provided the trigger mechanism for the statement was still operative. The fact that the statement was made in response to a question is but one factor to consider under this heading.

(4) Quite apart form the time factor, there may be special features in the case, which relate to the possibility of concoction or distortion. In the instant appeal the defence relied on evidence to support the contention that the deceased had a purpose of his own to fabricate or concoct, namely a malice ... The judge must be satisfied that the circumstances were such that, having regard to the special feature of malice, there was no possibility of a concoction or distortion to the advantage of the maker or the disadvantage of the accused.

(5) As to the possibility of error in the facts narrated in the statement, if only the ordinary fallibility of human recollection is relied on, this goes to the weight to be attached to and not the admissibility of the statement and is therefore a matter for the jury. However, here again there may be special features that may give rise to the possibility of error. In the instant case there was evidence that the deceased had drunk to excess. Another example would be where the identification was made in circum- stances of particular difficulty or where the declarant suffered from defective eyesight. In such circumstances the trial judge must consider whether he can exclude the possibility of error. (at 300–301)

Thus, while approximate contemporaneity is required, the emphasis is on the reliability of the statement. The shorter the time gap between the event and the statement, and the more dramatic and unusual the event is, the less likely it is that there has been concoction or distortion. In *Andrews* the time gap was some 15 minutes. It was, however, emphasised that the *res gestae* doctrine should not be used to avoid calling witnesses who can give direct evidence of the matter (see also *Edwards and Osakwe v DPP* [1992] Crim LR 576).

In *Tobi v Nicholas* [1987] Crim LR 774, the accused was convicted of failing to stop after an accident. The evidence was that the accused's car had collided with a coach and had failed to stop. Some 20 minutes after the accident a police officer went to a house where the damaged car was parked, and there heard the coach driver identify the accused as the driver of the car which had collided with him. The officer was allowed to give evidence of this oral identification, the court ruling that it was admissible under the *res gestae* doc- trine. The conviction was quashed on the ground that the coach driver, who was available, had not been called to give evidence. It was also said that the event was not so dramatic as to have dominated the mind of the maker of the statement. This, together with the fact that the statement was made some 20 minutes after the event, did not rule out the possi- bility of error or concoction. The fact that the evidence was excluded partly because it came 20 minutes after the event does not mean that this is the upper limit of approximate contemporaneity. Had the event been more dramatic or unusual, the mind of the maker might still be dominated by it. A minor road accident was neither of these.

In *R v Carnall* [1995] Crim LR 944, the accused was charged with the murder of V, a person who knew him very well. Part of the evidence against him was what V had said after the attack and before his subsequent death. Two witnesses had seen V in the street outside their house. He was bleeding and asking for help. He said he had been attacked with knives and a baseball bat, and it had taken him about an hour to crawl from his home to the house. The witnesses asked him who had attacked him, and he named the defendant. A police officer went with the victim to the hospital. In reply to the officer's questions, the victim named the accused, and gave details of the attack and the background to it. The trial judge admitted both statements as part of the *res gestae*. On appeal it was argued that he had been wrong to do so, first, because of the time which had elapsed between the attack and the making of the statements, over an hour between the attack and the first statement and nearer two hours in respect of the second statement, coupled with the fact that the statements had been made only in response to questions; secondly, the victim had acted dishonestly in the past and could not be relied upon; and thirdly, the victim had lost a lot of blood, which resulted in loss of oxygen to the brain which could cause confusion.

Dismissing the appeal, it was held that the crucial question was whether there was any real possibility of concoction or distortion, or whether the judge felt confident that that the thoughts of the maker of the statements were at the time so dominated by what had happened that what he said could be regarded as unaffected by ex post facto reasoning or fabrication. In answering this question the judge had taken account of the of the appalling nature of the attack itself, the frightful injuries that were inflicted, the pain that the victim was undergoing, and the obsession he had at the time with getting help and trying to stay alive. The time factor was not conclusive. As to the question of dishonesty, the judge had properly taken the view that the question was not whether the victim had been honest throughout his life, but whether in the context of this particular situation there was anything to suggest he would do otherwise than tell the first person he saw who had inflicted this appalling injury on him. Thirdly, counsel relied on medical evidence about the possible effect of the loss of blood. The judge had rightly taken the view that this was theoretical, there being no evidence to suggest that the victim was suffering from anoxia. It can be assumed that the central issue here was not one of time, but whether there was a real possibility of concoction or distortion as a result of the lapse of time or any other proven factor.

In *R v Newport* [1998] Crim LR 581, the facts were similar to those in *Ratten* (see p 188 above). The defendant's wife left the house after an argument. Newport, who was holding a bread knife, having been making a sandwich, pursued her down the road. The wife suffered a stab wound, which caused her death. The prosecution case was that the accused deliberately stabbed her to death. He denied this and claimed the death was an accident. Evidence was admitted of a telephone call made by the wife to a friend on the evening of her death. The friend said that the wife was agitated and frightened, and had asked if she could come to the friend's house if she had to flee in a hurry. This evidence was admitted as part of the *res gestae* and the accused was convicted. (The relevance of this evidence lies in the deceased's agitated and frightened state and the claim that she might need to flee her husband. Since he claimed the death was an accident, evidence that the wife was in fear and preparing to flee contradicted this and was clearly relevant.) The Court of Appeal found that the evidence of the telephone call had been admitted on the basis that it had been made immediately before the wife left the house, when in fact it had been made 20 minutes earlier. In view of that, it was held that the evidence was not a spontaneous and unconsidered reaction to an immediate impending emergency and should not have been admitted. However, in view of the other evidence before the jury the conviction was not unsafe.

As these cases make clear, the admissibility of spontaneous exclamations as *res gestae* is governed by the test laid down in *Andrews*. There is no longer a strict requirement of contemporaneity between the event and the exclamation. What is essential is that the trial judge is satisfied that the 'possibility of concoction or distortion can be disregarded', which involves considering whether 'the event was so unusual or startling or dramatic as to dominate the thoughts' of the declarant.

In *Attorney-General's Reference (No 1 of 2003)* [2003] Crim LR 547, the defendant was charged with causing grievous bodily harm to his mother. The prosecution told the court that they thought the accused's mother might not give true evidence, and sought to call witnesses who had heard her call out to them, saw her in distress and heard her identify the accused as her attacker. The trial judge refused to admit this evidence as *res gestae* because the better evidence of the victim was available. The Court of Appeal held that there was no rider to the *res gestae* exception that it was not applicable when better evidence was available. Nonetheless, while the prosecution had not sought to disadvantage the defence by not calling the victim, it was unfair to the defence not to call her and rely on *res gestae* evidence. However, had the prosecution not called the victim, the trial judge could have excluded the *res gestae* evidence under s 78 of the Police and Criminal Evidence Act 1984 as being in breach of the fair trial provisions of Article 6(1) of the European Convention on Human Rights. One way around this kind of problem might have been be to call the victim and, if she did not give the expected evidence, to call the other witnesses, whose evidence would then be admissible under the *res gestae* exception.

While most statements admitted under the *res gestae* principle are made by victims who are not able to give evidence, the rule applies to statements made by the accused as well. Where those statements involve an admission they are admissible as a confession, but the *res gestae* principle could apply to statements not amounting to an admission. Thus in *R v Glover* [1991] Crim LR 48, a man assaulted another man and was forcibly restrained by other persons present. He shouted, 'I am David Glover', and made threats to shoot the man and his family. There was a possibility that the man was not David Glover but, having considered that possibility and discounted it, the judge admitted evidence from witnesses of hearing the accused shout his name and make the threats. If one takes the facts of *Bedingfield* (above), where the accused was in a room alone with the deceased victim who was stabbed, the fact that the victim was heard to shout, 'Put that knife down Harry' would be admissible to prove that Bedingfield had a knife and used it to kill the victim, as would a statement by Bedingfield if he had been heard to say, 'I'm Harry Bedingfield and I've come to do for you'.

Section 118(1) 4 (b) – Statements that accompany and explain acts of the maker
In order to be admissible, the statement must relate to, accompany and explain the act, which must itself be relevant; and must be made contemporaneously with the act and by the actor. A simple example is that of a person who runs off on the approach of a police officer. In isolation it looks like a guilty act; however, if it is accompanied by the words, 'Sorry, I must run, the last bus leaves in two minutes', it takes on a different meaning. Most examples of this exception are to be found in the civil law. Thus in order to prove that money was a gift, a witness would be allowed to say in evidence that she heard the claimant say, on handing over money, 'This is for your birthday'.

In *R v McCay* [1990] 1 WLR 645, the Court of Appeal applied this principle to the admission of evidence concerning the identification of the accused at a pre-trial identification parade. The identifying witness, who viewed the parade through a one-way glass screen, said to the police officer, 'It's number 8', but he could not remember that number when he came to give evidence at trial. The police officer was permitted to give evidence that the witness had said 'It's number 8', because those words accompanied and explained a relevant act.

The same result could have been achieved using the means suggested above in *R v Osbourne and Virtue* [1973] QB 678. Here, an eyewitness had identified Osbourne at an identification parade, but at trial claimed that 'she did not remember that she had picked out anyone on the last parade'. The prosecution had to call a police inspector to confirm the positive identification. The Court of Appeal upheld the trial judge's decision to admit the evidence, although it preferred a somewhat doubtful application of the *res gestae* principle as the basis of its decision. The decision compares unfavourably with that in *Kearley* (see pp 196–197 above), where the telephone calls and words of the personal callers could fit into the *res gestae* exception if the offence was seen as a continuing offence during the time the officers were in the flat so that those words accompanied the continuing act. However, little attention was given to this possibility. In an unreported case involving the manslaughter of a young man, a witness was allowed to give evidence that the deceased, who was seen running from a group of young men and who was later found at the foot of a cliff having apparently run over the edge, had told him he was running away from the defendant who was out to get him. That statement would also come within *Andrews* exception if made contemporaneously with the events leading to his death, which demonstrates that there is degree of overlap between the three categories of *res gestae*.

Section 118(1) 4 (c) – Statements of the maker's own contemporaneous state of mind
Statements by a person which indicate the physical or mental state of that person are admissible on the basis that only that person knows how he feels, and there would be no way of proving such feelings unless his statement were admissible. The rule regarding contemporaneity is more flexible in this area. It may, for example, include a statement about the maker's physical or mental condition yesterday, or at some earlier point in time. Statements have been admitted on matters such as a person's political opinion, marital affection, the dislike of a child and, more recently, to prove, for the purposes of what is now s 116(2)(e) (see pp 208–214 above) that a witness who will not give evidence was in fear. It also seems that a statement of the intention of a person at the time he made the

statement is admissible under this head, and that such a statement is admissible to support an inference that the intention referred to existed at a time prior to or after that statement had been made. Where the statement expresses an intention to do an act, the authorities conflict as to whether it can be relied upon to prove that the act referred to was done.

In *R v Buckley* (1873) 13 Cox CC 293, the defendant was charged with the murder of a police officer. A statement made by the deceased officer to a senior officer, that he intended to watch the accused's movements on the night he was killed, was admitted to prove the accused had committed the offence. In *R v Moghal* (1977) 65 Cr App R 56, the accused's defence to a charge of aiding and abetting S (his mistress, who had already been tried and acquitted) to murder V, was that S committed the offence and he was merely a spectator. The Court of Appeal expressed the opinion that a tape-recorded statement made by S some six months before V's death, that she intended to kill V, would have been admissible. Note, however, that in *R v Blastland* [1986] AC 41 it was doubted whether this statement would have been relevant to the issue as to whether Moghal aided and abetted S. It would have been relevant if S had said that she planned to kill V alone because Moghal would have no part of it, and on that basis might have been admissible. Indeed, in *R v Wainwright* (1875) 13 Cox CC 171, a statement by the murder victim that she was going to the accused's premises was held to be inadmissible because it was only a statement of intention, which she might or might not have carried out. Similarly in *R v Thompson* [1912] 3 KB 19, the statement by a woman that she intended to abort herself, and the statement after her miscarriage that she had done it herself, was held to be inadmissible hearsay on a charge against the accused of using an instrument to procure an abortion. The difference may lie in the fact that the police officer in *Buckley* was seen to be more reliable than the murder victim and the aborted women.

If the woman's statements had been in documentary form (written or tape-recorded), they might now be admissible under s 116 of the Criminal Justice Act 2003 (see pp 201–215 above). The most recent case on this form of *res gestae* is *R v Gilfoyle* [1996] 3 All ER 883. The defendant had been convicted of the murder of his wife, who had been found hanging from a beam in the garage of her house. There was a note in her handwriting, in which she said she was going to take her own life, so it was at first thought to be a suicide. Later, a friend of hers made a statement to the police in which she said that the deceased had been told her that her husband, who was an auxiliary nurse, was doing a project on suicide at work and he had asked her to help him by writing examples of suicide notes. Two other friends made similar statements to the police. These three statements had been ruled inadmissible by the trial judge, but the defendant was nevertheless convicted.

The Court of Appeal ruled that these three statements ought to have been admitted. The statements attributed to the deceased by her three friends threw light on her state of mind, which was one of the principal issues in the case, and hearsay evidence to prove the declarant's state of mind was an exception to the rule against hearsay which had been accepted by the common law for many years. Accordingly, their Lordships were satisfied that, if considered necessary in the interests of justice, the fact that the statements were made could be used to show that, when the deceased wrote the notes, she was not in a suicidal frame of mind and that she wrote them in the belief that she was assisting the appellant in the course of work.

There was a clear hint here that the Court of Appeal was prepared to extend the category of hearsay involving spontaneous statements about the events in issue, of which *Andrews* (above) is the leading case. The Court held that evidence of the wife's statements was admissible to prove that she was not in a suicidal frame of mind when she wrote the notes, and that she wrote them in the belief that she was helping her husband with his course work. The 'state of mind' exception does not extend to statements proving facts other than the state of mind of the declarant; in this case, the fact that the husband asked her to write the notes and told her what to write. *R v Ratten* and *R v Andrews* were cited, and at one point the Court stated:

> In this case the statements themselves suggested that the events which prompted them were still dominating [the wife's] mind. The statement was made the morning after the letters had been written as soon as would ordinarily have been expected. The possibility of invention or unreliability could be discounted and there was little room for inaccuracy in the reporting of the statement.

This suggests that the court was applying *Andrews*. The wife's alleged suicide was a fact in issue, and the notes she made were circumstantial evidence that she had committed suicide. If it was an application of *Andrews*, it extends that category of *res gestae* to cover all three of the headings considered here.

In *R v Gilfoyle* [2001] 2 Cr App R 5, the Court of Appeal rejected a further appeal by Gilfoyle based on what was described as a 'psychological autopsy' of the deceased wife in order to show that she was in fact suicidal. The Court refused to accept as fresh evidence a psychological profile of the deceased carried out by Professor Canter, a psychologist who is a pioneer of the idea of psychological profiling as an aid to detection of criminals, such evidence not yet being accepted by the scientific community as being able to provide accurate and reliable opinion.

Evidence of the telephone call made by the deceased wife in *Newport* (considered at p 224 above) should also have been admissible under this head. The defendant husband claimed the stabbing was an accident, but the wife's telephone call to a friend suggested an ongoing argument, which had made her so agitated and frightened that she was contemplating almost immediate flight from the matrimonial home. Evidence of this state of mind was then clearly relevant to rebut the defence of accident under this exception to the hearsay rule. One may note that this exception assumed a new importance, being relied upon to prove the state of mind of a witness is who is said to be unable to give evidence through fear in order that it may be admitted under what is now s 116 of the 2003 Act.

Section 118(1) 7 – statements made by a party to a common enterprise

Where two or more persons conspire to commit an offence, a statement of one may be admissible in evidence against the other alleged conspirator, as well as against the person who made the statement. If the statement contains facts upon which the prosecution rely, those facts are admissible as an exception to the rule against hearsay. However, a condition of admissibility is that the statement must have been made in pursuance of the conspiracy subject of the charge. Where there is more than one conspiracy charged, as where A is alleged to have conspired with B and B is alleged to have conspired with C, a statement made by A in pursuance of his conspiracy with B is not admissible in relation to the alleged conspiracy between B and C.

The leading case in this area is *R v Blake and Tye* (1844) 6 QB 126. The defendants were convicted of fraudulent conspiracy to evade payment of customs duties. The prosecution case was that Blake, a customs official, and Tye, an agent for a importer, falsified documents, by declaring a smaller amount of goods than was actually imported, to avoid full payment of the amount due on imported goods. The conspiracy was largely proved by entries in a book kept by Tye, which showed the true amount of goods imported. It was held that these entries were properly proved against both conspirators, being statements made in pursuance of the conspiracy. However, entries on cheque book stubs by Tye, recording the division of spoils between Tye and Blake, were not admissible, because when they were made the conspiracy had been completed. They could not therefore have been made in pursuance of the conspiracy.

The decision regarding the cheque stubs in the above case may be compared with that in *R v Davenport* [1996] 1 Cr App R 221. Here, a document dealing with the proposed division of the proceeds from the alleged conspiracy was held to be admissible against all the parties concerned, on the basis that it was compiled before the conspiracy was complete and was made in pursuance of it. In *R v Jenkins and Starling* [2003] Crim LR 107, the defendants, directors of a company, were charged with conspiracy to defraud a local authority by falsely claiming a refund of business rates. It was alleged that they had conspired either with a council employee, or with an employee of the computer servicing company. They received a cheque for £62,733. At the trial, Exhibit 1 was a document bearing the word 'refund request' with the word 'overpayment' endorsed on it. The signatories of the document were not called as witnesses. On appeal, the prosecution conceded that the document was hearsay, but argued that it was admissible as a document made in pursuance of a conspiracy. The Court of Appeal disagreed. Allowing the appeal, it was said that to be admissible there had to be an assertion by the signatory that he knew the contents to be true. Additionally, there was no evidence as to when the document had been prepared. If prepared after the cheque, it was not made in pursuance of the conspiracy, which would by then have been complete.

The principle that a statement made by a party to a common enterprise is admissible against the maker and the other parties to the common enterprise, though mainly used in conspiracies, is not confined to such offences which involve a common enterprise. In *R v Gray* [1995] 2 Cr App R 100, the Court of Appeal approved and adopted the dictum of Dixon CJ in the Australian case of *Tripodi v R* (1961) 104 CLR 1, to the effect that the rule also applied to substantive offences committed by two or more persons with a common purpose. The Court attempted to define the application of the rule on the basis of a statement found in *Phipson on Evidence*:

> *Where two [or more] persons engage in a common enterprise, the acts and declarations of one in pursuance of that common enterprise are admissible against the other(s). The principle applies to the commission, by one or more people acting in concert, of a substantive offence or series of offences, but is limited to evidence which shows the involvement of each of the defendants in the commission of the offence or offences.*
> (14th edn, 1990, at para 25-10)

As with conspiracies, the acts or declarations must be made in pursuance of the common enterprise, so that statements made after the completion of the enterprise are admissible only against the maker. Some writers argue that statements by the parties to common enterprises involving substantive offences are admissible under other exceptions either as part of the *res gestae*, or as informal admissions. *Cross and Tapper on Evidence* classify them as 'admissions by agents', while *Andrews and Hirst on Criminal Evidence* see them as a species of *res gestae*.

Section 118(1) 8 – expert evidence

The exception for expert evidence permits an expert to give evidence of any relevant matter which forms part of his professional expertise (although not acquired through personal experience) and to draw upon technical expertise widely used by members of the expert's profession. However, s 127 of the 2003 Act also makes provision for expert witnesses to base an opinion on or draw inferences from statements prepared by other experts, and for the expert who did the preparatory work to be called to give evidence in appropriate cases.

Section 119 – previous inconsistent statements

Section 119(1) of the Criminal Justice Act 2003 clarifies the relationship between hearsay evidence and previous statements. This provides that if a witness admits that he has made a previous inconsistent statement, or it has been proved that he made such a statement, it is not only, as it was previously, evidence which undermines his 'credibility' (as someone who makes inconsistent statements) but will for the future also be evidence of the truth of its contents (see **Chapter 4**). Section 119(2) provides:

> *If in criminal proceedings evidence of an inconsistent statement by any person is given under section 124(2)(c) (to attack the credibility of the person), the statement is admissible as evidence of any matter stated in it of which oral evidence by the witness would be admissible.*

The provision envisages the following type of situation. A makes a statement to the police that she saw B 'outside the jewellers' at midday on Monday'. A is unavailable to testify at trial, but her statement is admitted under s 116 (discussed at pp 201–215 below) which provides that in these circumstances evidence can be admitted to attack the credibility of A. Section 124(2)(c) provides that evidence can be admitted to prove that A made another statement inconsistent with this statement (for example, A had said earlier that she did not see B at all on Monday). Section 119(2) provides that if there is such an inconsistent statement, it goes not only to the credibility of A, but also is admissible as to the truth of its contents (ie, that A did not see B on Monday).

Section 120 – other previous statements of witnesses

This section was discussed in Chapter 4 (see pp 97–99 above) and will not be revisited here. See also s 122, which provides that as a general rule statements admitted under this section or s 119, and produced as exhibits, should not accompany the jury when they retire.

Section 121 – additional requirements for multiple hearsay

This section has been discussed above in the contexts of ss 116 and 117. 'Multiple hearsay' is where the information passes through more than one person before it is recorded. Where the person seeking to give such evidence has no personal knowledge of the fact stated, the statement is said to be multiple hearsay. Thus if we seek to prove that A said that an event had occurred, if A had no personal knowledge of that event but is relying on what B had told him, A's statement is said to be multiple (or second-hand) hearsay (it could be third- or fourth-hand, or more, depending on the length of the com-munication chain, which only serves to underline the potential unreliability). Assuming no hearsay exception applies, A could not give oral evidence of the event. Under the Law Commission's proposals, A's statement about what B told him would not be admissible under their unavailability exception (which is now s 116) even if A was unavailable, such evidence being too unreliable to be admitted. Section 121 enacts this.

A similar view was taken of the cumulative use of a hearsay exception by the common law. Thus, to take the facts of *Andrews* (see p 222 above), if A, having been fatally stabbed, staggered to B's door and told B that D had stabbed him, B could give evidence of what A told him under s 116 and the *res gestae* exception preserved by s 118. But if B told C what A had told him, and B died before trial having made a statement to the police, C's state-ment would not be admissible as evidence that D stabbed A under the unavailability exception in s 116.

The Law Commission's view was that C's statement should not be admissible in such cir-cumstances because it thought it would be going too far to permit B's hearsay statement to be proved by another hearsay statement, since the risk of error or fabrication increased with each additional step in the chain. Section 121 gives statutory effect to this reasoning, so that the statement by C that B said that A said that D stabbed the deceased, would not be admissible under s 116, even if A and B are unavailable for one of the reasons set out in s 116. Section 121(1)(a) requires that in such a case the statement of the unavailable declarant, A, must be proved by evidence admissible other than under s 116, for example under ss 117, 119 or 120. Section 121(1)(b) allows such evidence to be admissible if all the parties agree, while s 121(1)(c) allows the court to admit it if highly reliable and the interests of justice require that it be admitted. This last head is similar to s 114(1)(d) and (2), though under s 121(1)(c) there is no requirement to consider the wider range of fac-tors set out in s 114(2); however, it is unlikely that a court exercising the power under s 121(1)(c) would not also consider most (if not all) of those factors.

The fact that s 116 permits documentary evidence to be admitted raises a question not clearly answered by s 116 and s 121. Suppose, as in the example given above, A, having been fatally stabbed, staggered to B's door and told B that D had stabbed him. B makes a statement to this effect to the police, who record it in the form of a witness statement. B dies before trial. The question is whether B's statement in a document is admissible under s 116? There is no doubt that had B survived, his statement that A told him that D stabbed him would be admissible under s 116, which extends to oral statements as well as state-ments in a document, and s 118(1) 4 (a), the *res gestae* exception. Does the fact that B is dead and unavailable make his statement inadmissible? All the requirements of s 116(1)(a) to (c) appear to be satisfied: oral evidence given in the proceedings would be admissible as evidence of the matters stated either directly by A had he survived, or by B relying on the *res gestae* exception; the person who made the statement (the relevant person, in this case A if we mean the original oral statement, or B if we mean the written statement of what A told B) can be identified to the satisfaction of the court; and one of the conditions set out in s 116(2) is satisfied as the relevant person (A or B) is dead.

However, this statement is 'multiple hearsay', excluded from the operation of s 116 by s 121. B's statement in a document is a hearsay statement intended to prove the fact that an earlier hearsay statement was made and, unless admissible under s 124(1)(a), (b) or (c), is not admissible. B's statement in a document may be no less reliable because he has died, therefore the only argument for excluding the written statement is the inability to cross-examine B about the circumstances in which the statement was made and the credibility of A and B where B is unavailable. However, that is a factor in all hearsay statements admitted in documentary form, and s 124 seeks to compensate for this. The court may well feel justified in admitting B's written statement in such circumstance under s 124(1)(c), if satisfied that the reliability is so high that the interests of justice require that it be admitted.

Section 122 – documents produced as exhibits

The section is self-explanatory. If a statement is admitted as a previous inconsistent statement or other previous statement of a witness under ss 119 or 120, and is produced as an exhibit, it should not normally accompany the jury when they retire unless the court considers it appropriate, or all the parties agree. The concern is that the jury may give too much weight to statements which they are permitted to take with them when they retire, hence the restriction.

Section 123 – capability to make a statement

This section provides that an out-of-court statement cannot be admitted under ss 116, 119 or 120 if the person who made the statement was not legally capable of making a statement at the time the statement was made; more simply, the statement maker must have been a competent witness at the time the statement was made. In *R v Setz-Dempsey; R v Richardson* (1994) 98 Cr App R 23, a case under s 23 of the 1988 Act which used the phrase 'unfit to attend as a witness through physical or mental illness', the defendants appealed against their conviction on the ground that the trial judge was wrong to admit the statement of an important witness, who had appeared in court but was unable through mental illness to recall the relevant events even after refreshing his memory from the statements he had made. Having heard evidence from a doctor that the witness was unable to recall events in a logically coherent way, the judge ruled that the witness was indeed 'unfit to attend as witness'. The appellants argued that a witness who had actually attended court could not be 'unfit to attend as a witness'. The Court of Appeal rejected this argument, holding that it was obvious that the words of the section were not intended to apply only to the physical act of getting to court. However, the Court was satisfied that the doctor's evidence had undermined the quality of the evidence contained in the statement, and for that reason it could not have been fairly admitted.

In this case the mental disorder had occurred before the events subject of the trial, and the first statement to the police was made the day before the witness was admitted to a mental hospital as an in-patient. The implication of the Court of Appeal's decision that the quality of the evidence had been undermined, is that the witness was probably incompetent from the outset. If the witness was of sound mind when he made the statements, his subsequent mental deterioration should not affect the quality of the evidence. The Court of Appeal appeared to be saying that the witness was incompetent through mental illness when the statements were made. If similar facts were to arise under the 2003 Act, applying s 116(1) the statement would be inadmissible because the relevant person lacked the competence to be a witness.

Section 123(2) provides that a statement may not be admitted under s 117 (business documents) if any person who supplied or received the information, or created or received the document, did not have the required capability or, where that person cannot be identified, cannot reasonably be assumed to have had the required capability.

Section 123(3) reflects the test for witness competence to give evidence in criminal proceedings under s 53 of the Youth Justice and Criminal Evidence Act 1999.

Section 124 – credibility

This section makes provision for challenges to the credibility of the maker of the hearsay statement who does not give oral evidence in person in the proceedings and is therefore not available for cross-examination. If such hearsay statements are admitted as evidence of a matter stated, s 124 provides that the person against whom the hearsay statement has been admitted can adduce, in specified circumstances, evidence to discredit the maker of the statement, or to show that he has contradicted himself. The section provides a replacement for the provision in s 28(2) of and Sch 2 to the Criminal Justice Act 1988, now repealed. One presumes that the absent witness will be protected against the admission of bad character evidence to the same extent as a witness who gives oral evidence in person. See further the discussion in **Chapter 4** concerning s 100 of the 2003 Act, dealing with a non-defendant's bad character.

Section 125 – stopping the case when the evidence is unconvincing

Section 125(1) imposes a duty on the court to stop a case and either direct the jury to acquit the defendant, or discharge the jury, if the case against him is based wholly or partly on an out-of-court statement which is so unconvincing that, considering its importance to the case, a conviction would be unsafe. The issue only arises in relation to jury trials (and by virtue of para 4 of Sch 7 to service courts) because, in other cases, the finders of fact, such as a magistrates' court, would be bound to dismiss in these circumstances, or order a retrial if appropriate.

Section 126 – court's general discretion to exclude evidence

This section provides a further discretion to exclude superfluous out-of-court statements if the court is satisfied that the value of the evidence is outweighed by the undue waste of time which its admission would cause. Section 126(2) preserves both the existing common law power for the court to exclude evidence where its prejudicial effect outweighs its probative value, and the discretion contained in s 78 of the Police and Criminal Evidence Act 1984 in relation to the exclusion of evidence which would have such an adverse effect on the fairness of the trial that it ought not to be admitted.

Further reading

Birch, D, 'Criminal Justice Act 2003: (4) Hearsay – same old story, same old song?' [2004] Crim LR 556.

Law Commission, *Evidence in Criminal Proceedings: Hearsay and Related Topics* (1997, Law Com 245).

Pattenden, R, 'Conceptual Versus Pragmatic Approaches to Hearsay' (1993) 56 MLR 138.

Taylor, G, 'Two English hearsay heresies' (2005) 9(2) E & P 110.

7 Confessions

One of the most important common law exceptions to the rule against hearsay is the informal admission (ie, an incriminating statement made by an accused other than such a statement made while giving evidence or more formally under s 10 of the Criminal Justice Act 1925). An informal admission is admissible at common law as evidence of the truth of its contents on the basis that a person is likely to be telling the truth when he says something against his own interest. At common law, when such an admission is made by an accused person before his trial and to a person in authority (usually the police), it is known as a confession.

The modern test for the admissibility of a confession is contained in ss 76 and 76A of the Police and Criminal Evidence Act (PACE) 1984. Section 76(1) provides that a confession made by an accused person is admissible against him in so far as it is relevant to any matter in issue in the proceedings and is not excluded by the court in pursuance of that section. Section 76(2) provides that the prosecution can be required to prove, beyond reasonable doubt, that the confession that they propose to introduce in evidence was not obtained by oppression (s 76(2)(a)) or in circumstances of unreliability (s 76(2)(b)). Section 76A, added by s 128 of the Criminal Justice Act 2003, makes similar provisions for the admissibility of a confession made by an accused person on behalf of a co-accused, though a co-accused need only prove on the balance of probabilities that the confession was not obtained by oppression or in circumstances of unreliability. Even if the prosecution successfully clear these hurdles, there remains s 78, which provides a broad judicial discretion to exclude prosecution evidence if it would have such an adverse effect on the fairness of the proceedings that it ought not to be admitted. Before considering these provisions in depth, it may be useful to address the question of what constitutes a confession.

What constitutes a confession?

Confession to whom?

Section 82(1) of the Police and Criminal Evidence Act 1984 defines a 'confession' as inclusive of 'any statement wholly or partly adverse to the person who made it, whether made to a person in authority or not and whether made in words of otherwise'. The definition includes any informal admission made out of court. A confession (or informal admission) is evidence only against its maker unless the maker repeats the confession from the witness box while giving evidence, in which case it is evidence against anyone implicated by it.

It is now immaterial to whom the confession is made. At common law only confessions made to a person in authority were subject to the test of admissibility. Under s 82(1), a confession made to anyone – wife, friend, social worker, or police – is subject to the test of admissibility under s 76 of the 1984 Act. For example, *The Times* (20 May 2000) carried a report of an article in *Le Figaro* in which Sid Ahmed Rezala, then undergoing extradition proceedings from Portugal to France where he was accused of three murders, was said to have confessed to the killing of three girls, including a British student Isabel Peake. That statement admitting the killings, made to a journalist who paid him for the interview, would be a confession within the definition contained in s 82(1). If introduced in evidence in an English criminal trial, its admissibility would undoubtedly be the subject of a challenge (because of the payment) under s 76(2)(b) of the 1984 Act but might well be admitted. The same edition of *The Times* reported the conviction for murder by an American court of a mother and son despite the fact that the prosecution failed to find the body. The son had kept detailed notes of the plot to kill the victim, a Manhattan socialite, in order to gain control of her $7 million town house using forged documents. The notes were admitted as a confession in that trial, and would also constitute a confession within s 82(1). In the trial of youths for the murder of Damilola Taylor in March 2002, the prosecution led evidence of admissions (confessions) made to other inmates of a detention centre in the presence of a member of staff. These confessions were challenged under s 76(2)(a) as being unreliable, but were nevertheless admitted. The jury who acquitted the defendants did not appear to accept the alleged confessions as reliable (at one point in the trial the jury went to the detention centre and listened to conversations to establish whether one of the inmates could have heard one of the defendants who was in another room).

The Privy Council, comprising Law Lords who also sit as members of the Judicial Committee of the House of Lords, has recently warned that juries must be cautious before accepting a cell confession allegedly made by the accused to a fellow prisoner, particularly an untried prisoner. Such prisoners might well have something to gain from assisting the prosecution and their evidence was inherently unreliable (*Benedetto v The Queen and Labrador v The Queen* [2003] 1 WLR 1545).

The great majority of confessions are made to the police or other investigative bodies such as Customs and Excise, but a letter written by the defendant to his wife (see *Rumping v DPP* [1964] AC 814) might be seen as a confession, as might a letter of apology written by the defendant to the alleged victim. In *R v Ellaray* [2003] 2 Cr App R 11, the defendant was convicted of rape solely on the basis of admissions made to a probation officer preparing a pre-sentence report. His appeal against conviction, based on the argument that the judge was wrong to admit the statements made to the probation officer, was dismissed. The Court of Appeal held that in the case of admissions or confessions made in circumstances such as those in the present case, the prosecution should carefully consider whether it was right to rely upon evidence provided by conversations between a probation officer and an offender, and rely upon it only if it was in the public interest to do so. The court should bear in mind the contrast between an interview involving the police and the offender and an interview between a probation officer and the offender. There was a need for frankness between the offender and the probation officer, there might not be a reliable record of what was said, and the offender had not been cautioned and was not legally represented. Section 78 of the PACE 1984 was available to ensure no unfairness occurred (discussed at pp 268–288 below).

Form of the confession

A confession may be made orally, in writing, by conduct or in any other way of communicating information. Thus if the defendant, by words or conduct, indicates that he accepts an accusation made by the victim of a crime, or by someone else who is on an equal footing, then to the extent that he has accepted it, the statement becomes his own (*R v Christie* [1914] AC 545). The re-enactment of a crime by an accused that is videotaped by the police is clearly a confession within s 82(1) of PACE 1984 in so far as it is adverse to him, eg he demonstrates how he stabbed the victim (*Li Shu-Ling v R* [1989] AC 270). The failure to reply to an accusation is not normally evidence against the person accused, though this common law rule is now modified by ss 34, 36, 37 and 38 of the Criminal Justice and Public Order Act 1994 (see **Chapter 2**).

Exceptionally, the failure to reply may at common law be admissible as evidence against the person who remains silent in the face of an accusation to which he would normally be expected to respond. The 'even terms' rule was expressed by Cave J in *R v Mitchell* (1892) 17 Cox CC 503, at 508, thus: 'Undoubtedly, when persons are speaking on even terms and a charge is made, and the person charged says nothing, and expresses no indignation, and does nothing to repel the charge, that is some evidence to show that he admits the charge to be true.' The principle was applied in *Parkes v The Queen* (1977) 64 Cr App R 25. Parkes was charged with the murder by stabbing of a young woman. The victim's mother found her bleeding from her wounds and saw Parkes nearby holding a knife. She twice accused him of stabbing her daughter. He did not reply. She then took hold of him saying she was going to hold him until the police arrived. He made to strike her with the knife, cutting her finger. The Privy Council upheld the judge's direction to the jury that they could take the defendant's reaction and his silence into account when determining whether he was or was not guilty of murder.

A more modern example is to be found in the evidence given by a witness in the trial of Barry George for the murder of Jill Dando, the television presenter (*The Times*, 5 May 2001). Lenita Bailey was a customer at a hairdresser's near Mr George's flat. She knew him and recalled a conversation with him. George came into the salon and claimed police were harassing him over the death of Dando. They had searched his home and his mother's house. Ms Bailey said to him, 'Did you do it?'. George remained silent and stared at the floor. She repeated the question twice more and asked him to look at her. She said, 'His lips moved as if he was thinking of an answer but none was forthcoming'. Her evidence of the discussion, or lack of it, was admitted. George was convicted.

The defendant and the mother in *Parkes* and the witness and defendant in the Dando trial were clearly on equal terms, and it was reasonable to expect a denial of the accusation if that was the position. However, a suspect arrested by the police will not usually be seen as being on equal terms with the police, although in *R v Chandler* (1976) 63 Cr App R 1 it was held that a suspect interviewed by police in the presence of his solicitor was on even terms, and therefore a failure to respond to an accusation before caution could be taken into account by the jury. That decision has now been overtaken by events, and in particular the requirement under Code C of PACE 1984 that a suspect be cautioned when he is suspected of involvement in a crime before the actual arrest.

Whatever the position might be at common law in relation to the above, it does not apply in situations where a defendant refuses to leave his prison cell to be interviewed by police and thus remains silent (*R v Gilbert* (1977) 66 Cr App R 237; *R v Johnson and R v Hind* (2005) *The Times*, 3 May). This is a very different situation from one where, for example, the defendant fails to offer an explanation for the fact that he was in possession of stolen goods (*R v Raviraj* (1986) 85 Cr App R 93).

Inculpatory, exculpatory and mixed statements

The content of a confession can range from a full, signed admission of guilt, to an incriminating comment, to a mixed statement containing admissions and exculpations. By confining the definition to 'adverse' statements, s 82(1) of the 1984 Act does not cover exculpatory statements but does cover 'mixed statements' – those containing both incriminating and exculpating elements. For example, the statement, 'Yes, I drove the getaway car but I had no idea they [the others implicated] were going to do a robbery' is a confession so far as its maker admits being the driver of the getaway car, but is exculpatory in seeking to show he had no idea he was involved in a robbery. *R v Sharp* [1988] 1 All ER 65 recognised that excluding the exculpatory part would often be unfair to the accused, therefore it was decided that the whole statement should be admitted but the jury warned that the exculpatory parts carried less weight than the incriminatory parts. However, in *R v Sat-Bhambra* (1988) 88 Cr App R 55, Lord Lane CJ stated that the provisions of s 82(1), and therefore s 76 of PACE 1984, do not apply to statements such as 'I had nothing to do with it'. Such a statement made on arrest may be admitted not as a confession, but as showing the suspect's reaction when accused of the offence and arrested.

The House of Lords, in *R v Hasan* [2005] 2 WLR 709, has recently confirmed this principle. Hasan was convicted of aggravated burglary, which he admitted subject to the defence of duress. He had been the minder of a female prostitute, but had been replaced in that role by X who was a drug dealer with a reputation for violence. Hasan's evidence was that X had boasted that he had committed three murders, and X used these assertions to back up a threat to Hasan and his family if he did not carry out the burglary. He alleged that an associate of X, who said he had a gun and remained nearby while Hasan committed the burglary, had taken him to the scene. The prosecution were permitted to cross-examine Hasan and call rebuttal evidence concerning a confidential 'off the record' conversation with the police regarding X's activities, which took place after Hasan had been charged, the content of which was alleged to be inconsistent with his evidence in some material respects.

On appeal Hasan's conviction was quashed, the Court of Appeal holding that the conversation should not have been admitted. Statements made by Hasan during that conversation were adverse to him within the meaning of s 82(1), and thus constituted a confession within s 76(2). The prosecution had not proved that the confession had not been obtained in breach of s 76(2)(b). The statements were made only in response to a promise of confidentiality and in circumstances likely to render them unreliable, in that the police officers said they were interested in the activities of X, not the involvement of Hasan in the burglary. However, on appeal by the Crown to the House of Lords, the court allowed the appeal, reinforcing the decision in *Sat-Bhambra* that s 82(1) does not cover exculpatory or neutral statements.

The exclusion of confession evidence

Section 76(1) of PACE 1984 provides that:

> *In any proceedings a confession made by an accused person may be given in evidence against him in so far as it is relevant to any matter in issue in the proceedings and is not excluded by the court in pursuance of this section.*

'Proceedings' means criminal proceedings, including courts martial (s 82(1)). However, in *R v Beckford* [1991] Crim LR 833, the subsection was held to apply only to confessions tendered by the prosecution. This was confirmed by the House of Lords in *R v Myers* [1997] 3 WLR 552, where it was held that a co-accused could make use of a confession made by another co-accused, even if it incriminated that co-accused and was inadmissible against him on behalf of the prosecution having been excluded under s 76. This was seen by many to be unfair to the accused whose confession had been excluded as against the prosecution either because it was obtained by oppression, or because it was potentially unreliable.

Section 128 of the Criminal Justice Act 2003 amends the law to prevent any potential unfairness by inserting a new s 76A into PACE 1984. This new section provides an almost identical regime for the admissibility of a confession made by an accused on behalf of another co-accused. The only difference between the sections is that s 76A(1) refers to an accused and co-accused, and in s 76A(2) the co-accused who seeks to rely on the confession of another co-accused must prove on the balance of probabilities that the confession was not obtained by oppression or in circumstances of unreliability, whereas the prosecution must do so beyond reasonable doubt. It follows that everything said about s 76 applies equally to s 76A, subject to that exception.

General principles

Breaches of PACE 1984 and Code of Practice C, which govern the detention and questioning of suspects, and Code of Practice E, which requires the tape-recording and/or the video-taping of interviews with suspects, are likely to be the grounds for seeking exclusion of a confession, together with the manner of questioning. The custody record, which is created in respect of every person arrested and taken to a police station, details every action in respect of the suspect. This record, together with the tape-recording and/or the video-recording of interviews with the suspect, may provide the defence with evidence of any breach, which they can then use to put the prosecution to proof that s 76 or s 78 of the 1984 Act have not been breached.

Any breach of procedure outside the police station may also be grounds for excluding a confession. In these circumstances, there are two overriding, but difficult, principles to apply. First, as soon a police officer has grounds to suspect that a person has committed an offence and wishes to question him, he must caution that person 'You do not have to say anything. But it may harm your defence if you fail to mention when questioned something which you later rely on in court. Anything you do say may be given in evidence.' Secondly, an interview with a suspect, which is questioning after caution about involvement in an offence, should normally take place in a police station after arrest, where the suspect will have all the protections of the 1984 Act and Codes of Practice (particularly Codes C and E), which include access to legal advice and the recording on audio or video tape of the interview.

The importance of these two principles lies in the fact that a caution when the officer has 'grounds to suspect' comes at a stage before arrest, which requires 'reasonable grounds to suspect' involvement in an offence. It follows that the on-street questioning which precedes an arrest should only be of the kind which provides the reasonable grounds for arrest. Once the officer has such reasonable grounds the questioning should cease, and should continue, if detention is authorised after arrest, only at an interview conducted in accordance with Codes C and E. Any attempt to circumvent the protections provided by the Act and Codes is likely to be met by exclusion of any evidence thus obtained.

The scope of s 76(2)

The issue of whether or not a confession is to be admitted takes place in the absence of the jury in what is known as a trial within a trial (a *voir dire* – see **Chapter 1**). Sometimes this will take place before the trial proper, but more often the jury will be sent out at the point where the prosecution intend to call the police officer(s) to whom the confession was made.

Section 76(2) provides:

> If, in any proceedings where the prosecution proposes to give in evidence a confession made by an accused person, it is represented to the court that the confession was or may have been obtained—
>
> (a) by oppression of the person who made it; or
>
> (b) in consequence of anything said or done which was likely in the circumstances existing at the time, to render unreliable any confession which might have been made by him in consequence thereof, the court shall not allow the confession to be given in evidence except in so far as the prosecution proves to the court beyond reasonable doubt that the confession (notwithstanding that it may be true) was not obtained as aforesaid.

Section 76A(2) is identical, except for the reference in the first line to 'a co-accused' rather than the prosecution and the final clause, which read as follows: 'The court shall not allow the confession to be given in evidence for the co-accused except in so far as it is proved to the court on the balance of probabilities that the confession (notwithstanding that it may be true) was not so obtained'. It follows from the lower standard of proof that a confession that is ruled inadmissible for the prosecution could be admitted for a co-defendant.

Section 76(2) is prospective

If a confession is admitted at what might be an early stage in the trial, and evidence given later casts doubt on the admissibility of that confession, s 76 (and s 78 which is similarly prospective) cannot be used to exclude the confession. Instead the common law discretion to exclude evidence (preserved by s 82(3) of PACE 1984) must be relied upon (*Sat-Bhambra* (1988) 88 Cr App R 55). However, it must be noted that, unlike s 76, s 78 and the common law discretion apply only to prosecution evidence.

Burden and standard of proof

The onus lies on the defence to 'represent' to the court that the confession was or may have been obtained in breach of s 76(2)(a) or (b). It means that the defence must produce sufficient evidence to suggest that the confession was or may have been so obtained. The court must then investigate the circumstances in which the confession was obtained and, as the section makes clear, the prosecution will be required to prove beyond reasonable doubt that the confession was not obtained in breach of s 76(2)(a) or (b). The phrase 'was or may have been obtained' suggests that the evidence need not amount to a prima facie case, still less a requirement to prove on the balance of probabilities. The evidence may appear on the face of the custody record, a detailed record of everything said or done to the defendant while in police detention, by revealing prolonged periods of questioning or lack of entitlements under the PACE 1984 or Codes of Practice, or from the tape-recording of the interview (see *R v Paris and others* (1993) 97 Cr App R 99 ('The Cardiff Three', discussed at pp 248–250 below).

Often it will require evidence from the police officers who conducted the interview and/or evidence from the defendant himself. The defence will intimate their intention to challenge the admissibility of the confession before counsel for the prosecution makes his opening address; the prosecution will then make no reference to it in their opening address. Depending on the importance of the confession to the case, the issue of its admissibility may be decided before any prosecution evidence is given. If a confession is central to the prosecution case but is excluded, the trial judge may then withdraw the case from the jury and direct an acquittal.

The section makes it clear that the burden of proving that the confession was not obtained in breach of s 76(2)(a) or (b) is on the prosecution to prove 'beyond reasonable doubt'. If they fail to discharge this burden the trial judge has no discretion – 'the court shall not allow the confession to be given in evidence'. Where a confession has been made to the police, as the vast majority are, an accused seeking to rely on a confession made by a co-accused will have to prove on the balance of probabilities that what the police said or did, which is alleged to have been oppressive or likely to render any confession made unreliable, was neither. It is then possible that the prosecution fail to prove beyond reasonable doubt that a confession was not obtained in breach of s 76(2)(a) or (b), while a co-accused succeeds in proving that the same confession was not obtained in breach of s 76A(2)(a) or (b). The confession may then be relied upon by the co-accused and will be evidence against the accused who made it. It will then assist the prosecution in proving their case against that accused, while undermining their case against the co-accused in whose favour the confession was admitted.

Admissibility of a confession is a matter of law

The admissibility and relevance of a confession are questions of law to be decided by the judge, whereas how much weight is to be given to the confession is a question of fact for the jury. In a magistrates' court, the bench is involved in both questions, but if the confession is ruled inadmissible, it must of course perform the difficult task of removing the alleged confession from its mind when deciding guilt. Even if the confession is admitted, the defence may still raise the issue again before the jury by, for example, cross-examining police officers as to the detail of the interrogation that led to the confession. It is for the jury to determine the weight, if any, to be given to an admissible confession and it is possible, on hearing how the confession was obtained, that the jury will take a different view of the confession to that of the judge and disregard it or give it little weight. In acquitting the accused persons the jury appeared to have given little weight to alleged confessions made to inmates at a detention centre). It is for this reason that s 76(2)(b) of the PACE 1984 deals with a hypothetical confession rather than the actual confession (discussed at pp 252–265 below).

If it is represented that a confession was or may have been obtained in breach of s 76(2)(a) or (b) a *voir dire* must normally be held (*R v Millard* [1987] Crim LR 196). The defence can of course give evidence, but the defendant cannot be compelled to testify (*R v Davis* [1990] Crim LR 860). In practice, however, there will be many cases in which the accused must testify if he is to stand any chance of getting the confession excluded. In the *voir dire*, the sole issue for the court is the admissibility of the confession. It may be declared inadmissible even if it is true, the section being concerned only with the question whether it was obtained by oppression or in circumstances of unreliability. This is understandable when oppression is used, but less so when the issue is the likely reliability of the confession. The fact that it is true is the best measure of its reliability, but the truth is not in issue within the *voir dire*. Evidence led, or cross-examination conducted, by the prosecution designed to show that the confession is true is therefore irrelevant to the issue of admissibility.

Thus in *R v Cox* [1991] Crim LR 276, the defendant, who was mentally handicapped, was interviewed in the absence of an 'appropriate adult' (an independent person who must be present to protect the interests of juveniles and the mentally handicapped as required by Code C, paras 3.6–3.14) and therefore in breach of Code C. During the interview he admitted being involved in two burglaries. At the *voir dire*, the defendant gave evidence and admitted his involvement in one of the burglaries. This persuaded the judge that the confession was reliable and should be admitted. The Court of Appeal held that the trial judge had applied the wrong test. The essential question was not whether the confession was true, but whether the breach of the Code was likely in the circumstances to produce an unreliable confession.

Corroboration is not required

In spite of several *causes célèbres* in recent years involving the quashing of convictions based on false or unreliable confessions, and calls to emulate the Scottish system, the Royal Commission on Criminal Justice (1993) rejected a requirement of corroboration of a confession as a condition of admissibility. However, in practice, there have been sufficient examples to caution courts against the ready acceptance of confessional evidence alone, and to remind the police and Crown Prosecution Service of the desirability of supporting evidence. (Principle (b) of the *Principles of Investigative Interviewing* encourages police to seek supportive evidence, and the courts look for it in respect of mentally disordered defendants.)

A confession may be admitted if it is 'relevant to any matter in issue in the proceedings' (s 76(1)), most obviously as regards the offence charged, but also in relation to other conduct (eg, as evidence of the accused's disposition where the court has decided to allow such evidence). Subject to its passing the relevance threshold, a confession may be used as evidence of any matter, including any matter favourable to its maker. However, the evidential value of self-serving extracts from a confession may be slight and the judge may well comment on their lack of weight.

Since an accused is generally neither competent nor compellable for the prosecution, an out-of-court statement by D1 against his co-accused, D2, who is being jointly tried, is inadmissible as evidence against D2. However, this is subject to the recent House of Lords decision in *R v Hayter* [2005] 1 WLR 605 (see also *R v Spinks* (1982) 74 Cr App R 263; *R v Hickey*, unreported, 30 July 1997, CA; *R v Rhodes* (1972) 56 Cr App R 23 and Metzer, A, (2005) 10 SJ 149, 290–1). The issue in *Hayter* arose in the context of what is known as a contract killing. Three defendants were charged with murder and jointly indicted as principals. The first defendant, Bristow, wanted to arrange a contract killing of her husband. The second defendant, Hayter, was the go-between who engaged and paid the third defendant, Ryan, to kill the husband. Bristow's husband was shot in the head at point blank range, dying instantly. The evidence against Ryan, the killer, was solely based on a confession which he allegedly made to his girlfriend. The trial judge directed the jury to consider in logical phases the case against Ryan, the alleged killer, then against Bristow, the woman who allegedly procured the killing, and finally against the middleman, Hayter.

The trial judge directed the jury in clear terms that the confession that Ryan allegedly made to his girlfriend was only evidence against him and not evidence in the separate cases against Bristow and Hayter. In his summing up he also told the jury that they should consider the case against Ryan first. If they found him guilty of murder they could then use that finding of guilt in their consideration of the case against Bristow and Hayter while taking care not to allow anything in the girlfriend's evidence of Ryan's confession to play any part in their consideration of the case against either. The jury found all three guilty and the House of Lords dismissed the appeal establishing that where the prosecution case against D1 is dependent upon the prosecution proving the guilt of D2, and the evidence against D2 consisted solely of his own out-of-court confession, then such a confession would be admissible against D1, but only in so far as it went to proving the guilt of D2. If D1 goes into the witness box and admits his part in the offence and incriminates his co-defendant, that is evidence against D2. Similarly if D1 ceases to be a defendant, where, for example, the prosecution offer no evidence against D1 or file a *nolle prosequi* in relation to D1, D1 can then give evidence for the prosecution against D2. As s 76A now makes clear, a confession made by an accused may be admissible on behalf of a co-accused if the provisions of that section are satisfied.

Breaches of the Code etc, during one interview followed by properly conducted interview(s)

If a confession is excluded under s 76 (or s 78) because of breaches of the Codes of Practice, subsequent interviews, in which the confession is repeated, will also be inadmissible if they stem from the original one, otherwise s 76 can be flouted by subsequent compliance with the rules (*R v Blake* [1991] Crim LR 119; *R v Ismail* [1990] Crim LR 109).

It is a question of fact and degree in each case as to whether a later unobjectionable interview should be excluded. Much will depend upon the objections raised to the earlier interview, and whether those objections were of a fundamental and continuing nature. Thus in *R v Conway* [1994] Crim LR 838, the defendant alleged that during a visit to his cell by a police officer he had been promised that if he admitted the offence he could go home to his sick mother. There was no record of the visit in the custody record, no caution was given and no note of the conversation was made. The defendant then confessed in an interview some 20 minutes later. The prosecution did not seek to rely on the interview in the cell, but the defence sought to exclude the later interview upon which the prosecution did rely. The trial judge's decision that there was no oppression or unreliability was overturned on appeal. The cell interview would have been excluded as unreliable, and there was nothing in the intervening 20 minutes to suggest that the effect of the earlier breaches had ceased to have any effect on the defendant.

In *R v Neil* [1994] Crim LR 441, police took a witness statement from the defendant in which he admitted giving a knife to the man who stabbed the deceased and then driving him from the scene. He was then arrested, cautioned and kept in custody overnight before being interviewed as a suspect when he made the same admission. The witness statement was excluded under s 78, but the second interview was admitted. The defendant's appeal was allowed. The defendant had no opportunity to seek legal advice before being interviewed as a suspect, and may well have felt bound by the admissions in the earlier statement.

Other factors may come into play which suggest that the breaches cannot be rectified by a later interview. In *R v Wood* [1994] Crim LR 222, the defendant, who was of limited mental capacity, was charged with manslaughter of a child by striking him a heavy blow. During an interview with no solicitor, no caution and no contemporaneous record, he admitted striking the boy on the day before his death. In a second, properly conducted interview he repeated this. The medical evidence agreed that the blow that killed the boy had been delivered on the day of his death, not on the previous day. This in itself suggested unreliability, and the absence of a record of the earlier interview made it impossible for the prosecution to prove that the second interview was not tainted by the first.

Occasionally it may be possible for the Crown to prove no connection between the interviews. For example, the defendant is oppressed and confesses. He is released on bail, but sometime later returns to the station with his lawyer and confesses (see *R v Gillard and Barrett* [1991] Crim LR 280 in relation to s 78; or, as is suggested in the commentary to *Conway* (above), if the defendant had seen a solicitor in the period between the breaches and had been made aware of his rights, and told that the earlier interview did not count).

Criteria for admissibility

The prosecution may be required to jump up to three hurdles before a confession can be admitted in evidence. The first is 'oppression' under s 76(2)(a); the second, 'unreliability' under s 76(2)(b). In respect of these hurdles, they must prove beyond reasonable doubt that the confession was not obtained by 'oppression' or in circumstances of unreliability. The third hurdle is the general discretion provided for by s 78, where the trial judge must be satisfied that admitting the confession would not have 'such an adverse effect on the fairness of the trial that the court ought not to admit it'. Usually a defendant will allege a breach of s 76(2)(a) and/or (b). Occasionally the defence look solely to s 78. Exceptionally, a defendant might represent that a confession ought to be excluded under all three by representing, first, s 76(2)(a), then (if that fails) s 76(2)(b) and then (if that fails) s 78, though the Court of Appeal has held that if the prosecution succeed in discharging the burden under s 76(2)(a) and (b), prima facie there are no grounds for exclusion under s 78 (see *Halawa v Federation Against Copyright Theft* [1995] 1 Cr App R 21, discussed at p 269 below).

Section 76(2)(a) – oppression

The defence may represent to the court that the confession 'was or may have been obtained ... by oppression of the person who made it'. This reflects the views of the Criminal Law Revision Committee (11th Report), and those of the Royal Commission on Criminal Procedure (Cmnd 8092, 1981), that society's abhorrence of methods of investigation amounting to oppression should be signalled by the automatic exclusion of a confession obtained thereby, even if the confession turns out to be true. It also reflects the late development of the common law, which first established oppression as a ground of inadmissibility of confessions in *Callis v Gunn* [1964] 1 QB 495. This was then incorporated, but not defined, in the revised Judges' Rules of 1964.

Defining 'oppression'

The common law did provide a definition of 'oppression'. At common law the test for the admissibility of a confession was that it was voluntary and not forced from the mind by pressure of threats or inducements (*R v Priestly* (1965) 51 Cr App R 1). The characteristics of the accused were of particular significance to the common law, which recognised that conduct which might not have been oppressive in the case of an experienced person, for example, a man with a criminal record and well used to police methods, might well be oppressive in the case of an inexperienced young man or woman, or a person who is vulnerable for other reasons. As we shall see, such characteristics are similarly relevant to the statutory test.

Section 76(8) of PACE 1984 offers a non-exhaustive statutory definition of the term 'oppression' and states that 'oppression' includes 'torture, inhuman or degrading treatment and the use of threat of violence (whether or not amounting to torture)'. The phrase 'torture or inhuman or degrading treatment' derives from Article 3 of the European Convention on Human Rights. Torture is undoubtedly the most severe form of oppression and, according to a resolution of the United Nations in 1975, 'constitutes an aggravated and deliberate form of cruel, inhuman or degrading treatment or punishment' (Resolution 3452). It suggests a systematic and premeditated course of action rather than a spontaneous act of violence. The *Shorter Oxford English Dictionary* defines torture as 'the infliction of excruciating pain, severe or excruciating pain of body, anguish, agony' and, given the courts' predilection for giving words their ordinary dictionary meaning (see *Fulling* [1987] QB 426, below), this may be preferred.

However, the terms of s 76(8) (or Article 3) are well established in international law (eg, Article 5, UN Declaration of Human Rights 1948). Thus in the 1984 United Nations Convention against Torture and Other Cruel, Inhuman and Degrading Treatment or Punishment, torture is defined as 'any act by which severe pain or suffering, whether physical or mental, is intentionally inflicted on a person for such purposes as obtaining from him or a third person information or a confession' (Article 1). 'Inhuman treatment' has been described by the European Commission of Human Rights as covering 'at least such treatment as deliberately causes severe suffering, mental or physical' (*The Greek Case* (1969) 12 Yearbook 1 at 186). In *Ireland v UK* (1978) 2 EHRR 25, the European Court of Human Rights described the interrogation techniques (prolonged wall-standing, hooding, subjection to white (ie high-pitched) noise, deprivation of sleep, and rationing of food and drink) employed by British security forces in Northern Ireland as 'degrading', because they were 'such as to arouse in their victims feelings of fear, anguish and inferiority capable of humiliating and debasing them and possibly breaking their physical or moral resistance' (see also *Soering v UK* (1989) 11 EHRR 439). It is thus clear that psychological, as well as physical, acts are included.

The alleged maltreatment of 'illegal combatants' at Guantanamo Bay, Cuba, and at Abu Ghraib prison, Baghdad, would undoubtedly fall within the definition of 'inhuman treatment' if not 'torture'. It would clearly be 'oppression' within s 76(2)(a) (see *Fulling*, above), and may explain why the US was reluctant to allow the British prisoners held at Guantanamo Bay to be repatriated and tried in the UK. Applying s 76, any confessional evidence obtained from the prisoners while in custody would be inadmissible in an English court. Section 76(8) is not an exhaustive definition, therefore subtle distinctions between its terms are unnecessary and it serves simply to illustrate the type of conduct outlawed by s 76. Indeed, the expansive view of oppression taken by the Court of Appeal in *Fulling* has meant that the narrow terms of s 76(8) are virtually redundant.

The facts of *Fulling* were that the defendant was convicted of obtaining property by deception. The defendant staged the burglary of her flat with her boyfriend and claimed some £5,000 from an insurance company. The pair were arrested. In seeking to exclude a confession made after a number of interviews, the defendant claimed that during a break in the final interview, a detective had told her that her boyfriend had been having an affair with a girl called Christine, who had also been arrested and was in the cell next to her. This, she said, caused her distress and, she claimed, amounted to oppression. The police denied telling her this. The trial judge made no finding as to whether she or the police were telling the truth, but was prepared to assume for the purpose of argument that the defendant's version was true. Ruling that the confession was admissible, the trial judge remarked (at 429–30):

> *Bearing in mind that whatever happens to a person who is arrested and questioned is by its very nature oppressive, I am satisfied that in section 76(2)(a) of the Police and Criminal Evidence Act 1984 the word oppression means something above and beyond that which is inherently oppressive in police custody and must import some impropriety, some oppression actively applied in an improper manner by the police. I do not find that what was done in this case can be so defined and, in those circumstances, I am satisfied that oppression cannot be made out on the evidence I have heard in the context required by the statutory provision.*

The Court of Appeal adopted this part of the ruling (applying the prinicples set out in *Bank of England v Vagliano Bros* [1891] AC 107 at 144–5) and held that 'oppression' in s 76(2)(a) should be given its ordinary dictionary meaning, taking the third definition of that word in the *Oxford English Dictionary*, which runs as follows: 'exercise of authority or power in a burdensome, harsh, or wrongful manner; unjust or cruel treatment of subjects, inferiors etc; the imposition of unreasonable or unjust burdens'.

Such a wide definition more than embraces s 76(8) and extends oppression well beyond that partial definition. The Lord Chief Justice also added this gloss: 'We find it hard to envisage any circumstances in which such oppression would not entail some impropriety on the part of the interrogator' (at 432). He implicitly adopted the trial judge's ruling that 'oppression' means something above and beyond that which is inherently oppressive in police custody, and must import some degree of impropriety on the part of the police.

The requirement of impropriety initially focuses the court's attention on what the investigator has done rather than on the effect of his conduct on the suspect. It will be noted that the prosecution must prove beyond reasonable doubt that the suspect was not oppressed. If the court is persuaded that the confession was or may have been obtained by oppression of the person who made it, the confession is inadmissible. It follows that no one need prove that the suspect was oppressed. The prosecution must prove beyond reasonable doubt that he was not oppressed or, if he was, that there was no causal connection between the conduct alleged to have been oppressive and the obtaining of the confession. If a co-accused seeks to rely on a confession by another co-accused, he must prove the above on the balance of probabilities.

In order to come within s 76(2)(a) there must be some impropriety on the part of the police (possibly others), which must be serious impropriety if it is to come within the above definition. Lesser impropriety, or something said or done by the police or others that does not amount to impropriety, is more likely to come within s 76(2)(b). Whilst a breach of the Code of Practice may be seen as wrongful, it is unlikely to amount to oppression unless it amounts to an accumulation of breaches which together form a gross breach (*R v Davison* [1988] Crim LR 442). Tricks, such as covert tape-recording of a suspect, do not therefore amount to oppression (*R v Parker* [1995] Crim LR 233).

In *Fulling*, Lord Lane seems to suggest that, 'impropriety' is a synonym for 'wrongful' as used in the definition, but serious wrongdoing rather than minor breaches of procedure, though a number of such breaches together may amount to oppression. *Davison* (above) contained a catalogue of improprieties. The defendant was arrested at 6.25 am for handling a stolen ring. At the police station, he agreed to be interviewed in the absence of a solicitor but made no admissions. The judge found that by 11.00 am, the police had no evidence against the defendant and should have released him under s 34 of PACE 1984. In fact the custody continued, and an entry in the custody record at 1.15 pm purported to authorise further detention to allow further interviews and charges to be made. That was a breach of s 37 of the Act. By 3.00 pm the police had learnt that the defendant had provided information to a third party that led to a serious robbery, and then sought the authority of a superintendent to delay access to a solicitor under s 58(8) of PACE 1984. When the defendant did ask to see a solicitor this was denied, and there were then no grounds under s 58(8) to authorise delay.

At 4.30 pm a confrontation took place between the defendant and the robbery suspects, followed by a 'conversation' in which the police told the defendant he was being questioned about an armed robbery. He was not arrested for that offence as required by s 31 PACE 1984, therefore there was a breach of that section. Both the confrontation and the conversation were recorded in the police officers' notebooks, but no attempt was made to show the defendant the notes and obtain his confirmation, a breach of Code of Practice C. At 5.10 pm he was interviewed in the absence of a solicitor and made admissions. The trial judge found that the defendant had been unlawfully detained from 11.00 am, and there was a total failure to arrest him for the armed robbery. The police powers were being exercised in a 'wrongful manner', in the light of *Fulling*, capable of amounting to oppression. The judge therefore excluded all the evidence after the first interview under s 76(2)(a).

The method of questioning

The method of questioning may amount to oppression as defined in *Fulling*. In *R v Mason* [1987] 3 All ER 481, the defendant was falsely told that forensic evidence had been found linking him to the crime. Although the Court of Appeal felt that this fell short of the dictionary definition of oppression approved in *Fulling*, it may exceptionally do so if, for example, the defendant is unaware that her mother is near to death, and the police tell her this in order to put pressure on her to confess. This deliberate misuse of the truth could amount to 'harsh' or 'improper' treatment (per *Fulling*) and therefore oppression.

The abuse of power is essential. Thus in *R v Miller* (1986) 83 Cr App R 192 (a pre-PACE decision), the defendant, a paranoid schizophrenic, confessed to killing his girlfriend. The confession contained delusions mixed with facts. A psychiatrist testified that the questioning had triggered delusions. The judge's decision that the questioning was not oppressive, not being designed to induce delusions, was upheld by the Court of Appeal, and doubtless would not be oppressive under the present law (*Fulling* requires 'some oppression actively applied'), but may be within s 76(2)(b) (see pp 252–265 below). Had the police been aware of the defendant's mental state and deliberately set out to induce delusions, that would be likely to constitute oppression within s 76(2)(a).

There is no doubt that persistent, heavy-handed or bullying questioning interspersed with misrepresentations could qualify. For example, in *R v Beales* [1991] Crim LR 118, a confession extracted during a 35-minute interview was excluded because the officer had invented evidence against the defendant and forcefully confronted him with it, repeatedly misrepresented the defendant's answers and 'hectored and bullied [him] from first to last'.

In *R v West (Timothy)* unreported, 2 May 1988, Gloucester Crown Court, there was oppression when the interviewing officer interrupted the suspect on a large number of occasions before he had finished his reply, often vigorously and rudely with a raised voice, and used obscenities to indicate that he was lying. It was clear to the court that the officer had made up his mind that the defendant had committed the offence, and would continue to question him until he admitted this.

Much more clearly oppressive was the conduct of the interviewing officers in *R v Paris, Abdullahi and Miller* (1993) 97 Cr App R 99 (dubbed 'The Cardiff Three'). There, the officers shouted at one suspect and told him what they wanted him to say, despite his denying involvement some 300 times. The suspect was of low intelligence, which made such questioning more obviously oppressive. It is, indeed, a matter of degree whether aggressive and hostile questioning amounts to oppression. It is more likely to do so if the suspect is a weak or vulnerable person. In this sense, there is a subjective element to the test for oppression. Though initially concentrating on the conduct of the police, the characteristics of the person on the receiving end of that conduct are also important, as are the particular circumstances in which the conduct takes place. Thus in *R v Seelig* (1992) 141 NLJ 638, the Court of Appeal held that the trial judge was right, in determining whether there was oppression, to take into account the fact that Seelig was an experienced merchant banker, intelligent and sophisticated. (See also *R v L* [1994] Crim LR 839, which indicates that other factors, such as the weakness of the case against the defendant apart from the confession and the initial failure to allow access to a solicitor, must be considered, rather than concentrating solely on the hostile questioning. There, the questioning was not oppressive, nor likely to induce unreliability.)

The availability of a tape-recording (as in *Beales, West* and *Paris, Abdullahi and Miller*) will be crucial in helping a court to decide whether the questioning has reached a sufficient degree of impropriety to be described as oppressive. Lord Taylor LCJ was clearly shocked after listening to the tape-recording of the interview with Miller (the third of The Cardiff Three), and expressed the view that short of physical violence, it was hard to conceive of a more hostile and intimidating approach by police officers to a suspect. The three defendants were accused of the murder of a prostitute, Lynette White, who was stabbed some 50 times. After a trial in which the prosecution relied on the evidence of two discredited witnesses and admissions made by Miller after exhaustive interviews, all three were convicted. Miller was described by a defence doctor as 'on the borderline of mental handicap' with an IQ of 75, a mental age of 11 and a reading age of 8. The following extract from the one of 19 taped interviews totalling 13 hours over 5 days, may provide something of the flavour of the interview. More so if you imagine the officer shouting in a frustrated manner, thumping the table and spluttering in his indignation so much that he failed to finish sentences:

Miller:	'I wasn't there.'
DC Greenwood:	'How can you ever ...?'
Miller:	'I wasn't there.'
DC Greenwood:	'How you ... I just don't know how you can sit there, I ...'
Miller:	'I wasn't ...'
DC Greenwood:	'Really don't ...'
Miller:	'I was not there, I was not there.'
DC Greenwood:	'Seeing that girl, your girlfriend, in that room that night like she was. I don't know how you can sit there and say it.'
Miller:	'I wasn't there.'
DC Greenwood:	'You were there that night.'
Miller:	'I was not there.'
DC Greenwood:	'Together with all the others, you were there that night.'
Miller:	'I was not there. I'll tell you already.'
DC Greenwood:	'And you sit there and say that.'
Miller:	'They can lock me up for 50 billion years, I said I was not there.'
DC Greenwood:	'Cause you don't wanna be there.'
Miller:	'I was not there.'
DC Greenwood:	'You don't wanna be there because if ...'
Miller:	'I was not there.'
DC Greenwood:	'As soon as you say you were there you know you're involved.'
Miller:	'I was not there.'
DC Greenwood:	'You know you were involved in it.'

Miller:	'I was not involved and wasn't there.'
DC Greenwood:	'Yes you were there.'
Miller:	'I was not there.'
DC Greenwood:	'You were there, that's why Leanne is come up now ...'
Miller:	'No.'
DC Greenwood:	'Cause her conscience is ...'
Miller:	'I was not there.'
DC Greenwood:	'She can't sleep at night.'
Miller:	'No. I was not there.'
DC Greenwood:	'To say you were not there that night ...'
Miller:	'I was not there.'
DC Greenwood:	'Looking over her body seeing what she was like ...'
Miller:	'I was not there.'
DC Greenwood:	'With her head like she had and you have got the audacity to sit there and say nothing at all about it.'
Miller:	'I was not there.'
DC Greenwood:	'You know damn well you were there.'
Miller:	'I was not there.'

And so on for many pages.

Having heard the entire tape, the court had no doubt that it was oppression within the meaning of s 76(2). A solicitor was present from the third interview. Quashing the convictions, Lord Taylor LCJ was severely critical of his failure to intervene and prevent the oppression of his client. That criticism led to a change in the training and authorisation of solicitors who attend police stations. The police were also prompted to retrain their officers in interrogation (interviewing) techniques so that this kind of questioning is unlikely to be repeated. Given that the *Fulling* definition of oppression means that extreme and improper conduct is required, the style of questioning will more often fall for consideration under s 76(2)(b), but where it falls short of oppression it will not necessarily be regarded as likely to render any confession unreliable; it remains a matter of degree, and the circumstances, including the characteristics of the suspect, are all important.

The Times (5 July 2003) reported the conviction of one Jeffrey Gafoor for the murder of Lynette White. After the conviction, South Wales police announced that they would hold another inquiry, overseen by the independent Police Complaints Commission. In May 2005, this investigation into the original conviction of the 'Cardiff Three' resulted in five retired police officers finally being arrested on suspicion of false imprisonment, conspiracy to pervert the course of justice and misconduct in public office after an investigation into this conviction (*The Times*, 19 May 2005.) In total nine former police officers and 13 other people have been arrested. The 13 other people, including former Cardiff prostitutes and pimps, have been questioned about information that they provided to the police (see also *Statewatch* March–April 2005, Vol 15, No 2; and for a detailed early account of the case see S Seker, *Fitted In: the Cardiff 3 and the Lynette White Inquiry* (1998)).

Additional points to note

The following additional points on s 76(2)(a) should be noted:

(a) The confession must have been obtained by oppression. If the defendant confesses before being subjected to oppressive treatment, s 76(2)(a) does not apply. More realistically, there may be occasions when the police have used oppression but the accused confesses for other reasons unconnected with it, for example after a night in a cell, following oppressive treatment, when he decides to get the 'matter off his chest' and save further anxiety to his family. However, the defence will in all probability raise the issue of oppression, in which case it will be extremely difficult for the prosecution to rebut the alleged causal connection between the police conduct and the confession; indeed, the night in the cell may be seen as an opportunity for the oppressive treatment to take effect by giving the accused time to think over his options.

(b) A confession which a court decides was, or might have been, obtained by oppression, *must* be excluded even if it is true. For example, the defendant, a suspected paedophile, is severely beaten up by enraged neighbours, and confesses to serious sexual offences against young children. The oppressive and improper conduct need not emanate from the police (despite Lord Lane's reference in *Fulling* to impropriety on the part of the interrogators, and the trial judge's reference to 'some oppression actively carried out by the police'). The defendant's confession will be excluded if it is shown that the oppression caused him to confess. It is, of course, possible that the defendant will make a second confession which is not induced by the oppression, but that will be a question of fact for the court to determine. This would also apply where a defendant was threatened by an IRA/Loyalist punishment squad and ordered to confess to his crimes. A causal connection must be shown between the oppression and/or something said or done which induces an unreliable confession, and the period in custody away from the threats of others may break the chain of causation.

(c) The defendant can be oppressed by the use of threats or violence against others (eg, a spouse, children or close friends) of which he is aware. Such psychological pressure can overlap with the question of reliability (see s 76(2)(b), below) and can be excluded on that basis as well.

(d) Since oppression must be the consequence of some improper conduct by the oppressor(s), acts the unintended consequence of which is oppressive are probably not within s 76(2)(a) unless they are improper acts. Proper acts which cause a person to be oppressed are not within s 76(2)(a), but may be within s 76(2)(b).

(e) If a confession is obtained by oppression, the things said or done will also render the confession unreliable under s 76(2)(b) (though that subsection need not be relied upon). However, things said or done which do not amount to oppression may nevertheless render the confession unreliable under s 76(2)(b) (ie, the greater para (a) includes the lesser para (b), but the lesser does not necessarily include the greater). Note that under s 76(2)(b), a confession may be invalidated where there is no suspicion of impropriety.

(f) It should be remembered that 'oppression' is not confined to conduct which took place at the police station. Questioning or conduct that occurred at the time of arrest or while the person was being conveyed to a police station may be similarly relevant. In any event, the court will wish to hear an account of the whole proceedings that took place between the police and the accused, before deciding whether there has been oppression.

251

(g) While, unlike the common law test, the *Fulling* test of oppression excludes the inherent oppression involved in arrest and custody, the characteristics of the suspect can be considered in determining whether a confession was obtained by oppression and in determining the related question of whether the conduct was 'burdensome', 'harsh' or 'cruel' within the definition of oppression (see *Seelig* and *R v L*, above). In *Paris, Abdullahi and Miller*, the fact that one of the suspects was below normal intelligence and on the borderline of mental handicap was taken into consideration, though the method of questioning in that case might have oppressed a man of average intelligence.

When considering whether the wrongful refusal to allow a suspect access to a solicitor is grounds for exclusion under s 76 or s 78, the Court of Appeal has adopted a similar subjective test in holding that where the suspect was an experienced criminal who knew his rights, the absence of a solicitor did not affect him and the resulting confession was not unreliable, and there were no grounds for exclusion under s 78 – see *R v Alladice* (1988) 87 Cr App R 380 and *R v Dunford* (1990) 91 Cr App R 150. Conversely, the fact that the suspect was vulnerable and in need of protection is evidence of unreliability or a ground for excluding under s 78 – see *R v Franklin* (1994) *The Times*, 16 June (discussed below).

Section 76(2)(b) – reliability

Section 76(2)(b) of PACE 1984 stipulates that a confession will be inadmissible if it

> *was or may have been obtained ... in consequence of anything said or done which was likely, in the circumstances existing at the time, to render unreliable any confession which might be made [by the person] in consequence thereof.*

What constitutes 'anything said or done'?

As with s 76(2)(a), once it is represented that the confession was or may have been obtained in circumstances of unreliability, the burden passes to the prosecution to prove beyond reasonable doubt that it was not so obtained. Therefore, while the trial judge must initially determine the likelihood of unreliability, if the confession is admitted, the jury will also do so in reaching their verdict. In order to avoid the embarrassment of a jury in effect overruling the judge by reaching a different conclusion, on the issue of admissibility the judge is concerned not with the actual confession but with any confession the defendant might have made in consequence of what was said or done.

The phrase 'anything said or done' is potentially very broad in scope. It can certainly encompass conduct which amounts to oppression under s 76(2)(a), but stretches well beyond that. It can include threats or promises, or the holding out of some hope of advantage directed towards the accused, which was a key feature of the previous common law. Everything said or done before and during the period of detention must be considered – the whole picture, rather than selective parts of it. Thus in *R v Barry* (1992) 95 Cr App R 384, the defendant was interviewed over two days. On the first day he was told that it would be beneficial to him to assist the police to recover certain property. On the second day he was interviewed and confessed. The judge's conclusion that the statement on the first day had no effect on the confession made on the second day, was rejected by the Court of Appeal. The Court set out the necessary steps under s 76(2)(b):

(a) The first step is to identify what was said or done and this should include everything said or done.

(b) The next step is to decide whether what was said or done was likely to render a confession unreliable; all the circumstances should be taken into account. The test is hypothetical.

(c) Finally, the judge should ask whether the prosecution had proved beyond reasonable doubt that the confession had not been made as a result of what was said or done.

In the context of this case, the promise of some benefit on the first day was something said which had to be taken into account. It was likely to render any confession made unreliable, and the fact that the defendant had some time to think about it made it more likely that he would be influenced by it. This is not to say that something 'said or done' cannot be rendered ineffective by time; much depends on what was said or done and the particular circumstances. A connection, or causal link, must be established between what was said and done and the obtaining of the confession; a delay between what was said or done and the obtaining of the confession may weaken that connection.

Something said or done can also embrace conduct that is directed towards a person other than the accused but which is designed (or is likely) to make his confession unreliable. This would include, for example, a threat or suggestion that official action will be taken against the defendant's family unless he or she confesses. Examples from the cases include allegations that threats were made to have children put into care, to prosecute a girlfriend or someone in the suspect's family, or to report the suspect's or a related person's activities to the Inland Revenue or Benefits Agency. While these things may properly be done, if used as a threat to obtain a confession they will fall within s 76(2)(b).

It has been held that the phrase does not refer to things said or done by the accused but must be something external to him which then raises the possibility of unreliability. Thus, the court will not consider the motives of the person making the confession as 'something said or done'; neither, it seems, will it consider self-inflicted drug addiction, which could prompt the defendant to agree to anything in order to get bail and to feed the addiction, as 'something said or done' within s 76(2)(b). There is, however, some confusion in the cases as to whether interviewing a suspect suffering from the withdrawal symptoms of self-induced drug addiction can be within s 76(2)(b), as a number of cases indicate.

In *R v Goldenberg* (1989) 88 Cr App R 285, a heroin addict was convicted on a charge of conspiracy to provide diamorphine. Following a search of the defendant's premises, where heroin and some £1,600 in cash were found, the defendant was arrested. After an initial interview, the record of which the defendant refused to read or sign, he was remanded in custody. Five days later the defendant requested another interview – his motive, according to the defence, being to obtain credit for helping the police and to get bail when he could continue to feed his habit – during which he allegedly gave information about the man who had supplied him with heroin. He also refused to read or sign the record of this interview.

On appeal against conviction it was argued that s 76(2)(b) was concerned with the objective reliability of the confession and not merely with the conduct of the police or other person to whom the confession was made. Accordingly, the Court might have to look at what was said or done by the person making the confession, because the confession might have been made 'in consequence' of what he himself had said or done, and his words or actions might indicate that this confession was or might be unreliable. In rejecting this argument the Court stated:

> *In our judgement the words 'said or done' in section 76(2)(b) of the 1984 Act do not extend so as to include anything said or done by the person making the confession. It is clear from the wording of the section and the use of the words 'in consequence' that a causal link must be shown between what was said and the subsequent confession. In our view it necessarily follows that 'anything said or done' is limited to something external to the person making the confession and to something which is likely to have an influence on him.*

In *Goldenberg*, the Court was concerned more with the motives of a suspect for making a confession, rather than with a suspect who was suffering the immediate effects of withdrawal. However, in *R v Crampton* (1991) 92 Cr App R 369, the Court was faced with a defendant drug addict more immediately affected by withdrawal symptoms, who, it was alleged, was prepared to say anything in order to get out of the police station and 'get a fix'. The defendant was convicted of conspiracy to supply heroin. The police were aware that he was an addict and put off interviewing him until lunchtime on the day after his arrest. Exercising their own judgement, they decided he was fit to be interviewed, then interviewed him after he had been in custody for 19 hours. He was asked whether he wanted a solicitor and if he was feeling all right. He replied that he did not want a solicitor and that he was feeling all right. He made a number of admissions during this interview. After the interview, on returning to the custody officer, he complained that he was suffering withdrawal symptoms. A doctor was called and, though he found only a high pulse rate and a suggestion in the pupils of the eyes that there was a very small amount of the drug in the body, he prescribed tablets to deal with any withdrawal symptoms. A second doctor repeated the prescription some five hours later. The second doctor described withdrawal symptoms as subjective, appearing eight to 16 hours after the last dose and worsening for up to 24 hours, but that the sufferer would be lucid with no mental confusion, though manipulative and lying in order to obtain more drugs. The first doctor also agreed that withdrawal symptoms do not affect the intelligence. In the trial within a trial, the defence argued that the confession should be excluded as unreliable under s 76(2)(b) or as unfair under s 78, relying on the fact that the defendant had been interviewed while suffering from withdrawal symptoms. Both doctors gave evidence, and they and the police agreed that an addict withdrawing would or might be unreliable in what he said in view of his desire for a further fix. Despite this, the trial judge admitted the confession and the defendant was convicted.

On appeal, counsel for the defence sought to distinguish *Goldenberg* on the basis that in this case the police decided when the interview should be conducted and it was not at the request of the appellant. The Court of Appeal doubted that the mere holding of an interview at a time when the appellant was experiencing symptoms of withdrawal from heroin addiction was something said or done within s 76(2)(b), but was prepared to assume that it was for the purpose of the appeal. The reason for the Court's doubt was that s 76(2)(b) is concerned with the nature and quality of the words spoken, or things said or done, which are likely, in the circumstances existing at the time, to render the confession unreliable in the sense that it is not true. The Court went on to uphold the decision of the trial judge that the confession had been correctly admitted (at 372):

> *It is plain that the experienced officers, who dealt with drug addicts, considered that he was fit to be interviewed. More important, perhaps, Dr Koppel [the first doctor to see*

the defendant] said that when he saw the appellant he considered he was then fit to be interviewed. It follows a fortiori that the appellant would have been fit at the time of his interview which occurred earlier ... In our judgement, the position is this. Whether or not someone who is a drug addict is fit to be interviewed, in the sense that his answers can be relied upon as being truthful, is a matter for judgement of those present at the time.

The Court also referred to Code C, Note C9B, which concerns mainly the condition of the defendant in the police station and the need to call a doctor if the police are in any doubt as to whether or not the defendant is well enough to be interviewed:

If the police had summoned Dr Koppell, and he had seen the appellant before the interview, the doctor would have certified that he was fit to be interviewed. That is the evidence that he effectively gave and the evidence which the trial judge accepted. It is then for the judge at the trial within a trial to decide whether the assessment of those present at the time was correct. The mere fact that someone is withdrawing, and may have a motive for making a confession, does not mean the confession is necessarily unreliable. (at 374)

The Court went on to cite the observations of the Lord Chief Justice in *Rennie* (1982) 74 Cr App R 207, 212:

Very few confessions are inspired solely by remorse. Often the motives of an accused are mixed and include a hope that an early admission may lead to an earlier release or a lighter sentence. If it were the law that the mere presence of such a motive, even if prompted by something said or done by a person in authority, led inexorably to the exclusion of a confession, nearly every confession would be rendered inadmissible. This is not the law. In some cases the hope may be self-generated. If so, it is irrelevant, even if it provides the dominant motive for making the confession. In such a case the confession will not have been obtained by anything said or done by a person in authority. More commonly the presence of such a hope will, in part at least, owe its origin to something said or done by such a person. There can be few prisoners who are being firmly but fairly questioned in a police station to whom it does not occur that they might be able to bring both their interrogation and their detention to an earlier end by confession.

The *Crampton* case does not exclude the possibility that the fact that the defendant is withdrawing can be a circumstance within s 76(2)(b) which could render any confession made in consequence unreliable. The important question is whether the confession was made in consequence of the withdrawing. As the following case makes clear, the subsection is viewed objectively. It is not a question of what the police believe to be the facts, that the defendant is not withdrawing and is fit to be interviewed, but what the facts actually are (or would have been) as ascertained by a doctor who examines the suspect.

In *R v Everett* [1988] Crim LR 826, the defendant, though aged 42 years, had a mental age of 8 when he pleaded guilty to indecent assault. He lived with a family who had known him for some years. He was left alone with a 5-year-old boy and a 6-year-old girl. The mother returned to find that the boy's track suit bottoms were pulled down and his underpants crumpled. She told the police, describing the defendant as slightly mentally defective and slow in his speech. He was arrested and on the way to the police station was asked a number of questions; he said that he had touched the boy's 'willy' and had then touched himself. At the police station, the police, having failed to appreciate that he was mentally handicapped, interviewed him on tape in the absence of an appropriate adult or solicitor. In the course of this interview the defendant admitted indecently touching the boy. The tape of the interview was the only evidence at his trial. There was medical evidence that mentally the defendant was in the bottom 2% of the population, with an IQ of 61. Had the police been aware of this, they would have been obliged by the Code of Practice to call an appropriate adult to look after his interests while at the police station and while being interviewed. However, they were not and did not. The trial judge decided to ignore the medical evidence and admitted the interview tapes. The Court of Appeal held that he was wrong to do so and quashed the conviction as it was clear that s 76(2)(b) was specially designed for the judge to have regard to certain circumstances when considering whether the prosecution has discharged the burden cast upon them. This obviously included the mental condition of a suspect which existed at the time when the confession or confessions came into being. In regarding those circumstances the court was in no doubt that the test to be applied is an objective one. Therefore it was not what the police officer thought, if they gave any thought to it at all, about the mental condition of the person they were asking questions of which was material, but, what was subsequently ascertained from doctors about the mental condition of the appellant.

Thus there is no doubt that the mental condition of the suspect is a relevant circumstance within s 76(2)(b), though in the case of Everett it was not a self-induced condition, as it would be in the case of drug addicts.

In *R v Walker* [1998] Crim LR 211, the Court of Appeal had to consider the case of the suspect with a personality disorder and a drug habit. The defendant, a prostitute, was convicted of robbery. It was alleged that she took the car keys from a man and demanded money for their return, showing the man a knife in her waistband. At the police station following her arrest, she was seen by a police doctor. She told him she was a heroin addict and was taking methadone. She was prescribed methadone and valium. In her interview she denied having a knife, but admitted that she had tried to frighten the victim into giving her money. At her trial the defence sought to exclude the confession. At the *voir dire*, the defendant gave evidence that she had smuggled crack cocaine into the police station and was under its influence when she was interviewed. Psychiatric evidence was called to the effect that the defendant suffered from a severe personality disorder. Having listened to the tapes of the interview, the psychiatrist expressed the opinion that her condition might render her admissions unreliable because she might elaborate inaccurately on events without understanding the implications; and this effect was likely to be exacerbated if she was a user of crack cocaine. The police claimed that her condition before she said she took the crack cocaine and during the interview appeared to be the same. The judge concluded that there was no evidence of mental impairment or subnormality in terms of IQ, and he did not accept that the personality disorder rendered the interview unreliable. He did not believe the defendant's evidence that she had smoked crack cocaine in the police station.

On appeal it was argued, first, that the trial judge had adopted the wrong approach to s 76(2)(b); and, secondly, that there was new evidence from the duty solicitor that the defendant had smoked crack cocaine earlier in the day. Allowing the appeal, the Court of Appeal held as follows:

(a) The evidence of the psychiatrist was uncontradicted. In his analysis of the evidence, the trial judge appeared to limit the question of whether the defendant's personality disorder was such as to render the confession unreliable, by reference to previously decided cases of what he termed 'mental impairment' or of 'impairment of intelligence or social functioning' such as that in *Everett*; and, whether as an extension of that class or as a separate category, to cases where it could be shown that the defendant had a very low IQ. The judge was entitled to reject the evidence of the psychiatrist, but in accepting the evidence but attempting to avoid its implications by reference to *Everett*, he adopted the wrong approach to s 76(2)(b). The test in the subsection replaced the old common law and did not require that there be wrongdoing by the police. The defendant's mental condition was one of the circumstances to be taken into account (*Everett*), and nothing in that case limited or defined the particular form of mental or psychological condition or disorder upon which the defendant could rely to show that his confession was unreliable – any mental or personality abnormalities may be of relevance.

(b) Having come to that conclusion, it was not necessary to rule on the new evidence, although the Court had considerable reservations as to whether there was a reasonable explanation for not adducing the evidence at trial. Had it been available to the judge, it must have been influential on his decision on the factual issue of whether or not she took the drug. However, that issue was not central to the evidence of the psychiatrist, which was principally concerned with the pre-existing disorder.

(c) Having decided that the approach of the judge was flawed, the Court was in no position to substitute its own discretion and rule on the admissibility of the evidence. The original ruling was rightly based on oral evidence.

It is unfortunate that the Court did not consider the effect of the new evidence, which might have led to a clarification of the question whether, and if so in what circumstances, self- administration of drugs and/or the symptoms of withdrawal can be a relevant consideration. *Goldenberg* was not considered in *Walker*. Therefore the *Goldenberg* case remains authority for the proposition that 'anything said or done' in s 76(2)(b) does 'not extend so as to include anything said or done by the person making the confession', but rather these words are 'limited to something external to the person making the confession' and to something that is likely to have some influence over him.

While *Goldenberg* was not directly concerned with a suspect under the influence of drugs or suffering withdrawal symptoms, there is no doubt that the taking of a drug and its subsequent effect is something done by the person making the confession and is not external to him, even if it is likely to have some influence on him. There is some dispute among the medical fraternity as to whether withdrawal from drugs has any effect on the intelligence. In *Crampton*, one doctor said withdrawal did not affect intelligence, while the other stated that the sufferer would be lucid with no mental confusion but manipulative and lying in order to get more drugs. *Crampton* appears to assume that interviewing a heroin addict in withdrawal can be something, 'said or done which was likely in the circumstances existing at the time, to render unreliable any confession which might be made in consequence thereof'. If the doctor's evidence had been that the defendant was a heroin addict in withdrawal and that those symptoms could influence him in such a way that any confession would be unreliable, there seems little doubt that it would come within s 76(2)(b).

In her commentary on the decision in *Walker*, Professor Birch ([1998] Crim LR 211) notes:

> *In order to give effect to the purpose of the subsection, which (as the present case acknowledges) is not to attach penalties to police misconduct at interview, but rather to prevent reliance on potentially unreliable material, the better approach would be to include the drugged (or drug-dependent) state of D as potentially relevant 'circumstances', and to concede that even the perfectly ordinary interviewing of somebody in such a state might be 'something said or done' which is conducive to the making of an unreliable confession. This seems to be the approach taken in the present case (though without consideration of the effect of Goldenberg) and it would seem, with respect, to be right.*

The Home Office recently commissioned a survey of those arrested in five areas (Bennett, *Drugs and Crime: The Results of Research on Drug Testing*, 1998 RDS No 183). Among the key findings were that 61% of arrestees had taken at least one illegal drug: 46% tested positive for cannabis; 18% for opiates/heroin; and 10% for cocaine/crack. Nearly half the arrestees across all five areas said their drug use was connected with their offending. Therefore, given that the number of people arrested whilst on drugs is so high, there may be an element of policy behind the decision to exclude self-induced incapacity, if withdrawal symptoms are in fact an incapacity. However, if the medical evidence is correct in saying that the intelligence of drug-dependent suspects who are withdrawing is not affected, and that they would be manipulative and lying in order to obtain more drugs, then it is arguable that the drug-dependent suspect is in no different position from the suspect who is desperate to get bail for other, equally compelling reasons. *Goldenberg*, *Crampton* and *Rennie* accept that suspects confess for many reasons. If they do so in a self-generated hope of some benefit then that is not within s 76(2)(b). The drug-dependent suspect may then be no different from the suspect who wants bail for some pressing personal reason. If the police do not say or do anything to suggest that he will be bailed in return for a confession, and the defendant confesses in the hope or belief that he will get bail, that is not within s 76(2)(b) any more than the drug-dependent suspect who similarly confesses, without prompting, in the hope or belief that he will get bail and be in a position to feed his habit.

Other 'circumstances' inducing unreliability

There may be other conditions which, perhaps coupled with low intelligence, might be a 'circumstance' in which an interview might be 'something said or done' to induce an unreliable confession. In *R v McGovern* (1991) 92 Cr App R 228, a woman aged 19, six months pregnant and of low intelligence, was arrested on a charge of murder and interviewed in the absence of a solicitor. The subsequent confession was excluded because of the absence of a solicitor but, that apart, one can readily accept that the factors of age, pregnancy and limited intelligence combine to create a circumstance in which an interview could produce an unreliable confession.

One might further note that both mentally handicapped and juvenile suspects must be interviewed in the presence of an 'appropriate adult', whose role is not simply that of observer. He or she is there to advise the vulnerable suspect, to see whether or not the interview is being conducted fairly and properly, and to facilitate communication between the suspect and police (Code C, para 11.16). The absence of an appropriate adult may then be something done which in the circumstances is likely to result in any confession made being unreliable.

Although the point has not been considered directly, it might be noted that that 'anything said or done' may include omissions. *McGovern* involved the failure (omission) to allow access to a solicitor; *R v Cox* [1991] Crim LR 276 involved the failure to call an appropriate adult; and *R v Doolan* [1988] Crim LR 747 involved the failure to caution and record the interview.

Something 'said or done' need not emanate from the police

The most obvious external event which is 'said or done' is the conduct of the police. However, the 'something said or done' need not emanate from a police officer. In *R v Harvey* [1988] Crim LR 241, the defendant confessed after hearing her lover confess to murder. She was of low intelligence and suffering from a psychopathic disorder. Doctors suggested that she might have confessed in a child-like attempt to protect her lover. Though the police had acted properly throughout, the prosecution were unable to prove beyond reasonable doubt that hearing her lover confess did not cause her to confess. Other conduct external to the police would include a threat by a father to his son that the latter had better tell the truth or he will be beaten, or a promise by an employer to an employee that if he admits the misconduct he will not be dismissed, or a threat by a head-master to a pupil that unless the latter tells the truth to a police officer, he will be disciplined. There must be a causal connection between what was said or done and the obtaining of the confession, and in these cases the prosecution may be able to prove that there was no such connection, particularly if they are aware of what was said or done and take steps to ensure that the suspect is no longer influenced by it when interviewed.

In *R v Wahab* [2003] 1 Cr App R 15, the accused was arrested for conspiracy to supply class A prohibited drugs together with members of his family. He was interviewed in the presence of his solicitor and after the third interview he authorised his solicitor to approach the police to see whether the members of his family who were also in custody would be released if he confessed. The solicitor approached the police who made it clear that no promise could be made and no guarantee could be given. The solicitor then told his client that if he confessed police would look at the whole picture and if the evidence against his family was 'borderline' they would be released. At the fourth interview Wahab confessed to his part in the conspiracy but only as a middleman. At his trial, the accused challenged the admissibility of the confession on the basis that he had been incompetently advised by his solicitor. He called another solicitor to show that the conduct of his solicitor had fallen below the proper standard of professional competence. The trial judge upheld the prosecution submission that the solicitor had properly outlined the factors to be con-sidered and ruled that the confession was admissible. Following his conviction Wahab appealed arguing that the confession should not have been admitted. Dismissing the appeal the Court of Appeal held:

(a) Advice properly given by a solicitor did not normally provide a basis for exclusion of a subse-quent confession under s 76(2).

(b) One of the duties of a legal adviser is to give the client realistic advice. That emphatically did not mean the advice had to be directed to 'getting the client off' or simply making life difficult for the prosecution though it had to be sensibly robust considering the advantages the client might derive from evidence of remorse and a realistic acceptance of guilt, or the corresponding disadvantages of a no comment interview.

(c) In the instant case the cross-examination of the second solicitor was not relevant to the reliability of Wahab's confession, it was not necessary and inappropriate. Following *Goldenberg* the competence of the solicitor did not influence Wahab's decision to confess.

Proper conduct by the police

It can be argued that the phrase 'anything said or done' implies something out of the ordinary, for the proper exercise of normal police powers and procedures, as set out by Parliament, can hardly be allowed to trigger s 76(2)(b) (note that in *Fulling* the inherent oppression involved in arrest and custody is not enough for s 76(2)(a)). However, in contrast to oppression under s 76(2)(a), no impropriety on the part of the police is required under s 76(2)(b) (see *Harvey* and *R v Morse* [1991] Crim LR 195). This is clearly the correct approach – the emphasis of s 76(2)(b) lies on the reliability or otherwise of the confession and not   the propriety of police conduct per se. The fact that 'something said or done' in s 76(2)(b) includes almost anything external to the suspect and does not require any impropriety on the part of the police, encourages the defence to raise the issue of unreliability in many more circumstances than were possible under the previous law. A narrow dividing line can separate legitimate police responses from illegitimate ones. At common law answers to questions from the suspect such as 'If I make a statement will I be given bail now?' (*R v Barry* (1992) 95 Cr App R 384) led to the exclusion of a confession, as did the statement that the police had no objection to taking a number of offences into consideration, rather than prosecuting each separately, in response to the suspect's question before he confessed to a number of additional burglaries (*R v Phillips* (1988) 86 Cr App R 18).

Code of Practice C, para 11.5 seeks to prevent proper responses to such questions being seen as something 'said or done' within s 76(2)(b) by providing that 'proper and warranted.' responses would not be seen as falling within s 76(2)(b). Regardless of the provisions of the Codes, it is for the court to decide whether a proper response to a suspect's question was likely to induce an unreliable confession in the particular circumstances. In practice it is unlikely that the courts will find that a proper response is likely to induce an unreliable confession. It may often be the case that the suspect is merely seeking support for his own motives for confessing (see *Rennie*, above and *Wahab* in relation to proper advice by a solicitor) having recognised that a confession will bring an end to the interrogation and to his release on bail. Nonetheless, a police officer would still be well advised to think twice before responding to a suspects questions lest the answer be seen as improper and an inducement to confess (see *R v Howden-Simpson* [1991] Crim LR 49 where the police officer promised to charge the defendant with only two offences if he confessed, more if he did not, clearly a promise and a threat. The confession was excluded under s 78 (considered below) but it is more properly seen as something said or done which was likely to induce an unreliable confession under s 76(2)(b).

Breaches of the Code of Practice

Where police impropriety is present it will usually involve a breach of the Codes of Practice, but even a serious breach may not result in exclusion of a confession. Much depends on the nature of the Code provision which has been breached. The gravity of each and every breach of PACE and the Codes is more likely to influence the court towards exclusion (eg *DPP v Blake* [1989] 1 WLR 432; *R v Trussler* [1988] Crim LR 446), as is the type of breach which can be described as *significant or substantial* (ie, those which are more likely to affect the reliability of a confession such as the presence of an appropriate adult when interviewing juveniles or the mentally handicapped). The police conduct can clearly include the physical treatment of the suspect. For example, in *Trussler* the denial of a rest period, as prescribed in Code C, para 12.2), was a crucial factor leading to exclusion under s 76(2)(b). To this extent, the category overlaps with oppression in s 76(2)(a) but goes further by covering conduct which lacks the gravity of oppression but which still has, or is likely to have, an effect on the particular suspect such as to produce an unreliable confession. Two other broad categories of police conduct which could lead to unreliability within s 76(2)(b) may be noted.

The denial of a defendant's protective rights
It is not every breach of PACE 1984 which may affect the reliability of confessions. Thus in *R v Sparks* [1991] Crim LR 128, a failure to caution and to record the interview were breaches of Code C (and may be dealt with under s 78, see pp 277–279 below), but were held not to be likely, without more, to affect reliability. However, there are some provisions in the Code C which are designed to protect the suspect against himself, especially vulnerable suspects, and breach of which may influence the reliability of what he said. These provisions concern the physical presence of an adviser for the suspect, the most obvious of which is a lawyer (see *McGovern*, at p 258 above).

For the vulnerable groups of suspects for whom the Code of Practice require the presence of an 'appropriate adult' (see Code C, para 11.14) the presence of such an adult is crucial (see *Cox* at p 259 above). Moreover, the presence must be effective and a person called as the appropriate adult may himself be totally incompetent as in *R v Morse* [1991] Crim LR 195 where the father was of very low intelligence and virtually illiterate. The custody record and the tape-recording of interviews goes some way to discovering such cases.

The denial of access to a solicitor
Failure to allow access to a solicitor will not necessarily lead to unreliability. If the suspect is vulnerable, a juvenile or mentally disordered, or as in *McGovern*, young, of low intelligence and pregnant, it may do so and almost certainly will do so, especially if coupled with a failure to provide an appropriate adult (*R v Moss* (1990) 91 Cr App R 371). The seriousness of the offence under investigation will also be a factor, the protective presence of a solicitor being more necessary the more serious the offence.

Despite the decision in *R v Samuel* [1988] QB 615, which severely restricted police power to delay access to a solicitor under s 58(8) and described the right to access legal advice as 'one of the most important and fundamental rights of a citizen', wrongful delay in permitting access to a solicitor is seldom considered as likely to lead to unreliability under s 76(2)(b) when the suspect is an adult and not vulnerable for any reason. Instead, s 78 is often relied upon (see pp 275–277 below). The character of the accused is important in determining whether the suspect has been prejudiced by the absence of a solicitor; for example, the suspect who is familiar with the criminal justice system is not prejudiced by the absence; whereas a suspect who is unfamiliar with the system may be considered vulnerable and prejudiced by the absence of a solicitor. Where the vulnerable suspect is denied access it is often seen as having such an adverse effect on the fairness of the trial that the evidence, a confession or admission, ought not to be admitted. However, the absence of a solicitor in such a case may well produce an unreliable confession which should be dealt with under s 76(2)(b). For example, in *R v Sanusi* [1992] Crim LR 43, a confession made by a foreigner with no knowledge of our legal system was excluded under s 78 because he was wrongly denied access to a solicitor but any confession made in those circumstances is almost certain to be unreliable (see also *R v Beycan* [1990] Crim LR 185, where the suspect was also a foreigner unfamiliar with our system. Both cases should have been dealt with under s 76(2)(b) but demonstrate the judicial tendency to ignore s 76 in favour of s 78 so that the courts are being asked to exercise a discretion to exclude what is likely to be a confession that is inadmissible under s 76(2)(b).

Recording and tape-recording of interviews and cautions

The recording provisions of Code C are designed to protect the accused against abuse by 'verballing', ie attributing to the accused words he never said or taking words out of context to attribute to them a different meaning. The requirement to tape record interviews reduces the importance of the Code C requirement that written records of the interview be kept. That provision was directed at the pre-tape recording era when the requirement was that the interview be recorded in writing, read to and signed by the suspect. If the police then failed to record the interview or to show it to the suspect for approval, and the suspect later disagrees with the officer's recollection of the record, he is effectively saying that the confession is untrue and that the police have fabricated or misrepresented the confession (eg, *R v Waters* [1989] Crim LR 62; *Doolan* (above)). The lack of a written record agreed by the suspect makes it virtually impossible for the police to prove that the defendant confesses as alleged.

The failure to record, coming after the confession was made, could not be something said or done within s 76(2)(b), but the thing done which is alleged is the making up of a confession, or the doctoring of it. Whether this is so or not, the failure to record deprives the prosecution of evidence which might be used to rebut the allegation. The failure to caution the defendant will also not inevitably trigger s 76(2)(b); the defendant would have to show an extra ingredient which suggests that what he said is unreliable. Note that, as from June 2002 (see Code of Practice F), many interviews must now be video recorded. This adds an additional protection for the suspect and for the police officers conducting the interview. The suspect sometimes alleges physical intimidation that will not show on the tape recording. The police will sometimes be accused of mistreating a suspect who screams and shouts on tape. The video recording will not only record what was said but also how it was said and the circumstances in which it was said.

The method of questioning

The tape recording or video recording of interviews has meant that the method of questioning is now much more important than it was before such recording took place (see *Paris, Abdullahi and Miller*, at p 248 above). The oppressive nature of the questioning in that case became apparent when the court listened to the tape-recording. Indeed the bench of Court of Appeal in that case, none of whom had heard an actual interrogation before, were appalled and had no hesitation in finding that it was oppressive within s 76(2)(a). However, s 76(2)(b) clearly encompasses a much wider range of lesser conduct that would not be considered oppressive but which might lead to an unreliable confession. If then the method of questioning as revealed by the tape or video recording is not so obviously oppressive, as it should not be since the reforms which followed the above case, it would be sensible for the defence to plead both limbs of s 76. This may encourage a court, as *Beales* (above), to decide that even if s 76(2)(a) does not apply, the lesser s 76(2)(b) does.

The question thus arises as to how far s 76(2)(b) extends. The key lies in deciding whether what was 'said or done' was likely to render a confession 'unreliable'. This requires that the court look carefully at the circumstances of the detention and interview and the characteristics of the particular suspect and, if the judge putting himself in the position of the suspect decides that any confession made in those circumstances is likely to be unreliable, it is then for the prosecution to prove beyond reasonable doubt that he spoke in order to give a reliable account and not for other motives.

Clearly the method of questioning may produce an unreliable confession in that the suspect may speak for a variety of motives other than that of telling the truth (eg he wants to protect someone; he wants to leave the police station and is prepared to say anything, in the hope of retracting it later; he is suggestible and seeks to please his interrogator; he becomes confused and mistakenly incriminates himself; he is persuaded to speak because of promises or threats made to him). In *Fulling* (see p 246 above), the Lord Chief Justice decided that the following definition of oppression (cited with approval in *R v Prager* [1972] 1 All ER 1114), was insufficient for s 76(2)(a) but suggested that some of it could fall within s 76(2)(b) in stating that '... questioning which by its nature, duration or other attendant circumstances (including the fact of custody) excites hope (such as the hope of release) or fears, or so affects the mind of the subject that his will crumbles and he speaks when otherwise he would have stayed silent.'

This does of course put the court (and initially the prosecution) in a very difficult position in trying to fathom the defendant's motives for speaking. It is easier if the defendant falls within a group identified by PACE 1984 and the Code as 'vulnerable' (eg, juveniles, the mentally handicapped). Such persons may be suggestible or readily manipulated, with the consequence that certain styles of questioning are likely to produce unreliable confessions. In these types of cases, the prosecution can face an uphill task. Thus, in *R v Delaney* (1989) 88 Cr App R 338, the interviewing officer had throughout suggested to the defendant that he really needed psychiatric help, and that if he owned up, people would help him. The officer played down the criminal offence and falsely aroused the defendant's hopes of treatment. As the Lord Chief Justice put it, 'he might, by the same token, be encouraging a false confession'. In a less extreme case, the evidence, or speculation, of psychiatrists or psychologists as to the likely effect of police conduct on the defendant could readily sow sufficient seeds to raise a reasonable doubt (see also *R v Harvey* [1988] Crim LR 241, where psychiatric evidence suggested that the defendant might have confessed in a vain attempt to save her lover).

As for the 'ordinary' suspect, the court must consider all the circumstances of the interrogation and what was said by the police, or any other relevant person (eg parent, friend, co-accused, or even a solicitor who suggests that the evidence is stacked against the accused and that a confession and guilty plea will result in a lesser sentence); and the likely effect of what was said on the mind of the accused taking into account his characteristics.

This requires an understanding of the pressures that a police station can engender. See the observation of the Lord Chief Justice in *Rennie*, and see also *Goldenberg* and *Crampton*.

Tricks and misrepresentation

In some cases the evidence of persistent questioning and misrepresentation by the officer may be clear enough to suggest a state of confusion or hopelessness on the part of the suspect such as is likely to produce unreliable statements (see *R v Beales* [1991] Crim LR 118). What about tricks or misrepresentations practised on the suspect? For example, what the defendant is told, falsely, that his voice has been recognised on a tape as in *R v Blake* (at p 243 above) or that forensic evidence links him to the crime as in *Mason* (at p 248 above)? In the right circumstances, this could induce the defendant falsely to confess. The difficulty is that deceptions which suggest that there is conclusive evidence of guilt may lead to a reliable confession, rather than an unreliable one. In *Blake* the trial judge found unreliability within s 76(2)(b), but in *Mason* where the defendant was falsely told that his fingerprints had been found on a part of a bottle used as a petrol bomb, s 76(2)(b) was not argued, presumably because in the circumstance the confession was reliable. Section 78 was invoked on the basis that the deceit practised on the solicitor led him to advise his client on the basis of false facts which effectively denied the accused the benefit of the right of access to a solicitor and thus had such an adverse effect on the fairness of the trial that the confession ought not to be admitted (the judgement does not state this explicitly but it seems to be a fair inference).

In other cases of deception in undercover operations such as *R v Christou and Wright* [1992] 1 QB 979 and *R v Smurthwaite and Gill* [1994] 1 All ER 898, and other deceptions such as covert bugging of cells (*Shaukat Ali* (1991) *The Times*, 19 February, discussed in *R v Bailey and Smith* (1993) 97 Cr App R 365) or houses (*R v Khan (Sultan)* [1997] AC 558), the emphasis has been on reliability as a condition of admissibility and, reliability being established, s 76(2)(b) did not come into play.

Further examples of things said or done which the defence can raise under s 76(2)(b) include:

(a) a threat to charge the person with a more serious offence or with more offences unless he makes a statement (see the facts of *R v Howden-Simpson* (above), though decided under s 78);

(b) a promise to charge him with a less serious offence or not to prosecute at all, if he confesses;

(c) a promise to 'put in a good word for him at the trial or before the prosecuting solicitor';

(d) a promise to take another offence into consideration at the trial rather than prosecute him separately for that offence (*R v Northam* (1968) 52 Cr App R 97);

(e) a threat to, or promise not to, prosecute the accused's spouse or mistress or other close relation (cf *R v Middleton* [1974] 2 All ER 1190), the more remote the relationship, the less likely it is that there will be a causal connection between the threat/promise and the making of the confession;

(f) a threat to inform a third party unless the accused confesses (eg to inform his wife of a charge of indecent assault, or his employer of a shoplifting allegation, or social services or the Inland Revenue of his financial activities);

(g) a threat to prosecute the defendant on a charge unrelated to the one under investigation or to inform another agency about a prosecution (cf *Commissioners of Customs and Excise v Harz and Power* [1967] 1 AC 760).

Facts discovered as a result of an excluded confession

Section 76(4)–(6) deal with the problem that arises in relation to evidence discovered as a consequence of an excluded confession. For example, if during the investigation of a theft a confession is forced out of the defendant by oppression and he tells the police where they can find the stolen goods, can the prosecution (a) produce the goods at the defendant's trial, and (b) link their discovery to what the defendant told the police? The Criminal Law Revision Committee had unanimously recommended an affirmative answer to (a) and, by a majority, to (b). The 1984 Act opted for a halfway house. On the one hand, the prosecution can use in evidence 'any facts discovered as a result of the confession' even if the confession is itself inadmissible (s 76 (4)(a)). On the other hand, proof that those facts were discovered as a result of a wholly or partly inadmissible confession is not admissible (s 76 (5) and (6)), unless the accused himself gives evidence that they were so discovered (s 76 (5)). This places the old common law rule in *R v Berriman* (1854) 6 Cox CC 388 upon a statutory footing.

The policy underlying this rule is that it is unfair for the inadmissibility of a confession to be negated by the admissibility of the 'fruits of the crime', unless the accused so chooses. This must be right where confessions are obtained by oppression but less supportable when unreliability is involved given that the finding of the stolen goods where the defendant said they would be is a good indication of reliability. Be that as it may, the law states that the prosecution can produce the stolen goods at trial but cannot show that they were discovered as a result of the defendant's confession, unless the defendant in examination in chief or cross-examination admits that he told the police where to find them. Where the stolen goods can be linked to the defendant without the aid of the confession, eg they were found on his premises or his fingerprints are on them, there is no difficulty for the prosecution. The difficulty thus arises when a link to the defendant can only be established by reference to the confession, eg the stolen goods were found in a field off the motorway after the defendant had told police where to find them. If the confession is excluded the finding of the stolen goods in the field is not evidence against the defendant and it is hard to imagine a case in which the defendant would go into the witness box and give evidence that he told the police where to find the stolen goods.

Note that where only a part of a confession is excluded, perhaps one interview out of a number, evidence found as a result of the admissible part is admissible (s 76(6)(b)).

Those parts of a confession which are relevant as showing that the accused 'speaks, writes or expresses himself in a particular way' are admissible for that purpose (s 76(4)(b)). The object of this exception is illustrated by *R v Voisin* [1918] 1 KB 531, where the body of a murder victim had been found alongside a piece of paper bearing the words 'Bladie Belgiam'. The accused was asked by the police to write the words 'Bloody Belgian' and he happily wrote 'Bladie Belgiam'. This evidence was held to be admissible. *R v Voisin* did not involve a confession but it will be noted that s 76(4)(b) can apply even if the confession was improperly obtained and therefore inadmissible. In a modern day example, the defendant, a pupil at a regularly vandalised school, was suspected of spraying graffiti. He was asked to write the sprayed words 'Mr Brown is a homosexual'. He wrote, as had the graffiti artist, 'Mr Broun is a homeosexal'. The limitation is that the confession can only be used to identify the characteristics mentioned in the subsection and not to establish the truth of anything said or written or to show that the accused had some special knowledge which only the offender could have had.

If the accused has written his own confession which is excluded that may be used as a sample of his handwriting where relevant. If the defendant is charged with kidnapping and the victim states that the kidnapper spoke with a local accent and stammered, the non-incriminating parts of the defendant 's excluded tape-recorded confession can be used for voice comparison (see *R v Robb* (1991) 93 Cr App R 161 and *R v Deenick* [1992] Crim LR 578 for the admissibility of voice recognition evidence by a non expert such as a police or customs officer).

Confessions by the mentally handicapped

Section 77 of the PACE 1984 provides:

Where at such a trial (on indictment)—

(a) *the case against the accused depends wholly or substantially on a confession made by him; and*

(b) *the court is satisfied;*

(i) *that he is mentally handicapped; and*

(ii) *that the confession was not made in the presence of an independent person,*

the court shall warn the jury that there is a special need for caution before convicting the accused in reliance on that confession.

Code C, para 11.14 provides that no interview with a mentally disordered or mentally handicapped person should take place unless an appropriate adult is present. The Code mentions juveniles along with the mentally disordered or mentally handicapped and uses the phrase 'appropriate adult'. This is correct in respect of juveniles when the appropriate adult may be a parent, friend or anyone else deemed appropriate. However, the independent person referred to in s 77 must be independent of the person to whom the confession is made, thus a confession to a friend is not to an independent person (*R v Bailey* [1995] Crim LR 723). This suggests that the 'independent person' must be independent of the police, the solicitor and the mentally disordered/handicapped suspect.

Therefore s 77 should apply only in exceptional circumstances, since any confession made in the absence of an independent person is likely to fall foul of s 76(2)(b) and be excluded as unreliable. For example, in *R v Moss* (1990) 91 Cr App R 371, a mentally disordered person was interviewed nine times over a long period before confessing. The trial judge admitted the confession and gave a s 77 warning but the Court of Appeal thought it should have been excluded under s 76(2)(b). There the Court of Appeal suggested that the section was directed at two types of cases: those where the interview had been in the emergency circumstances envisaged by Code C, para 11.1; and secondly where the interview was in breach of Code C, para 11.14 but consisted of not more than one interview over a short period. The second set of circumstances envisaged by the Court may be doubted as there is no reason why an appropriate adult should not be present however short the interview. It is, nonetheless, sometimes difficult for the police to determine that a suspect is mentally disordered/handicapped but the test is objective, it is not what the police think, if they gave it any thought, but what was subsequently ascertained from doctors (see *Everett*, at pp 255–256+ above).

In *R v Law-Thompson* [1997] Crim LR 674, the accused suffered from an autistic psycho-pathic condition, Asperger's Syndrome. It was characterised by marked obsessionality, extreme rigidity of thought and strict adherence to rules and rituals. One manifestation was that he thought his mother was evil. One morning he attacked his mother with a meat cleaver shouting, 'I'm going to kill you'. He was restrained and the police were called. A sergeant asked Law what the cleaver was for and Law replied, 'It's my duty to kill her'. On being cautioned he said, 'I won't harm you. I only intend to kill my mother'. At the police station a psychiatrist found him fit to be interviewed. The police had arranged for an appropriate adult (the terminology used in the report) to be present but the social worker advised that it was not necessary. Law was then interviewed in the presence of a solicitor and made it clear that his intention had been to kill his mother and would try again given the opportunity.

At trial, the remark made to the police before caution was excluded, although the inter-view itself was admissible. A psychiatrist stated that, although Law had a personality disorder, he was not mentally ill. He understood the nature and quality of his action but not that they were wrong. 'Not guilty by reason of insanity' was the recommended plea. Law chose not to plead insanity and was convicted of attempted murder. He then appealed, one ground being the absence of an appropriate adult (independent person) at the interview which, according to the defence, rendered the interview inadmissible. Dismissing the appeal, the Court of Appeal held that it was not easy to apply s 76(2) of PACE 1984 to these facts, since there was nothing to suggest that the interview was obtained in consequence of the absence of an appropriate adult, or that such absence rendered the confession unreliable. The focus was then on s 78 which gave the judge a discretion to exclude which was at least as wide as that at common law. In support of exclusion, defence counsel argued that the prosecution were in breach of Article 6 of the European Convention on Human Rights. While accepting that the trial judge would have been entitled to consider Article 6 had his attention been drawn to it, the Court said that his focus had to be on s 76 and s 78. Even if there had been a breach of Article 6 it did not lead to the conclusion that evidence thus obtained must be excluded.

Section 77 was not argued in this case, presumably because, even if Law was mentally ill, the case did not depend wholly or substantially on his confession. In practice a prosecu-tion is most unlikely when the prosecution case depends 'wholly or substantially' on a confession obtained in the circumstances envisaged by s 77. There will usually be other evidence taking the case outside the section (see *R v Campbell* [1995] 1 Cr App R 522).

In *R v McKenzie* (1993) 92 Cr App R 369, the defendant, a mentally disordered man with a personality disorder was convicted of two offences of manslaughter and two of arson. The prosecution case on the manslaughter charge depended almost entirely on his unsup-ported confession while the arson charges were supported by other evidence. Quashing the convictions for manslaughter, the Court of Appeal held where the defendant suffers from a 'significant degree' of mental illness and the case against him depends wholly upon confessions which are 'unconvincing to the point where a jury properly directed could not convict upon them', then the trial judge (assuming he has not already excluded the confessions) should withdraw the case from the jury. The confessions were unconvincing because they lacked the incriminating details which would have made them reliable and because the defendant had confessed to twelve other killings which no one believed he had committed. There was also the possibility that he had confessed to ensure that he stayed in the secure hospital where he was detained (see also *R v Wood*, at p 244 above). The effect of these decisions is that cases are unlikely to proceed solely on the basis of a confession from a mentally disordered person obtained in the absence of an independent person.

Confessions and s 78

It was initially thought that s 76 of PACE 1984 provided a strict regime for the admissibility of confessions and if the prosecution succeeded in discharging the burden of proof under that section there was little room for discretionary exclusion. Therefore, it was doubted whether s 78 would apply to confessions. These doubts were not shared by the courts, and in *Mason* (see p 248 above) the Court of Appeal made it clear that the word 'evidence' in s 78 included a confession and held that the trial judge had wrongly exercised his discretion under s 78 by failing to take account of the deceit practised on the appellant and his solicitor. Without explaining how that deceit had such an adverse effect on the fairness of the trial that the confession ought not to be admitted, the Court made it clear that the conviction must be quashed:

> It is obvious from the undisputed evidence that the police practised a deceit not only on the appellant, which is bad enough, but also on his solicitor, whose duty it was to advise him. In effect, they hoodwinked both solicitor and client. That was a most reprehensible thing to do. It is not however because we regard as misbehaviour of a serious kind conduct of that nature that we have come to the decision soon to be made plain. This is not the place to discipline the police. That has been made clear here on a number of previous occasions. We are concerned with the application of the proper law. The law is, as I have already said, that a trial judge has a discretion to be exercised of course upon right principles to reject admissible evidence in the interests of a defendant having a fair trial. The judge in the present case appreciated that... So the only question to be answered by this Court is whether, having regard to the way the police behaved, the judge exercised that discretion correctly. In our judgement he did not.

There clearly is an element of disciplining the police in this decision but the exercise of the s 78 discretion can be justified on the basis that the provision of false information led the defendant's solicitor to mis-advise the defendant. This is effectively a denial of the defendant's fundamental right to legal advice based on the true facts. While the use of s 78 was justifiable in the *Mason* case on the basis that the deceit induced a reliable confession, thereby excluding the operation of s 76(2)(b), s 78 has been relied upon to exclude confessions in many cases in which its use was less justifiable and in circumstances in which s 76 appeared to be more appropriate. While accepting that s 78 does apply to confessions the Court of Appeal is now coming around to the view that where a confession satisfies s 76, that is it was not obtained by oppression and there are no circumstances of unreliability, there are prima facie no grounds for exclusion under s 78. It would seem that something more is needed in order to persuade the court that the admission of the confession would have such an adverse effect on the fairness of the trial that it ought not to be admitted. Unfortunately, there are few explanations in the cases of how the police actions, or inactions, have such an adverse effect on the fairness of the trial that the confession ought not to be admitted.

An example of the use of s 78 rather than s 76(2)(b) is seen in *R v Howden-Simpson* [1991] Crim LR 49 where the interviewing officer told the accused that he would only be charged with two offences if he confessed. If he did not, many charges would be brought. This is precisely the sort of threat or inducement with which s 76(2)(b) was intended to deal, although in that case the trial judge considered and rejected it. The Court of Appeal, however, decided that s 78 should have been relied upon to exclude the confession because the officer had indicated what action he would take if the defendant did not confess in breach of Code C, para 11.3 – this surely should have qualified as 'something said or done' under s 76(2)(b). Similarly in *R v Fogah* [1989] Crim LR 141, a juvenile was questioned in the absence of an appropriate adult. The latter's presence is required by the Code C 11.14, partly in order to protect the vulnerable juvenile from making unreliable admissions, yet the court used s 78 to exclude them.

It is submitted that the correct vehicle for handling this type of case is 76(2)(b). In relying on s 78 the Court risks excluding inadmissible evidence which is not the function of s 78 (see comments of Ralph Gibson LJ in *Halawa v Federation Against Copyright Theft* [1995] 1 Cr App R 21, 33). As suggested above, it is sensible to conceive s 76 and s 78 as a series of hurdles (see Birch [1988] Crim LR 95) over which the prosecution can be made to jump, and which should be approached in order unless it is obvious that one or more does not apply. The first hurdle is oppression under s 76(2)(a). As indicated above this requires serious impropriety and it will rarely be the case that the prosecution fail to clear this hurdle. The second hurdle is s 76(2)(b). Since this requires no impropriety, includes anything said or done in the particular circumstances which include the personal characteristics of the accused and can often be evidenced by breaches of the Code, it is an extremely broad hurdle made more difficult by the requirement that the prosecution prove beyond reasonable doubt that the confession was not obtained in breach of that subsection.

If the prosecution succeed in discharging that heavy burden there is the third hurdle of s 78. Though often labelled 'unfairness' the section requires that the judge be persuaded that in all the circumstances, including those in which the evidence was obtained, the admission of the evidence would have such an adverse effect of the fairness of the trial that the court ought not to admit it. Under s 78 there must be sufficient evidence to persuade the court that the challenged evidence would have such an adverse effect on the fairness of the trial that it ought not to be admitted. In seeking to persuade the judge the parties have to clear this hurdle from opposite sides, the prosecution seeking to persuade the judge that there would no adverse effect in admitting the confession and the defence seeking to persuade him that there would be such an adverse effect that he ought not to admit it.

In deciding whether to rely on s 76 or 78 (or both, since *Alladice* established that they may be used by the defence consecutively), one must examine all the circumstances in which the confession was alleged to have been made, including the relevant characteristics of the accused. It should be noted that the element of 'fairness of the proceedings' refers to fairness to the prosecution as well as fairness to the defence. The court will then look at the entire process in determining whether admitting the evidence would have such an adverse effect on the fairness of the proceedings that it should not be admitted. Note that the section refers to 'such an adverse effect'. An adverse effect will not be enough, the word 'such' importing a degree of adverse effect over and above the baseline of 'adverse effect'. What that degree is has yet to be determined.

The following guidelines are suggested:

(a) If there is serious impropriety which may be oppressive within the *Fulling* definition, s 76(2)(a) should be relied upon in the first instance.

(b) If the impropriety amounts to something said or done (or not done) which was likely in the circumstances to lead to an unreliable confession, s 76(2)(b) should be relied upon.

(c) If what is said or done does not involve police impropriety, or is not said or done by the police (cf *Harvey*, above), but is nevertheless likely to lead to an unreliable confession, s 76(2)(b) should be relied upon.

(d) If the manner in which the confession was obtained does not amount to something said or done but is nevertheless likely to lead to an unreliable confession; or is something not done after the confession was made, eg no contemporaneous record, or record not shown to the accused, which puts a question mark on the accuracy of the recording, and therefore the reliability, of the confession, s 76(2) does not apply and s 78 must be relied upon.

(e) If the manner in which the confession was obtained does amount to something improperly said or done but which is not likely in the circumstances to lead to an unreliable confession (cf *Mason* where the deception induced a truthful and therefore reliable confession), s 78 must be relied upon. One may note that under s 78, unlike s 76, the truth of the confession can be relied upon to demonstrate the reliability of the confession, but the fact that it is true does not mean that admitting it will not have an adverse effect on the fairness of the trial.

(f) There are some circumstances in which Code C cannot apply in its entirety, eg undercover operations. Here the courts are more concerned with the reliability of any statements made than the conduct of the police. If there is an unassailable record of what was said and done, or evidence supporting its reliability it is unlikely that the courts will see the police conduct as likely to lead to an unreliable confession (see, eg *Smurthwaite and Gill* (above); *R v Dixon and Mann* (1994) *The Times*, 31 December; *R v Khalid Latif* [1995] 1 Cr App R 270). The course are also unlikely to exercise their discretion under s 78.

(g) Other tricks, like covert bugging of cells or other places (see *R v Khan* [1996] Crim LR 733 where the House of Lords held that evidence obtained following the trespassory entry onto premises was admissible), or setting traps to catch thieves, appear to be acceptable if the resultant evidence is reliable, as it usually is in such circumstances where video and tape recordings are made. This too may be seen as something done which was not likely to lead to unreliable confessions therefore s 76(2)(b) does not apply and s 78 is unlikely to apply (see eg, *R v Jelen and Katz* (1989) 90 Cr App R 456; *Bailey and Smith* (above); *Williams and O'Hare v DPP* [1993] Crim LR 776; *R v Christou and Wright* (above); *R v Roberts* [1997] 1 Cr App R 217).

(h) In a number of recent cases the Court of Appeal has expressed the view that once the judge had decided that there was nothing to require the exclusion of a confession under s 76, it was difficult to see why the evidence should have been excluded under s 78 (see *R v Weeks* [1995] Crim LR 52 and *R v Campbell* (above)). As the commentary to the latter case states: 'Admissible confessions are often excluded; but the fact that the confession passes the s 76 test certainly suggests that, prima facie, its admission would not have an adverse effect on the fairness of the proceedings'. This supports the three-hurdle approach suggested above.

The discretion to hold a *voir dire*

When s 78 is raised, the court has a discretion as to whether to hold a *voir dire* (*Carlisle v DPP* unreported, 9 November, 1987, QBD). How it should exercise that discretion is unclear. If, as it often will be, the confession is the central plank of the prosecution's case, its admissibility should be raised early on in the trial and argued in a trial within a trial where it may be coupled with an application to exclude under s 76. In *R v Keenan* [1990] 2 QB 54, Hodgson J distinguished three situations in which the appropriate procedure may vary:

(a) Where evidence of police irregularity is plain for all to see (eg, on the custody record) and the prosecution concede the conduct and argument follows as to whether the confession evidence should be excluded under s 78.

(b) Where there is prima facie evidence of irregularity and the prosecution seek to justify it and argue against exclusion. The defence may wish to call evidence, occasionally even the defendant himself.

(c) The comparatively rare case where the alleged breaches can probably be established only by the evidence of the defendant himself.

Hodgson J also posed the problem that, in determining the effect, if any, of the evidence on the fairness of the trial under s 78, if objection it taken early on in the trial, the judge is unlikely to know the defendant's likely defence and is in a difficult position to decide whether admissibility of the evidence will adversely affect the fairness of the proceedings.

The provisions of the Criminal Procedure and Investigations Act 1996, which require that the defence provide the prosecution with a statement setting out the general nature of their defence, may operate to overcome this difficulty. The alternative is to require more from the defence at the trial within a trial. Indeed, if the defendant's case is thin, the onus lies on him (see below) to establish the adverse effect alleged, if necessary, by giving evidence (see the commentary to *Rajakuruna* [1991] Crim LR 407). Where magistrates are faced with an application to exclude evidence under s 78, the magistrates must deal with it when it arises or leave the decision until the end of the prosecution case, including the disputed evidence (possibly the better course given that the issue under s 78 is to be determined 'having regard to all the circumstances'), with the objective of ensuring a trial which is fair and just to both sides (*Halawa v FACT* [1995] 1 Cr App R 21).

The burden of proof under s 78

The Divisional Court in *R (Saifi) v Governor of Brixton Prison* [2000] 1 WLR 1134 stated that the concept of burden of proof has no part to play under s 78. The situation when a judge is considering whether or not to exercise his discretion under the section is not like that within the trial proper. The judge must be satisfied that to admit the evidence would have such an adverse effect on the fairness of the trial that it ought not to be admitted.

He will hear argument from both parties and exercise the discretion to exclude if he is satisfied that admitting the evidence will have such an adverse effect, or he will not exercise the discretion if he is not so satisfied.

The following points should be noted:

(a) Like s 76, s 78 applies only to the evidence on which the prosecution proposes to rely. This means that in a jury trial it must be argued before the evidence which it is sought to exclude is given. On summary trial it may be argued at that point or at the end of the prosecution case including the disputed evidence (*Halawa v FACT*, above).

(b) The evidence must adversely affect the fairness of 'proceedings' and these are defined (s 82(1)) as criminal proceedings (including a court martial), and 'proceedings' in this context probably means the trial.

(c) Although it is the adverse effect of the evidence on the fairness of the proceedings which concerns the court, the whole of the investigatory stage is open to scrutiny in order to ascertain whether the circumstances in which the evidence was obtained could have such an adverse effect on the fairness of the trial that it ought not to be admitted.

(d) Section 78 is quite separate from the common law power to exclude confessions (s 82(3); *R v Sat-Bhambra* (1988) 88 Cr App R 55, see further below), although that, too, is concerned with the fairness of the trial (*R v Sang* [1980] AC 402).

(e) In *Mason*, it was clearly established that s 78 may apply to confessions and that they are not the sole preserve of s 76 (*Mason* [1987] 3 All ER 481).

(f) The relevant confession has usually been made to the police but this is not essential. Section 78 can be used to exclude a confession made to others (eg a doctor as in *R v McDonald* [1991] Crim LR 144 or a probation officer as in *R v Ellaray* [2003] 2 Cr App R 11).

(g) In reaching its conclusion the court must consider all the circumstances, which goes beyond simply the circumstances in which the confession was obtained, and includes the amount of other evidence against the accused and the characteristics of the accused (see *R v Bailey* [1995] 2 Cr App Rep 262).

(h) The court exercises a discretion and this gives the trial judge some leeway. Provided that he interprets the 1984 Act and the Codes correctly, and professes to consider all the circumstances of the case (in *Mason* the Court of Appeal was able to intervene because the trial judge had wrongly exercised the s 78 discretion), the chances of a successful appeal are considerably diminished (*R v O'Leary* (1988) 87 Cr App R 387). In *R v Quinn* [1995] 1 Cr App R 480, Lord Taylor CJ stated at 487: 'Before this Court could reach the conclusion that the judge was wrong [to exercise his discretion under s 78 as he did] we would have to be satisfied that no reasonable judge, having heard the evidence that this learned judge did, could have reached the conclusion that he did.'

This principle is one that guides the present Court of Appeal and was applied in *R v Dures and others* [1997] 2 Cr App R 247. Here, the trial judge's refusal to exclude evidence of interviews held in the cell, which were not contemporaneously recorded nor confirmed and signed by the second appellant, was upheld on the basis that it was not a decision which no reasonable judge could have reached.

The existence of this discretion also means that it should not be fettered by the erection of rules, since each decision rests on its particular facts (*R v Canale* [1990] 2 All ER 187 and *R v Gillard and Barrett* [1991] Crim LR 280). If an appellate court concludes that the discretion has been wrongly exercised (or not exercised at all), it may be able to put itself in the position of the trial judge and consider whether or how the discretion should have been exercised (see *Mason*).

(i) Subsections 76(4), (5) (evidence found in consequence of an inadmissible confession) are applicable only to a confession excluded under s 76. There is no equivalent provision in s 78, although it is open to a court to decide that to admit evidence found in consequence of a confession that has been excluded under s 78 would have such an adverse effect on the fairness of the trial that it should not be admitted and to also exclude it under that section.

(j) Judges are fond of remarking that it is not the court's function to punish/discipline the police for failure to observe PACE 1984 and the Codes (see *Delaney* (above); *Mason* (above); and *R v Fennelley* [1989] Crim LR 142). However, it is suggested that such reasoning is disingenuous for, no matter how the court expresses it, an inevitable consequence of exclusion of evidence is that the police are disciplined by the collapse of a prosecution. Hodgson J, it is submitted, came closer to the mark in *Samuel* (above) when he described police disciplinary procedures as 'a much less secure method of ensuring compliance' with PACE 1984 than s 76 and s 78 (see also the trenchant criticism of police conduct by Lord Lane CJ in *R v Canale* [1990] 2 All ER 187 and more recently of officers of Customs and Excise whose disregard of Code C caused the Court in *R v Weerdesteyn* [1995] 1 Cr App R 405 some concern). It is therefore likely that there is an element of discipline/punishment in some of the decisions under s 78. That may be no bad thing but an honest acceptance of that principle would assist in understanding the application of the section.

Interpreting s 78

The terse terms of s 78 give little help as to the proper interpretation of the section and the courts have displayed a range of approaches. Three general points can be made. First, the section is to be construed widely (*R v Keenan* [1990] 2 QB 54). Secondly, the test is fairness of the proceedings, not fairness to the defence. In other words, fairness to the prosecution and to the court (that it be able to hear all the relevant evidence) must also be considered (*DPP v Marshall* [1988] 3 All ER 683; *R v Quinn* [1990] Crim LR 581; *R v Kerawalla* (above)). Thirdly, as Auld J remarked in *R v Jelen and Katz* (1990) 90 Cr App R 456, at 465: 'The circumstances of each case are almost always different, and judges may well take different views in the proper exercise of their discretion even where the circumstances are similar. This is not an apt field for hard case law and well founded distinctions between cases.' (Approved in *R v Roberts* [1997] 1 Cr App R 217, considered at p 279 below).

In *R v Oliphant* [1992] Crim LR 40, the Court of Appeal further emphasised the need to consider the facts of each case against the statutory language of PACE 1984 when it stated, per curiam that '[i]t is important, in deciding admissibility of evidence under PACE, not to be diverted by other decisions of the court, often on different facts, from considering the statutory language' (see also commentary to *R v Campbell* (above)).

Factors influencing the decision to invoke s 78

Whilst recognising the unpredictable nature of s 78, it is possible to identify factors which have influenced its use. The most common trigger for the application of s 78 is where the defence can show that there has been a breach of PACE 1984 or the Codes of Practice. In principle, breach of the former should be treated more seriously since the Codes are not binding on the courts (the point was raised but not pursued in *Keenan*), but what should matter is the relevance of the breach to the fairness of the proceedings. In practice breaches of the Codes are usually of greater relevance for the reception of confessions. It has been clearly established that not every breach of correct procedures will be greeted with exclusion of evidence. Thus in *R v Walsh* (1990) 91 Cr App R 161, it was said that a breach of Code C meant that prima facie at least the standards of fairness set by Parliament have not been met and any evidence admitted in such circumstances must have an adverse effect on the fairness of the trial, but his does not mean that in every case of a significant and substantial breach exclusion under s 78 was automatic: 'The task of the court is not merely to consider whether there would be an adverse effect on the fairness of the proceedings, but such an adverse effect that justice requires the evidence to be excluded' (see also *Keenan* (above); *Delaney* (above); *R v Waters* [1989] Crim LR 62).

Much depends on the type and extent of the breach. Thus, exclusion is more likely if the breach is flagrant (*R v Canale* [1990] 2 All ER 187, where the Lord Chief Justice found a cynical disregard of the rules governing the contemporaneous recording of interviews); or wilful (*R v Nagah* (1991) 92 Cr App R 344 where, although the defendant agreed to an identification parade, he was released so that a street identification could more easily be made); or in bad faith (see the remarks by Lord Lane CJ in *R v Alladice* (1988) 87 Cr App R 380 that a court might find it easier to employ s 78 if bad faith on the part of the police is proved). However, in *Walsh* it was made clear that breaches which are in themselves significant and substantial are not rendered otherwise by the good faith of the officers concerned. Correspondingly, mistaken conduct on the part of the police carried out in good faith may tilt against the use of s 78 or at least be a neutral factor in the equation (see *R v Clarke* [1989] Crim LR 892 where the officers did not realise that the defendant was deaf, but the breach of what is now Code C, para 13.5 could still be considered; *R v Younis* [1990] Crim LR 425 where the suspect 'volunteered' most of the remarks in the police car and there was no evidence of deliberate police prompting; *R v Kerawalla* (1991) Crim LR 252 where the absence of bad faith was a factor). However, unlike s 76(2)(a), impropriety is not essential (*R v O'Leary* (1988) 87 Cr App R 387; *Samuel* (above)) and good faith does not remedy a significant breach of PACE procedures.

If the procedure is regarded by the court as an important one, it does not matter whether lack of adherence to it was wilful or through ignorance, the effect on the proceedings being the same in either case. For example, in the case of *Walsh*, the denial of legal advice, omitting to note the reason for not recording an interview contemporaneously, and failure to show the defendant the record of interview, were regarded as significant and substantial breaches which were not cured by good faith. This case has become the standard reference point for cases involving breach of PACE 1984 and the Codes, particularly those involving wrongful exclusion of a solicitor, but, as Woolf LJ pointed out in *Oliphant*, the words 'significant' and 'substantial' are not terms of art but are simply offered as guides to ruling out of consideration those merely technical breaches which have no adverse consequences. Similarly in *R v Foster* [1987] Crim LR 821, the officer failed to appreciate that his brief chat with the defendant in the street was an interview for PACE purposes and therefore did not make a contemporaneous record of it (for a similar mistake by an inexperienced officer, see *R v Sparks* [1991] Crim LR 128).

One of the key factors is thus the particular type of PACE procedure that has been breached. It should be noted that 'the mere fact that there has been a breach of the Codes of Practice does not of itself mean that evidence has to be rejected' (*per* Lord Lane CJ in *Delaney* (1989)). A link between the breach and fairness to the proceedings must be established (eg *R v Hughes* [1988] Crim LR 519; *R v Dunford* (1990) 91 Cr App Rep 150). If the PACE procedure is an important safeguard for the suspect, an adverse effect on the fairness of the proceedings is inevitable and that effect is likely to be so adverse that justice demands the exclusion of any evidence thus obtained. In this context most important are the provisions designed to prevent verballing of the suspect (ie concocted admissions), see *R v Keenan* [1990] 2 QB 54. Transgression of these standards often leads to exclusion under s 78 because it is unfair to deprive the defendant of his rights (especially legal advice) and it is unfair to the court since it is deprived of a more accurate record of an interview (eg a contemporaneous record) and it is unfair for the criminal process since admission of the confession would allow one side (the prosecution) to win by foul play.

These reasons appear throughout the cases, although they are often not clearly articulated. Indeed, sometimes the courts, despite what was said in *Walsh*, proceed almost automatically to apply s 78 where improprieties have been established without first considering the statutory language (*R v Hughes* [1988] Crim LR 519).

Cases involving breaches which have been the subject of s 78 can be broadly classified into one of two major categories: first, those cases involving the lack of or delay to legal or other advice; and secondly, those cases involving the absence of an the accurate recording of an interview either by a contemporaneous record or by showing the defendant a summary of the interview together with failure to caution and other breaches of the Code of Practice.

Provision of legal or other advice
A feature of the law before 1986, when PACE 1984 came into force, was the fact that an accused rarely had access to a solicitor. Section 58 of PACE 1984 gives the suspect a legal right of access to a solicitor while in police detention, although the legislation stipulates that access may be delayed during the 36 hours of police-authorised detention provided one of the conditions set out in s 58(8) is satisfied.

However, as previously noted the decision in *Samuel* places a severe restriction on the ability of the police to lawfully delay access to a solicitor under s 58. Here, the defendant, who was arrested on suspicion of armed robbery, was interviewed twice and after the second interview he asked to see a solicitor. His request was refused by a superintendent who certified that there was a likelihood of other suspects being alerted inadvertently (a valid ground for delay under s 58(8)). Two further interviews followed after which he confessed to two burglaries. Later his solicitor telephoned the police station and was told that his client had been charged with two burglaries and that he was not allowed to see him. The defendant was then interviewed again and he confessed to the robbery. He was then charged and allowed to see his solicitor after 29 hours of detention.

The Court of Appeal allowed the defendant's appeal against conviction and held that access had been wrongly denied after the defendant had been charged with the burglaries since Code C makes it clear that the right to delay access ceases when the accused is charged with an offence. Furthermore, s 58 gave a person detained by the police a 'fundamental right' to obtain legal advice. Delaying the grant of that right could only be authorised on one of the specific grounds set out in s 58(8). In the present case the super-intendent had to show pursuant to s 58(a) or (b) that the solicitor in question would deliberately or inadvertently so act that other suspects would be warned or the recovery of stolen property would be hampered. The Court pointed out that the words in s 58(8) state that the superintendent must believe that allowing access to a solicitor 'will' lead to one of the consequences mentioned, not 'may' do so. If a solicitor were to cause interference with witnesses, warn other suspects or do anything to hinder the recovery of stolen prop-erty, he would be committing a serious offence. All solicitors are officers of the court and it will rarely be the case that a police officer could genuinely believe a solicitor could act in one of those ways, wittingly or unwittingly. The belief had therefore to apply to a particu-lar solicitor, not solicitors in general. In reality the police were adopting a standard procedure to deny access to a solicitor.

In this particular case, the appellant's solicitor was an experienced criminal practitioner and there were no grounds for believing he would act in such a way. Furthermore, the Court pointed out that if there were a genuine belief about a particular solicitor it would be a simple matter to offer the suspect a duty solicitor. It would be difficult to justify the belief required under s 58(8) so as to be able to delay consultation. The police should either call a solicitor chosen at random from a list or, more likely, simply call the duty solicitor.

Accordingly, the trial judge had wrongly decided that that the refusal of access to a solici-tor prior to the final interview was justified. Furthermore, if he had held that the refusal of access to the solicitor was unjustified and that in consequence the final interview was unlawful, he might well have found that it was so unfair that he ought not to admit it. Quashing the conviction, the Court concluded that denial of 'one of the most important and fundamental rights of a citizen' – legal advice – could well have an adverse effect on the proceedings. This conclusion was assisted by the finding that, if the solicitor had been allowed access, he would probably have advised silence.

The result of the decision in *Samuel* is to virtually make the right of access to a solicitor an unfettered right of access to a solicitor, though access to a particular solicitor may be delayed if there is the genuine belief that he is sufficiently corrupt or naive as to do one of the things mentioned in s 58(8). The decision also emphasises that denial of legal advice per se is not enough. It must also be shown that the denial produced an adverse effect. The point was made again in *Alladice* (above) where a solicitor was wrongly denied access (a clear breach of s 58 of PACE 1984 and Code C); the interview was otherwise conducted properly, the solicitor would probably have reminded the defendant of his right to silence but the defendant, being used to police interviews, already knew that (indeed he exercised it at times during the interview), therefore the solicitor's presence would not have made a difference and there was no unfairness to the proceedings (see also *Dunford* (above), where the improper denial of legal advice was balanced by the defendant 's knowledge of his rights and ability to cope on his own).

In *R v Chahal* [1992] Crim LR 124 the defendant said he did not want a solicitor and later confirmed this. However, unknown to him his family had instructed a solicitor who attended but was told the defendant did not want a solicitor. His appeal against convic-tion was dismissed. The defendant was a mature businessman who knew what he was about and had suffered no prejudice. This may be compared with *R v Franklin* [1994] *The*

Times, 16 June. The defendant, a young unemployed man, initially said he did not want a solicitor. Ten minutes later he asked that his father be informed of his arrest and that he get a solicitor for him. He was then interviewed twice, having agreed to be interviewed without a solicitor being present, and made admissions. In the meantime the defendant's father had telephoned the police station but the defendant was not told of this, though it was recorded in the custody record. The father instructed a solicitor who attended at the police station but was told that the defendant would not be informed because he did not want a solicitor (see now Code C 6.15, which requires that the defendant be informed that the solicitor has attended). Two further interviews followed at which the defendant was reminded of his right to legal advice but not told that a solicitor had attended. The trial judge admitted the evidence of all four interviews believing he was bound by *Chahal*. The Court of Appeal disagreed. There were significant differences between the two cases. In *Chahal* the solicitor had merely telephoned and Chahal was a mature businessman. In this case the solicitor actually attended and the defendant was a young unemployed man who had never been in a police station before. The trial judge had therefore exercised his discretion wrongly, but the case against the defendant was overwhelming and the proviso was applied and the appeal dismissed.

Other cases in which denial of access to legal advice led to exclusion of the confession include: *R v Vernon* [1988] Crim LR 445, where the defendant was not told of the duty solicitor scheme or that a solicitor was on the way; *R v Absolam* [1989] Cr App R 332, where the defendant was not told of his right to legal advice and proceeded to make damaging admissions, and, to similar effect, *R v Williams* [1989] Crim LR 66; *R v Beycan* (above), where D was wrongfully denied a solicitor being told 'we usually interview without a solicitor' (this decision seems particularly unfair since the suspect was a foreigner with poor English and therefore vulnerable).

The complexity of the offence under investigation may increase the need for legal advice and the adverse effect of its denial (see *R v Guest* unreported, 20 January 1988, Leeds Crown Court). The potential for inferences to be drawn from silence under the Criminal Justice and Public Order Act 1993 also increases the need for legal advice in the police station and the adverse effect of the lack of it. Even the Alladices of this world may not fully appreciate their potential effect. The Youth Justice and Criminal Evidence Act 1999 has amended ss 34, 36 and 37 of the Criminal Justice and Public Order Act 1994 so that inferences cannot be drawn under those sections unless the defendant had access to a solicitor before the request for facts or an explanation of marks on his person or clothing or of his presence at the scene of a crime is required. This amendment, together with the decision in *Samuel*, means that rarely will the decision to deny a suspect immediate access to a solicitor be made, or if made be lawful.

Accurate recording, failure to caution etc
Since the advent of tape and video-recording of interviews under Code E, the failure to record interviews in police stations is rare, and one may note that many of the cases referred to below precede PACE 1984. Nowadays any failure to record will usually relate to statements made outside the interview room. In *R v Canale* [1990] 2 All ER 187, where the interviews were not contemporaneously recorded and the reason given on the subsequent record of interview was 'bw' (ie 'best way' for the police but not the suspect). This

'lamentable attitude' (Lord Lane CJ) towards proper police procedures strongly influenced the Court of Appeal's decision to use s 78 (though in the absence of such a record the statement was likely to have been unreliable). In contrast, in *R v Dunn* (1990) 91 Cr App R 237, there had been a failure to record a conversation – prima facie a reason for exclusion of it, but this was balanced by the presence of the defendant's legal adviser during the interview. Likewise, in *R v Matthews* [1990] Crim LR 190, where the defendant 's comments were noted after the interview ended but the note was not shown to her, The Court of Appeal accepted that there had been a clear breach of the Code C but did not disturb the trial judge's refusal to use s 78, apparently on the basis (or lack of it) that he had considered all the circumstances and his discretion could not be challenged

However, similar subsequent cases the Court of Appeal has not hesitated to state that such evidence should have been excluded. In *R v Scott* [1991] Crim LR 56, the defendant made an incriminating remark, unprompted by the police, which was noted but not shown to the defendant for his immediate denial or confirmation. Instead he was forced to deny it at trial, thus exposing himself to prejudicial cross-examination and this was held to be unfair for s 78 purposes. Similarly, in *R v Maloney and Doherty* [1988] Crim LR 523, interviews outside and inside the station were not contemporaneously recorded, notes of the interviews were not shown to the suspects and, although they could not read, no lawyer or third party was made available to assist them. It was held that these should have been excluded under s 78. In *RSPCA v Eager* [1995] Crim LR 59, the accused Eager was interviewed in her home by RSPCA inspectors who made up their record of the interview in their car afterwards giving Eager no opportunity to read it or sign it as correct. Again, the Court held this should have been ruled out. In contrast, in *R v Courtney* [1995] Crim LR 63 customs officers intercepted parcels of herbal cannabis and posed as a postman to deliver them to the defendant's address. A note of the defendant 's comments on the doorstep was made but was not shown to the defendant. In this instance, the breach was not significant or substantial and the note was admitted.

In *R v Sparks* [1991] Crim LR 128, the failure to caution (and to record the interview) was a substantial breach of Code C and warranted exclusion of the conversation under s 78. The Court of Appeal also found a substantial breach in *R v Saunders* [1988] Crim LR 521, where the key component of a caution (that the defendant need not say anything) was omitted. On the other hand, failure to tell / remind the defendant that he is a volunteer and free to leave (Code C, para 10.2) is not necessarily a substantial breach (*R v Rajakuruna* [1991] Crim LR 460, particularly where the defendant ought to have known that he was a suspect in an investigation.

Some cases will involve both an improper denial of access to legal advice plus some other failure to abide by PACE requirements. In *Walsh* (above), legal advice was improperly denied, the interview was not contemporaneously recorded and the eventual record was not shown to the defendant. These were significant and substantial breaches of PACE procedures, and the good faith of the officers could not prevent the application of s 78, the effect on the trial being the same whether the officers acted in good or bad faith (cf *R v Williams* [1989] Crim LR 66). In contrast, there are many minor provisions in the Code, breach of which will have no effect on the fairness of the trial, such as a failure to supply meals and drink on time or a failure to record the time when an interview finished and to allow 8 hours of continuous rest. In *R v Deacon* [1987] Crim LR 404, these failings were considered by the court but clearly did not weigh heavily); and the courts have frequently remarked that it is not every breach of the Code that will lead to exclusion under s 78. As suggested in *Walsh* and many subsequent cases, the breaches must be significant and substantial to justify exclusion. Those provisions that are mandatory are more likely to be so and to warrant exclusion than those which are directory (*R v Grier* (1989) LAG April, p 14). Also, there may an accumulation of minor breaches of procedure which together justify the exercise of the s 78 discretion (eg *R v Moss* (1990) 91 Cr App R 371).

Deceiving a solicitor or suspect

Section 78 has also been used to condemn the tactics and content of police questioning. In fact this was the concern of the first leading case on the section, *R v Mason* (see above). The Court of Appeal was enraged that the defendant 's solicitor had been hoodwinked ('a most reprehensible thing') thereby affecting the advice he gave his client, and used s 78 to exclude the defendant's confession. This does not mean that deceit practised on the defendant alone is legitimate. On the contrary, the court issued a stern rebuke against such deception but has since distinguished the deception involved in undercover operations (see *Christou and Wright; Smurthwaite and Gill; Bailey and Smith; and Khan Sultan*).

In *R v Roberts* [1997] 1 Cr App R 217, the accused was arrested on suspicion of robbery of a building society and two banks. Roberts was interviewed over a number of days, remained silent but was nevertheless charged with two of the robberies. C was arrested on suspicion of involvement in one of the robberies with Roberts. He was also interviewed a number of times and implicated himself in a number of offences including conspiracy to rob, supplying drugs, large scale shoplifting and escaping from police custody, but he denied involvement in the robbery for which he had been arrested but was charged with that offence. Later there were a number of breaches of the Codes of Practice in relation to C.

Roberts asked to share a cell with C and later when visited by a police officer, without prompting, C asked to be put in a cell with Roberts so that he could get Roberts to admit the robbery with which C was charged and to clear him of involvement. A note was made of this conversation but in breach of Code C it was not read to or signed by C. The officer in charge of the inquiry obtained permission to bug the cells of both Roberts and C. C, who did not know the cell was bugged was later placed in a cell with R and their conversation was recorded. C pressed Roberts to clear him of the robbery and asked questions about the other robberies. In response, Roberts admitted the two robberies with which he was charged and other offences. Evidence of the conversations were admitted at his trial and Roberts was convicted of the two robberies and the other offences he had admitted.

On appeal Roberts claimed there had been a material irregularity in the trial in so far as the judge had wrongly permitted the prosecution to adduce evidence of the covert tape recordings of the conversation in the police cell where C, a police stooge, was placed to obtain admissions from Roberts in breach of the Code of Practice. No solicitor was present and he alleged that he had been deceived into believing his conversation was in private. Dismissing the appeal, the Court of Appeal held that it was not part of the purpose of the Code of Practice to protect an accused in relation to breaches of the Code in respect of another suspect and that, accordingly, since there was no causal link between the breaches of the Code and the appellant's subsequent spontaneous admissions. As such, the judge was right to regard those breaches as insignificant in relation to the appellant. Furthermore, each case of this kind was to be decided on its own facts and it was inappropriate to draw a distinction between mere eavesdropping and putting a person in the cell with the suspect. The true test was whether the conduct of the police, either wittingly or unwittingly, led to unfairness or injustice. The proper adjudicator of this question being the trial judge himself, and in the instant case the trial judge's exercise of his discretion could not be faulted.

In *R v Chalkley and Jeffries* [1998] 2 All ER 155 the prosecution sought to rely on covertly obtained tape recordings of conversations between the defendants, charged with conspiracy to rob. In order to obtain the recordings police arrested Chalkley and his partner on unrelated charges and, in their absence, entered their house and planted a listening device. The defence argued for exclusion of the tape recordings under s 78 of PACE 1984. The trial judge looked for guidance to cases relating to the dismissal of prosecutions for abuse of process, and concluded that he was obliged to conduct a balancing exercise between the interests of justice and the effective prosecution of offences and the public interest in discouraging the abuse of police power. He concluded that the balance lay with the effective prosecution of offences and admitted the evidence. The defendants then changed their plea to guilty.

On appeal, the primary question was whether in these circumstances the Court of Appeal had the power to quash a conviction following a guilty plea. The Court concluded that it did not, and whilst that was enough to determine the outcome of the appeal, the Court went on to consider the arguments put forward in relation to s 78. It concluded that there was no basis for the defence submission that admission of the taped conversations would have such an adverse effect on the fairness of the proceedings that they ought to have been excluded. Accordingly, the appeals were dismissed on that ground as well. In doing so, the Court of Appeal disapproved of the way in which the trial judge came to the same conclusion using a balancing exercise based on abuse of process cases, and made further observations on the scope and effect of s 78. In particular, the court noted that the reference in s 78 to 'the circumstances in which the evidence was obtained' was not intended to widen the common law rule stated by Lord Diplock in *Sang* to the effect that the judge has 'no discretion to refuse to admit relevant and otherwise admissible evidence solely on the ground that it was obtained by improper or unfair means' (see also *Khan*, discussed in depth below). The quality and reliability of the evidence had to be considered therefore the trial judge had been wrong to apply the balancing process applicable to abuse of process cases when applying s 78. Chalkey took his case the European Court of Human Rights claiming a breach of Article 6(1), but the Court found that proper procedure had been followed and it was not unfair to admit the surveillance evidence (*Chalkey v UK* [2003] Crim LR 51).

The decision in *Chalkley and Jeffries* was applied in *R v Hardy and another* [2003] 1 Cr App R 30. Undercover officers answered an advertisement by BH. They met and discussed the smuggling of cannabis from the continent. Conversations and telephone calls between BH and the undercover officers were recorded. One of the officers drove BH's lorry to Holland and collected a consignment of cannabis. On arrival in England, the load was swapped for dummy packages before delivery to BH. BH and others were then arrested and charged with conspiracy to supply cannabis. At the trial the defence sought disclosure of the authority for surveillance. The judge refused because the surveillance was clearly properly authorised and therefore of no help to the defence. However, the prosecution did disclose the authorities in reduced form. The defence submission, that the tape-recording was an interception of communications which was neither in conformity with the Regulation of Investigatory Powers Act 2000 nor with the ECHR, was rejected by the trial judge. Hardy's appeal against conviction was dismissed. The tape-recording was not an interception of communications but was the same as a face-to-face recording. It was properly authorised and was properly admitted.

Bugging meetings with a legal adviser

Bugging a meeting between solicitor and client, which is legally privileged, is likely to be considered even more reprehensible than deceiving the solicitor and lead to the almost certain exclusion of any evidence thus obtained under s 78. As stated by Lord Taylor in *R v Derby Magistrates' Court, ex p B* [1996] AC 487, 507, '[l]egal privilege is … much more than an ordinary rule of evidence … [i]t is a fundamental condition on which the administration of justice rests.' The Court of Appeal have recently confirmed this principle (*R v Grant* [2005] EWCA Crim 1089) and that this area of common law mirrors the jurisprudence of the European Court of Human Rights (see *Lanz v Austria* App No 24430/94, 31 January 2002; *S v Switzerland* (1992) 14 EHRR 670; *Niemitz v Germany* (1992) 16 EHRR 97; *Brennan v UK* (2002) 34 EHRR 18). Thus a breach of Article 5 of the European Convention on Human Rights can be found even if it cannot be proved that the accused did not have a fair trial as long as it is shown that there was an infringement of the right to confidential legal advise. The discretion to prevent a prosecution for abuse of process is similar to s 78 but the issue is whether the prosecution should proceed rather than whether evidence should be excluded. In *R v Sutherland and Others*, unreported, 29 January 2002, Mr Justice Newman, sitting at Nottingham Crown Court, held that the prosecution of five men for murder could not proceed being an abuse of process. Police in Grantham, Lincolnshire, suspecting the defendants had murdered a fellow criminal but having no evidence of substance, were granted permission under the Regulation of Investigatory Powers Act 2000 to place listening devices in the cells and communal areas at two police stations where the defendants were to be held following their arrest. In the event a listening device was also placed in the exercise area and conversations between the defendants and their solicitors were also recorded in breach of the defendants right to legal privilege. The prosecution did not seek to use these conversations in evidence, therefore s 78 could not be relied upon. However, although the police denied listening to the taped conversations between lawyer and client or making any use of them, the trial judge did not accept this. He held that knowledge of the conversations must have informed their decisions and their use of the privileged conversations prejudiced the defendants and amounted to an abuse of process. Applying the balancing test referred to above, the trial judge concluded that 'in this case justice had been affronted in a grave way' and said he was satisfied that there could be no fair trial into all the issues to which the trial gave rise.

Bluff and counter-bluff

Interrogations are sometimes akin to a game of poker in which one side seeks to persuade the other that he has a stronger hand than he actually has. The courts appear to be saying that police should not tell a direct lie while accepting that other forms of deceit such as covert bugging of cells, meetings with the defendant's family and the like are permissible. Thus an interviewing officer should not tell the defendant and/or his solicitor falsely that a co-accused has already confessed and spilled the beans; or that he has forensic or other evidence of the defendant's involvement when he has not. He may, however, bug the cell or place a police officer in the cell pretending to be a fellow criminal, and use any incriminating evidence thus obtained. Though any evidence obtained by bugging of conversations between solicitor and client would not be admitted – see *Sutherland* and *Grant* above.

One may, it seems, also make proper use of the truth without any risk of impeachment. Thus an officer may truthfully tell the defendant and / or his solicitor that another person or even a lover has already confessed. That would probably not constitute oppression within s 76(2)(a) (see *Fulling)*, is unlikely to produce unreliability within s 76(2)(b), and, in the light of *Mason*, would not trigger s 78. However, as indicated in the discussion of oppression, one can misuse the truth in order to put improper pressure on an accused by, for example, telling a suspect that his mother is seriously ill with the intention of increasing the pressure on him to get out of police detention through the door marked 'confession'.

The characteristics of the suspect

The suspect's character and the effect of police conduct on him may be important. If he is of strong disposition, well versed in criminal procedure and able to look after himself in interviews, the s 78 discretion may not be exercised (*Canale; Alladice; Dunford*). If, however, the suspect is for any reason a vulnerable adult breaches of PACE 1984 and the Code of Practice may have much greater significance for the fairness of the trial (see eg *Beycan* and *Sanusi*). As already indicated, the fact that the defendant is mentally disordered or handicapped is always relevant circumstance to be taken into account and the presence of an appropriate adult and a solicitor will almost always be required to balance the perceived disadvantage they would otherwise suffer.

The presence of other evidence against the defendant should not affect the decision whether there is unfairness (that aspect is the preserve of s 2(1) of the Criminal Appeals Act 1968, the proviso to which can counterbalance any refusal to exclude evidence under s 78 – see *Walsh*)). However, where there is enough other evidence to convict the defendant, the court might be more easily persuaded to exclude the peripheral and disputed evidence whilst still allowing the rest to go before the jury (*Waters; Keenan*). By contrast, the absence of other evidence, apart from the disputed area, could be crucial to the fairness of the trial (in *Canale* the disputed interviews were the only effective evidence against the defendant and in *R v Cochrane* [1988] Crim LR 449, the interviews were the only evidence against the defendant and, since s 58 had been transgressed, it was unfair to use them). That other evidence may even be linked to and infected by the disputed area. In *Beycan* it was held that once admissions at the station had been excluded under s 78, it was unfair to admit statements made in the car en route there. Indeed, as with s 76 an earlier improper interview may affect a subsequent, proper one sufficiently to warrant the exclusion of all the interview evidence. This may be because the impropriety still influences the later interview, or because the court is determined not to let the police flagrantly flout the rules and then 'get away with it' by obeying them (*Canale*). However, the court, in exercising its discretion may find that the later interview is not so tainted and can refrain from using s 78 (see *R v Gillard and Barrett* above; the distinction between this case and *Canale*, above, is narrow and seems to depend on the degree of flagrancy of the misconduct).

Fairness of the proceedings

As has been seen, police misconduct is the most regular reason for exclusion under s 78. This does not mean that fairness to the accused is the criterion for its use. Fairness of the proceedings is the criterion, which means that the trial judge must balance the effect of admitting the evidence on the trial as a whole, including the effect on the prosecution and the public interest in ensuring that all relevant evidence is admitted. Thus, in *R v Hughes* (above), it was decided that the defendant had genuinely consented to an interview without a solicitor and that balancing the interests of the prosecution and of the defence did not require exclusion under s 78 (see also *Oliphant*). As the court pointed out in *Kerawalla*, the overall fairness of the proceedings has to be judged.

The common law

Before PACE 1984 came into force, a trial judge who found that a confession had been obtained by oppression or as a result of threats or inducements from a person in authority which rendered it involuntary, would exclude it as a matter of law (*Ibrahim v R* [1914] AC 599). There was also a discretion to exclude a confession obtained in breach of the Judges' Rules, the precursor of what is now Code C. Whether such a breach rendered the confession involuntary and therefore inadmissible as a matter of law, or whether the judge had a discretion to exclude a voluntary confession obtained in breach of the Judges' Rules, was never very clear, nor was the basis of any discretion to exclude confessions.

So far as non-confessional evidence was concerned the common law was not concerned with how it was obtained but only with the effect that the evidence had on the fairness of the trial. In *R v Sang* [1980] AC 402 the House of Lords held that there was no defence of entrapment and there was therefore no power to exclude otherwise admissible evidence on the ground that if the offence was committed it was at the instigation of an *agent provocateur*. Their Lordships accepted that a judge in a criminal trial has a general discretion to refuse to admit evidence where its probable prejudicial effect so outweighed its probative value as to make its admission unfair to the accused, but went on to say that, 'save with regard to admissions and confessions and generally with regard to evidence obtained from the accused after commission of an offence, the judge has no discretion to refuse to admit relevant and otherwise admissible evidence solely on the ground that it was obtained by improper or unfair means' (at 437).

The common law discretion to exclude evidence applied only to prosecution evidence and was concerned not with how the evidence was obtained but with the effect of the evidence on the fairness of the trial. Section 78 now provides a broad discretion to exclude any evidence, including confessional evidence obtained in a manner which while not rendering it unreliable would have an adverse effect on the fairness of the trial if admitted (*Mason*). It is broader than the common law discretion in that it can take into account the manner in which the evidence was obtained in determining its effect on the fairness of the trial but like the common law is concerned with the effect the evidence has on the fairness of the trial. It is narrower than the common law in that it only applies to evidence upon which the prosecution proposes to rely. Neither it, nor s 76, can be exercised to exclude evidence once it has been admitted.

Section 82(3) of 1984 PACE preserves any power of a court to exclude evidence. In the light of s 78 is there any role left for the common law discretion? One use was suggested in *R v Sat-Bhambra* (1988) 88 Cr App R 55. As indicated above, s 76 and a 78 are incapable of applying retrospectively, but the common law discretion allows the court to remedy earlier unfairness to the accused by excluding a previously admitted confession (after a voir dire the defendant's confession had been admitted, but later on hearing further medical evidence the judge changed his mind). The common law discretion thus remains as a separate head for excluding evidence but in almost all cases where evidence could properly be excluded at common law it can be excluded under s 78 before it is actually admitted (see Lord Lane CJ in *Delaney*, May LJ in *O'Leary*, and *Matto v Wolverhampton Crown Court* (1987) RTR 337).

It may also be the case that where the improperly obtained evidence, other than confessional evidence, would not be excluded at common law it will not be excluded under s 78. Thus, in *R v Stewart* [1995] Crim LR 500, it was argued that evidence of meter tampering which proved the offence of fraudulent abstraction of electricity, should be excluded under s 78 because of breaches of s 16 PACE and Code B in the manner in which a warrant of entry under the Rights of Entry (Gas and Electricity Boards) Act 1954 was executed. In dismissing the appeal the Court of Appeal found it unnecessary to decide whether PACE 1984 or the Code applied and whether the entry was unlawful, but, even assuming that they did and it was, the Court found no unfairness in admitting the evidence which was there for all to see whether the entry was effected properly or not. This is consistent with the common law's approach to the exclusion of real evidence. There is no question of unreliability, the evidence speaks for itself and whilst admitting it may operate unfortunately for the accused it does not operate unfairly. Elsewhere it is suggested that the common law has no role to play since s 76 and s 78 have not only supplemented it but have also extended the court's powers to exclude confessions.

Other forms of improperly obtained evidence

In *R v Khan (Sultan)* [1997] AC 558, the House of Lords upheld the decision of the lower courts to admit evidence obtained by placing an electronic listening device (a bug) to the outside wall of a private house without the knowledge of the owner or occupiers. Although not strictly concerned with confessions, the decision sheds light on the general approach to the exclusion of evidence in England and Wales and supports the contention above that s 78 was not intended to and did not change the law on the exclusion of illegally obtained evidence. The opportunity to clarify the law on the exclusion of evidence at common law and in particular the proper interpretation of s 78 was missed largely because Liberty were permitted to appear before their Lordships to argue that a court in exercising its exclusionary discretion under s 78 was obliged to have regard to the European Convention on Human Rights and the jurisprudence of the European Court of Human Rights.

The defence contention was that a private conversation in a private house was analogous to a private telephone call, the interception of which is governed by the Interception of Communications Act 1986 and the decision of the European Court of Human Rights in *Malone v United Kingdom* (1984) 7 EHRR 14. Section 9 of the 1986 Act forbade the use in evidence of material used by the interception of communications and a similar restriction should be applied to materials obtained by aural surveillance devices. Lord Nolan, giving the judgement of the House of Lords, rejected this argument because it required the formulation of two new principles: (a) that the appellant enjoyed a right of privacy in respect of the taped conversation; and (b) that evidence of a conversation obtained in breach of that right was inadmissible. There was no such right of privacy in English law, and even if there were, evidence obtained improperly or even unlawfully, remained admissible, subject to the trial judge's power to exclude it at his discretion.

Turning to the issue of whether the judge should have exercised his discretion to exclude the evidence in the exercise of his common law discretion or under s 78, Lord Nolan said the only relevant element of the common law discretion was that part which authorised the judge 'to exclude evidence if it is necessary in order to secure a fair trial for the accused'. It was unnecessary to consider the common law position separately from that under s 78 (which is also concerned with securing a fair trial). Liberty contended that if the evidence had been obtained in breach of the European Convention (which under Article 8 does include a right to privacy) then that should be regarded as grounds for excluding what was otherwise admissible evidence. Section 78 required the court to have regard to 'all the circumstances' in which the evidence was obtained. If the circumstances included an invasion of the right to privacy protected by Article 8 of the European Convention on Human Rights then this was something to which the court must have regard in exercising its exclusionary discretion.

Lord Nolan stated that while the principles reflected in the European Convention could hardly be irrelevant to the exercise of the s 78 power under English law there was nothing unlawful about a breach of privacy (note that the case was decided well before the Human Rights Act took effect). The appellant's case rested wholly upon the lack of statutory authorisation for the particular breach of privacy (it then being authorised under administrative guidelines laid down by the Secretary of State) and the consequent infringement of Article 8. In these circumstances the appellant could no more succeed on this second issue than he could on the first. Even if the evidence had been obtained in breach of Article 8 or, for that matter, in breach of the law of a foreign country, that fact would be of no greater significance per se than if it constituted a breach of English law. Upon the facts of the instant case, their Lordships considered that the judge was fully entitled to hold that the circumstances in which the relevant evidence was obtained, even if they constituted a breach of Article 8, were not such as to require the exclusion of the evidence. Lord Nolan went on to say that it would be a strange reflection of our law if a man who had admitted his participation in the illegal importation of a large quantity of heroin should have his conviction set aside on the ground that his privacy had been invaded. While the American exclusionary principle does permit the guilty man to go free if his privacy or other rights are infringed, the English common law principle, and the statutory power under s 78, does not.

In *Khan v United Kingdom* (2001) 31 EHRR 45, the European Court confirmed that the use of a secret listening device in the *Khan* case was a breach of Article 8 because the domestic law of the United Kingdom failed to regulate the use of covert listening devices: they were then regulated only by administrative guidelines. The use of such devices is now regulated by the Regulation of Investigatory Powers Act 2000, therefore the decision is of only of historical significance. As was made clear by the House of Lords, the fact that evidence is obtained in breach of the Convention or domestic law is not the issue when deciding whether to admit the evidence; rather it is the effect on the fairness of the trial which the admission of such evidence might have.

The refusal to exclude real evidence, even if obtained unlawfully, was continued in *R v Khan, Sakkaravej and Pamarapa* [1997] Crim LR 508. Pamarapa, a Thai diplomat, brought into the UK drugs worth some £5 million. He was met at Heathrow airport by Sakkaravej. Pamarapa was wearing his diplomatic identity card but despite this he was arrested. His suitcase had already been searched in the hold of the aircraft and on arrest his hand luggage was searched The prosecution case was that Khan's father had organised the importation and Khan had overseen it because his father was terminally ill. The Thai government waived Pamarapa's diplomatic immunity. At the trial it was argued that the search of Pamarapa's suitcase was in breach of Article 36(2) of the Vienna Convention on Diplomatic Relations 1961, which is given the force of law in the UK by the Diplomatic Privileges Act 1964. Under the Convention the search should have taken place in Pamarapa's presence and then only if the customs/police had serious grounds to believe it contained prohibited goods, which, it was argued, they did not have. It was also argued that the arrest was unlawful and the subsequent search of his bag also unlawful. The trial judge refused to exclude the evidence of the search under s 78 or at common law. He found that there were grounds to believe the bags contained drugs, the only illegality was the absence of Pamarapa when the search took place. The Convention provided a right to search which implied a right to detain therefore there was no unlawful arrest. Even if the second search was unlawful there would be no unfairness in admitting it.

The Court of Appeal, dismissing the appeal, upheld the trial judge's exercise of his discretion. If the second search had been illegal, the trial judge had a discretion, not an obligation, to exclude it. Section 78 modified the principle laid down in *R v Sang* [1980] AC 402 by enlarging a judge's discretion to exclude evidence obtained by unfair means. However, it is the effect on the fairness of the trial which is relevant, and only then when the unfairness leads the court to conclude that the evidence should not be admitted. The trial judge correctly found that the first search did not taint the second, but even if there had been some lingering illegality, or further illegality in respect of Pamarapa's arrest, it had no effect on the quality of the evidence, or the fairness of admitting it. The only recorded case in which real evidence had been excluded, *R v Fennelly* (above, which concerned a failure to comply with PACE 1984 stop and search requirements) was doubted.

In *R v Loveridge (William); R v Lee (Charles Sonny) and R v Loveridge (Christine)* (2001) *The Times*, 3 May, the three defendants were convicted of robbery after the prosecution had been allowed to introduce in evidence a film made by video recording of the three defendants taken in the holding area of the magistrates' court. An expert witness compared the video recording with film taken by a surveillance camera at the scene of the robbery and concluded that the defendants were those depicted in the surveillance camera. The trial judge accepted that the video film taken in the magistrates' court contravened s 41 of the Criminal Justice Act 1925, which makes filming in the precincts of a court unlawful. However, while not approving or encouraging the tactics adopted by the police, the judge decided that to admit the video film would not have an adverse effect on the fairness of the trial.

On appeal the Court of Appeal agreed. It was accepted that filming in the court was unlawful being a breach of s 41 of the 1925 Act, that there might have been a breach of Code D which deals with the taking of photographs of arrested persons, and that the secret filming was unlawful being a breach of Article 8 of the European Convention on Human Rights. However, so far as the outcome of the appeal was concerned, the breach of Article 8 was only relevant if it interfered with the right of the defendants to a fair hearing. Giving full weight to the breach of the Convention their Lordships were satisfied that the contravention of Article 8 did not interfere with the fairness of the hearing. The judge had been entitled to rule as he did. The position under s 78 of the 1984 Act was the same. Collectively the evidence of the involvement of each of the defendants was overwhelming. The trial was fair and the convictions were not in any way unsafe.

In the absence of a right to privacy in English law there has been little discussion of the suspect's right to privacy in a police station. Article 8 of the European Convention on Human Right does protect the privacy of the individual and in *PG and JH v United Kingdom* [2002] Crim LR 308 the European Court of Human Rights held that the use of covert listening devices in a police station violated Article 8 of the Convention. Here, police received information that a robbery was to take place 'somewhere' in early March 1995. Visual surveillance of B's home began but no robbery took place. Later the information was received that the robbery would take place on 9 March. Authorisation was given for listening devices to be placed in B's flat. B and others with him discovered the listening devices and left the flat. No robbery took place. B and others were arrested on March 16 in a stolen car containing two black balaclavas, five black plastic cable ties, two pairs of leather gloves and two army rucksacks. In order to obtain speech samples to compare with the tapes from the flat, police applied for and were granted authorisation to use covert listening devices in the cells and on the police officers who were to be present when B and others were charged. Evidence derived from the listening devices was admitted at their trial for conspiracy to rob. They were convicted and their appeal to the Court of Appeal was rejected.

The Strasbourg Court held that the use of a covert listening device in B's flat was not in accordance with the law existing at the time as there was no statutory provision for surveillance. The Home Office Guidelines which existed were not in accordance with law under Article 8 (although statutory provision is now made under the Regulation of Investigatory Powers Act 2000). Similarly, the Court held that there was a breach of Article 8 in respect of the use of covert surveillance devices in the police station although no breach was found in respect of Article 6, the right to a fair trial. The taped evidence was not the only evidence against B and the others. There was ample opportunity to challenge both the authenticity and the use of the recordings. It was clear that had the domestic courts been of the view that the admission of the evidence would have given rise to substantive unfairness, they had a discretion to exclude it under s 78. The Court further considered that there was no unfairness in leaving it to the jury, on the basis of a thorough summing up by the trial judge, to decide where the weight of the evidence lay. The defence claim that the use of voice samples to compare with other recordings was a breach of their right not to incriminate themselves was rejected the Court which saw these as akin to the use of blood or other samples used in forensic analysis to which that right did not apply. This decision is consistent with those considered above where the fact that the evidence was obtained unlawfully does not necessarily mean that admitting it will have such an adverse effect on the fairness of the trial that it ought not to be admitted.

Further reading

Hartshorne, J, 'Defensive use of a co-accused's confession and the Criminal Justice Act 2003' (2004) 8(3) E & P 165.

Hirst, M, 'Confessions as Proof of Innocence' (1998) 57 CLJ 146.

Mirfield, P, *Silence, Confessions and Improperly Obtained Evidence* (1997).

Munday, R, 'Adverse denial and purposive confession' [2003] Crim LR 850.

Index